Multiple Commitments
in the Workplace
An Integrative Approach

Series in Applied Psychology

Edwin A. Fleishmann, George Mason University
Jeanette N. Cleveland, Pennsylvania State University
Series Editors

Gregory Bedny and David Meister
The Russian Theory of Activity: Current Applications to Design and Learning

Michael T. Brannick, Eduardo Salas, and Carolyn Prince
Team Performance assessment and Measurement: Theory, Research, and Applications

Jeanette N. Cleveland, Margaret Stockdale, and Kevin R. Murphy
Women and Men in Organizations: Sex and Gender Issues at Work

Aaron Cohen
Multiple Commitments in the Workplace: An Integrative Approach

Russell Cropanzano
Justice in the Workplace: Approaching Fairness in Human Resource Management

Russell Cropanzano
Justice in the Workplace: From Theory to Practice, Second Edition

James E. Driskell and Eduardo Salas
Stress and Human Performance

Sidney A. Fine and Steven F. Cronshaw
Functional Job Analysis: A Foundation for Human Resources Management

Sidney A. Fine and Maury Getkate
Benchmark Tasks for Job Analysis: A Guide for Functional Job Analysis (FJA) Scales

J. Kevin Ford, Steve W. J. Kozlowski, Kurt Kraiger, Eduardo Salas, and Mark S. Teachout
Improving Training Effectiveness in Work Organizations

Jerald Greenberg
Organizational Behavior: The State of the Science, First Edition
Organizational Behavior: The State of the Science, Second Edition

Uwe E. Kleinbeck, Hans-Henning Quast, Henk Thierry, and Hartmut Häcker
Work Motivation

Martin I. Kurke and Ellen M. Scrivner
Police Psychology Into the 21st Century

Manuel London
How People Evaluate Others in Organizations
Job Feedback: Giving, Seeking, and Using Feedback for Performance Improvement, First Edition
Job Feedback: Giving, Seeking, and Using Feedback for Performance Improvement, Second Edition

Robert F. Morrison and Jerome Adams
Contemporary Career Development Issues

Michael D. Mumford, Garnett Stokes, and William A. Owens
Patterns of Life History: The Ecology of Human Individuality

Kevin R. Murphy
Validity Generalization: A Critical Review

Kevin R. Murphy and Frank E. Saal
Psychology in Organizations: Integrating Science and Practice

Erich P. Prien, Jeffery S. Schippmann, and Kristin O. Prien
Individual Assessment: As Practiced in Industry and Consulting

Ned Rosen
Teamwork and the Bottom Line: Groups Make a Difference

Heinz Schuler, James L. Farr, and Mike Smith
Personnel Selection and Assessment: Individual and Organizational Perspectives

John W. Senders and Neville P. Moray
Human Error: Cause, Prediction, and Reduction

Frank J. Smith
Organizational Surveys: The Diagnosis and Betterment of Organizations Through Their Members

Multiple Commitments in the Workplace

An Integrative Approach

Aaron Cohen
University of Haifa, Israel

LEA LAWRENCE ERLBAUM ASSOCIATES, PUBLISHERS

2003   Mahwah, New Jersey   London

Lawrence Erlbaum Associates, Inc., Publishers
10 Industrial Avenue
Mahwah, NJ 07430

Cover design by Kathryn Houghtaling Lacey

Library of Congress Cataloging-in-Publication Data

Cohen, Aaron, 1952–
    Multiple commitments in the workplace: an integrative
approach / Aaron Cohen.
        p. cm. — (Series in applied psychology)
    Includes bibliographical references and index.
ISBN 0-8058-4234-9 (cloth: alk. paper)
ISBN 0-8058-4368-X (pbk.: alk. paper)
1. Organizaitonal commitment. 2. Organizational behavior.
    3. Employee loyalty. 4. Commitment (Psychology). I. Title.
    II. Series.
HD58.7 .C621352002
158.7—dc21   2002075263
                                                        CIP

Books published by Lawrence Erlbaum Associates are printed on acid-
free paper, and their bindings are chosen for strength and durability.

Printed in the United States of America
10   9   8   7   6   5   4   3   2   1

*This book is dedicated to
Itai, Maor, and Avigail
who brightened some dark days.*

Contents

Series Foreword

Edwin A. Fleishmann, George Mason University
Jeanette N. Cleveland, Pennsylvania State University
Series Editors

There is a compelling need for innovative approaches to the solution of many pressing problems involving human relationships in today's society. Such approaches are more likely to be successful when they are based on sound research and applications. This *Series in Applied Psychology* offers publications, which emphasize state-of-the-art research and its application to important issues of human behavior in a variety of societal settings. The objective is to bridge both academic and applied interests.

Individuals in organizations have a number of commitments, which affect their behavior and attitudes in and out of the workplace. These include employee commitments to the organization, to the work group, to the occupation, to the union, and to the job. People in the workplace are exposed to more than one commitment at a time. Their work behavior, therefore, is affected by several commitments, not only one. In the last several years a sizable body of information has accumulated on issues related to such multiple commitments in organizations. This knowledge needs to be marshaled, its strengths highlighted, and its importance, as well as some of its weaknesses, made known. Enough evidence now exists to show the potential of this multidimensional approach.

The purpose of Aaron Cohen's book, *Multiple Commitments at Work: An Integrative Approach*, is to summarize this knowledge, as well as to suggest ideas and directions for future research and application. This book addresses a number of important aspects of commitment by applying this multidimensional approach. It covers the differences among the various forms of commitment, the definition and boundaries of commitment foci, their interrelationships, and their effects on outcomes, mainly work outcomes. It also examines the relationships of commitment foci to aspects of nonwork domains and to cross-cultural aspects of commitment foci.

The book provides a provocative and innovative approach to the conceptualization and understanding of multiple commitments in the work place. It includes a thorough review of the existing research on multiple commitments, and analyzes the relationships among commitment forms and how they might affect behavior at work. Topics rarely covered in multiple commitment research are reviewed, such as cross-cultural aspects of commitment and the relationship between commitment forms and nonwork domains. The author includes all the available scales of commitment forms that can assist researchers and practitioners in measuring the different kinds of commitment. He also presents conceptual models for multiple commitments that can further increase our understanding of these important concepts.

The author has been a leader in this field. He received his PhD in Management at the Technion-Israel Institute of Technology and taught three years at the University of Lethbridge, Alberta, Canada. He is currently Associate Professor in the Department of Political Science, University of Haifa, Israel. His current research interests include, multiple commitments at work, organizational commitment and union commitment, work/nonwork relationships, organizational citizenship behavior, and the relationship between politics and work. His work has been published in *Academy of Management Journal, Journal of Management, Journal of Vocational Behavior, Journal of Business Research, Administration and Society, Journal of Organizational Behavior, Human Relations, Applied Behavioral Science, and Political Psychology.*

This volume should interest students, researchers and practitioners in the field of human resources, and organizational behavior, and can be used in graduate courses in these areas. It is a landmark publication in this important and emerging area.

Preface

Commitment is a force that binds an individual to a course of action of relevance to one or more targets. As such, commitment is distinguishable from exchange-based forms of motivation and target-relevant attitudes, and can influence behavior in the absence of extrinsic motivation or positive attitudes (Meyer & Herscovitch, 2001, pp. 301–302). The concept of commitment in the workplace has attracted the attention of academics and practitioners since the 1950s. There are many definitions of commitment, but predominately, it is viewed as an attitude that reflects feelings like attachment, identification, or loyalty to the object of commitment (Morrow, 1993). Commitment was first proposed as a concept to replace or strengthen the somewhat disappointing findings regarding the effects of job satisfaction on work behaviors such as turnover and absenteeism (Mowday, Porter, & Steers, 1982). Lack of commitment, or loyalty, is cited as an explanation for employee absenteeism, turnover, reduced effort expenditure, theft, job dissatisfaction, and an unwillingness to relocate (Morrow, 1993).

Interest in commitment has also been heightened by a widespread perception that Americans are no longer greatly committed or loyal to their work, a circumstance for which various reasons have been cited. Some have suggested that corporate America has not met its obligations toward its employees. Business leaders have been all too willing to dismiss employees, reduce employee hours, and find other ways to cut employee compensation. Another possible explanation is that societal values are changing and the present labor force values work less than did the previous generation (Morrow, 1993).

Curiosity about the secrets of the motivated and successful Japanese workforce likewise increased research on commitment. Researchers believed that commitment was a key factor accounting for the hard work and the low turnover of Japanese workers. Today it is apparent that neither was explained in the way the researchers anticipated. Commitment was found to be a modest predictor of turnover, certainly not of the magnitude expected. The differences between the Japanese and the American workforces were not as wide as expected, and commitment played only a minor role in them. It is disappointing that after so many years of research many issues and aspects of the process, determinants, and outcomes of commitment still remain unanswered. Indeed, some researchers questioned the need for future research on this concept (Randall, 1990).

Naturally, researchers sought alternative ways to understand commitment in order to enhance its contribution in both theory and practice. One of the important alternatives was to perceive commitment as a multidimensional concept. For example, Rotondi (1975), argued that the need to differentiate identification targets in organizations such as occupational activities, task groups, or reference groups was essential. This approach was advanced by Morrow (1983) and later in the works of Reichers (1985, 1986), Becker (1982), Cohen (1989; 1993a, 1999a, 1999b, 2000), Blau and his associates (1993), and others.

The growing interest in multiple commitments among researchers and practitioners is evinced by the greater attention in the literature to the broader concept of work commitment. This includes specific objects of commitment such as organization, work group, occupation, the union, and one's job (Blau, Paul, & St. John, 1993; Cohen, 1993a, 1999a; Randall & Cote, 1991). Perhaps most critical for an appreciation of the multiple commitment approach is the extent to which it has *added value*. That is, if the recognition that we live in a multiple commitment world is to have either theoretical or practical importance it must be shown that examining commitment to various constituencies and domains refines our understanding of work-related behavior (Morrow, 1993; Meyer & Allen, 1997). Randall and Cote (1991) emphasized the importance of such research: "A multivariate approach to work commitment research will advance the understanding of how various pieces of the commitment puzzle fit together and how constellations of work commitment constructs influence outcome variables" (p. 209). Indeed, commitment forms have been shown to predict important work outcomes such as withdrawal, performance, absenteeism, and tardiness (e.g., Wiener & Vardi, 1980; Blau, 1986; Cohen, 1993a, 1999b, 2000). This is one of the main reasons for the growing interest in the concept of multiple commitments.

What is the meaning of being committed to multiple foci in the workplace? Very few definitions have been advanced for the notion of commitment to multiple foci. Morrow (1983; 1993) proposed the idea that many foci of commitment exist, and the organization is only one of several entities in the workplace that employees can be committed to. They may be committed to their job, profession, union, or work in general. Morrow (1993) argued that at a minimum, *work commitment*, a concept referring to multiple commitment at the work place, would seem to involve loyalty to several different entities, including the actual work, one's career or profession, one's job, and one's employer or organization. Note too, that in this book *work commitment* is used as another term for *multiple commitments*. It should be understood differently from the term *work involvement*, which refers to one specific form of commitment; work commitment concerns the idea of multiple commitments.

The main idea behind the multidimensional approach to commitment is that people in the workplace are exposed to more than one commitment at a time. Therefore, their behavior is affected by several commitments, not only one. Employees may be affected differently by different foci of commitment. For some, commitment to the organization may be the most important; for others, it may be commitment to the occupation, and for others still, it may be both. In each case the resulting behavior may differ according to the magnitude of the effects of a given set of commitments. Therefore, there is a need conceptually and empirically to distinguish different commitment constructs, to recognize that employees are committed simultaneously to different constituencies, and to ground commitment constructs in important employee behaviors (Vandenberg & Scarpelo, 1994).

This idea leads to a different insight on commitment, that has been overlooked. Diverse questions may arise as a result of such an approach, for example, what are the relevant commitment foci one is exposed to in the workplace? How do they differ? How are they related, and which given set of commitments is related to a given outcome? Such questions diverge from the traditional approach that focuses on one given commitment at a time, most often organizational commitment. But because the traditional approach is hard pressed to demonstrate the utility of commitment in explaining employees' behavior at work, the multidimensional approach potentially can better explain the concept of commitment at the workplace, hence provide better prediction of behaviors by commitment.

A large body of knowledge analyzing a variety of different foci of commitment separately constitutes current commitment research. Most work centers on organizational commitment as a unidimensional or multidimensional construct. Much of this knowledge is summarized in two books; is thorough review of organizational commitment as a unidimensional construct and is based on the works of Mowday et al. (1982). The other assembles the work of Meyer and Allen (1997) and their approach to organizational commitment as a multidimensional construct. The first book attempts to demonstrate the need for a multidimensional approach to commitment by Morrow (1983), who drew attention to the range of commitment foci being examined by researchers and the possibility of concept redundancy among these foci. In a special issue of the journal devoted to multiple commitments, Morrow and McElroy (1993) expressed their disappointment with the submissions they received as follows:

> The use of inferior/homemade measures of work commitment, when better/more established measures are available, is still commonplace. There was also uneven interest in the various forms of work commitment, with work ethic endorsement and career/occupational commitment under-represented. Consequently, our understanding of these concepts lags behind organizational commitment considerably and delays resolution of how various forms of work commitment are related to one another (p. 2)

A step toward the advancement of the multidimensional approach to commitment was taken by Morrow (1993). A major contribution of her book is that it directs researchers to the importance of commitment foci other than organizational commitment. For Morrow's reason, much space in her book was devoted to separately summarizing knowledge on each of the commitment foci. Because organizational commitment had captured most of the attention in commitment research there was a need to familiarize readers with the other commitment foci in the workplace. That is one reason why only a small portion of Morrow's (1993) book focused on the purely multidimensional approach, namely, how constellations of commitments are related to each other, differ from each other, and affect work outcomes.

OVERVIEW OF THE VOLUME

The multidimensional approach to commitment is the main focus of the volume. Particularly since the 1980s, a sizable body of research has accumulated on the multidimensional approach to commitment. This knowledge needs to be marshaled, its strengths highlighted, and its importance and some of its weaknesses made known, with the aim of guiding future research on commitment to be based on a multidimensional approach. Enough evidence exists to show the potential of this approach.

The purpose of this book is to summarize this evidence and suggest ideas and directions for future research. Only a small part of the book describes commitment foci separately, and this is simply to acquaint the reader with these forms before they are presented as part of the multidimensional approach. Most of the book addresses what seems to be the important aspects of commitment by a multidimensional approach: the differences among these forms, the definition and boundaries of commitment foci as part of a multidimensional approach, their interrelationships, and their effect on outcomes, mainly work outcomes. Two chapters concern aspects rarely examined but that I believe could and should be important topics for future research. These are the relation of commitment foci to aspects of nonwork domains and cross-cultural aspects of commitment foci.

Part I is an introduction that familiarizes the reader with the concept of commitment. Part I includes, in addition to this Preface, chapter 1, that discusses the importance of the concept of commitment; what commitment is in general and what the importance of commitment is at work. The volume moves on to a comprehensive discussion of the main theme: Multiple commitments at work. What is the importance of the multiple commitment approach? Why is it important to look at a constellation of commitments and not only one commitment at a time, as most research has done? Chapter 1 emphasizes the difference between the approach of this book and other research that tested and presented one commitment at a time, presents the conceptual framework of commitment forms and their effect on employees' behavior at work, and concludes with a description of the goals and the structure of the book.

Part II deals with important conceptual considerations in multiple commitment research. The main idea here is to introduce the reader to the concept of multiple commitments in greater depth. Chapter 2 reviews commitment forms (e.g., organizational commitment, career commitment, job commitment, group commitment, and union commitment), which of them should form the concept of work commitment. Each commitment form is defined and its development and characteristics are described. The goal of chapter 2 is to set forth the different concepts of commitments. The account is brief because this task was already accomplished in Morrow's (1993) book. However, it is necessary, as the reader should be made familiar with the different terms and concepts of commitment at work before the multiple commitment approach is introduced in the subsequent chapters.

After the reader has become acquainted with the different concepts of commitment at work, chapter 3 considers how the commitment forms differ. Can employees differentiate commitment to the organization from commitment to the work group or from the other forms of commitment? Are multiple commitments a concept developed by scholars for scholars but do not actually exist in the workplace? Or can employees make meaningful distinctions between their commitment to one object, such as the occupation, and another object, such as the organization? What does research tell us about these questions? Chapter 3 reviews and discusses research findings on the discriminant validity of commitment forms, and concludes with the implications of this research for the definition and measurement of commitment forms.

Part III moves to theoretical developments in multiple commitment research. Chapter 4 focuses on different typologies to commitment forms. These typologies deal with the definition and boundaries of the concept of multiple commitment and review existing models of the way multiple commitment should be viewed and analyzed. The issue of how to integrate the different commitment forms into one model is important for clarifying what is meant by multiple commitments. The importance of these typologies is that they present the main effort at conceptualizing multiple commitments. Several such models are presented: those of Reichers (1985, 1986), Morrow (1993), Meyer and Allen (1997), and Cohen (1993a). Chapter 4 reviews and analyzes these models and their advantages and disadvantages. The chapter tackles questions about differences between multiple commitments and multiple dimensions of one commitment, and the implications of these questions for ongoing research of multiple commitments.

Chapter 5 discusses an important, interesting question that exemplifies the concept of multiple commitments: How are the different commitment forms interrelated? Are some commitment forms determinants of others? What are the implications of this interrelationship for our understanding of the development of commitment forms among employees? What are its implications for the relationship between commitment forms and employees' behavior, particularly work outcomes? What theory or theories underlie this interrelationship? Chapter 5 proposes several models and theories for the interrelationships among commitment forms.

The four chapters in Part IV and discuss current research in multiple commitments. Chapter 6 studies how commitment forms affect work outcomes such as turnover, absenteeism, performance, and Organizational Citizenship Behavior. It presents conceptual arguments for their relationship and reviews research findings. The emphasis is on the combined and joint effect of commitment forms on work outcomes. This differs from past research that has focused on the effect of one commitment form on work outcomes. Chapter 6 is an important one, as it has practical implications for research on multiple commitments.

In chapter 7, different profiles of commitment forms and their effects on work outcomes are considered. For example, the most common profile is Gouldner's (1957) concept of *local* versus *cosmopolitan*. This refers to a combination of two commitment forms: commitment to the organization versus commitment to the profession. By this approach, employees with a high level of organizational commitment and a low level of professional commitment, termed *local*, represent a different type of employee, from one with a high level of professional commitment and a low level of organizational commitment, who is termed *cosmopolitan*. Another important profile developed in the literature is dual commitment: to the organization as against the union. How do those with high commitment to the organization and low commitment to the union differ from those with low commitment to the organization and high commitment to the union? A third profile of commitment proposed in the literature is a combination of commitment to the organization and commitment to the job. This chapter reviews and discusses the different profiles presented in the literature and their possible effects on employees' behavior, and questions the possibility of other profiles.

Chapter 8 deals with one of the new research directions in recent years, namely nonwork domains and their relation of with working in general and multiple commitments in particular. However, here the focus is the relationship between dimensions of nonwork domains such as work–nonwork conflict, coping strategies, organizational support, and commitment forms. The chapter outlines the conceptual framework of the relation between dimensions of nonwork domains and commitment forms (mainly the positive nonwork-to-work spillover approach), and surveys research that has examined which dimension of nonwork domain is related to which commitment form. Here too, the emphasis is on an integrative approach: how constellations of dimensions of nonwork domains are related to constellations of commitment forms.

Chapter 9 approaches a somewhat neglected yet notably important topic in multiple commitment research, namely multiple commitments in a crosscultural setting. Chapter 9 explains the reasons for the importance of understanding commitment in crosscultural settings, and then describes the main conceptual framework applied for understanding commitment in a crosscultural setting. Because very few crosscultural studies exist on multiple commitments, this chapter reviews those conducted on separate commitments. Many of the crosscultural studies were performed on organizational commitment in Japan, or in comparison to Japan, and these are reviewed first. They are followed by a survey of research on organizational commitment in other cultures and crosscultural research on other commitment forms. Thereafter, the little existing research on multiple commitments in a crosscultural setting is presented.

The volume concludes with Part V, consisting of chapter 10, assembles suggestions and recommendations for future research based on the knowledge that has accumulated so far on multiple commitments. It summarizes what has been learned about multiple commitments in the book, and points out issues that need to be addressed in future research.

All the aforementioned should provide the reader with updated knowledge on commitment in a multidimensional perspective. Such knowledge can be used to teach organizational behavior in classes where commitment is one of the issues discussed, or to encourage research on commitment by a multidimensional approach. Such knowledge can also be helpful for practitioners who are interested in a better understanding of their employees' attitudes and behaviors. The main theme of the book is that understanding commitment by a multidimensional approach can overcome many of the limitations of research on commitment by a multidimensional approach. I believe that convincing researchers and practitioners of the validity of this theme increases our understanding of the concept of commitment and encourages research on this important concept.

—*Aaron Cohen*

I

Introduction

1

The Importance
and Meaning of Multiple
Commitments

Commitment is a general phenomenon that occurs in all social systems. As a research topic, commitment is important regardless of its setting because increasing our comprehension of the phenomenon may assist us in better understanding the nature of the psychological process through which people choose to identify with different objects in their environment and how they find purpose in life. In this way, we increase our understanding of society (Mowday et al., 1982, chap. 1). Not surprisingly therefore, research has investigated commitment to a variety of objects such as religion (Lensky, 1961; Anderson, 1998; Hovemyr, 1996; Hillstrom & Stracham, 2000), programs (Neubert & Cady, 2001), friends and spouse (Huston & Levinger, 1978; Johnson, 1973; Rusbult, 1980a, 1980b; Sprecher, Metts, Burleson, Hatfield, & Thompson, 1995), the community (Antonovsky & Antonovsky, 1974; Kanter, 1968, 1972), one's goals (Busch, 1998; Donovan & Radosevich, 1998), one's decisions (Dooley & Fryxell, 1999; Dooley, Fryxell, & Judge, 2000; Greer & Stephens, 2001), or one's employees (Lee & Miller, 1999; Miller & Lee, 2001).

THE IMPORTANCE OF STUDYING COMMITMENT
IN THE WORKPLACE

This book addresses perspectives of commitment in one of the foremost domains of our lives, the workplace. Several reasons can be advanced for the

3

ance of studying commitment in this setting. First, not only does a better understanding of commitment in the workplace have the potential to make us happier and more productive employees, but also insights gained in the study of commitment forms may spill over into other areas (e.g., how to foster or manage commitment to one's family, religion, nation, marriage, and so on). (Morrow, 1993).

Second, the quality of individuals' linkages with organizations to which they belong also affects society at large. For example, the larger society may need to be concerned with whether its members have sufficient commitment to its institutions including, albeit not exclusively, work organizations. If the general quality of members' attachment to work organizations were low, this would doubtless carry certain implications for the basic fabric of society. Among these is the fact that without some employee commitment organizations simply would not work. Individuals would also lose one very basic source of identity and belonging, namely their employers. When quality of membership and membership status linkages are low in a large number of work organizations, the level of productivity and the quality of products and services in the society would be affected. Although slow growth in productivity rates may be due to a number of complex factors, the quality of employee linkages to organizations is often said to be the core of the problem (Mowday et al., 1982).

Another reason is that identification of people with the organization, for example, can create a larger whole that can be a driving force behind a firm's performance, its workers' well being, and the resilience of both the firm and the workers in times of change (Meyer & Herscovitch, 2001). In turbulent organizational environments, it is important to ask whether workers still identify with organizations, what forms such identification may take, and what factors shape it. Worker identification occurs through both individual and firm-level forces. Individuals have a strong drive to believe that they are part of the settings in which they work and their members' identification enhances the success of firms on the basis of coordinated corporate action in particular (Morrow, 1993; Morrow & McElroy, 2001; Rousseau, 1998). These arguments point to the importance and potential contributions of understanding and studying commitment in the workplace.

Multiple Commitments as a Relevant Concept

A question also raised by several authors (Mowday et al., 1982; Meyer & Allen, 1997) is whether the concept of commitment is relevant, or still relevant. For example, it can be argued that the world of work is changing, becoming characterized by increased global competition, rapid developments in information technology, and re-engineering of business.

Because of these changes much greater emphasis is falling on flexibility and efficiency. To be competitive, companies must be able to adapt to changing conditions and to cut costs. Many strategies used to achieve these objectives, such as the introduction of new technology, consolidation of operations, and contracting out involve the job losses. Consequently employees are advised not to become too attached to their employers, but to look out for themselves to ensure that they remain employable in the event of a layoff. Apparently, neither employers nor employees are or should be committed to one workplace any longer.

Yet there are several important reasons for the relevance of studying current forms of commitment and why research on multiple commitments should be pursued vigorously. The first has to do with changes in employment practices stimulated by the need to be more competitive. Whereas external pressures on work organizations caused practices like layoffs, downsizing, and mergers that might result in reduced organizational commitment, this may also adversely impact on other forms of commitment. For example, corporate restructuring of jobs may lead to lower job involvement, which in turn is linked to low levels of product or service quality. Restoring quality may therefore be connected with improvements in job involvement. Similarly, changes in employment practices may cause employees to prioritize their commitments differently. When a long-term, individual–organizational exchange relationship is disrupted, work ethic endorsement may ultimately become a less central value for the individual concerned. Career commitment may take priority over organizational commitment, particularly in the case of temporary or part-time employees.

The second reason has to do with the common opinion that many management–employee relations are poor. The changes in employment practices noted previously are used to explain the diminishing sense of reciprocity between employees and employers and low employee commitment. A better understanding of the various types of work commitment may therefore be useful for people seeking to re-establish or sustain work commitment. For example, if workers are perceived to be uncommitted because they are bored with their jobs, techniques for enhancing job involvement become of interest. It is also seems conceivable that one form of commitment might be used to elevate another, thereby improving employee–employer relations.

The third rationale is based on the growth in team-based management methods. The expanding use of these means, such as self-managed work teams and quality circles, is another justification for continuing interest in commitment forms. Like union commitment, work group commitment could conceivably evolve into a universal form of work commitment. The fourth factor is changing labor force participation patterns and anticipated labor shortage. These processes are reasons for concern with work commitment. More and more employees anticipate and realize lifelong paid employment. This expectation alone will probably cause people to view their occupation in career-oriented terms. Organizations that appreciate these shifts in expectations and values may be better equipped to manage employee commitment levels, hopefully by striking a better balance between individuals and organizational interests. On the assumption that the predicted, demographically induced shortage of labor is realized, future workers will also have more options in choosing their careers, jobs, and organizations. Organizations may need to adopt more of a "customer orientation" toward workers, as the latter "shop" for employers. To secure and retain the very best employees, organizations will be obliged to meet their expectations (Morrow, 1993).

The fifth reason stems from the argument that organizations are not disappearing. They may be becoming leaner, but they must maintain a core of people who are the organization. As organizations slim down, those who stay in them become more important. Once the fat is gone, the remaining employees represent the heart, brain, and muscle of the organization. All the more important, therefore, that the organization be able to trust the employees to do what is right, something that commitment arguably ensures. Also, organizations that contract work out to other companies or individuals will still be concerned about the commitment of these contractors. The organizations' own success might depend on it.

The last reason is based on the argument that commitment develops naturally. There is reason to believe that people need to be committed to something; the opposite of commitment is alienation, and alienation is unhealthy. If they become less committed to organizations, as a result of the changing nature of careers (Sullivan, 1999) from traditional to boundaryless (defined by DeFillippi & Arthur, 1996, p. 116 as "… a sequence of job opportunities that go beyond the boundaries of a simple employment setting"), employees may channel their commitment in other directions. In addition to being of relevance for the understanding of the individual's own well being, the behavioral consequences of these commitments might have implications for employees' relations with their organizations. For example, employees who are reluctant to develop a commitment to an organization that cannot or will not reciprocate might instead become committed to their occupation/profession or to the industry in which they work (Meyer & Allen, 1997). Although there might be additional reasons to those mentioned here, those presented here show that all in all understanding commitment and how it develops is as important now as it ever was.

The Rationale for a Multiple-Commitment Approach

The last argument set out above provides good justification for the approach adopted by this book, namely a *multiple-commitment approach*. That is, if employees are less committed to one aspect in the workplace (i.e., the organization), they may be more committed to another aspect (the job or the occupation). This may be one important reason to justify the need for the growing interest in the broader concept of work commitment. Such an approach shows the usefulness of multiple commitments, in contrast to focusing on one or another isolated form of commitment. People must be committed to something: if it is not the organization it will be another entity in the work setting. Therefore, the debate among some researchers about the relevance of organizational commitment is not that crucial if we know that employees who are not committed to the organization are probably committed to another focus at work. This likelihood does increase the usefulness of the multiple commitments approach. We want to know which other entity our employees are committed to—is it the profession, the job, the union? What are the determinants of these commitments? Which outcomes, such as turnover, performance, and absenteeism, do they affect?

A multiple approach is much more useful in dynamic, changing times like those we are experiencing now. In a dynamic environment employees may be committed to different entities in different settings. Magnitudes of commitments may differ across time, industries, professions, and cultures. All this can be captured if we apply a multiple commitment approach, but we may miss it if we concentrate on one commitment. This probably constitutes one reason for the broadening consensus among commitment theorists and researchers that commitment is a multidimensional construct.

Individuals are not committed to only one group or organization, because various social structures, including work organizations, place people in "multiple," nested collectivities where they are simultaneously members of at least two groups, one encompassing the other (Lawler, 1992). Because an individual is simultaneously committed to several environments, it would not be surprising that a single commitment to a single group guarantees little control over that individual's behavior. A person acts on the implications of commitments as a function of the salience of the implication and the strength of the commitment. If the implications of some behaviors are not salient their impact is less than if they are. If a certain social group is not salient the commitment to that group is less relevant to ongoing behavior than if the group is salient.

Consequently, people may be simultaneously committed to a variety of units, such as the union, the family, the organization, social groups, and so forth. An individual's commitment to one life sphere may prevent his/her commitment to another (e.g., to family as against organization; Mowday et al., 1982). Accordingly people invest their behaviors in many social environments at the same time, and the demands from these various groups may conflict. Although most problems of conflicting roles and commitments are probably handled by the relative salience of each, sometimes individuals may actually have to choose among them. The choice would mirror the degree of commitment to the alternative groups (Salancik, 1977a, 1977b).

Several examples to multiple commitments or conflicting commitments were already advanced in early research on commitment. Gouldner (1957, 1958) acknowledged that an individual can be committed to more foci than one, and emphasized the height of the levels of commitment to the two objects. Gouldner discussed differences in commitment levels based on a person being "local" (organizationally oriented) versus "cosmopolitan" (professionally oriented). Being "local" means that one is more intensely committed to the organization than to the profession or occupation and being "cosmopolitan" means the reverse. Stagner (1954, 1961) and Purcell (1954) studied unilateral versus dual commitment to the union and to the firm, an approach to studying commitment that has recently gained fresh prominence (Magenau, Martin, & Peterson, 1988; Fukami & Larson, 1984). The rationale is similar to that advanced by Gouldner but it highlights two different foci. The question of compatibility is central to research probing the links between these two pairs of commitments.

The above studies indicated that individuals are subject to demands from several groups (e.g., union and firm) or entities (e.g., occupation or organization), and this may in turn affect their commitment to each. Consequently, a focus is needed on the concept of work commitment, which examines multiple commitments simultaneously, rather than one commitment at a time. An employee may experience simultaneously different levels of commitment to different objects in the work environment, such as organization, occupation, the union, and their job. Consequently, the question of what the employee is committed to cannot simply be answered by "organizational goals and values."

Conceptual Framework for Multiple Commitments

The Conflict Approach.   Although the previously mentioned literature acknowledges the existence of multiple commitments, little conceptual or theoretical work has been done on this issue. The literature has suggested two main conceptual frameworks for an understanding of multiple commitments. One embraces the potential conflict among various commitment objects. This approach posits a carryover effect among foci of commitments. That is, an individual who identifies with his or her task group also tends to identify with the larger organization, because the task group is an integral part of the larger organization. However, successful commitment transference often depends on an individual's perception of compatibility among alternative targets, in terms of such criteria, as need satisfaction and goal congruency. In the absence of perceived compatibility among alternative targets of commitment, different targets quite plausibly do indeed represent competing sources for identification. Historically, commitment to one value system was deemed inherently incompatible with commitment to another value system (Rotondi, 1975).

The conflict approach postulates that the potential for conflicts that may exist among commitments is perhaps the most significant question in the multiple-commitment approach. To the extent that organizations pursue the conflicting goals of multiple constituencies, individuals committed to them may suffer on account of conflicts over the direction that their energies and loyalties should take. Commitment to one group may imply the necessary abandonment of other identifications with other groups. This form of conflict may be more fundamental than a simple role conflict concerning appropriate job-related behaviors. The potential conflict among multiple commitments involves the self-concept and identity of individuals because the set of identifications and commitments an individual experience is an integral part of the self (Reichers, 1985). Moreover, this approach argued that if commitment behavior is not typically transferred from subgroups to the total organization, dysfunctional behavior might exist among personnel of any subgroup whose goals are in conflict with the goals of the total organization (Rotondi, 1975; Vandenberg & Scarpello, 1994).

One of the most important demonstrations of this approach is the expected inverse relation between occupational commitment and organizational commitment. Accordingly, occupational self-control was seen as incompatible with bureaucratic control and organizational loyalty was considered to be inconsistent with client loyalty. Gouldner's (1957, 1958) concept of "local" versus "cosmopolitan" applies to predominately organizational or occupational foci. Gouldner concentrated on the notion of a hidden conflict between one's orientations toward one's organization as against one's occupation. Stagner (1954, 1961), Purcell (1954), and more recently Angle and Perry (1986) and Magenau, Martin, and Peterson (1988), suggested similar conflicts between union and organizational commitment. This conflict was studied on the basis of the concept of unilateral versus dual commitment to the union and one's firm, a concept partially supported by this research.

The positive correlations found among union, occupational, and organizational commitment (Mathieu & Zajac, 1990; Wallace, 1993; 1995a; 1995b; Vandenberg & Scarpello, 1994) do not support the notion of hidden conflict between these commitments. Particular attention should be paid to the meta-analysis findings of Wallace (1993) which, in a study of 25 samples, revealed a relatively strong average corrected correlation of .45 between occupational and organizational commitment. However, the positive effect of occupational commitment, against the negative effect of organizational and job commitment on job and organization withdrawal intentions, does in some way support the notion of conflict between commitment objects in and outside the organization (occupation, union). The notion of conflict as a conceptual framework for work commitments as suggested by Gouldner (1957, 1958) and by Angle and Perry (1986) has some empirical support.

The Exchange Approach. The second conceptual approach, exchange theory, was proposed mainly for understanding the determinants of organizational commitment (Mowday et al., 1982), and also those of union commitment (Magenau, Martin, & Peterson, 1988). According to this approach a positive exchange relationship with one object of commitment and a negative relationship with another may also affect work behavior outcomes (Magenau et al., 1988).

A good demonstration of the exchange approach was advanced by Brown (1996), who argued that all commitments have an object or focus, a party to which the commitment is made. This may be a person, a group of persons, an entity made up of people, an idea, or a cause. All commitments also include some idea of terms, namely, an understanding of what must be done by a committed party to uphold the commitment. The first element allows us for the time being to direct discussion to an organizational focus as opposed to other foci. The second element, terms, clarifies the agreement and enables a person to make more than one commitment to a particular party.

Brown contended that evaluating one's commitments, in light of competing demands and options for involvement, is a natural and continuous process. A person's current circumstances and feelings, influenced by recall of the development process, affect how that person evaluates a commitment. Many factors affect attitudes and feelings, which in turn affect a person's evaluation of a commitment, but the bottom line is an ongoing subjective appraisal of the worthiness of the commitment in light of the other options. This evaluation can affect the relative strength of the commitment, and through that, the actions a person takes with regard to meeting the terms. According to Brown, positive attitudes lead to positive evaluations, supportive behaviors, and quite possibly an enhancement of the understood terms. Persistent doubts and negative attitudes, in most cases, lead to an unfavorable evaluation, a desire to minimize the terms, and possibly an attempt to withdraw from the commitment. Or they may cause a person to downplay the commitment by shifting the focus to other commitments.

In recent literature, the exchange approach was presented through the concept of psychological contract. This is an unwritten agreement between an individual and the organization where the terms of employment are entered into (Millward & Hopkins, 1998). The psychological contract signifies issues of exchange and of mutual expectations in the link between individuals and the organizations for which they work. It can be conceptualized as a sophisticated set of expectations and rules that form the psychological basis for the continuing commitment of an employee to his or her employer (Cavanagh, 1996). More formally, the psychological contract was defined as an individual's belief in paid-for promises or a reciprocal obligation between the individual and the organization (Rousseau, 1995). A demonstration of such an approach that is more relevant to organizational commitment is based on supervisor–employee relations, showing that bosses secure greater commitment from selected subordinates by providing them with greater discretion, attention, influence, support, information, and other resources. Subordinates reciprocate by offering organizationally desired contributions such as commitment (Mottaz, 1988; Nystrom, 1990).

Rousseau (1998) argued that once particularistic rewards are exchanged and identification begins, individuals are likely to become concerned with the broader interests of the organization including its reputation, survival, and continued success, that generates activity and resource exchanges (reflecting enhanced concern between firm and employee) that foster further identification. However, Rousseau contended that the problem with this simple model is that it ignores the symbolic aspects of many economic resource exchanges that convey meaning to the parties to the exchange regarding the nature of their relationship.

Rousseau (1998) suggested that a conceptually rich framework for characterizing resource exchange is Foa and Foa's (1974) resource theory, which distinguishes resource types. One dimension of this framework is particularly relevant to commitment, namely particularism/universalism. *Particularism*, in the sense of Foa and Foa, means that the value of a given resource is influenced by the particular people involved in the exchange and their mutual relationship. Three resources they identify as particularistic are love, status, and information. In all three cases, the origin of the resource affects its meaning for and acceptability by the receiver. Particularistic resources can only be provided when trust exists between the parties, typically in the context of relations characterized by interactions over time.

By contrast, universalistic resources such as money or goods can be exchanged in almost any type of interaction. The constraints that a relationship places on the exchange of particularistic resources means that employers are only able to offer a broad array of resources when their employees are willing to accept them. Where workers identify with the organization, the organization is able to offer (as well as receive) particularistic and universalistic rewards. When identification is low, only universalistic rewards can in effect be exchanged. Rousseau (1998) showed that not only are employees more likely to perceive assurances of caring and concern as genuine when identification exists but their willingness to reciprocate such concern is enhanced. Such increased levels of discretionary effort displayed on the organization's behalf can generate positive organizational responses (e.g., recognition of the employee as a valued member), which can act further to strengthen deeply structured identification with the organization.

Rousseau's (1998) framework allows us to apply the exchange more easily to the context of multiple commitments. That is, the exchange relation with some forms of commitment is more universalistic in nature, or, in a combination of universalistic and particularistic, places stronger emphasis on universalistic rewards (e.g., the organization or the union). The exchange relation with other forms of commitment is more particularistic in nature, or a combination of the two lays stronger emphasis on particularistic rewards (e.g., the occupation or the job).

It seems that the exchange approach is the dominant one in understanding multiple commitments. First, most research findings showed positive correlations among commitment forms. This contradicts the basic argument of the conflict approach, which expects negative relations among any given combination of commitment forms. Second, although the conflict approach is more relevant for understanding the interrelations among commitment forms, the exchange approach is also useful for understanding the antecedents of commitment. Different commitment forms have different exchange relations with different potential determinants.

The State of Research on Multiple Commitments

Two of the leading studies on work commitment have been conducted by Morrow, one published in a paper in 1983, the other in a comprehensive book that appeared in 1993. These works of Morrow (1983, 1993) have been at the forefront in the advancement of a multivariate approach to multiple commitments. In them, Morrow compared the definition and measurement of different forms of commitment such as the organization, job, career, union, and work values. She focused on the problems of concept redundancy among different definitions and measures of work commitment and recommended additional research to examine the problem of overlap of commitment measures. Using a comprehensive analysis of the different forms of commitment in the work setting, Morrow (1983) proposed three recommendations for future research on commitment forms. Because of the finding that some forms of commitment were partly redundant and insufficiently distinct to warrant continued separation, Morrow's first recommendation was for a more rigorous examination of the differences among the various forms of commitment. Her second recommendation was more empirical examination of the forms of commitment as dependent variables. Third, Morrow concentrated on the need for conceptual re-evaluation of commitment. This re-evaluation should concentrate on examining similarities and differences among the various forms of commitment, on the assumption of the small likelihood of a single, unidimensional generic concept and measure of commitment being devised.

Of these three recommendations only the first has received much attention in the literature. Most research into work commitment has concentrated on the discriminant validity of different measures of work commitment forms in an attempt to clarify empirically whether concept redundancy exists among its various manifestations (Blau, Paul, & St. John, 1993; Morrow & McElroy, 1986; Morrow & Wirth 1989; Morrow, Eastman, & McElroy, 1991; Brooke, Russell, & Price, 1988; Mathieu & Farr, 1991; Blau, 1985). Other studies proposed and tested new measures (e.g., Cohen, 1993a) or changes in established measures (e.g., Blau, Paul, & St. John, 1993) for improving the discriminant validity of work commitment constructs.

Only minimal research has been conducted regarding Morrow's other two recommendations. Most of the work on multiple commitments has been methodological as opposed to conceptual. Meyer, Allen, and Smith (1993) rightly stated that until then no systematic attempt had been made to develop a multidimensional conceptualization of commitment applicable across domains, and noted that the development of such a conceptualization would help to foster communication among researchers studying commitment within their various domains.

Because most of the work dealing with multiple commitments has been methodological and not conceptual, little progress has occurred in the understanding of the conceptual relations among the different commitment forms, how they differ in their effects on work outcomes, and how they differ as dependent variables. Research examined the effects of commitment forms on work outcomes such as turnover, turnover intentions, performance, job satisfaction, and prosocial organizational behaviors (Becker, 1992; Cohen, 1993a, 1999b; Wiener & Vardi, 1980). The research indicated that a multivariate approach to commitment could predict work outcomes better than each commitment could predict separately. Little research has been conducted into the differences among the different forms of commitment as dependent variables, or has tried to explore the relations among them. In short, more research on work commitment is needed because our understanding of commitment processes increases by an examination of more than one commitment at a time (Reichers 1985).

This volume begins where Morrow's work ended. Morrow (1983, 1993) thoroughly reviewed each of the commitment foci, its definition, measurement determinants, and outcomes. Because of the need for a simultaneous presentation of the different foci of commitment, most of her book concentrated on such presentation. Only in the last part of it did the author emphasize the need for understanding and analyzing commitment by a multiple approach. As mentioned, Morrow's book ends with important recommendations for future research on work commitment adopting such an approach.

This volume is mostly devoted to the multiple commitment approach, and investigates the concept of work commitment from an integrative perspective. Namely, it studies how these commitments relate together, how distinct or similar they are, how they affect work outcomes, and what the determinants are that affect them. An adequate body of research exists analyzing commitment at the workplace from an integrative approach. As most of this work so far has concentrated on separate commitment forms, the need arises to discuss, review, propose, and summarize research on the joint effect of these commitments on employees' behavior and attitudes. Taking the multiple-commitment approach as more conducive to the understanding of commitment in the workplace raises several interesting questions: What defines the boundaries for the various foci? What determines the foci to which an employee becomes committed? Under what conditions are commitments to these different foci likely to be compatible or to conflict? How do these multiple commitments combine to shape employees' behavior? These are some of the major issues that this volume addresses.

II

Conceptual Considerations in Multiple Commitment Research

2

Commitment Forms: Descriptions and Characteristics

Before dealing with the mutual effects and interrelations of work commitment forms they should be reviewed. Our understanding of the meaning of the interrelations among the different forms and their effects on work outcomes expands if we familiarize ourselves with what each of the individual foci of commitment represents. A more thorough review of each of these can be found in Morrow's work (1993) which, however, mostly examines each commitment focus separately. This volume elaborates on the integrative approach so its review of each commitment focus is much briefer. The technical aspects of the different scales such as their psychometric properties are not addressed; these too can be found in Morrow's study.

Furthermore, the measurement scales of the main approaches to commitment foci are set out in Appendix A; readers no doubt can better understand each form of commitment with the relevant scales before them. This also allows deeper comprehension of the complexity of the integrative approach, which uses several of these scales to measure more than one commitment form in the same study. In addition, it facilitates the researcher's decision on whether to use this scale or that scale in his or her own research.

Morrow and McElroy (1993) in their summary of a special issue on work commitment, mentioned some major limitations in work commitment research noted in the papers published in that issue. One of these was the uneven interest in the various forms of work commitment, with emphasis on the work ethic whereas career and occupational commitment was somewhat neglected. In consequence, they argued, our understanding of these concepts lags behind that of organizational commitment considerably, delaying a grasp of how various forms of work commitment are related. To understand fully the integrative approach familiarity with all the relevant commitment forms is essential. Accordingly, throughout the volume I elaborate on those commitment forms that have not received attention as organizational commitment.

ORGANIZATIONAL COMMITMENT

The concept of *organizational commitment* (OC) has grown in popularity in the literature of industrial and organizational psychology and organizational behavior (Mathieu & Zajac, 1990). Of all the forms of commitment, the organizational form still receives most attention (Griffin & Bateman, 1986, p. 166). This interest is apparent from the numerous studies that have examined the relations between OC and its antecedents and outcomes (e.g., Mathieu & Zajac, 1990; Mowday et al., 1982). This high degree of attention, it is argued, stems from the fact that OC "is theory based, broad in focus, holds significant integrative potential, and may be more manageable than other forms" (Griffin & Bateman, 1986, p. 166). Another reason is the perception that OC can predict turnover better than other work attitudes, especially job satisfaction (Williams & Hazer, 1986; Clugston, 2000). Moreover, it is argued that organizations whose members have higher levels of commitment show higher performance and productivity and lower levels of absenteeism and tardiness (Bateman & Strasser, 1984; Morris & Sherman, 1981).

Approaches to Organizational Commitment

Growing interest in OC has probably contributed to the conceptual richness of its definition. This has, correspondingly, led to diverse approaches to measuring this construct (Griffin & Bateman, 1986; Morrow, 1983; Mowday et al., 1982; Reichers, 1985). The differences among measures of OC have generally paralleled the distinction between two theoretical approaches to the construct: the "side-bet" ,or, calculative approach and the moral or attitudinal approach (Cohen & Lowenberg, 1990; Cohen & Gattiker, 1992; Ferris & Aranya, 1983; Griffin & Bateman, 1986; McGee & Ford, 1987).

The calculative approach rested on the side-bet theory of Howard Becker (1960), who used the term to refer to the accumulation of investments valued by the individual that would be lost or deemed worthless if he or she were to leave the organization. Becker argued that over a period of time certain costs accrue that make it more difficult for the person to disengage from a consistent line of activity, namely, maintaining membership in the organization. The threat of losing these investments, along with a perceived lack of alternatives to replace or make up for them, commits the person to the organization. According to this view, the individual is bound to the organization by extraneous factors such as income and hierarchical position, and internal factors such as "knowing the ropes" and interpersonal relations (Cohen, 1993b; Cohen & Gattiker, 1992; Cohen & Lowenberg, 1990; Meyer & Allen, 1984; Wallace, 1997). The loss of friendships and seniority rights also can be a factor when employers are changed. Becker (1960) phrased his argument as follows:

> The man who hesitates to take a new job may be deterred by a complex of side-bets: the financial costs connected with a pension fund he would lose if he moved; the loss of seniority and "connections" in his present firm, which promise quick advance if he stays; the loss of ease in doing his work because of his success in adjusting to the particular conditions of his present job; the loss of ease in domestic living consequent on having to move his household, and so on. (pp. 38–39)

The measure based on this theory attempted to reflect the basic arguments of this approach. They were first developed by Ritzer and Trice (1969), with some methodological modifications added later by Hrebiniak and Alutto (1972), and Alutto, Hrebiniak, and Alonso (1973). These measures question the respondents on the likelihood of their leaving the organization, given various levels of inducement in pay, status, responsibility, job freedom, and opportunity for promotion. The revised measure, presented in Appendix A, is used often, especially in research on the side-bet theory (e.g., Fukami & Larson, 1984; Hunt, Chonko, & Wood, 1985; Parasuraman & Nachman, 1987; Wittig-Berman & Lang, 1990).

The second approach sees commitment as affective or attitudinal, and has been called the "organizational behavior" (Staw, 1977) or "psychology" (Near, 1989) approach. It regards the individual as identifying with the organization, hence committed to retaining membership to pursue his or her goals. The origins of this treatment of commitment perhaps lie principally in the work of Porter and his associates (e.g., Porter, Steers, Mowday & Boulian, 1974; Mowday et al., 1982); and has been termed *affective commitment* (Meyer & Allen, 1984) and *value commitment* (Angle & Perry, 1981). This approach developed the most commonly used measure of OC, the attitudinal Organizational Commitment Questionnaire (OCQ) introduced by Porter and Smith (1970).

This scale, displayed in Appendix A, also known as the Porter et al. measure (1974), is "the most visible measure of affective commitment [and] has enjoyed widespread acceptance and use" (Griffin & Bateman, 1986, p. 170).

It consists of 15 items (a shortened version has nine positively phrased items) reflecting the three dimensions of the definition of commitment as suggested by Porter et al. (1974). These are (a) a desire to maintain membership in the organization, (b) belief in and acceptance of the values and goals of the organization, and (c) willingness to exert effort on behalf of the organization. Although Mowday et al. (1982) and Mowday, Steers, and Porter (1979) demonstrated the well-proven psychometric properties of this measure; they also noted that the relations between their measure and some attitudinal variables such as job satisfaction and job involvement were too high for an acceptable level of discriminant validity. Later, in separate examinations of the OCQ characteristics, Morrow (1983), Blau (1985, 1987), and Commeiras and Fournier (2001) supported the general conclusion that it contains good psychometric properties.

Despite the existence of alternative conceptualizations and measures of OC such as the side-bet approach (Becker, 1960), the OCQ dominated the literature from the early 1970s to the mid-1980s. Most OC findings are based on this measure, as are the conclusions and future research agenda. Furthermore, the many studies about OC and its relations with antecedents and work outcomes have, meanwhile, been subjected to several meta-analyses (Mathieu & Zajac, 1990; Cohen, 1991, 1992; 1993d; Cohen & Gattiker, 1994; Randall, 1990; Gaertner, 1999) that quantitatively summarized the findings on the concept. But recently some criticism has arisen regarding Porter et al.'s (1974) measure, the OCQ. The basic difficulty is that two of the dimensions of commitment of the OCQ, a strong desire to maintain membership in the organization and a willingness to exert considerable effort on behalf of the organization, overlap with intentions of outcome behaviors such as withdrawal and performance (Reichers 1985; O'Reilly & Chatman, 1986; Bozeman & Perrewe, 2001). The response to that criticism has taken two directions. First, researchers have tended to use the 9-item version of the OCQ more frequently than the full 15 items to avoid the 6 problematic negatively phrased items of the measure that dealt with withdrawal and performance (Beck & Wilson, 2000; Iverson, 1999). Second and possibly of equal importance, a new trend has started to evolve in the definition and measurement of OC.

On the argument that OC can be better understood as a multidimensional concept, Meyer and Allen (1984) proposed a two-dimensional measure of OC. Conceptually, their distinction between the two dimensions paralleled that between the side-bet calculative approach of Becker (1960) and the attitudinal approach of Porter and his colleagues (1974). The first dimension was termed affective commitment, and was defined as "positive feelings of identification with, attachment to, and involvement in, the work organization" (Meyer & Allen, 1984, p. 375). The second was termed continuance commitment, and was defined as "the extent to which employees feel committed to their organizations by virtue of the costs that they feel are associated with leaving (e.g., investments or lack of attractive alternatives)."

McGee and Ford (1987) in their factor analysis found that the continuance commitment scale is a two-dimensional construct. One subdimension represents sacrifices made by the employees by staying in the organization and was termed *high sacrifice*, and the other represents available employment alternatives, and was termed *low alternatives*. Meyer, Allen, and Gellatly (1990) replicated this finding. In subsequent research, Allen and Meyer (1990) added a third dimension, termed normative commitment, that was defined as the employees' feelings of obligation to remain with the organization. All three scales are shown in Appendix A, this volume.

The factor analysis of Allen and Meyer (1990) supported the proposed three-dimensional scales. In their assessment of the scales Hackett, Bycio, and Hausdorf (1992) generally supported the existence of three dimensions. But based on a LISREL model, a better fit with the data was found for a four-component model, with the continuance commitment being divided into two dimensions along the lines suggested by McGee and Ford (1987). However, certain studies (Jaros, 1997; Ko, Price, & Mueller, 1997) indicated problems with the dimensionality of commitment based on Meyer and Allen's (1990) scales. In a later study, Ko et al. (1997) found that reliabilities of the affective commitment and the normative scales were acceptable, whereas the reliability of the continuance commitment scale was low. The three scales had acceptable convergent validity, but the affective and the normative scales lacked discriminant validity. The construct validity of the affective commitment was supported whereas the construct validities of the continuance commitment and the normative commitment scales were questionable. The authors concluded that a new measure should be devised for continuance and normative commitment.

MEASURES OF ORGANIZATIONAL COMMITMENT

The need for research that examines the measurement of OC was identified by Mowday et al. (1982), who stated, "Little evidence exists of any systematic or comprehensive efforts to determine the stability, consistency, or predictive powers of the various instruments" (p. 219). Griffin and Bateman (1986) supported this position: "With regard to commitment research, much work on scaling needs to be done" (p. 180). They argued that more empirical work was requisite for an enhancement of investigators' ability to make comparisons and contrasts across studies, and to improve their ability to draw inferences regarding generalizability.

Some information on the common OC scales has been provided above, so this section concentrates mainly on comparisons among the different scales. Despite the important theoretical and practical implications of these arguments, few empirical studies have compared different measures of OC. Ferris and Aranya (1983) compared two measures, the OCQ and the Hrebiniak and Alutto (1972) measure for the results of several antecedents and outcomes of OC. They found the correlations and the explained variance to be generally stronger between the 10 antecedents and the attitudinal measure (the OCQ) than between these same antecedents and the calculative measure (the Hrebiniak & Alutto measure). The OCQ was found to predict turnover intentions better than did the Hrebiniak and Alutto measure, but no difference was found between the two regarding actual turnover.

Meyer and Allen (1984) and McGee and Ford (1987) compared the Hrebiniak and Alutto scale, the Ritzer and Trice scale, the Porter et al. scale, and two scales developed by Meyer and Allen (one an affective scale, the other a continuance scale). Meyer and Allen's (1984) analysis focused on the relations among the different scales. They also examined the relations between the five scales and age and tenure; their main conclusion was that the two assumed continuance commitment measures (Hrebiniak & Alutto, 1972; Ritzer & Trice, 1969) "reflect primarily affective commitment rather than continuance commitment" (p. 376). Meyer and Allen concluded that the continuance measure, which they had developed, was a more appropriate measure for the side-bet theory was than that of Hrebiniak and Alutto (1972) of Ritzer and Trice (1969). McGee and Ford's (1987) reexamination of their findings supported Meyer and Allen's conclusion, but the findings of a later study (Ko et al., 1997) contradicted it. The conclusions of these studies assert that almost all existing measures of OC are attitudinal.

O'Reilly and Caldwell (1980) found the OCQ to correlate more strongly with intrinsic and extrinsic factors in the choice of a job than did a behavioral scale using two items of tenure intentions. In another study (O'Reilly & Caldwell, 1981), variables reflecting aspects of job choice processes such as explicitness of formal contract and explicitness of employer expectations, were found to be related quite similarly to both attitudinal (Porter et al., 1974) and behavioral (tenure intentions) scales of OC. This behavioral measure also proved to have a stronger relation with actual turnover than did the attitudinal scale. Wiener and Vardi (1980) found that the Hrebiniak and Alutto scale related more strongly to job satisfaction than did the normative scale they had developed. They found no marked difference between the two scales in their ability to predict organizational outcomes such as effort, attachment, and performance. Finally, Kacmar, Carlson and Brymer (1999) compared the OCQ with a three-dimensional measure developed by

Balfour and Wechsler (1996) and found little overlap between them. They concluded that Balfour and Wechsler's scale measured components of OC not captured by the OCQ.

The measure used in most research on OC is Meyer and Allen's (1984) 8-item affective commitment scale. Recent empirical research suggests that this is superior to the Porter et al.'s (1974) OCQ scale (Blau et al., 1993). Moreover, some literature has argued that affective commitment is the most important component of OC in predicting turnover (Jaros, 1997; Somers, 1995). However, accumulated data on these scales indicated some problems, particularly with continuance commitment and normative commitment scales. Allen and Meyer (1996), in a thorough review of research on their scales mentioned possible problems with the dimensionality of the continuance commitment dimension and the similarity of the normative to the affective commitment. They suggested the use of a 6-item revised form of the normative commitment scale (Meyer & Allen, 1997; see Appendix A). However, their revised scale includes some items referring to withdrawal cognition that are more consequences of commitment. Ko et al. (1997) concluded from their findings that the 3-component model of commitment contained conceptual problems which were the main reason for the difficulties with the psychometric properties of the continuance commitment and normative commitment scales. Vandenberg and Self (1993) found in a longitudinal design that the factor structure of affective commitment and continuance commitment was profoundly changed, and attributed this to conceptual problems in the two scales.

Finally, several authors have devised their own measures, in addition to the two main approaches to the measurement of organizational commitment. "Most of these measures consist of from two- to four-item scales that are created on an a priori basis and for which little or no validity and reliability data are presented" (Mowday et al., 1982, p. 219). These scales were developed and adjusted to meet the needs of specific research designs, and most were not used by later researchers (e.g., Antonovsky & Antonovsky, 1974; Baba & Knoop, 1987; Bhuian, Al-Shammari, & Jefri, 1996; Brager, 1969; Brown, 1969; Currivan, 1999; Decotiis & Summers, 1987; Ferris, 1981; Franklin, 1975; Gouldner, 1960; Gregerson, 1993; Grusky, 1966; Hall & Schneider, 1972; Hall, Schneider, & Nygren, 1970; Hudson & Sullivan, 1985; Jauch, Glueck, & Osborn, 1978; Kalleberg & Mastekaasa, 2001; Koch & Steers, 1978; Landy & Guion, 1970; Lee, 1969, 1971; Marsh & Mannari, 1971, 1972, 1977; Moon, 2000; Nogradi & Koch, 1981; Organ & Greene, 1981; Patchen, 1970; Rotondi, 1975a, 1975b, 1976; Rubenowitz, Norrigren, & Tannenbaum, 1983; Schneider, Hall, & Nygren, 1971; Sheldon, 1971; Templer, 1982; Thornton, 1970; Wiener & Vardi, 1980; Werbel & Gould, 1984; Yoon, Baker, & Ko, 1994).

OCCUPATIONAL AND PROFESSIONAL
AND CAREER COMMITMENT

Definition and Terminology

Occupational and professional commitment focuses on the employee's profession, occupation, or career. Morrow (1983, p. 490) emphasized the importance of this commitment focus: "... it is one of the few commitment concepts that attempts to capture the notion of devotion to a craft, occupation, or profession apart from any specific work environment, over an extended period of time" Blau (1985) argued that in order not to making this commitment form redundant with other concepts (e.g., work involvement, job involvement, organizational commitment) the focus of this form should be more specific than "work in general" and have broader referents than "job" and "organization." Career, profession, and occupation represent somewhat different entities. Yet all three foci are seem to be in accord with Blau's argument that they are more specific than "work in general" and broader than job or organization. Note that the terms *occupation, profession,* and *career* were used somewhat interchangeably in the commitment literature (Meyer, Allen, & Smith, 1993). All three seem to capture a similar notion, as argued by Morrow (1993), namely the importance of one's occupation.

Because the three terms greatly overlap, analyzing them as separate commitments increases concept redundancy among commitment foci. Accordingly, Morrow's suggestion to treat them as one commitment focus is adopted here. A related question is which of the three terms should be used in specifying this commitment. Some argue that the term *career commitment* is ambiguous because "career" can be defined as a planned pattern of work from entry into the workforce to retirement (Meyer et al., 1993). Others held that professions are a special type of vocation. Perhaps "profession" should only be applied to vocations that are consistently high on characteristics of professionalism. If so, fewer professional occupations can be designated simply as "vocations" (Blau, 1988). According to this argument the definition of career commitment could be slightly revised, to "one's attitude towards one's vocation, including a profession" (Blau, 1988; p. 295), because a profession is a special type of vocation. The emphasis is on the vocation itself rather than specific jobs within the vocation.

Because we are interested in assessing commitment to a particular line of work, the term *occupation* is more appropriate. However, as Blau (1988) argued, a question for future research pertains to the necessary minimum levels of professionalism characteristics, below which a measure of career commitment is no longer useful. For example, could career commitment be reliably and validly operational with samples of factory workers, custodians, or mechanics? Following the previous arguments, we use the term *occupa-*

tion (for example, in occupational commitment) and not *profession*. This usage rests on the belief that professionals and nonprofessionals can experience commitment to the work that they do.

Conceptual Approaches to Occupational Commitment

Conceptually, this form of commitment has two main approaches. The first is based on the concept of professionalism, namely, the extent to which individual members identify with their profession and endorse its values. One of the earliest typologies based on this approach was advanced by Becker and Carper (1956). From data they collected from interviewing students in different disciplines, they isolated four elements for identification with an occupation: (a) occupational title, and associated ideology; (b) commitment to task; (c) commitment to particular organizations or institutional positions; and (d) significance for one's position in the larger society. Becker's (1960) side-bet theory, which was largely applied to the concept of organizational commitment, was also presented as the theoretical basis for professional commitment. The reason is that Becker originally conceptualized the side-bet model as applying to both occupational and organizational commitment (Wallace, 1997).

As noted earlier, Becker (1960) used "side-bets" to refer to the accumulation of investments valued by the individual that would be lost if he or she were to leave the organization or the occupation. Becker suggested that commitment to a course of action develops as one makes such side-bets. Several studies have tested occupational commitment using Becker's theory, and assessing the validity of this theory for both organizational and occupational commitment (Alutto et al. 1973; Aranya & Jacobson, 1975; Aranya et al. 1981; Ritzer & Trice, 1969). These studies applied the measurement of organizational commitment to occupational commitment by substituting "relevant occupation" for organization.

Another approach to occupational commitment arises from the notion of career. This approach defined career commitment as the magnitude of an actor's motivation to work in a career he or she chose (Hall, 1971) or as the degree of centrality of one's career for one's identity (Gould, 1979). Our knowledge on career commitment lacks a precise and systematic approach (e.g., Layder, 1984; Louis, 1980; Tziner, 1983). One of the important contributions to our understanding the concept of career commitment is the work of Greenhaus and his colleagues (Greenhaus, 1971, 1973; Greenhaus & Simon, 1977; Greenhaus & Sklarew, 1977). Greenhaus tried to rectify the relative dearth in research on career commitment by defining and developing a 28-item scale for what he termed *career salience*. It referred to three broad areas: general attitudes toward work; degree of vocationally relevant planning and thought; and the relative importance of work. This scale was validated mostly in samples of students (Greenhaus, 1971, 1973). Subsequently other measures of career salience were advanced, such as that of Sekaran (1982, 1986).

The work of Greenhaus and his colleagues (1971, 1973) focused mostly on occupation and job search, not the work setting. Their approach is chiefly criticized in that its definition and measurement of career salience overlaps with other commitment foci, particularly "job involvement" and "work involvement" (Blau, 1985; Morrow, 1983; Wiener & Vardi, 1980). Greenhaus's approach and scales are not regarded as foremost in research on commitment forms. The overlap problem just mentioned prevents re-searchers from applying this scale for measuring multiple commitments.

The following two approaches seem more dominant and relevant for the integrative principle. The problems outlined previously led Blau (1985) to argue for an alternative approach and scale. Blau posited that research on concepts related to career commitment such as professional commitment, occupational commitment, and career orientation suggested both a concep-tual definition of career commitment and a way to operationalize that defi-nition. He defined career commitment as one's attitude to one's profession or vocation. Blau's (1985, 1988, 1989, 1999) findings showed encouraging results in the psychometric properties of his scale, particularly in the scale's discriminant validity. In a later study, Blau, Paul, and St. John (1993) devel-oped a revised occupational commitment scale intended to fit better with the other scales of commitment forms. In this scale, occupational commit-ment was defined as "one's attitude, including affect, belief, and behavioral intention, toward his/her occupation" (p. 311).

Carson and Bedeian (1994) criticized Blau's scale in three ways. First, the high correspondence reported by Blau between career commitment and ca-reer withdrawal cognition may be due to items in his measure emphasizing one's intention-to-remain in one's vocation. Second, in developing his scale Blau (1985) extracted the best items from two existing instruments empha-sizing work attitudes and career orientation. Whereas such an approach is generally considered acceptable in generating an initial pool of items, unless final item selection is based on systematic development procedures there is no assurance that an intended measure possesses content validity. Third, Blau's measure was developed by the extraction of the best items from two existing instruments. Consequently, beyond its uncertain content validity, the internal (inter item) statistics of the Blau measure may well represent upper bound or inflated estimates. Carson and Bedeian (1994) proposed a conceptualization and measurement based on Hall's (1971) definition of ca-reer commitment as one's motivation to work at a chosen vocation. They also argued, on the grounds of London's (1983, 1985) work, that it could be deemed a multidimensional construct of three components: career identity, namely establishing a close emotional association with one's career; career planning, namely determining one's developmental needs and setting career goals; and career resilience, namely, resisting career disruption in the face of adversity.

2. The second approach that fits the integrative principle in occupational commitment was advanced by Meyer et al. (1993). This simply applied to occupational commitment Meyer and Allen's (1991) three component scales of organizational commitment discussed earlier. Namely, the three dimensions of affective commitment, continuance commitment, and normative commitment were applied to occupational commitment by substitution of "organization" by "occupation." Meyer et al. concluded from their data that preliminary evidence existed for the generalizability of Meyer and Allen's three-component model of commitment. This conclusion was based on their finding that the occupational commitment showed good psychometric properties and the three components were found to be differentially related to variables considered antecedents or consequences of commitment. Blau (2001) argued that more work using longitudinal design is needed to establish the discriminant validity among the three components of this measure.

Measures of Occupational Commitment

The inconsistency in the way occupational commitment was defined and conceptualized was also reflected in the way it was measured. This inconsistency seems to prevail in recent research too, and it certainly prevents research on occupational commitment from advancing valid, generalizable conclusions. Conclusions are hard to draw from diverse research findings; when one knows that many of these conceptualize and define occupational commitment differently and that the variety in definitions and scales might affect research findings. This problem is vividly demonstrated in the many scales of occupational commitment developed for one study or another (Baird, 1969; Brief & Aldag, 1980; Gardner, 1992; Jauch et al., 1978; Nogradi & Koch, 1981; Patchen 1970; Thornton, 1970; Gould, 1979). Many of these scales are based on respondents' answers to questions about their attitudes to their profession or their involvement in professional activities.

Other scales of occupational commitment are based on a more defined, focused approach. One of these referred to the concept of *professionalism*. According to this, professional commitment is part of the larger concept of professionalism (Bartol, 1979a, 1979b; Norris & Niebuhr, 1983; Tuma & Grimes, 1981). Another approach was founded on the concept of *career* (White, 1967; Gould 1979). The usual scale for the career approach to occupational commitment is Greenhaus's (1971, 1973), discussed previously.

As noted, the main criticism of this measure was its overlap with other commitment scales, such as job and work involvement, and with Dubin's work centrality measure (Morrow, 1983). Some of the items of this measure refer to nonwork domains, increasing the concept redundancy of this scale.

Blau's (1985) scale of career commitment, outlined above, was revised in his later studies (1988, 1993, 1999). The 1988 version has seven items; it is presented in Appendix A together with the 1985 version. In the later study, Blau et al. (1993) presented an elaborated scale with items from four others: those of Blau (1988), Sekaran (1982), Greenhaus (1971, 1972), and Good (1979). This scale, shown in Appendix A, has 11 items and is based on the findings of factor analysis of items from four career commitment and career salience scales. In general, Blau's scales seem to be one of the better approaches to defining and measuring occupational commitment. As mentioned, Carson and Bedeian (1994) criticized them, and developed a 12-item scale meant to overcome their limitations. Carson and Bedeian's criticism of Blau et al.'s (1993) latest scale is important. Blau et al.'s combined use of items from different scales, each with its own conceptual definition and background, can cause serious concept redundancy. This exists whenever the link between a conceptual definition and a measurement procedure is less than perfect.

Carson and Bedeian (1994) conceptualized career commitment as one's motivation to work at a chosen vocation. As stated, it is a multidimensional construct of three components: career identity, career planning, and career resilience. In this study, the authors set out acceptable psychometric properties of this scale and the findings supported its dimensionality. This scale is also shown in Appendix A. Note, however, that research on multiple commitments has favored Blau's scales. Carson and Carson (1998) used only three items from the Carson and Bedeian's (1994) scale, each representing one dimension. This, of course, is not enough to provide any indication of the validity and reliability of the Carson and Bedeian scale, mainly because only part of it was used. More research on this scale is needed before a firm conclusion can be reached as to which of the occupational commitment scales should be applied in multiple commitment research.

Another common approach to the measurement of occupational commitment adopts the common definitions and scales of organizational commitment. Here "organization" is replaced by the term of the relevant occupation. Some studies adopted the approach and measurement of organizational commitment on the basis of Becker's (1960) side-bet theory (Alutto et al., 1973; Aranya & Jacobson, 1975; McElroy, Morrow, Power, & Iqubal, 1993; Parasuraman & Nachman, 1987; Ritzer & Trice, 1969; Vrendenbuagh & Trinkaus, 1983). Some adopted Porter at al.'s common attitudinal approach and scale (Amernic & Aranya, 1983; Brierley, 1996;

Colarelli & Bishop, 1994; Dolen & Shultz, 1998; Hoff, 2000; Lachman & Aranya, 1986a, 1986b; Wallace, 1995a; 1997; Vandenberg & Scarpello, 1994). A more recent work (Meyer et al., 1993) adopted the three-dimensional approach to organizational commitment developed by Meyer and Allen (1984). This scale is also presented in Appendix A. Finally, Shuval and Bernstein (1996) used Lodhal and Kejner's (1965) job involvement scale to measure professional commitment by replacing the word "job" by the word "profession."

JOB INVOLVEMENT

Definition and Approaches

Relatively much attention has been paid to the concept of job involvement, particularly in the industrial psychology research. The early approach to job involvement was that advanced by Lodhal and Kejner (1965). This approach, more particularly its resulting scale, exerted a similar impact on the relevant literature as did Porter et al.'s (1974) OCQ. Because Lodhal and Kejner proposed their scale, hundreds of empirical studies have been conducted on this form of commitment (Brown, 1996). Lodhal and Kejner (1965) argued that job involvement is the internalization of values about the goodness of work or the importance of work for the person's worth. On the one hand, described the job-involved person as one for whom work is a very important part of life, and who is personally greatly affected by his or her entire job situation. On the other hand, the nonjob-involved worker makes a living off of the job. Work is not as important a part of her or his psychological life. His or her interests lie elsewhere, and the core of her or his self-image, the essential part of one's identity, is not greatly affected by the kind of work one does or how well one does it. Based on the definition that job involvement is the degree to which one's work performance affects one's self-esteem, Lodhal and Kejner (1965) developed a 20-item attitudinal scale for job involvement (presented in Appendix A).

Starting out from Lodhal and Kejner's definition, Rabinowitz and Hall (1977) argued that job involvement had been defined and conceptualized in two different ways: performance-self-esteem contingency and component of self-image. The first class of definitions might be considered as the extent to which self-esteem is affected by level of performance. The second definition describes job involvement as the degree to which a person is identified psychologically with their work, or the importance of work in their whole self-image. Wiener and Gechman (1977) added a third way of conceptualizing job involvement: A value orientation to work learned early in the socialization process. They argued that although all of these definitions focus on interpersonal, attitudinal processes, the definitions seemed to suggest distinct psychological processes; in short, the definition of job involvement labored under considerable confusion.

Lodhal and Kejner's (1965) approach was criticized in that it did not clarify which of the two kinds of process the authors perceived as the main concept behind job involvement. The resultant confusion among researchers was not confined to the theoretical level but proliferated into empirical studies of involvement. There, job involvement was viewed in three ways: as an individual difference variable, as a situationally determined variable, and as a person–situation interaction variable (Rabinowitz & Hall, 1977). Another criticism of Lodhal and Kejner's (1965) measure is that it was not devised with any a priori definitions or theoretical frameworks in mind, and it contained items reflecting the two definitions provided (Morrow, 1983). The variety of definitions of job involvement posed several difficulties. First, the terminology was somewhat imprecise. For example, it was not clear how identification with work related to general theories of psychological identification. Second, there were no clear-cut criteria for selecting one of these three distinct attitudinal processes as the most useful definition of job involvement. Third, it was somewhat unclear how these different definitions of involvement related to satisfaction, motivation, and situational factors. Finally, no relations were suggested between the attitudinal processes of job involvement and concrete, operational work behaviors (Wiener & Gechman, 1977).

The aforementioned problems and limitations of the concepts and definitions of job involvement generated criticism of Lodhal and Kejner's (1965) approach and scale, and the formulation of an alternative approach by Kanungo (1979, 1982). According to this author, the major source of conceptual ambiguity lay in the use of the construct "job involvement," which carries excess meaning. This caused problems of validity in the construct's measurement. Kanungo identified the excess meaning of the job involvement construct in four different ways. First, past conceptualizations of this construct confused it with the issue of intrinsic motivation on the job. Second, in dealing with the construct researchers confused the issue of identifying the antecedent conditions of job involvement with its subsequent effects. Third, job involvement was described as both a cognitive and a positive emotional state of the individual. Finally, earlier conceptualizations of job involvement failed to distinguish two different contexts in which an individual can show personal involvement: In a specific or particular job context and in a generalized work context.

Kanungo (1979) asserted that involvement in a specific job is not the same as involvement in work in general, and therefore, argued for a reformulation of the involvement construct eliminating the problems of excess meaning (Kanungo, 1979). Such a reformulation (Kanungo, 1979, 1981) would conceptually distinguish job and work involvement. The two could not be measured with the existing instruments, so Kanungo developed separate scales for each. These scales and that approach became more current and acceptable than those of Lodhal and Kejner (1965).

The Measurement of Job Involvement

From the review above, two measures of job involvement have clearly dominated the literature. Other, different, job involvement scales, developed for particular studies, of course exist (Alutto & Acito, 1974; Gomez-Mejia, 1984; Lefkowitz, Somers & Weinberg, 1984; McKelvey & Sekaran, 1977; Reitz & Jewell, 1979; Wiener & Gechman, 1977; Van Ypreen, Hagedoorn, & Geurts, 1996). Most of these scales have not been replicated in other studies and their impact on the commitment literature has been limited.

Lodhal and Kejner's (1965) widespread scale started with 120 items. After empirical examinations the final measure had 20 items; presented in Appendix A. Lodhal and Kejner (1965) concluded from their findings that the 20-item job involvement scale was a multidimensional attitude that could be scaled with adequate but not high reliability. In an attempt to shorten the 20-item scale for use in long, densely packed questionnaires, Lodhal and Kejner (1965) recommended a shorter version of 6 items, loading highest on the first (unrotated) principal component in both the engineers' and nurses' sample (these were items 3, 6, 8, 11, 15, and 18 of the 20 items given in Appendix A). This scale became the common one for job involvement and was applied in almost every study that examined job involvement in its long or short version. In practice, users of the Lodhal and Kejner (1965) scale have usually employed the shortened version (Brown, 1996). This was specified by Lodhal and Kejner (1965) and by Hall (1971) as best representing the psychological identification dimension of job involvement. But some research still uses the long version (Thompson, Kopelman, & Schriesheim, 1992).

Two other prevalent scales, albeit not as common as Lodhal and Kejner's, should be mentioned. The first is the four-item subscale of Lawler and Hall (1970), which appears in Appendix A. These items focus on the degree of daily absorption individual experiences in work activity, and they are closely aligned with the psychological identification definition of work offered by Lodhal and Kejner (1965). Despite its brevity, the Lawler and Hall scale is not altogether independent of the other forms of work commitment. It directly overlaps with the first career salience subscale, and at least latently co-varies with both work as a central life interest and the third career salience subscale that contrasts commitment spheres (Morrow, 1983). Another measure is that of Saleh and Hosek (1976), which proposed a multidimensional scale of job involvement reflecting four dimensions: (a) work as a central life interest, (b) the extent of a person's active participation in the job, (c) extent of performance–self-esteem contingency, and (d) consistency of job performance with the self concept. However, the Saleh and Hosek scale was strongly criticized as reflecting not only the psychological state of the individual but also the antecedent circumstances and consequent outcomes of this psychological state. The measure incorporates considerable extraneous conceptual content in addition to the core meaning of the cognitive state of psychological identification of one's job (Kanungo, 1979, 1982).

Kanungo's scale, presented in Appendix A, is considered the most commonly used for job involvement (Brown, 1996). It was devised to eliminate several specific dimensions of excess meaning in Lodhal and Kejner's (1965) scale. Kanungo's (1979, 1982) scales separate the definitions and measurement of job involvement from those of work involvement, and are based on the clearest and most precise conceptualization of the construct. The job involvement scale clearly identifies the core meaning of the construct as a cognitive state of the individual, is not contaminated by items tapping concepts outside this core meaning, and separates job involvement from antecedents and consequent constructs. Blau (1985a) who compared Kanungo' scale to the Lodhal and Kejner's one concluded that the Kanungo's measure is the superior one. From all this it is only natural that Kanungo's scale of job involvement should be the one included in research on multiple commitments.

Work Values

It can be argued that research on work values stemmed from early research on the work/nonwork relationship, which emphasized the need for further empirical explorations of how the nonwork domain is related to behavior and attitudes in the workplace (Goldthorpe, Lockwood, Bechhofer, & Platt, 1968, 1969, 1971; Blauner, 1964, 1969). Some of this research (Goldthorpe, Lockwood, Bechhofer, & Platt, 1968) predicted that in the future workers would emphasize their nonwork needs on account of their commitment to their employer. Work as a central life interest can be viewed as one of the earliest forms of commitment. This concept refers to an individual's preferred locale for carrying out activities. It is measured by respondents' being asked to choose between work and nonwork settings for engaging in an activity that is as likely to take place in one setting as another (Morrow, 1983).

Another line of research on work values concerns commitment to nonfinancial employment (Warr, 1982), or the "lottery" question (Morrow, 1993), which was first advanced by Morse and Weiss (1955). It asked whether a person would continue working if he or she won a lottery or inherited a large sum of money. This concept seems to reappear every decade or so, when researchers wish to discover whether the workforce in a certain country has become more committed or less committed than the previous decade's workforce (Morrow, 1993). It is seen as a way to measure how much a workforce or society values work, and is therefore quite similar to the concept of work ethic endorsement (Morrow, 1993). In earlier studies (Morse & Weiss, 1955; Tausky, 1969), most participants in samples in the United States said that they would continue to work even if they had no need to earn a living. But later studies (Campbell, Converse, & Rodgers, 1976; Vecchio, 1980) found a notable drop in the percentage of those who would do so. More recent studies (Harpaz, 1998) found that the relatively low value placed on work in the 1970s rose.

Early studies regarding work as a central life interest (Dubin, 1956; Orzack, 1963; Kornhauser, 1965) are perhaps the first empirical research directly on the relationship between one form of commitment and nonwork domains. Dubin's (1956) work on central life interest provided insight into the importance of work in people's lives. At first glance central life interest appears to capture the broad concept of the centrality or importance of work in general rather than involvement in a job. However Dubin's measure of central life interest seemed inconsistent with his conceptual definition of the construct; the items actually measured the extent to which the work setting was preferred for performing behaviors that could also be performed elsewhere (Paullay, Alliger, & Stone-Romero, 1994). Therefore, response to this instrument appeared to be influenced by present job attitudes. Another problem of central life interest is concept redundancy, because items that represent work and nonwork domains are included in the same scale that measures this concept, thus hindering evaluation of how one domain is related to or affected by the other (Morrow, 1983).

Protestant Work Ethic (PWE) is the more common and acceptable form of work values. It is the oldest work commitment concept reviewed, with origins dating back to the 1905 publication of The Protestant Ethic and Spirit of Capitalism by Max Weber (Morrow, 1993). This is also one of the few concepts that span nearly all social sciences (Furnham, 1990). Note that although "Protestant" work ethic is still more widely recognized, based on changes in work attitudes resulting from the Protestant Reformation (Weber, 1958), research indicates that work ethic is applicable across all religious affiliations (Blau & Ryan, 1997). Some researchers suggested erasure of the word "Protestant." and reference to the concept only as "work ethic" (Blau & Ryan, 1997; Morrow, 1993). However, research on this concept relative to other commitment forms is sparse; it may be considered it a neglected commitment form (Blau & Ryan, 1997).

The essence of this concept is the belief that hard work is intrinsically good and is an end in and of itself. Personal worth and one's moral stature are to be gauged by the willingness to work hard. One's job, career, organization, or union is merely a setting in which to exert high levels of effort (Morrow, 1983). The PWE is nearly always referred to as a set or system of beliefs mainly, but not exclusively, concerning work. It is of course, much more than that, being multidimensional and related to various aspects of social, political, and economic life. Psychologists tend to treat the PWE as a belief system, a set of values and attitudes concerning work and related issues such as money. It has been suggested that PWE beliefs are learned at various periods of life hence may be changed. More important, it is suggested that these beliefs are related to behavior (Furnham, 1990).

It can be argued that understanding the theoretical foundation for the work ethic construct requires study of Weber's (1958) original work (Blau & Ryan, 1997). Weber (1958) seemed to emphasize four dimensions comprising a more secular work ethic construct: belief in hard work, nonleisure, independence, and asceticism. Blau and Ryan (1997) observed that behavioral scientists have supported this multidimensional conceptualization. The multidimensionality and the ambiguity in the definition, and hence, in the measurement of work values, considerably impedes combining the concept with the other commitment foci in an integrative approach. A concept that overlaps other commitment forms and aspects of nonwork domains, and that is not clear-cut in its dimensionality, can increase conceptual and methodological problems when used with other commitment forms that are far more sharply defined and clearly measured. Yet regardless of the other forms of work values, PWE is the concept that attracts most attention in commitment research. Most empirical research on multiple commitments has used PWE as representing work.

Unlike the other forms of commitment much less construct validation or substantive research attention has been given to the work ethic facet (Blau & Ryan, 1997). Several attempts have been made to improve the way work values are conceptualized and measured so that they conform better to a multiple commitment approach. One attempt was by Blau and Ryan (1997), who relied on Furnham's (1990) work in an effort to strengthen the epistemic correlation for work ethic by recommending a parsimonious construct-valid measure. Their study, using items from the usual work ethic scales, resulted in an 18-item measure addressing four dimensions: hard work, nonleisure, independence, and asceticism. Each of the four dimensions accords with Weber's (1958) theoretical discussion of work ethic. Blau and Ryan's work contributed to the development of PWE scale that suited the other commitment form scales. However, Blau and Ryan seem to have been intent on developing a short, convenient scale, in contrast to the long scales advanced previously. Still, it is a multidimensional scale, and needs to be tested for its relation to the measures of other commitment foci. An interesting and fruitful avenue is the development of an Islamic work ethic scale that will fit the Arab culture better than the Protestant work ethic scale (Ali, 1988, 1992; Darwish, 2000). A similar attempt was by Miller, Woehr, & Hudspeth (in press) who developed a new multidimensional measure of work ethic.

Another attempt is through the concept of work involvement. This concept was developed by Kanungo (1979, 1982), who emphasized the difference between this construct and job involvement on the one hand, and the Protestant work ethic on the other. Job involvement is a belief about the current job and tends to be a function of how much the job can satisfy one's immediate needs. But involvement in work in general is a normative belief about the value of work in one's life, and is more a function of one's past cultural conditioning or socialization. The work involvement construct can represent work values even better than PWE because the latter is a multidimensional construct concerning the importance of work and also a rejection of leisure and excess money (Morrow, 1993). The use of this three-dimensional construct with the other commitment foci can needlessly complicate the models and analysis. Work involvement is a unidimensional construct, hence a more appropriate scale to apply with other commitment foci as representing work values.

Measure of Work Values

Central Life Interest. One of the most common scales to measure central life interests is Dubin's (1956) scale. Dubin defined *central life interest* as the expressed preference for a given locale in carrying out an activity. The original instrument comprised 40 items but was subsequently reduced to 32. The items require a respondent to select one of three alternatives for a specified activity: One alternative typically represents a preference for a work setting, another a preference for a specific setting outside work, and a third indicates indifference to the location. The items are designed to cover four areas: membership of formal organizations, technological aspects of the environment, informal personal relations, and general everyday experiences (Cook, Hepworth, Wall, & Warr, 1981). Other scales examined central life interests or similar constructs (Fineman, 1975, Gordon, 1973; Super, 1970), but these were not as common as Dubin's. Two more recent works (Paullay et al., 1994; Hirschfeld & Field, 2000) presented a shorter 12-item scale of work centrality that attempts to overcome the limitations of the common Dubin's (1956) scale. Findings of these studies revealed acceptable psychometric properties of this measure. However, central life interests scales have hardly been used in research on multiple commitments, so little attention is devoted to them in this book.

Protestant Work Ethic. As stated, the work values scales have been more usually applied in work commitment research, and many of them were thoroughly reviewed by Furnham (1990). Furnham noted seven work scales: Protestant ethic (Goldstein & Eichorn, 1961), Protestant Work Ethic (Mirels & Garrett, 1971), pro-Protestant Ethic and non-Protestant Ethic (Blood, 1969), Spirit of Capitalism (Hammond & Williams, 1976), Leisure Ethic and Work Ethic (Bucholz, 1977), Eclectic Protestant Ethic (Ray, 1982), and Australian Work Ethic (Ho & Lloyd 1984). To these the development of an Islamic work ethic scale can be added (Ali, 1988, 1992). Two of these scales are more prevalent in work ethic research in general and commitment research in particular, namely those of Blood (1969) and Mirels and Garrett (1971). Blood (1969) describes a person with ideals of the Protestant ethic as one who feels that personal worth results from self-sacrificing work or occupational achievements. The scale was designed to measure the strength of this orientation along with the extent to which individuals dissociate themselves from such values. It is thus composed of two subscales, labeled pro-Protestant ethic and non-Protestant ethic, each consisting of four items. The scale is shown in Appendix A. Mirels and Garrett (1971) interpreted the Protestant Ethic as a dispositional variable characterized by a belief in the importance of hard work and frugality, which acts as a defense against sloth, sexuality, sexual temptation, and religious doubt. Accordingly, they set out to construct an instrument with a relatively broad focus (Cook et al. 1981). Their scale has 19 items, and it is presented in Appendix A.

An interesting attempt to understand better the Protestant ethic scales was made by Furnham (1990), who content-analyzed and then empirically factor-analyzed the 77 items of the seven work ethic scales mentioned above. In a sample of 1021 respondents, Furnham found empirical evidence for five factors: belief in hard work, leisure avoidance, religious and moral belief, independence from others, and asceticism. This analysis resulted in 59-item scale, which is impractical for research purposes. Blau and Ryan (1997) used 25 of the items of Furnham's final list of items. Their goal was to recommend a more construct-valid and parsimonious measure of the work ethic concept with a stronger epistemic correlation than previous measures, for potential incorporation into a general work commitment index. As mentioned earlier, their survey ended up in an 18-item measure that is described in Appendix A. They also suggested a shorter, 12-item measure by selecting the highest three-item loadings from each factor. These items are listed in Appendix A. More empirical work on this scale is needed to examine how well it fits with the other commitment measures. But note that even the shorter 12-item scale is multidimensional in nature.

Work Involvement. An alternative that should be considered in commitment research is the work involvement scale of Kanungo (1982), shown in Appendix A. The work involvement scale is based on Kanungo's (1979, 1982) conceptual and methodological distinction between job involvement and work involvement. The rationale for this distinction is presented in the section dealing with job involvement. However, the six-item work involvement scale does capture the notion of work values, is unidimensional and relatively short. In addition it has demonstrated good psychometric properties. A researcher attempting to test several commitment forms, including one of the work value forms, is recommended to consider the work involvement scale as such a representative.

Group Commitment

Group commitment, defined as an individual's identification and sense of cohesiveness with other members of the organization (Randall & Cote, 1991), is one of the new concepts in multiple commitment research (Morrow, 1993). Traditional studies tended to focus on group commitment as an important characteristic of the work group. Ellemers, van Rijswijk, Bruins and de Gilder (1998), for example, observed that highly committed group members seem to maintain solidarity with their fellow group members when faced with group threat. Ellemers, Kortekaas, and Ouwerkerk (1999) posited that group commitment is one of the three dimensions that contribute to one's social identity. The first is a cognitive component, the second is an evaluative component, and the third is an emotional component, a sense of emotional involvement with the group, namely an affective commitment. The key proposal of social identity theory is that the extent that people identify with a particular social group determines their inclination to behave in terms of their group membership. In this sense, these authors held, social identification is primarily used to refer to a feeling of affective commitment to the group.

Many of the writings on group commitment related it to organizational commitment conceptually or empirically. Randall and Cote (1991) maintained that the importance of work-group commitment is its enhancement of social involvement, and this reinforces the social ties the individual develops with the organization. They explained that on being hired, one's initial reference group gratifies one's needs for guidance and reassurance and exerts a lasting influence over individual attitudes to the organization. Another reason for analyzing group commitment together with organizational commitment was the need to demonstrate the distinction between the two commitments and to show that group commitment is an independent concept in addition to organizational commitment. Reichers (1985, 1986), who advanced the notion of a multidimensional perspective of the concept of organizational commitment, proposed group commitment as one of the important dimensions to be considered in such a conceptualization. Riechers argued that an individual's commitment to a workplace cannot be adequately explained by commitment to the organization alone because the coalitional nature of organizations makes employee commitment multidimensional.

A more recent and thorough approach to group commitment was advanced by Zaccaro and Dobbins (1989), who applied a distinctive scale to measure group commitment and from their findings asserted that commitment to the organization and to the work group are distinct constructs. Zaccaro and Dobbins (1989) focused on the differences between group and organizational commitment. Their findings showed that the major correlates of group commitment are group-level variables such as cohesiveness, while organizational commitment was correlated more with variables such as role conflict and met expectations. They concluded that there is a conceptual distinction between group and organizational commitment.

Another recent approach to group commitment is that of Ellemers, de Gilder, and van den Heuvel (1998), who examined the relation between group commitment, among other commitment forms, and work outcomes. They emphasized group commitment, which they termed *team-oriented commitment,* as representing commitment to a common goal, as distinct from commitment foci such as career commitment, which represents a personal goal. One of their important contributions was a clear definition of and measurement for group commitment and the exposure of differences and similarities between this form and organizational and career commitment.

Few studies considered commitment to the workgroup as another focus of commitment. March and Simon (1963) were among the first to do so in early research on commitment. Another example is the early work of Rotondi (1975), who found positive correlations between group commitment and organizational and occupational commitment. In later research, Randall and Cote (1991) decided to include this form of commitment in their multivariate model of work commitment. Becker (1992, 1993), who examined work-group commitment as one of the foci of commitment, followed this line of research. In an empirical examination, Becker (1992) found some interesting correlations between group commitment and various measures of performance. Becker's work is one of the few to test group commitment in relation to outcomes, and it showed a promising relation. Another notable study in this regard is that of Bishop, Scott, and Burroughs (2000) who used the term *team commitment.* They examined the mutual relation of organizational and team commitment for important outcomes such as performance, OCB, and turnover intentions, and concluded that each made a unique contribution to these outcomes. In another study, team commitment was found to positively affect a team's decision commitment and decision quality (Dooley & Fryxell, 1999). Thus, promising data exist on the effect of group commitment on work outcomes at the individual and the group level.

Measures of Group Commitment

The fact that group commitment is a relatively new form in multiple commitment research is the main reason why few measures of this focus exist. So far, no consistency has been observed in the way group commitment is measured and little evidence is forthcoming of its conformity with the other common, more established commitment forms. Most of the measures for group commitments were simplistic (Dooley & Fryxell, 1999), some, with only a one-item measure (Becker, 1992, 1993). Another approach to measure group commitment was to use items from organizational commitment scales and replace the term organization with work-group (Rotondi, 1975, 1976; Zaccaro & Dobbins, 1989; Bishop et al., 2000).

Two scales that attempted to measure group commitment by developing specific scales for this construct deserve to be noted. The first is that of Randall and Cote (1991), presented in Appendix A. Three of the six items of their scale were taken from Sheldon's (1971) social involvement scale. The authors developed three other items. The other scale, advanced by Ellemers et al. (1998), has seven items that the authors developed, also shown in Appendix A. The advantage of the two scales is that two were tested in research on multiple commitments and in this context, demonstrated acceptable psychometric properties. However much more research is needed to establish one of these scales as appropriate for multiple commitment research.

Union Commitment

Union Commitment has received scholars' attention already half a decade ago. In the early 1950s, the rise in unionism in the United States attracted the attention of researchers to many aspects of the phenomenon. One concern at that time was that unionization, and commitment to the union, would result in diminished loyalty to the employer. This concern started a series of studies on the concept of *dual commitment*, namely, to the organization and to the union (Dean, 1954; Derber et al., 1953, 1954; Gotlieb & Kerr, 1950; Purcell, 1954; Stagner, 1954, 1961). However, central findings were that dual commitment was a common phenomenon, and an employee's being a committed union member did not necessarily equal hostility toward the organization or vice versa. From the point of view of this volume, the research in the 1950s was perhaps the earliest to apply a multiple commitment approach although only two forms were applied, union and organizational commitment.

However, the extensive research of the 1950s and 1960s was followed by a steep decline in interest in the concept of union commitment, which was not renewed until the 1980s. The reason for the revival was mainly the expanding research on organizational commitment, which stimulated researchers to examine commitment to other foci as well. The starting point for the regenerated research was the work of Gordon, Philpot, Burt, Thompson, and Spiller (1980), which developed a new scale for measuring union commitment. Gordon and his colleagues (1980) argued that union commitment was analogous to organizational commitment; the only difference being that union commitment addressed a different situation. They adopted the assumptions and definitions of the prevalent Porter et al. (1974) organizational commitment scale, and defined union commitment by three dimensions: the wish to remain a member of the organization, willingness to invest much energy in the organization, and a firm belief in the organization's values and goals. A factor analysis of the Gordon et al. (1980) scale revealed basically four factors, representing four dimensions of union commitment. The first and preeminent dimension was union loyalty, in which two aspects were reflected. The first was a sense of pride in association with and membership of the union, the second a clear awareness of benefits accruing to the individual. The second dimension was responsibility to the union. It measured the degree of willingness to fulfill the day-to-day obligations and duties of a member to protect the union's interests. The third dimension was willingness to work for the union, namely, a member's expenditure of extra energy in the union's service. The fourth dimension was belief in unionism, namely a member's belief in the concept of unionization. The items for each of the factors are presented in Appendix A, where we may note that commitment to the union is the relevant concept in the case of the closed shop because varying degrees of commitment to the union can be seen in this situation.

The approach and measurement of Gordon and his colleagues (1980) are considered the dominant avenue to union commitment. Most studies on this subject somehow rely on their definition and measurement (Beauvais, Scholl, & Cooper, 1991; Fullagar & Barling, 1991; Fullagar, Gordon, Gallagher, & Clark, 1995; Johnson & Johnson, 1992; Johnson & Johnson, 1995; Kelloway & Barling, 1993; Mellor, Mathieu, & Swim, 1994; Sinclair & Tetrick, 1995; Thacker, Fields, & Barclay, 1990; Trimpop, 1995; Wetzel, Gallagher, & Soloshy, 1991). However, this approach has its limitations, most of them reflected in the way union commitment was measured, as may be seen in the next section.

The Measurement of Union Commitment

Early work in the 1950s and 1960s measured union commitment very simplistically by a single-item measure (Derber et al., 1953, 1954; Gottlieb & Kerr, 1950; Purcell, 1954; Stagner, 1954, 1961). Later studies used either a one-item measure (Dalton & Todor, 1981) or a several-item measure (Angle & Perry, 1986; Black, 1983; Cohen, 1993c; Cohen & Kirchmeyer, 1994; Sverke & Kuruvilla, 1995; Sverke & Sjoberg, 1994), all were developed for the purposes of a given study. Some other measures used the organizational commitment scales by replacing the word "union" by "organization" (Aryee & Debra, 1997; Dalton & Todor, 1982; Conlon & Gallagher, 1987). As noted, Gordon et al.'s (1980), scale has dominated the union commitment literature since it was presented; the four-dimension scale is presented in Appendix A. The scale demonstrated good psychometric properties and several subsequent investigations replicated Gordon and colleagues' factor structure (Ladd, Gordon, Beauvais, & Morgan, 1982; Fullagar, 1986; Liebowitz, 1983; Gordon, Beauvais, & Ladd, 1984; Tetrick, Thacker, & Fields, 1989; Thacker, Fields, & Tetrick, 1989; Thacker, Fields, & Barclay, 1990). Thacker, Fields, and Tetrick (1989) and Thacker, Fields and Barclay (1990) argued from their findings that the four-factor solution provides a good representation of the factor structure of union commitment. Moreover, the antecedents and outcome models offered varied results, depending on the factor examined. However, it was suggested that either the four- factor solution or commitment as a multidimensional construct might be used, depending on the research focus. Following this recommendation, Fullagar and Barling (1989) measured union commitment by using only the union loyalty factor derived in the aforementioned studies. Friedman and Harvey (1986), in a reanalysis of Gordon et al.'s data, questioned the dimensionality of the union commitment scale. Using goodness-of-fit indexes, they suggested two oblique, rather than four orthogonal, factors as a more a parsimonious solution. Oblique rotation revealed that union commitment was best represented by two factors: union attitudes and opinions and pro-union behavioral intentions. They concluded by recommending the use of a shorter version of the union commitment questionnaire. Klandermans (1989) arrived at similar findings and conclusions from his work with a Dutch sample, whereas Trimpop (1995) found some differences in the factors' structures in a German sample and attributed them to cultural and structural differences. Mellor (1990), for example, followed Friedman and Harvey's (1986) recommendation and used their short form of the union commitment scale identified in their factor analysis. The tendency to shorten the scale was emphasized by Kelloway, Catano and Southwell (1992) who, on the basis of their findings, proposed shortening the scale to 13 items measuring union loyalty, responsibility to the union, and willingness to work for the union. This shorter scale was applied in later research (Fullagar, Gordon, Gallagher, & Clark, 1995).

Another criticism mainly concerns the overlap of the union commitment scale and other forms of work commitment outcomes and determinants of

this construct (Morrow, 1983). The main problem of the union commitment scale of Gordon and his colleagues (1980) seems to be that some of the
factors reflect more outcomes or determinants of commitment. For example, Thacker, Fields, and Barclay (1990) found that the factor of willingness
to work for the union was strongly related to attendance at meetings, that is,
in a way, part of working for the union. Moreover, they provided an interesting distinction between the different factors of union commitment by defining *union loyalty* as a passive dimension of union commitment, and
willingness to work for the union as the active dimension. Liebowitz (1983)
found an additional factor of union commitment, which represents union
instrumentality, although many researchers used union instrumentality as a
predictor of union commitment. Moreover, Gordon and his colleagues
(1980) found that the strongest determinant of the overall scale of union
commitment was the item "I believe in the goals of organized labor," which
overlaps the factor "belief in unionism" in the union commitment scale.
Moreover, Gordon and his colleagues emphasized the instrumentality dimension of the main factor of their construct, union loyalty, whereas research on union commitment used union instrumentality as one of the
important determinants of union commitment (Fullagar & Barling, 1989).

SUMMARY AND DIRECTIONS FOR FUTURE RESEARCH

The multiple commitment approach depends on the definition and measurement of the different commitment foci covered by this approach. The
advancement of the integrative approach depends on the clarity and validity of the definition and measurement of each of the commitment foci. Research findings can be better generalized if one knows whether the
commitment foci scales were precise, reliable, and valid measures of the
commitment focus they were supposed to measure. However, one of the
problems is that commitment forms have not all received similar attention
in the literature. As a result, definitions and scales of some commitment
forms are more developed than others. Organizational commitment is the
form that has received the most attention, and much work on its measurement and scales has been performed. Less attention has been paid to group
commitment and much more work is needed in this area before an established way to define and measure is found. This is not an easy starting point
for researchers who want to examine several commitment forms in one research design. Although it is easier to choose a definition and scale from the
more established forms a researchers face a thorny dilemma when selecting
scales for less established forms such as group commitment or work values.
Some suggestions that may assist in making better decisions in that regard
are proposed next.

The existing literature on the foregoing commitment definitions and measures generally evinces two commitment foci that seem to be more established and reliable scales than the others. The Allen and Meyer (1991) multidimensional approach to organizational commitment dominates organizational commitment research. Some problems exist with the continuance commitment form in their approach because of the multidimensionality of this form and the ambiguity of its focus. But the affective commitment dimension seems to provide a practical, clear, and focused scale (Jaros, 1997). Consensus appears to prevail about the validity of this scale and there is no reason not to apply it consistently in multiple commitment research.

The same can be said about the job involvement facet. Kanungo's (1979, 1982) approach and scale for job involvement have become paramount in job involvement research. The distinction she made between job and work involvement clarified the focus of this scale, and it demonstrated good psychometric properties in the research to which it was applied. As Brown (1996) stated:

> Of the commonly used scales of job involvement, Kanungo's is based on the clearest and most precise conceptualization of the construct. It clearly identifies the core meaning of the construct as a cognitive state of the individual, is not contaminated by items tapping concepts outside of this core meaning, and separates job involvement from antecedents and consequent constructs.... (p. 236).

Accordingly, two valid and reliable scales can be used in multiple commitment research: the affective organizational commitment scale and the job involvement scale. All the other commitment foci carry conceptual and methodological problems.

The career commitment focus advanced significantly with Blau's work on this subject (1985, 1988). The scale proposed by Blau et al. (1993) in later work is not recommended because, as mentioned, it includes items from different scales, some of them career salience scales, and it is probably contaminated with problems of concept redundancy. The scales proposed by Blau in earlier studies (1985, 1988) solved some of the problems of previous scales. However, Carson and Bedeian (1994) pointed out several problems of this scale that must be addressed. The most severe is the overlap of items in the scales with possible outcomes such as withdrawal cognition. This was the main problem with the widely used Porter et al. (1974) scale of organizational commitment (OCQ), which caused its abandonment and eventual replacement by Meyer and Allen's (1990) scales. The scale proposed by Carson and Bedeian (1994) has to be applied more frequently before any conclusions about its validity can be reached. At this point, Blau's two scales (1985, 1988), for all their limitations, are the most appropriate for use in multiple commitment research. However, additional work is needed on the career commitment facet to establish a clear-cut scale for this important commitment focus.

More ambiguity exists with the form of work values. To date we have long and multidimensional scales, some of whose items overlap other commitment foci in and outside the workplace. There is some consensus that the Protestant Work Ethic is the appropriate form of work values that should be tested in multiple commitment research. But the existing scales suffer from those same problems mentioned previously: multidimensionality, excessive length, and overlap with other commitment foci. The work of Blau et al. (1997) acknowledged this problem and proposed a reasonable approach and scale for this form. Yet their scale, in its long and short form, is still multidimensional and can cause problems when the scale is used with other commitment foci. Besides, the scale has hardly been tested in commitment research, (or in any research), so there is very little evidence of its validity and reliability. A reasonable alternative for the work values facet could be Kanungo's work involvement scale (1979, 1982). This scale is unidimensional, clear, and short. It also demonstrated good psychometric properties in the samples in where it was tested.

Union commitment was rarely taken as one of the foci in research on multiple commitments. Mostly, it was associated with organizational commitment in the more recent research that has tested the concept of dual commitment (Angle & Perry, 1986; Bemmels, 1995; Barling, Wade & Fullagar, 1990; Conlon & Gallagher, 1987; Fucami & Larson, 1984; Johnson, & Johnson, 1995; Johnson, Johnson, & Patterson, 1999; Magenau et al., 1988; Martin et al., 1986; Thacker & Rosen, 1986). In a few cases, it was tested with other commitment foci (Cohen, 1993a). One reason for union commitment's omission from multiple commitment research is the complexity of the scale, as is reflected in its multidimensionality and length.

The union commitment focus presents similar problems as those of work values focus, but with a significant advantage. Consensus exists that the approach and measurement by Gordon et al. (1980) best represents this construct. But this scale is multidimensional, long, and some of its items overlap other commitment forms. Some of its dimensions do not seems relevant for a multiple commitment approach (for example, belief in unionism or willingness to work for the union); rather, they seem to overlap outcomes. Suggestions in the literature to shorten the scale are appropriate, and Kelloway et al.'s (1992) leaning toward this seems promising. Another suggestion proposed here is that researchers who wish to test union commitment together with other commitment forms use only the loyalty dimension in its long, or better, its short six-item form, as suggested by

Kelloway et al. (1992). This dimension seems more fitting as part of the multiple commitment approach because its definition is close to the notion and essence of other commitment forms. However, some of the loyalty dimension items seem to overlap outcomes such as withdrawal cognition ("Based on what I know now and what I believe I can expect in the future, I plan to be a member of the union as long as I am working in this branch of industry"), and should be omitted.

Although there are conceptual reasons for the slight use of this form in multiple commitment research if the scale were made shorter and simpler union commitment may well be applied more in this pursuit. Cohen (1993a) found that this form can predict important outcomes in the work setting, and Tetrick (1995) advanced a model suggesting that union commitment was related to organizational citizenship behavior. Abridging the scale as reviewed here could be one way of tempting researchers to apply it in multiple commitment research. Another is to simply use only the loyalty dimension of this scale, as in the examples of Barling et al. (1990) and of Fullagar, McCoy, and Shull (1992). This dimension is the foremost and the most distinct of the four, and its definition accords better with the concept of commitment in general. Also, the use of this dimension would obviate any problem of multidimensionality and the scale would be shorter and more practicable. It would have up to 16 items in Gordon et al.'s (1980) version and six items in Kelloway et al.'s (1992) abbreviated one.

The concept of group commitment is not yet developed, and much more work is needed before an established definition and scale of this form can exist. Therefore, it should be used with the utmost caution. Randall and Cote's (1991) scale or that of Ellemers et al. (1998) is the only acceptable alternative. However, both of these have hardly been tested in empirical research and there are minimal data on their psychometric properties.

In short, the integrative approach depends on conceptual and methodological development in each of the commitment forms. With some forms, far more work is needed to provide commitment researchers with better tools with which to examine multiple commitments. However, it seems that a core of acceptable scales for almost each commitment form exists in a way that allows research on multiple commitment with a minimum of measurement problems. For example, the following scales can be used together in research that examines five commitment forms: Meyer and Allen's (1991) scale for organizational commitment, Kanungo's (1982) scale for job involvement, Blau's (1988) scale for career commitment, Kannungo's (1982) work involvement scale for work values, and Gordon et al.'s (1980) loyalty dimension scale for union commitment. In a nonunionized setting, group commitment measured by Randall and Cote's (1991) scale can replace the union commitment scale.

3

Commitment Forms: How Distinct Are They?

Chapter 2 demonstrated the different commitment foci generally used in multiple commitment research. Naturally, not all the above forms figured in every study. The use of given set of commitment foci depended on the research question at hand. In some cases only two commitment forms were applied, for example, in an investigation of dual commitment to the union and company (Angle & Perry, 1986; Johnson et al., 1999). In others, it was commitment to the job and the organization (Blau & Boal, 1987, 1989; Keller, 1997) or commitment to the profession and organization (Aranya & Ferris, 1983, 1984; Wallace, 1993, 1995b). But there is a growing tendency to use more than two commitment forms in one study (Becker, 1992; Cohen, 1993a, 1999a, 1999b; Knoop, 1995; Randall & Cote, 1991; Riley, Lockwood, Powell-Perry, & Baker, 1998), a trend that will probably continue.

In any study, a relevant question is which of all possible work commitment forms should be tested so as to better reflect an individual's multiple commitments at work. Two suggestions were advanced in attempt to answer this question. Blau et al. (1993), who developed a general index of work commitment, suggested that a work commitment facet index should include at least job, organization, occupation, and value of work facets. Morrow (1993) proposed two forms of organizational commitment (OC) (affective and continuance) together with job involvement, career commitment, and work ethic as universal forms of commitment that can and should be examined together in multiple commitment research. To date, few studies have applied either suggestion. In most cases, the rationale for using these or other commitment foci has been the researcher's selection, not the result of an accepted or consistent approach regarding which commitment foci should be used in a given research question. More conceptual work needs to be done to elaborate the justifications for examining particular commitment foci in a given research.

Yet in addition to the conceptual considerations of using more than one commitment form, researchers should begin to prune the choices by using valid, reliable measures for each construct being investigated (Randall & Cote, 1991). Also, to prevent overlap, more attention should be paid to the way measures of commitment were conceptualized and operationalized (Morrow, 1983), particularly when several commitment measures are used in the same research. Certain forms of commitment are possibly somewhat redundant and insufficiently distinct to warrant continued separation. Therefore, a more rigorous examination of their differences is recommended (Morrow, 1983, 1993). This chapter discusses some methodological considerations that need to be addressed when commitment foci in a given research are chosen.

POTENTIAL PROBLEMS
IN MULTIPLE COMMITMENT RESEARCH

Because some of the conceptual and methodological problems in each commitment form were addressed in the previous chapter the focus next is on potential problems of using several commitment forms. The use of several commitments in a single study raises problems because in addition to the specific conceptual and measurement problems of each commitment, multiple commitment scholars might encounter difficulties such as concept redundancy, overlap of items and concepts across commitment foci, and lack of discriminant validity. Therefore, a review of the potential problems in multiple commitment research is necessary.

Concept Redundancy.   Concept redundancy was mentioned as one of the major problems (Morrow, 1983, 1993). It exists whenever concepts are not precisely defined to be mutually exclusive (i.e., they combine different forms of work commitment) or when the link between a conceptual definition and a measurement procedure is less than perfect (Morrow, 1993). *Concept redundancy* implies that concepts and/or their measures are not distinct from other concepts and their measures. It thus threatens the content- validity, unidimensionality, and discriminant-validity standards (Morrow et al., 1991).

Morrow (1993, pp. 109–113) provided good examples of definitions of commitment forms that overlap other commitment forms or items from commitment scales that refer to more than one commitment form. Redundancy was evident in the overlap of items supposed to measure different work commitment foci and in items not clear as to the commitment foci they were measuring. One possible explanation for such redundancy involved the considerable interchangeability of the words *job* and *work* within the various measures of commitment (Morrow & McElroy, 1986). For example, researchers used the word *work* when measuring commitment to the job and the word *job* when measuring commitment to the work. The problem is that researchers neglected the fact that work and job are two different entities and as such are two different foci of commitment. To avoid concept redundancy one should not refer to the job when measuring commitment to work or to work when measuring commitment to the job. Other problems concern the overlap of items supposed to measure different work commitment foci and items that are unclear about the commitment foci they are measuring (e.g., "My loyalty is to my work, not to the union"). More attention is warranted regarding the way the different measures of commitment are conceptualized and operationalized to prevent overlap of the concepts (Morrow, 1983).

Rater Naivety.   Another problem is rater naivety (Morrow et al., 1991). Are commitment items and measures meaningful, particularly for those academically naive raters who will be called on to handle these measures? Does this conceptual and analytical distinction among commitment forms actually result in better information, namely, more generalizable knowledge? Or are we perhaps creating measures of false precision? The potential problem here is whether the refinements in instrumentation, namely, defining more commitment forms, represents anything more than a scholastic artifact. Specifically, can respondents report their attitudes to related phenomena (e.g., different commitment forms in this case) without contamination? A possible implication of this question could be that perhaps researchers have been so ambitious in their propagation of additional concepts and measures that the incremental benefits they have achieved are perceptible only to other researchers. If potential participants of commitment research cannot distinguish these scales and their concepts, the capacity of these instruments to gather generalizable data is severely limited (Morrow et al., 1991). Research is needed here to clarify whether there is a gap between scholars' and employees' perceptions as to the existence of some commitment forms. This dilemma highlights the question of which commitment forms should be studied out of all the possible forms proposed in previous research.

Few studies have dealt directly with this issue. In one such interesting study, Morrow et al. (1991) presented to three groups of raters, namely researchers, undergraduates, and clerical staff, and items of five commitment foci (Protestant work ethic, job involvement, work as a central life interest, career salience, and OC). The raters were asked to classify items for each of five work commitment scales according to the construct it represented. The results showed that the commitment measures examined exhibited varying levels of redundancy, which proved increasingly problematic the less familiar raters were with the concepts at hand. The students consistently misclassified more items than the researchers, and the clerical employees misclassified more items than the students. The findings also showed that some measures of commitment were marked by a degree of concept redundancy. However, the significance of the redundancy issue appeared problematic for only three of the five measures of commitment used in this study. The OC and Protestant work ethic scales demonstrated the least redundancy, whereas job involvement, career salience, and work as a central life interest exhibited a high degree of redundancy with one another. In a later work, Singh and Vinnicombe (2000) interviewed Swedish and UK engineers about the meaning of commitment, and concluded that for their respondents the meaning of commitment was not inline with commitment as defined in the management literature. This finding provides important support for Morrow et al.'s (1991) finding that researchers and practitioners do not attribute the same meaning to commitment at work.

Morrow et al. (1991) justifiably concluded that researchers should persist in the careful, if tedious, work necessary to validate the concepts that drive their research; commitment forms in our case. Morrow et al.'s findings depended on the specific measures used in that study, hence are hardly generalizable. But the degree of overlap evinced in their study demonstrated that those least familiar with commitment-form concepts are least able to distinguish among them accurately. Their findings together with those of Singh and Vinnicombe (2000) completed us to caution researchers against using redundant commitment form measures. Researchers should also ask whether the measures they apply exhibit sufficient uniqueness to justify their use as independent instruments.

Discriminant Validity

The potential problems previously mentioned caused researchers to examine different forms of work commitment for concept redundancy. In fact, an important line of work commitment research, particularly in earlier studies, has concentrated on its discriminant validity. This line of research is important because it helps in the detection of commitment forms that are too similar to other forms. Such research can lead to reduction in the number of commitment forms that should be considered in multiple commitment research. In also points to items of specific commitment forms that are too ambiguous in terms of the commitment form into which they fit. This can aid researchers in omitting these items and developing clear, and valid scales of commitment.

The literature shows several methods for examining differences and similarities among commitment scales. Using exploratory and confirmatory factor analysis is one way of examining the discriminant validity of commitment scales, and essentially the main strategy in commitment research. Another method is to observe the correlations among commitment forms. High or too high correlations may indicate redundancy. A third course is to examine the relations between commitment forms and expected determinants and outcomes. If commitment forms differ, they should be related differently to work-related variables. All three methods have been applied in multiple commitment research and are reviewed here.

Factor Analysis.   This method is considered the most prevalent in the attempt to establish the discriminant validity of commitment forms. In the review below, studies are placed in two categories: first, studies that are more limited in their methodology, and second more advanced studies. The first group of studies is limited in the sense that they applied obsolete scales of commitment and/or used up to three commitment scales. These studies are reviewed in Table 3.1.

The general conclusion based on the findings of these studies is evidently that sufficient discriminant validity existed among most of the commitment forms that were examined. Some problems were revealed by Morrow and McElroy (1986) who concluded that job involvement, career salience, and work as a central life interest were marked by a fair amount of redundancy, whereas the Protestant work ethic and OC were independent forms of work commitment. Note that Morrow and McElroy's conclusion was based on obsolete measures used in their study. For example, Work as a central life interest has hardly been used as a commitment form. In fact it is not recommended for such use because of its low reliability and multidimensionality, and its overlap with other commitments in and outside the work setting. Mirels and Garrett's (1976) scale of Protestant work ethic (PWE) has conceptual and methodological problems, as noted in the previous chapter. Lodhal and Kejner's (1965) job involvement scale has practically been replaced by the Kanungo's (1979, 1982), as has Porter et al.'s (1974) scale of OC by Meyer and Allen's scale (1991). Therefore, it is hard to generalize from their findings on the discriminant validity of more common and established commitment forms used in more recent research. Other problematic findings presented in Table 3.1 are those of Carson and Bedeian (1994), who found some redundancy between the Blau's (1985) career commitment scale and a scale of career withdrawal. Regardless of some of the problematic

TABLE 3.1

Research Using Factor Analysis to Test the Discriminant Validity of Commitment Forms Using Few Forms or Obsolete Scales

Studies	Commitment forms that were examined	Method	Commitment forms that have acceptable discriminant validity	Commitment forms that have problematic discriminant validity	Sample
Morrow and McElroy (1986)	Protestant work ethic Career salience Central life interest Job involvement Organizational commitment	Exploratory factor analysis (Minres solution with varimax rotation)	Protestant work ethic Organizational commitment	Job involvement Career salience Central life interest	563 employees with supervisory responsibilities at a large public agency in a Midwestern state
Steffy & Jones (1988)	Organizational commitment Career commitment Community commitment	Principal component factor analysis using oblique rotations	Organizational commitment Career commitment Community commitment	None	118 married female nurses in a large psychiatric hospital in the Northwest
Paullay, Alliger, & Stone-Romero (1994)	Job involvement Work centrality Protestant work ethic	Confirmatory factor analysis using LISREL 7	Job involvement Work centrality Protestant work ethic	None	313 human service employees at a state psychiatric hospital
Carson & Bedeian (1994)	Career commitment measure of authors Career commitment measure of Blau (1985)Career withdrawal cognition	A principal-axes factor analysis with an oblique rotation	Career commitment measure of authors	Career commitment Blau (1985) Career withdrawal cognition	476 employees from a variety of occupations employed in a various work settings
Carson & Bedeian (1994)	Career commitment measure of authors Affective organizational commitment Job involvement	A principal-axes factor analysis with an oblique rotation	Career commitment measure of authors Affective organizational commitment Job involvement	None	476 employees from a variety of occupations employed in a various work settings

continued on next page

51

TABLE 3.1 *(continued)*

Studies	Commitment forms that were examined	Method	Commitment forms that have acceptable discriminant validity	Commitment forms that have problematic discriminant validity	Sample
Brooke, Russell & Price (1988)	Job satisfaction Job involvement Organizational commitment	Confirmatory factor analysis using LISREL 6	Job satisfaction Job involvement Organizational commitment	None	577 employees of a Veterans Administration Medical Center located in the upper-Midwest
Morrow & Goetz (1988)	Professionalism Job involvement Organizational commitment Work ethic	Exploratory factor analysis (Minres solution with varimax rotation)	Job involvement Organizational commitment Work ethic	Professionalism	325 accountants in public practice from 19 firms
Morrow & Wirth (1989)	Professional commitment Organizational commitment Job involvement	Exploratory factor analysis with varimax rotation	Professional commitment Organizational commitment Job involvement	None	728 employees of a Midwestern university who work in professional or scientific jobs
Mathieu & Farr (1991)	Job satisfaction Job involvement Organizational	Commitment Confirmatory factor analysis using LISREL 6	Job satisfaction Job involvement Organizational commitment	None	483 engineers from a variety of fields and from seven different organizations
Mathieu & Farr (1991)	Job satisfaction Job involvement Organizational commitment	Confirmatory factor analysis using LISREL 6	Job satisfaction Job involvement Organizational commitment	None	194 transit bus drivers from a large city in the Midwest
Bashaw & Grant (1994)	Organizational commitment Job commitment Career commitment	Principal component factor analysis and Confirmatory factor analysis using LISREL 7	Organizational commitment Job commitment Career commitment	None	560 industrial salespeople from 16 companies operating primarily in the Southeastern US
Gaither (1993)	Organizational commitment Job withdrawal intention Career commitment Career withdrawal intention	Confirmatory factor analysis using LISREL 7	Organizational commitment Job withdrawal intention Career commitment Career withdrawal intention	None	940 pharmacists who held license to practice pharmacy in the US. A nationwide random sample

results one important conclusion from these studies is that OC and job in-volvement are distinct concepts.

Although most of the these studies either used obsolete scales, applying ex-ploratory factor analysis or used only two or three commitment forms, several others and rather more recent investigations, constituting the second cate-gory noted earlier have taken a step forward by examining the discriminant validity of more than three commitment foci in one study. These studies mostly applied more current and established scales of commitment. More-over, the stated goal of some of them was to promote the development of a general scale of commitment forms. These studies also tended to use confir-matory factor analysis because the distinction in practice between exploratory and confirmatory analysis may be deemed an ordered progression.

An exploratory factor analysis, without prior specification of the number of factors, is exclusively exploratory. Using a maximum likelihood (ML) or gen-eralized least squares (GLS) exploratory programs represents the next step in the progression, in that a hypothesized number of underlying factors can be specified and the goodness of fit of the resulting solution can be tested. At this point there is a demarcation, with passage from an exploratory program to a confirmatory program. Although historically this has been termed *confirma-tory analysis*, a more descriptive term might be *restrictive analysis*, in that the values for many of the parameters have been restricted a priori, typically to zero (Anderson & Gerbing, 1988). In short, confirmatory factor analysis that supports the distinction among commitment foci by providing acceptable fit indexes will advance by one-step development in the definition and measure-ment of these scales. A summary of the findings of the more recent and ad-vanced studies is presented in Table 3.2.

The main conclusion of the findings presented in Table 3.2 is that there is good discriminant validity among commitment forms. In one study (Chang, 1999) a problem with the discriminant validity of continuance organizational commitment was found. In general it seems that for three commitment foci, organization, career, and job, there is sufficient evidence that all the three can be tested in the same research design with minimum risk of redundancy.

Several studies deserve specific and more detailed attention because of their potential and specific contribution to the development of valid scales to multiple commitments. Cohen (1996) conducted a detailed study on the discriminant validity of commitment forms that applied confirmatory factor analysis. The contribution there was the testing of five commitment foci in one study: career commitment, job involvement, work involvement, OC, and the (PWE). The study also dealt with two other important matters. First, which measure of OC should be included in the integrative approach to commitment: the Porter et al. scale, or, the multidimensional Meyer and Allen scale; and second, how was the continuance scale to be integrated

TABLE 3.2

Research Using Factor Analysis to Test the Discriminant Validity of Commitment Forms Using Established Scales

Studies	Commitment forms that were examined	Method	Commitment forms that have acceptable discriminant validity	Commitment forms that have problematic discriminant validity	Sample
Blau (1985)	Career commitment Job involvement Organizational commitment	A principal components factor analysis	Career commitment Job involvement Organizational commitment	None	119 registered staff nurses at a large hospital in a Midwestern city
Blau (1988)	Career commitment Job involvement Organizational commitment	A principal components factor analysis	Career commitment Job involvement Organizational commitment	None	137 nonunion first-level supervisors from the circulation department of a large eastern city newspaper
Blau (1988)	Career commitment Job involvement Organizational commitment	A principal components factor analysis	Career commitment Job involvement Organizational commitment	None	106 field office personnel in an insurance company in a large eastern city
Reilly & Orsak (1991)	Affective Organizational commitment Continuance Organizational commitment Normative organizational commitment Career commitment	Principal component factor analysis using a varimax rotation	Affective Organizational commitment Continuance Organizational commitment Normative organizational commitment Career commitment	None	520 full-time practicing nurses in the Pacific Northwest
Ellemers, de Gilder, & van den Heuvel (1998)	Career-oriented commitment Team-oriented commitment Organizational commitment	Confirmatory factor analysis with LISREL	Career-oriented commitment Team-oriented commitment Organizational commitment	None	690 people in the Netherlands who were employed at least 20 hours per week
Ellemers, de Gilder, & van den Heuvel (1998)	Career-oriented commitment Team-oriented commitment Organizational commitment	Confirmatory factor analysis with LISREL	Career-oriented commitment Team-oriented commitment Organizational commitment	None	287 workers at the job level in a large financial service organization in Belgium
Mueller, Wallace, & Price (1992)	Work commitment Career commitment Organizational commitment Intent to stay	Confirmatory factor analysis using LISREL 6	Work commitment Career commitment Organizational commitment Intent to stay	None	123 newly hired female nonsupervisory registered nurses at a large Midwestern teaching hospital

Study	Variables	Analysis	Variables	Notes	Sample
Blau, Paul, & St. John (1993)	Occupational commitment Organizational commitment Job involvement Value of work	Confirmatory factor analysis (Oblique solution) using LISREL	Occupational commitment Organizational commitment Job involvement Value of work	None	339 full-time registered nurses in three hospitals in a large Eastern city
Chang (1999)	Continuance organizational commitment Affective organizational commitment Career commitment	A principal components factor analysis	Continuance organizational commitment Affective organizational commitment Career commitment	Continuance organizational commitment	227 researchers working for 8 business or economic research institutes in Korea
Boshoff & Mels (2000)	Organizational commitment Professional commitment Job involvement Commitment to supervisor Intention to resign	A stepwise Exploratory factor analysis with oblique rotation	Organizational commitment Professional commitment Job involvement Commitment to supervisor Intention to resign	Some items from each scale were removed to increase reliability	382 chartered accountants, teachers and office administrative personnel
Cohen (1999)	Affective organizational commitment Continuance organizational commitment Job involvement Career commitment Protestant work ethic	Confirmatory factor analysis using LISREL 8	Affective organizational commitment Continuance organizational commitment Job involvement Career commitment Protestant work ethic	None	238 nurses (a response rate of 47%) from two hospitals in Western Canada, one medium size and one small
Hackett, Lapierre, & Hausdorf (2001)	Affective organizational commitment, work involvement, job involvement, occupational commitment	Principal axis component extraction followed by direct oblimin oblique rotation	Affective organizational commitment, work involvement, job involvement, occupational commitment	None	852 part-time and full-time employed Ontario nurses belonging to a 75,000-member nursing association
Blau (1989)	Career commitment Organizational commitment Job involvement	A principal components factor analysis	Career commitment Organizational commitment Job involvement	None	133 full-time bank tellers working for a large nonunionized bank based in a major Northwestern city

into a work commitment scale? The last issue is important because research has shown that the variable continuance organizational commitment has two dimensions: personal sacrifices and high alternatives (Dunham et al., 1994; Hackett, Bycio, & Hausdorf, 1994; McGee & Ford, 1987; Somers, 1993; Jaros, 1997; Iverson & Buttigieg, 1999; Hartman & Bambacas, 2000). Although Morrow did not refer to the possible implications of this bidimensionality for discriminant validity, Cohen (1996) tested and compared the full-scale models against models with each of its two dimensions separately. Accordingly, two measures of OC were compiled, namely the three eight-item scales of *affective*, *continuance*, and *normative* commitment of Allen and Meyer (1990), and the full 15-item version of the OCQ (Porter et al., 1974).

Another advantage of Cohen's (1996) study was that it applied more current and established scales than those used in previous research. Career commitment was measured by the eight-item measure developed by Blau (1985). Job involvement (10 items) and work involvement (6 items) were subjected to measures developed by Kanungo (1979, 1982). These measures were selected as they overcame the problem of Lodhal and Kejner's measure (1965), which failed to distinguish particular job context and generalized work context. The 19-item scale developed by Mirels and Garrett (1971) measured the PWE.

The sample consisted of 238 nurses (a response rate of 47%) from two hospitals in Western Canada, one of medium size and one small. Three confirmatory factor analyses were performed to test discriminant validity using LISREL VII (Joreskog & Sorbom, 1989). The first tested the discriminant validity of the three-component model of Meyer and Allen (1984). The second tested the discriminant validity of work commitment model, which included the Meyer and Allen scales together with four other forms of commitment, namely job involvement, career commitment, work involvement, and PWE. The third tested the discriminant validity of a work commitment model that included the OCQ together with the four forms of commitment just mentioned above.

The first confirmatory factor analysis aimed to establish the discriminant validity of Meyer and Allen's (1984) three-component commitment model. The results of this analysis showed a poor fit to the data of a one general-factor model ($X^2 = 119.46, p < .001; X^2/df = 4.42$; AGFI = 0.818), and a good fit to a three-factor model ($X^2 = 45.42, p < .01; X^2/df = 1.89$; AGFI = 0.919). In accordance with previous research (Hacket et al., 1994), the three-component model of OC was supported by the data. A confirmatory factor analysis for commitment forms with the Meyer and Allen scales was also conducted. Three alternative models were tested: a seven-factor model, representing Meyer and Allen's proposed model, a five-factor model, combining Meyer and Allen's three dimensions into one scale, and a one-factor model. The seven-factor model clearly proved to fit the data better than did the two others. All the fit measures in the seven-factor model were better: The X^2/df ratio was 1.73, RMSR was .384, and the GFI was .888.

Another confirmatory factor analysis examined commitment scales with the OCQ. Two alternative models were tested, a five-factor and a one-factor model. The five-factor model was shown to fit the data better than the one-factor model: The X^2/df ratio was 2.52, RMSR was .458, and the GFI was .889. However, the overall fit measures of the seven-factor model, which included the Meyer and Allen scales, were better than those of the five-factor model, which included the Porter et al. scale. For example, the X^2/df was below 2 for the Meyer and Allen (1.73) model and above 2 for the Porter et al. model (2.52). The RMSR and the AGFI were higher for the Meyer and Allen model than for the Porter et al. model.

In another study, Cohen (1999a) tested the discriminant validity of five commitment scales defined by Morrow (1993) as universal forms of commitment, namely, commitment forms that can be tested in any work setting: affective organizational commitment, continuance organizational commitment, career commitment, job involvement, and PWE. Here, too, confirmatory factor analysis using LISREL VIII (Joreskog & Sorbom, 1993) was performed to test the discriminant validity. Several alternative models were tested: A five-factor model which represented Morrow's one-factor model, 10 four-factor models, 10 three-factor models, and 3 models based on dividing continuance commitment into two dimensions. The findings clearly show that the five-factor model fitted the data better than the one-factor model, any of the four-factor models, and any of the three-factor models. The X^2/df ratio was 1.76, the TLI was .93, and CFI was .95. These fit indexes were much better than those in the one-factor model or any of the ten four-factor models, and showed an acceptable discriminant validity of the five forms of work commitment. Also, a chi-square difference test comparing the five-factor model with the ten four-factor models and the ten three-factor models revealed significant differences between the five-factor models and any of the other twenty. This finding shows a better fit with the data of the five-factor model than with any other.

The discriminant analysis also examined continuance organizational commitment and its dimensions at the item level. The findings of the chi-square test showed a significant difference between the five- and the six-factor models ($X^2 = 79.97$; df = 5; $p < .001$), with a better fit of the six-factor than the five-factor model. When each of the two dimensions of continuance commitment was analyzed separately as representing this construct, results of the chi-square test showed a significant difference between them and the five-factor model. This finding supports a better fit of models that use any of the dimensions of continuance commitment than of models that combine them into one scale. The chi-square test revealed no significant difference between the six-factor model and the models with the dimensions of continuance commitment. This showed that the fit of the two models with the data was not better than the fit of the six-factor model. Finally, the fit indices showed that the five-factor model with "low alternatives" as representing continuance commitment had a somewhat better fit with the data than the model with "personal sacrifices."

The findings of confirmatory factor analysis support the argument that the five commitment forms (i.e., continuance organizational commitment, affective organizational commitment, career commitment, PWE, and job involvement) advanced as universal by Morrow (1993) are distinct constructs. But they also show that the discriminant validity of the commitment forms is not perfect and can be improved. One way is by deciding which of the dimensions of the continuance commitment should be included in the model.

Blau and Ryan (1997) and Blau, Paul, and St. John (1993) took another step forward in the quest for the appropriate commitment scales to provide a parsimonious and valid index for commitment in the workplace. In their study Blau et al. (1993), in contrast to Cohen (1996, 1999a), took what might be termed a *two-step approach*. In the first step, they factor-analyzed (exploratory factor analysis) several commitment measures and in some cases, more than one form for each facet. They used the following scales: four career facet scales, Blau's (1985, 1988) career commitment scale, Gould's (1979) career involvement scale, Greenhaus's (1971, 1973) career salience scale, and Sekaran's (1982, 1986) career salience scale; one job facet scale, that of Kanungo (1982); two work values scales, Kanungo's (1982) work involvement scale, and Blood's (1969) four-item PWE scale; as well as one OC scale, that of Meyer and Allen (1984).

In an exploratory factor analysis with a sample of part-time MBA students, Blau et al. (1993) extracted a general index of commitment forms including five scales for each commitment facet. Naturally, in the commitment forms that were represented by two, three, or four scales, the final scale was a combination of more than one scale. For example, the final career commitment scale consisted of items of three scales: those of Blau (1985), Gould (1979), and Sekaran (1982). The work value scale consisted of items taken from two scales: work involvement (Kanungo, 1982) and PWE (Blood, 1969). An immediate question indicating a problem in Blau's findings is why were some commitment facets represented by several scales and others by one? The problem was strongly demonstrated in the work value scale. It is not clear why items were added to a work involvement scale that was considered valid, reliable, and unidimensional, particularly when the items added were from a PWE scale considered somewhat problematic.

The same can be argued about the final career commitment scale in Blau's finding that comprises three scales. Two of them (Gould, 1979; Sekaran, 1982, 1986) were somewhat problematic and less established than Blau's scale (1985). This may have been a source of contamination in the final scales. Each scale had its own conceptual definition. Combining items from several scales might create some ambiguity in the exact conceptual definition of the resulting new scales. A notable advantage of Blau's finding is that the model was tested twice and the findings indicated consistent results each time.

At the second step, Blau et al. (1993) administered the resulting 31 items comprising the general work commitment scale, which included five facets of commitment, to a sample of registered nurses and applied confirmatory factor analysis. The results of the confirmatory factor analysis (oblique solution) of the 31 commitment items showed an acceptable fit of the data to the four a priori facets. The chi-square to degree of freedom ratio was 1.97, goodness of fit was .92, adjusted goodness of fit was .90, and the root mean square residual was .06. All the item factor loadings were significant. Blau et al. (1993) concluded that occupational commitment, job involvement, value of work, and OC were distinct work commitment facets.

In the later study, Blau and Ryan (1997) developed a scale for Protestant work ethic intended to be parsimonious and better fitting a multiple commitment approach. This was akin to that of Blau et al. (1993) in combining items of different scales of work ethic and administering a questionnaire to respondents. They ended with an 18-item scale and a short version of 12 items. Blau and Ryan (1997) concluded that their 12-item (short-form) measure of work ethic could be combined with a 10-item job involvement scale (Kanungo, 1982), three eight-item measures of affective, continuance, and normative organizational commitment (Allen & Meyer, 1990), and an 11-item (Blau et al., 1993), or 12-item (Carson & Bedeian, 1994) measure of occupational or career commitment, to create a 57- or 58-item general indexD of work commitment of reasonable length.

Blau and Ryan's (1997) idea is a good one, but some problems exist with some of the scales they mentioned as appropriate for a general index of work commitment. The main problem concerns the scales based on a combination of scales: Each has its own and different conceptual definition and origin. I believe this causes concept redundancy, the main problem of the multiple-commitment approach (Morrow, 1983). Also, I believe that commitment research should rely on a purely attitudinal approach, not on definitions or items reflecting behavior or behavioral tendencies, otherwise, we increase the possibility that commitment scales might overlap with commitment outcomes. This was the case with the OCQ and it is the case with Blau's (1985, 1988) career commitment scales. Third, we should do our best to ensure that our scales are unidimensional in nature, and not multidimensional like the Carson and Bedeian (1994) career commitment scale. This leads to the main conclusion here. The best way to develop a general scale for commitment comprising a combination of commitment scales is to rely on established, valid, and reliable scales of each commitment form. Only such commitment forms can be part of a more general scale of commitment. I do not think that relying on scales that are not valid or composed of a combination of scales, of which some are not valid, will contribute to the advancement and development of a general index of commitment. The work should be done with each commitment form separately. Here valid and reliable scales should be elaborated, and from these we should choose the scales that best fit other commitment forms.

Interrelations Among Commitment Forms

Another way to examine concept redundancy among commitment forms is to examine their intercorrelations. "In the case of work commitment, redundancy would be evidenced by high, positive intercorrelations among the relevant measures. These correlations should be particularly high, say in the .6 to .8 range because of the common variance attributed to the derivement of all the measures from paper and pencil techniques ..." (Morrow, 1983, p. 496). Morrow (1983) argued that evidence of independence might be as high as .3 to account for the shared method error and the probability of some mutual antecedents. In her work, Morrow reported six studies that examined interrelations among the commitment forms.

The correlations presented in Morrow's (1983) study were relatively old and based on obsolete scales of commitment. However, the findings did not display exceptionally high or low intercorrelations. All those presented by Morrow (1983) were between .30 to .60. Morrow concluded that for this reason the data were inconclusive. Yet these correlations actually seem quite conclusive, considering, of course, the limitations of the period of publication and the obsolete scales, and the fact that only 5 of 21 possible combinations were observed. From Morrow's finding we can conclude that the intercorrelations provide no evidence for concept redundancy among commitment forms. Many more findings on the intercorrelations among commitment foci are needed to provide more valuable data on this important issue.

For greater conclusiveness on this important issue, a better way to examine the correlations among commitment forms is to meta-analyze them with corrections for sample size and measurement error (Hunter & Schmidt, 1990). This provides more conclusive findings about the true interrelations among commitment forms. The superiority of meta-analysis is due, according to Hunter and Schmidt (1990), to the traditional narrative review procedure being beset by three possible limitations: (a) the reviewer may not attempt to integrate findings across studies, (b) the reviewer may simplify the integration task by basing his or her conclusions on only a small subset of the studies, (c) the reviewer may actually attempt the task of mentally integrating findings across all studies and fail to do an adequate job.

Recent developments in meta-analysis (Hunter & Schmidt, 1990) made it possible to re-examine existing studies by quantitative review methods. These permit the statistical aggregation of research findings and the systematic assessment of interstudy moderators. Quantitative effects and samples can be cumulated and, consequently, commonalties beyond the scope of narrative reviews can be brought to light. Hunter and Schmidt's (1990) method is based on the following steps:

1. Introducing a more accurate estimate of effect-size through the use of sample weighted estimates.
2. Removing the artifactual attenuating effects of instrument unreliability and range restriction to correct effect size estimates.
3. Testing the hypothesis that the variance in observed effect-size is due solely to artifacts.

This meta-analytic procedure aggregates correlation coefficients across a collection of empirical studies and corrects for the presence of statistical artifacts to provide unbiased estimates of population relations. The method consists of three basic steps: the estimation of population means correlation and variance, the correction for statistical artifacts, and the analysis of moderating effect.

This section reviews existing findings of meta-analysis on the interrelation among commitment forms. However, because most research on commitment in the workplace was done on OC, most meta-analyses were performed on this form rather than other commitment forms. Therefore, in the case of other commitment forms, in addition to studies that used meta-analysis, empirical studies that did not use meta-analysis are also reviewed.

Organizational Commitment

The meta-analyses findings of research that examined the relationship between OC and other commitment forms are presented in Table 3.3. These show that the magnitude of the relation between OC and practically all the other commitment forms does not indicate any severe problem of concept redundancy. The highest true corrected correlation across 71 samples is between job involvement and OC, $r = .50$. With Morrow's criterion of size of correlations between .6 to .8 as evidence of overlap, no such conclusion can be reached, although note should be taken of the high correlation with the job involvement measure.

TABLE 3.3
Findings of Meta-Analyses that Examined the Relationship Between
Organizational Commitment and Other Commitment Forms.

Studies	Professional/ Occupational Commitment			Job Involvement			Work Values			Union Commitment		
	k	N	r_c	K	N	r_c	k	N	r_c	k	N	r_c
Cohen (1992)	22	9011	0.36	12	3424	0.37						
Meyer et al. (in press) (1)	13	3599	0.51	16	3625	0.53						
Cohen, Lowenberg, & Rosenstein (1990)							5	1047	0.39	5	1696	0.30
Wallace (1993)	25	8203	0.45									
Mathieu & Zajac, (1990)	22	5131	0.44	20	5779	0.44	7	1269	0.29	5	3407	0.21
Brown (1996)				71	26331	0.50						
Lee, Carswell, & Allen (2000)	49	15774	0.45									
Reed, Young, & McHugh, (1994)										76	15699	0.42
Johnson & Johnson (1999)										91	22012	0.32
Bamberger, Kluger, & Suchard, (1999)										41	17935	0.36

k = the number of samples in each analysis; N = the total number of individuals in the k samples;
r_c = the mean weighted corrected correlation.
(1) Only findings on affective organizational commitment are presented.

The only commitment form for which there are no meta-analysis data is the relation between OC and group commitment. The few empirical findings about this relation do not show high correlations, which might indicate concept redundancy. For example Rotondi (1975), found a correlation of −.06 among scientists and .23 among engineers. A slightly higher correlation between the two forms, r = .45, was found by Zaccaro and Dobbins (1989) who developed their own measure of group commitment. The highest correlations between group and OC was reported by Ellemers et al.

(1998), who found a correlation of .61 between the two commitment forms in one sample (a representative sample of the Dutch population) and a correlation of .57 in another (employees of a financial service organization in Belgium). Despite these two high correlations the overall findings we have thus far indicate no concept redundancy between OC and other commitment forms in the workplace based on the correlations between the forms.

The Meyer and Allen Scale of Organizational Commitment

Most of the findings presented above are based on the OCQ. Moreover other commitment forms are sometimes also measured by means of the OCQ. For example, Dolen and Shultz (1998) examined the intercorrelations among four commitment forms: academic commitment, OC, professional commitment, and university commitment. In all cases they used the OCQ scale, replacing the word "organization" in each question with "profession," "university," and "major." Their findings showed that none of the correlations among these forms exceeded .60. In fact only one of them, between OC and professional commitment, was higher than .40.

However the Meyer and Allen (1984) commitment scales are is today considered more valid scales to measure OC. There are very few meta-analysis data on the relation between this form and other commitment forms. Lee, Carswell, and Allen (2000) reported a corrected correlation of .45 between affective OC and occupational commitment (based on 49 samples), −.08 between continuance OC and occupational commitment (based on five samples), and .34 between normative organizational commitment and occupational commitment (based on three samples). Meyer, Stanley, Herscovitch, and Topulnytsky (in press) reported a corrected correlation of .53 between affective OC and TOB involvement (based on 15 samples), .03 between continuance OC and TOB involvement (based on 8 samples), and .40 between normative OC and TOB involvement (based on 4 samples). In a study that examined the Meyer and Allen scale and its relation with other commitment foci, Cohen (1996) found that the affective commitment dimension of Meyer and Allen evinced the highest correlation with other commitment forms such as job involvement ($r = .51$), career commitment ($r = .47$), and work involvement ($r = .41$). The correlation of normative commitment with other commitment measures did not exceed $r = 3$, thus providing support for the discriminant validity of that dimension. An interesting result is the lack of a significant relation between the continuance commitment dimension and any of the commitment measures. The correlations are extremely low and do not exceed .10. Reilly and Orsak (1991) also reported this pattern of findings.

Cohen (1996; 1999a) also examined the possibility that continuance commitment was multidimensional and that one dimension could fit a general index of commitment forms better than another dimension. In keeping with previous research (Dunham et al., 1994; Hackett et al., 1994; McGee & Ford, 1987; Somers, 1993; Jaros, 1997), the continuance commitment scale was divided into two: "high sacrifices" and "low alternatives." The correlations of the two subscales with work commitment constructs supported their distinction. For example, "high sacrifices" had a positive significant relation with affective organizational commitment ($r = .193, p < .01$), career commitment ($r = .130, p < .05$), and job involvement ($r = .159, p < .01$), whereas "low alternatives" had negative relations with affective organizational commitment ($r = -.201, p < .001$) and with career commitment ($r = -.272, p < .001$). The differential relations of the two subscales of continuance commitment with work commitment constructs explained the nonsignificant relations of the full scale with the same constructs.

Another finding in Cohen's (1996) research concerned the correlation between continuance commitment and the OCQ. Conceptually, Meyer and Allen (1984) argued that continuance commitment is not expected to be related to the OCQ because of the different conceptualizations of affective (OCQ) versus continuance commitment. Still, for the continuance dimension to demonstrate a convergent validity, one would expect some relation with the OCQ, even if the correlation were low. In Cohen's (1996) study, for example, the correlation was $r = .06$. In Meyer and Allen's sample of university employees (1984) the correlation was $r < -.06$, and these authors (1990) found a correlation of $-.02$ in a sample of non-unionized employees in three organizations.

In two other samples (Hackett et al., 1992) consisting of 2301 nurses and 100 bus operators the correlations were $r = -.10$ and $r = -.06$ respectively. Moreover, the continuance commitment was not related to OC measures, defined conceptually as continuance commitment, in a sample of university employees (Meyer & Allen, 1984); nor to the Ritzer and Trice scale (1969) or the Hrebiniak and Alutto scale (1972). In their literature review, Allen and Meyer (1996) also reported very low correlations between continuance commitment and the OCQ. In a meta-analysis study a corrected correlation of $-.02$ was found between continuance OC and the OCQ based on 10 samples (Meyer et al., in press). In addition, in many findings regarding the Meyer and Allen measure, low and mostly insignificant correlations were found between the continuance scale and the affective or normative scales (Jaros, 1997; Ko et al., 1997; Shore & Wayne, 1993). The few instances where the continuance measure was related to other commitment measures were in Randall et al.'s (1990) study, where the reported correlation was .28, and in a unique research design (Meyer & Allen, 1984, p. 374) where "students were presented with scenarios describing employees who were high or low in continuance commitment and high or low in affective commitment. After reading these scenarios, the subjects responded to several measures as they believed the employee in the scenario would respond."

Therefore, it can be argued that the continuance commitment dimension shows an unsatisfactory construct and convergent validity. It is true that the total independence of this dimension as demonstrated in both the correlations and the factor analysis can indicate good discriminant validity. But the absence of any significant relations of this dimension with any other commitment measures or with the outcome variables calls in question its being part of the work commitment construct at all. In light of these above findings, the way this dimension was defined, and the specific items compounding it, the continuance commitment dimension is arguably an elaborated measure of perceived employment alternatives, and is not a dimension of OC or part of the work commitment construct. A work commitment variable is not bound to have a high relationship (e.g., $r = .6$ to $r = .8$) with another work commitment to demonstrate that it is an independent construct. But some relation with some work commitment measures is needed for a demonstration of construct or convergent validity. The correlations found by Cohen (1996) and Reilly and Orsak (1991) showed that the continuance commitment dimension is not related to any of the other commitment foci. This is a highly uncommon finding in the work commitment literature. In addition to the present findings, all previous literature (Morrow & McElroy, 1986; Morrow & Goetz, 1988; Morrow & Wirth, 1989) has shown that a given commitment focus is related to at least one other, and usually to more. A finding that strengthens the above conclusion is by Singh and Vinnicombe (2000) who interviewed Swedish and UK engineers about the meaning of commitment. They concluded that the continuance element operationalized as one of the two key aspects of commitment by management literature seemed no longer to be an important aspect of commitment by engineering management in the global workplace of the 1990s. Naturally, more research is needed on continuance commitment and particularly on its bidimensionality before a final conclusion will be made about abandon it as part of the multiple commitments constructs.

Let us turn to the affective dimension of OC proposed by Meyer and Allen (1984). Because their scale for this is quite similar to the short version of the OCQ (Dunham et al., 1994), the OCQ-based meta-analysis findings presented above can be generalized, with some caution, to the Meyer and Allen (1984) scale. However, more meta-analysis research is needed on the relationship between OC as conceptualized and measured by Meyer and Allen (1990) and other commitment forms.

Job Involvement

The findings of an important meta-analysis study on the correlates of job involvement by Brown (1996) showed somewhat higher correlations of this form with other commitment forms. This research was based on 51 samples and provides important information on the relation between job involvement and other commitment foci. Brown's (1996) meta-analysis showed the following relationship between job involvement and other commitment forms: $r = .50$ with OC (71 samples); $r = .45$ with work ethic endorsement (13 samples); $r = .60$ with career commitment (10 samples); $r = .53$ with work involvement (6 samples). These corrected correlations can be defined as more problematic in terms of discriminant validity than those for OC. Although they do not exceed .60 they are very close to it, and in fact, reached .60 for career commitment. It seems that some potential for concept redundancy with most of the other commitment forms exists for job involvement. Other meta-analyses reported a corrected correlation of .52 between job involvement and occupational commitment based on 23 samples, (Lee et al., 1999), and a corrected correlation of .53 between TOB involvement and affective OC based on 16 samples (Meyer et al., in press).

An interesting result in Brown's (1996) study was that when the measurement of job involvement was controlled the moderator analysis showed that the relationship between job involvement and OC was lower with Kanungo's (1982) measure ($r = .44$ with 16 samples) than with the short or the long version of Lodhal and Kejner's (1965) measure ($r = .53$ based on 11 samples that used the short six-item version, and $r = .54$ based on five samples that used the long 20-item version). This finding showed that Kanungo's scale is superior to Lodhal and Kejner's in terms of concept redundancy. This finding is important in light of the high correlations found between job involvement and most of the other commitment forms. Controlling for the type of measurement in the other combinations, as was done for OC, might show that there is less danger of concept redundancy when Kanungo's scale is used. These important findings also demonstrated the need for more meta-analysis research on commitment forms that control for the measurement of these forms. Such research will provide important and useful information regarding commitment forms that are more promising than others in terms of concept redundancy.

In the following section, some of the interrelations among commitment forms examined by narrative review are surveyed. Only combinations of relations other than those set out above are presented because the meta-analysis findings are superior to narrative review. In particular, the survey emphasizes findings that showed exceptional relations among commitment forms, mostly findings that might indicate concept redundancy. An important source for such data is Morrow's (1993) review of commitment forms. In her review, Morrow (1993) also examined the correlations between given commitment forms and selected variables, among them other commitment forms.

Protestant Work Ethic

Not a single correlation between PWE and other commitment forms exceeded .60. Morrow reported that the correlation of PWE with work as a central life interest was .30, and with career salience .33. Other studies tended to support Morrow's findings. The only meta-analysis that also examined PWE reported a corrected correlation of .34 between it and occupational commitment based on five samples. Blau et al. (1993) found that the correlation between their measure of work values and occupational commitment was .36 and .39 on the two occasions it was tested in a sample of part-time MBA students, and .27 with registered nurses. A correlation of .23 between the two variables was found by Randall and Cote (1991) with university employees. Cohen (1998) found a correlation of .11 between career commitment and PWE with Canadian nurses. All the above research indicates that the magnitude of the relation between career commitment and PWE is not too high, and in general, no concept redundancy problem exists between the two concepts.

Data on the possible interrelation combinations among other commitment forms are too few to allow any explicit conclusion on concept redundancy. Union commitment was tested mainly in its relation to OC, and this was discussed earlier. Group commitment has hardly been tested in its relation with any commitment form. The few relations of this form with OC were also surveyed previously. Some of the findings on the relation between group commitment and occupational commitment do not indicate correlations high enough to suggest concept redundancy. For example, Cohen (1999b) found a correlation of .25 between the two in a sample of Israeli nurses, and Ellemers et al. (1998) found a correlation of .29 in one sample and a correlation of .37 in another. Becker (1992) found a correlation of .36 between a shorter version of Porter et al.'s (1974) scale and a one-item measure of group commitment.

Correlation Analysis

Convergence or divergence of the various commitment forms can also be examined by simple bivariate correlations. This procedure examines correlations between a set of work-related variables and the commitment forms. Assuming that the measures assess distinct constructs, we would expect measures of these constructs to relate differently to measures of demographic and other job-related variables. Besides the commitment measures several outcome variables have also been assembled. As Brooke et al. (1988) pointed out, this procedure represents a more rigorous test of discriminant validity. Very few studies examined the discriminant validity of commitment forms this way. Because correlates of commitment forms were also treated in Morrow's (1993) book, the issue need not be elaborated on here. However, some findings relevant to the discriminant validity issue and reports of studies that examined this issue directly are outlined here. In analyzing determinants of commitment forms, Morrow (1993) also focused on the determinants of each form separately. One reason for this was that little research had examined the relation between a set of workrelated variables and more than one commitment form simultaneously. Most of the existing research examined determinants of one form separately. Therefore, research that examines correlates of several commitment forms simultaneously is more valuable in terms of discriminant validity because it tests the relation in the exact same setting and increases our ability to reach valid conclusions about differences among commitment forms. This research is reviewed and elaborated on next.

Cohen (1999a) explained the rationale for some of the differences among commitment foci in their relationship to selected correlates. PWE determinants are felt to be primarily a function of personality and secondarily a function of culture (Morrow, 1983). The personality link is based on observation that ethic endorsement covaries with stable personality and demographic traits. The secondary impact of culture and socialization derives from studies that note greater acceptance of PWE ideas by rural workers and Protestants. The expectation is that the Protestant ethic is related to some of the demographic variables; it is not expected to be related to work experience variables or to work outcomes (Morrow, 1983). Furnham (1990) argued for a positive spillover between the PWE and nonwork, leading for example to the expectation of a positive relation between the PWE and life satisfaction (Cohen, 1999a).

There is a consensus that job involvement is a function of personality or individual difference, and the work situation (Morrow, 1993). Thus, demographic and work experience variables are expected to relate to job involvement. There is no evidence for a strong relation between job involvement and performance (Morrow, 1993) or between job involvement and nonwork domains. Hence job involvement is not expected to relate to performance or to variables representing nonwork domains. As for career commitment, individual differences and situational characteristics were suggested as the primary determinants of career commitment (Blau, 1985). Little research exists on the relationship career commitment and performance or between career commitment and nonwork domains, and very little research examined its relationship with nonwork domains and performance (Cohen, 1999a).

Affective organizational commitment was found to be related to a wide variety of correlates. The literature (Mathieu & Zajac, 1990; Meyer & Allen, 1991; Morrow, 1993) suggests that affective commitment is related to demographic characteristics (Cohen, 1993b; Cohen & Gattiker, 1992; Cohen & Lowenberg, 1990) and work experiences (Zeffane, 1994), and in professional settings, to structural characteristics (Cohen & Gattiker, 1994; Wallace, 1995). Affective commitment was also found to be positively related to performance (Meyer, Paunonen, Gellatly, Goffin, & Jackson, 1989). The literature also indicated positive spillover between variables representing nonwork domains and affective commitment (Kirchmeyer, 1992). Thus, all or most correlates discussed here were expected to relate to affective commitment. However, because the exchange approach is the main theory explaining the development of affective commitment (Mowday et al., 1982), variables that represent work experiences (such as met expectations or job satisfaction), and are therefore an important component of the exchange process, are expected to demonstrate a stronger relationship with affective commitment than are other correlates.

Continuance commitment, which reflects the recognition of costs associated with leaving the organization, should be related to anything that increases perceived costs. Direct or indirect investments in the organization, side bets, represent such costs most accurately and were operationalized mainly by variables like age, marital status, education, and tenure (Cohen & Gattiker, 1992; Cohen & Lowenberg, 1990; Wallace, 1997). Therefore, demographic variables and tenure are expected to demonstrate the strongest relation with continuance commitment. Meyer et al. (1989) found a negative relation between continuance commitment and performance based on the expectation that people who feel "stacked" in an organization would not exert much effort (Cohen, 1999a).

Finally, there has been little research on antecedents of the two dimensions of continuance commitment: personal sacrifices and low alternatives. The theoretical rationale behind the two constructs suggests that *personal sacrifices* are related to variables that represent side bets, namely, investments that might be lost if one leaves the organization. Demographic variables such as age and tenure are considered good indicators of such side bets (Becker, 1960; Cohen, 1993b; Cohen & Lowenberg, 1990; Wallace, 1997). For example older, veteran employees hesitate to leave the organization so as not to lose pension plans or other accumulated benefits. Conceptually, the *low alternatives* dimension represents a construct similar to withdrawal cognitions, and thus, is expected to relate to situational variables affecting stay or leave decisions like job satisfaction, performance, or job tension (Cohen, 1999a).

Research Findings. Similar to the examination of the interrelationship between commitment forms, meta-analysis findings that compare correlates of commitment forms yield perhaps the most valuable information for conclusions on discriminant validity. Brown (1996), who meta-analyzed correlates of job involvement, compared his findings with the meta-analysis findings of Mathieu and Zajac (1990) on correlates of OC. Twenty-five correlates were compared. According to the Bonferroni criterion, the strength of the relations with nine variables differed between job involvement and OC. By this criterion, the only relation that was significantly stronger for job involvement than for OC involved participative decision-making. Job involvement however, was substantially more strongly related to work ethic endorsement and skill variety than OC was. Job stress, communication, salary, supervisor, cowork-ers, pay satisfaction, promotion satisfaction, and turnover intentions were all more strongly related to OC than to job involvement. In addition, OC was substantially more strongly related to turnover than was job involvement.

Overall, the findings showed that job involvement tended to be somewhat more strongly related to job characteristics than OC. Of the five job charac-teristics measured by the Job Diagnostic Survey, only two—skill variety and autonomy—were common across the two meta-analytic studies. With re-spect to supervisory behaviors, participation was more strongly related to job involvement, but amount of communication was more strongly related to OC. Brown (1996) also showed that although relations with role-stress vari-ables were generally stronger for OC, the only significant difference was for job stress. Relations with all job satisfaction facets were stronger for OC. All the above findings indicate reasonable differences between OC and job in-volvement, and provide acceptable support for their distinctiveness.

No other meta-analyses of this kind exist that can provide such compara-tive and valuable information about correlates of commitment forms. An analysis of the correlates of commitment forms was presented by Morrow (1983, 1990). Some later research also compared the correlates of two or more commitment forms based on survey findings (Mueller & Lawler, 1999; Hirschfeld & Field, 2000; Bashaw & Grant, 2001). A summary of this re-search is presented in Table 3.4. The main conclusion to be drawn from this summary is that in general commitment forms are related differently to cor-relates. This was found in most of the studies presented in Table 3.4. The dif-ferential relations between most of the correlates and commitment forms support the distinctiveness of commitment foci.

Continuance Commitment. Finally, the fact that Morrow (1993) con-sidered continuance commitment an independent commitment focus ne-cessitates a specific discussion on this form. In many of the findings to date the continuance dimension has many insignificant correlations with poten-tial antecedents (Meyer & Allen, 1984; Allen & Meyer, 1990; Hackett et al., 1992; Ko et al., 1997; Reilly & Orsak, 1991). For example, Allen and Meyer (1990) found very low relations between the continuance scale and a large set of OC antecedents (e.g., job challenge, feedback, role clarity), most of them nonsignificant and none exceeding $r = .2$. The only fairly high cor-relation of the continuance dimension in that study was with the variable *perceived availability of alternatives* ($r = .43$). In some of the findings, the con-tinuance dimension had modest relations with age, tenure, education, and job satisfaction. Conceptually and logically, the demographic variables are expected to be related to perceived availability of alternatives, which is per-haps what the continuance dimension actually measures. The moderate re-

TABLE 3.4

Correlates of Commitment Forms

| | | | | Commitment Form Correlates | | | |
| | | | | | | | |
Studies	Sample	Organizational Commitment	Job Involvement	Career/Professional Commitment	Work Values	Group Commitment
Ellemers, de Gilder & van den Heuvel (1998)	690 people in the Netherlands who were employed at least 20 hours per week	Age, tenure, supervisory role, hours per week, work satisfaction		Hours per week, supervisory role, work satisfaction, age, tenure		Supervisory role, work satisfaction
Ellemers, de Gilder & van den Heuvel (1998)	287 workers at the job level in a large financial service organization in Belgium	Turnover intentions, contextual qualities, relational qualities		Age, education, internal turnover, number of internal applications		Turnover intentions, contextual qualities, relational qualities, overall performance
Steffy & Jones (1988)	118 female and married employees in a large psychiatric hospital located in the Northeast	Financial insecurity, relative pay, engaged in individual career planning		Marital satisfaction, relatives in vicinity, relative pay, financial insecurity, engaged in: dual-career planning, coping behaviors, individual career planning		
Blau (1985)	119 staff nurses working at a large hospital located in a Midwestern city	Tenure, role ambiguity, job withdrawal cognition	Tenure, role ambiguity, initiating structure, job withdrawal cognition	Tenure, marital status, growth need strength, locus of control, role ambiguity, consideration, initiating structure, career withdrawal cognition		

continued on next page

TABLE 3.4 (continued)

Commitment Form Correlates

Studies	Sample	Organizational Commitment	Job Involvement	Career/Professional Commitment	Work Values	Group Commitment
Carson & Bedeian (1994)	476 employees from a variety of occupations and variety of work settings	Career withdrawal cognitions, job withdrawal cognitions, age, career tenure, and organizational tenure	Career withdrawal cognitions, job withdrawal cognitions, education, age, career tenure, and organizational tenure	Career withdrawal cognitions, job withdrawal cognitions, education, age, and career tenure		
Thompson, Kopelman, & Schriesheim (1992)	A random sample of 330 employees drawn from the master alumni list of a large college in the Eastern USA	Self (as opposed to organizationally) employed have higher commitment	Not significant		Not significant	
Zaccaro & Dobbins (1989)	203 members of a traditional Cadet Corps at a large Southeastern University	Stronger correlations with: role ambiguity, role conflict, satisfaction with work, organization, progress, promotion chances, met expectations				Stronger correlations with: cohesiveness, task liking, task-process, and satisfaction with group members
Nogradi & Koch (1981)	139 administrators in Municipal Recreation Departments in Ontario	Related to participation in decision making		Not related to participation in decision making		
Parasuraman & Nachman (1987)	65 members of an Eastern Symphony orchestra	Gender, age, experience as professional musician, leadership attention, felt stress thoughts about quitting, intention to leave	Leadership attention, thoughts about quitting, intention to leave	Employment status, thoughts about quitting, intention to leave leadership attention, felt stress		

lation found between the continuance commitment and job satisfaction (Meyer et al., 1989) should be viewed in light of the negative relations between the two variables found in two other and different samples (Hackett et al., 1992). Many nonsignificant relations between continuance commitment and correlates such as work stress, negative affect, or emotional exhaustion were also found by Reilly and Orsak (1991).

Continuance commitment was also found to have low correlations with variables that are considered outcomes of commitment. Low correlations between the three dimensions of the Meyer and Allen's measure and intention to quit were found by Hackett et al. (1992). Jaros (1997) found that the continuance commitment was significantly correlated with turnover intentions in both samples, but did not independently predict turnover intentions in two samples, concurrently or longitudinally. For comparison, in a Ddifferent conceptualization of the continuance commitment proposed by Mayer and Schoorman (1992), a significant relation was found between their measure of the continuance commitment and intention to stay ($r = .38$) and quitting ($r = -.21$). Ko et al. (1997) found low correlations between the continuance commitment and intent to stay and search behavior. These correlations were much lower than those of normative and affective commitment with the two variables. Whitener and Walz (1993) found a weak effect of affective and continuance commitment on turnover when intent to turnover was controlled. Meyer et al. (1989) and Goffin and Gellatly (2001) found a negative relation between the continuance dimension and performance, and a positive relation between the affective dimension and performance. Shore and Wayne (1993) found a similar pattern of findings when the performance measure was Organizational Citizenship Behavior (OCB). Cohen (1996) found that the continuance dimension was not related to any of the outcome variables: intention to leave the organization, perceived effort, and perceived performance. What is puzzling is the lack of relation with the variable of intention to leave the organization; conceptually, this should be related to continuance commitment. Ruyter and Wetzels (1999) found a negative relation between continuance commitment and service quality. Conceptually it can be argued that employees with few employment alternatives might be unsatisfactory performers regardless of their level of OC. But alternative employment opportunities, which are what the continuance commitment dimension represents, and OC are two different concepts. One can also question the merit of studying a concept that predicts a negative relation with performance.

SUMMARY AND DIRECTIONS FOR FUTURE RESEARCH

The findings presented here shed some light on the question of how distinct are the commitment forms presented in this chapter. Some of Morrow's (1993) conclusions seem relevant here. First, job involvement operationalizations manifested the most overlapping with other measures. That is, the highest correlations between a given commitment focus and other commitment forms have been found between job involvement and the other forms. According to the correlations among commitment forms, some potential for concept redundancy might exist in the relation between job involvement and other commitment forms, particularly work involvement and career commitment. There is less danger of concept redundancy in the interrelations among other commitment forms. Future research should examine the role of the different scales used in commitment research in determining concept redundancy. This is based on these findings that lower correlations exist between job involvement and other commitment forms when job involvement is measured by Kanungo's (1982) scale.

Second, redundancy was found to be more a problem of instrumentation than of conceptual overlap, namely more a function of overlapping measures than overlapping concepts. This conclusion was strongly supported by the meta-analysis findings that showed that Kanungo's (1982) measure of job involvement is less redundant than is Lodhal and Kejner's (1965) measure.

In addition to these above conclusions, which are valid for Morrow's (1993) work and for this volume, several other conclusions were evinced here. Third, the Meyer and Allen (1984) scale of affective organizational commitment is a better measure of OC than the Porter et al. (1974) OCQ scale. The OCQ includes items that overlap with behavioral intentions (i.e., withdrawal cognition and performance) and therefore, overlap with other commitment forms more than does the Meyer and Allen scale, which is purely attitudinal. Fourth, the differing relation of commitment forms with work related correlates showed that basically each form has its uniqueness. There are different commitment forms in the workplace that are related differently to characteristics of the workplace. It is our task to better measure them, in a way that reduces concept redundancy.

Fifth, although Morrow (1993) included continuance commitment as one of the multiple commitment constructs, an important question is whether the continuance dimension as operationalized by Meyer and Allen (1984) is part of the large multiple commitments construct. The findings about the discriminant validity of this form do not support its inclusion as part of the multiple commitment constructs. As it is, this form is multidimensional and overlaps outcomes; its correlations, or perhaps lack of correlations, with many work-related variables indicate that it is not part of a general work commitment scale. In short, unlike Morrow (1993), who advanced continuance commitment as another form of multiple commitments, empirical findings showed than this form should not be included in multiple commitment research.

Several other recommendations for future work toward reducing concept redundancy are as follows: First, work on discriminant validity should rely on established scales, each with its own conceptual development, definition, and measurement having been tested several times and demonstrating good psychometric properties. This is a better approach than is using a combination of items from different measures of the same commitment construct and letting the statistical analysis decide for us which items to use. By using items from different scales to create a new measure for a given form, we simply shift the problem of redundancy from the measurement level to the conceptual level, where it is more severe. As Morrow (1983, p. 498) suggested, the existing redundancy of measures within each work focus must be eliminated first, followed by the elimination of between-work-foci redundancy.

Second, from these above recommendations and findings the suggested scales to be used for future research are Meyer and Allen's (1984) affective organizational commitment scale and Kanungo's job involvement and work involvement scales. The scales for the other commitment forms need more work and research to improve their psychometric properties and reduce concept redundancy. However, for the time being it is recommended Blau's (1985, 1988) career commitment scale be used, but with the omission of items referring to withdrawal cognitions (particularly item 1 in the 1985 and 1988 scales presented in Appendix A), and the union loyalty dimension of Gordon et al.'s (1980) union commitment scale in its long or short version (Kelloway et al., 1992), with the omission of the behavioral intentions item (item 2 of Gordon et al.'s scale presented in Appendix A). The recommendation to use only the loyalty dimension follows Morrow's (1993) argument that *work commitment*, a concept referring to multiple commitments at the workplace, would at a minimum seem to involve loyalty to several different entities. According to Morrow, loyalty is the minimum required dimension of commitment across different entities. As for group commitment, either Randall and Cote's (1991) scale or Ellemers et al.'s (1998) scale (without item 1, which has a behavioral orientation) can be used. It is difficult to recommend any of the work ethic scales because of their measurement problems. Blood's (1969) scale is the least problematic because it is short and unidimensional. Kanungo's (1982) work involvement scale can be a good replacement for the PWE scales.

Following the aforementioned recommendations, more research using confirmatory rather than exploratory factor analysis is required. If the process examines established scales, confirmatory analysis can inform us whether and how a combination of established commitment scales fit together. Naturally, more work is needed on commitment scales that cannot be defined as established. Such are the career commitment, group commitment, and PWE scales. Also, more work is needed to test the union commitment scale with other commitment forms. So far, it has been tested mainly with the OC scale. We need to know how it fits with other commitment forms. Another recommendation is that researchers test and use entire scales and not parts of scales. Using only several items from a given scale, without any conceptual or methodological justification, does not contribute to the advancement of the measurement of commitment forms. It is difficult to generalize from results deriving from partial scales to findings deriving from the complete scales. Most of the scales on commitment forms are relatively short and there is no reason to use only part of them.

Yet we can advance very little in our understanding of the discriminant validity of commitment forms if research applies obsolete scales or scales designed for some particular study. More necessary needful is testing of several commitment forms in one design with scales that are more current and promising in their psychometric properties, validity, and dimensionality. Future research should broaden the "sample" of commitment measures to examine within-category redundancy and to verify the nature of between-category redundancy (Morrow and McElroy, 1986).

Finally, Cohen (1993a) concluded that the findings of his study, and of the other studies on concept redundancy of commitment forms, have several implications that need to be addressed in future research. If the redundancy arises from methodological problems, research should continue the search for the appropriate methodology and measurement for assessing commitment forms (Randall & Cote, 1991). If the redundancy is because respondents cannot distinguish some concepts, a possible conclusion would be that "researchers have been so ambitious in their propagation of additional concepts and measures that the incremental benefits they have achieved are only perceptible to other researchers" (Morrow et al., 1991, p. 230). Morrow (1983) emphasized the importance of establishing whether respondents' discriminant abilities were sufficiently sensitive to allow them to report multiple work commitment attitudes accurately within a single data collection. Therefore, empirical tests showing that commitment foci assess distinct attitudinal constructs become vital.

The implication would probably be to reduce the commitment foci to those that respondents can discriminate. Morrow and Goetz (1988) suggested that the value, job, and organizational foci may be the only truly generic forms of work commitment. However, Cohen (1993a) also suggested that another possible implication is that some redundancy among the commitment forms should be tolerated. Conceptually, it can be argued that perfect interdependence does not reflect reality in the workplace. It makes more practical sense to suggest that forms of commitment are likely to be correlated and dependent simply because they are likely to be correlated within the mind of the employee. For example, Stagner (1956) described *dual commitment* to union and employer as a phenomenon arising from people's tendency to perceive their work situation as a unit rather than sharply differentiating the union role from the management role. The validity of commitment measures should be demonstrated not only by factor analysis, which is sample-specific and subject to common method-error variance problems (Morrow et al., 1991). Their predictive validity should also be evinced, as well as the differences among antecedents, which may be more useful in increasing our understanding of multiple commitments. Although the majority of the current literature examines discriminant validity among commitment forms, more research is necessary on outcomes and determinants of commitment foci by means of established or proposed measures of the concepts.

III

Theoretical Advancements in Multiple Commitment Research

4

Typologies
of Multiple Commitments

Morrow's (1983) work on multiple commitment stimulated thinking and research on this issue. In particular, Morrow pointed out the potential problems associated with examining multiple commitments, such as concept redundancy among commitment foci and measures within and between commitment forms. This is perhaps one of the reasons that there has been more methodological research on multiple commitments than conceptual studies. Still, Morrow's (1983) work eventually stimulated conceptual thinking on important aspects of multiple commitments. That is, what are the components of multiple commitments? How many and which commitment forms should be included in multiple commitment research? What are the boundaries of this concept? How should the different commitment foci be integrated into a meaningful concept? These are some of the questions that were asked in consequence of Morrow's (1983) work. Assuming that sooner or later the methodological problems of redundancy will be solved, these above questions are important for the progress of multiple commitment research. The answers may well determine its directions.

Since the appearance of Morrow's (1983) work, several conceptual frameworks on multiple commitments have been advanced. Some were presented as such and dealt directly with this issue whereas others approached it more indirectly. Some of the typologies presented here have a stronger conceptual justification, some a stronger methodological one. Not all of them are fully developed conceptually or methodologically. However, the progress of the concept of multiple commitments depends largely on the quality of the conceptual framework that attempts to integrate the different commitment forms. That is why it is important to present them, discuss their advantages and limitations, and suggest the best ways of integrating the separate commitment foci into one concept. This can make the difference between examining different foci without any clear justification for these rather than others and theory driven research on multiple commitment. A theory-driven study can justify any given selection of a combination of commitments in the workplace, and its findings and conclusions are probably be more meaningful and generalizable. As mentioned, several conceptual frameworks on multiple commitments have been advanced. In the following section the more common approaches are set out and analyzed.

Morrow's (1983, 1993) Framework: Commitment Forms as Analogous to Job Descriptive Index

In her proposed model, Morrow (1993) suggested that of all foci of work commitment five are basic in the sense of being relevant to the largest possible number of employees and termed them universal forms of work commitment. These are affective commitment to the organization, continuance commitment to the organization, work ethic endorsement, career commitment, and job involvement (see Fig. 4.1). Morrow (1993) concluded that these five forms appeared quite promising but needed more empirical substantiation. Her main rationale for selecting these particular forms was the growing need to identify forms of work commitment relevant to as many employees as possible. Morrow (1983) argued that because of the strong probability of shared antecedents and causal linkages among the components, these five forms could be viewed as dimensions of work commitment in the same way as the five dimensions of job satisfaction were viewed within the Job Descriptive Index (JDI; Smith, Kendall, & Hulin, 1969).

Morrow (1983) suggested the development of a commitment index analogous to the JDI (Smith et al., 1969) reflecting different foci. Morrow contended that this recommendation was consistent with the experience of researchers who, in dealing with the similarly complex notion of organizational effectiveness, elected to treat its constituent dimensions as separate concepts. According to Morrow (1993), the establishment of such an index should be a primary goal for researchers working in this area. Such an index would permit the formation of commitment profiles, allowing managers and others to pinpoint what forms of work commitment were less than optimal.

Before elaborating on Morrow's suggestion, a brief description of the Job Diagnostic Index is warranted. Smith et al. (1969) defined job satisfactions (in the plural) as "the feelings a worker has about his job," noting, "there are different feelings corresponding to differentiable aspects of the job" (p. 12). Their express goal was to measure the principal features of satisfaction, rec-

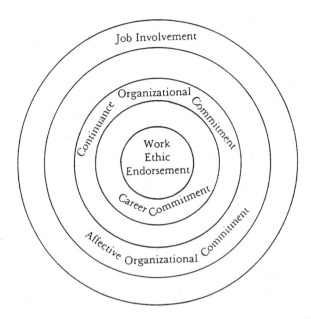

FIG. 4.1. Morrow's (1993) concentric circle model of work commitment. From *The theory and measurement of work commitment* (p. 163), by P. C. Morrow (1993). Greenwich: JAI Press. Copyright © by Elsevier Science. Reprinted with permission.

ognizing that not all components can be examined within a brief question-naire (Cook et al., 1981). The JDI was developed in the 1960s through several databased revisions from an initial pool of more than 100 items. The final version contains five separately presented subscales, covering Satisfaction with Type of Work (18 items), Pay (9 items), Promotion Opportunities (9 items), Supervision (18 items), and Co-Workers (18 items). Each of the 72 items is an adjective or phrase, and respondents indicate whether it describes the job aspect in question.

The question is whether a similar scale to the JDI can be developed for commitment forms. Morrow's (1983, 1993) idea is methodological in nature. According to this approach, what we need, is a parsimonious, practical, and above all flawless, not redundant, scale, that can easily be applied in multiple commitment research. However, a difference that exists between the JDI and the status of commitment research affects the idea of adopting the approach of the former to the latter. Each commitment form has its own research frame, definition, and history of conceptual and methodological development and scales. By contrast, the JDI is another measure, albeit common, for one of the most usual constructs in organizational behavior. The differences among commitment forms are more profound and have a more conceptual nature than do the differences among the various dimensions of job satisfaction. An attempt to develop a multiple commitment scale similar to the JDI might result in scales that are too simplistic and trivial or that disregard the conceptual framework and essence of each commitment. To tailor all commitment forms to one simple frame seems overly simplified. Morrow (1983, 1993) however, did not elaborate on how exactly to develop a multiple commitment scale that would parallel the JDI. She briefly suggested some examples on how it should be done but in general, the reader is left without enough information about how to develop such a scale. This left the door open to proposals from several researchers who tried to follow Morrow's general recommendation, each in the way he or she understood and interpreted it. As we review later, Morrow's suggestion was perceived and operationalized in entirely different ways by different researchers.

Cohen's (1993a) Model of a Multiple Commitment Matrix

One of Morrow's ideas (1993) was to "start from scratch" and develop an entirely new measure of work commitment embracing all five components. Such a strategy was advanced by Cohen (1993a) and was mentioned by Morrow (1993) as an example. In his approach, Cohen (1993a) used a definition of work commitment based on the approach suggested by O'Reilly and Chatman (1986). Accordingly, Cohen (1993a) defined *work commitments* as affective attachments to one or more of the objects of commitment (organization, occupation, job, and union). Work commitment can take one or more of the following three dimensions:

1. *Identification*—adoption of the goals and values of the commitment objects as one's own goals.
2. *Affiliation*—feelings of belonging to the commitment objects, being "part of it."
3. *Moral involvement*—internalization of the roles of the commitment objects expressed in feelings of care and concern for them.

Cohen's definition, as do definitions of commitment to multiple foci, takes a firmly attitudinal approach. The first and the third of these three dimensions of work commitment are similar to the identification and internalization dimensions developed by O'Reilly and Chatman (1986). However, their compliance dimension overlaps the calculative or continuance commitment as proposed by the side bet theory of Becker (1960) and its advocates (e.g., Meyer & Allen, 1984; McGee & Ford, 1987; Meyer, Paunonen, Gellatly, Goffin, & Jackson, 1989). Although continuance commitment is considered to represent psychological attachment, it tends to measure intentions to withdraw instead (e.g., Meyer & Allen, 1984; O'Reilly & Chatman, 1986; Mathieu & Zajac, 1990).

Diverging from such earlier work, Cohen proposed the affiliation dimension, which seems more consistent with the definition of work commitment as a psychological attachment.

Cohen (1993a) reported that to increase face and content validity of the work commitment measures, a number of preliminary steps were taken. The initial stage of the proposed instrument construction consisted of collecting items from common commitment scales and composing items that reflected the dimensions of all work commitments. Altogether, 40 items were collected. Each item was put in a general form, thus becoming usable for all types of work commitments (i.e., occupation, union, organization, and so on). A pre-test of these items with 110 employees was conducted to assess construct validity (Cohen, 1993a). Based on the analysis of these data, some ambiguous items were deleted from the instrument. Grounded in these qualitative and quantitative methods, the items were reduced to nine; three for each definition suggested for work commitment (identification, affiliation, and moral involvement).

The final list of items was organized in matrix form for the final survey instrument. This work commitment measure is presented in Fig. 4.2. The vertical portion of the matrix included the nine items that were phrased in general form, whereas the horizontal axis listed the types of work commitment measured in the study (occupation, organization, job, and union). The respondents answered the same questions for each of these four types of commitment. The items for the identification dimension were: "I find it very easy to identify with the objectives of this organization," "Most of the values I believe in are demonstrated by this organization," and "There are a lot of similarities between my personal goals and the goals of this organization," The items for the affiliation dimension were: "I talk to my friends about how great it is to work in/belong to this organization," "I am proud to work for/be a member of this organization," and "I feel myself a part of this organization." The items for the moral involvement dimension were: "I take personally any problem that occurs in the organization," " I become upset when things are not working out as they should in my organization," and "I really care about everything that happens in my organization." Respondents answered the same question for each type of commitment using a 7-point scale ranging from 1 (strongly disagree) to 7 (strongly agree).

Cohen's approach was tested in two studies. In the first (Cohen, 1993a), the relation between the four commitment forms (i.e., organization, occupation, union, and job) and work outcomes was tested in a sample of 129 white collar, unionized Israeli employees. The results demonstrated acceptable reliabilities of the commitment measures, ranging from .86 to .92. Item analyses (correlations between each item of a commitment scale and the total score less the item) indicated that each item had a positive correlation

Work Commitment Questionnaire
Instructions

Listed below are a series of statements that represent possible feelings that individuals might have about the following aspects of their work: organization, occupation, job, and union. With respect to your own feelings about each of the four particular factors, please indicate the degree of your agreement or disagreement with each statement regarding each of the four factors listed. Please use the following scale for indicating your response. Write the number that indicates your response in the squares to the right of each statement. You don't have to give the same for each square, but the scores in some squares may be the same.

1	2	3	4	5	6	7
Strongly disagree	Moderately disagree	Slightly disagree	Neither agree nor disagree	Slightly agree	Moderately agree	Strongly agree

Work Objects[1] Statements[2]	My Organization	My Occupation	My Union	My Job
1. I talk up to my friends about how great it is to belong to:				
2. I find that many of my values are very similar to the values of:				
3. I take personally any problems that occur in:				
4. I am proud to be a member of:				
5. Most of the things I believe in are exemplified by:				
6. I feel depressed when things are not working out as they should in:				
7. I feel myself a part of:				
8. There is a lot of similarity between my goals and the goals of:				
9. I really care about everything that happens in:				

[1]Giving the specific title for each of the commitment factors is highly recommended. For example, the name of the union, organization, occupation, job.

[2]affiliation   - Items 1, 4, 7
Identification   - Items 2, 5, 8
Moral Involvement   - Items 3, 6, 9

FIG. 4.2. Cohen's (1993) matrix format of measuring commitment forms. From Cohen, A. (1993), Work commitment in relation to withdrawal intentions and union effectiveness. *Journal of Business Research, 26,* 75–90. Copyright © 2002 by Sage Publications. Reprinted with permission.

with the total score for each of the commitment scales, with a range of average correlation from .60 to .81 for the union commitment, .40 to .73 for the organizational commitment, .27 to .65 for the occupational commitment, and .46 to .73 for the job commitment scale. These results suggested that the commitment scales were relatively homogeneous with respect to the underlying attitude constructs they measure.

Cohen (1993a) reported that some of the work commitment forms were highly correlated with each other, such as the relationship between organizational commitment and job commitment $r = .62$), or occupational commitment and job commitment $r = .65$). These two high correlations suggested that job commitment was redundant with other commitment forms. All the other intercorrelations of commitment measures were below $r = .40$. Cohen (1993a) also performed exploratory factor analysis, which provided another way to evaluate discriminant validity. If the four measures were reasonably independent, the factor structure should reflect such a pattern (Morrow & McElroy, 1986). The 36 items used to measure the commitment forms were factor-analyzed using the minres (principal axes with iterations) solutions with varimax rotation. The factor analysis yielded eight factors accounting for 65% of the total variance. The results suggested that in this sample, union commitment (Factor 1) and organizational commitment (Factor 2) were independent forms of commitment. Union commitment was completely independent, and organizational commitment had only a few common loadings on job commitment items. However, occupational commitment (Factor 4) and job commitment (Factor 5) were marked by some redundancy as evinced by common loadings, especially on Factor 3.

Despite some of the concept redundancy problems evident in Cohen's (1993a) approach, one of the advantages of his proposed measure was the predictive validity of the commitment scales tested in that research. For example, commitment forms predicted turnover intentions better than any commitment separately. Organizational commitment proved to be the strongest predictor of intentions to withdraw from the organization, together with occupational commitment, which exerted a positive effect on organizational withdrawal intention. Results for job withdrawal intention demonstrated that job commitment was the strongest predictor of job withdrawal intentions, although occupational commitment, like organization withdrawal, also positively affected withdrawal intentions. Only in the case of occupational withdrawal intentions did the findings show that job commitment was the only variable that affected occupational withdrawal intentions, whereas occupational commitment was hypothesized to be the best predictor of this outcome, along with other commitment forms.

In addition, the findings of this research strongly demonstrated the usefulness of commitment forms as a predictor of union effectiveness. Union commitment was the strongest predictor of union effectiveness, as suggested in the hypothesis. Other commitments also affected measures of union effectiveness. Job commitment positively affected union activity, and occupational commitment negatively affected union success. However, in the case of union militancy, union commitment was the only variable of any effect (Cohen, 1993a).

In his second study applying this approach, Cohen (1997b) surveyed 300 Canadian teachers in Western Canada and tested two commitment forms, using the same scales as in the first study. Cohen distinguished commitment to the specific organization for which one works, mostly schools, from commitment to the head office, (the school district covering all the schools.) Cohen (1997b) followed Gregersen and Black (1992), who examined the relation of several antecedents of commitment to the parent company and to the local work unit. Cohen (1997b) argued that the local unit and the head office represented different entities, so differences would exist in the level of commitment to each of them and in their antecedents. Because employees worked, spent their time, their daily experiences within their local unit, the level of commitment to the local unit could be expected to be higher than to the head office.

To test the possibility of concept redundancy, exploratory factor analysis was performed first. All the items of the two commitment forms were subjected to a principal component factor analysis and varimax rotation. A factor analysis of the 18 items was intended to indicate whether the two forms represented different dimensions and a distinct construct. The analysis revealed four factors. The first factor included six items of the commitment-to-school-district construct; the second factor included the same six items of the commitment-to-school construct. The six items represented the identification and the affiliation dimensions. The third factor included four items, two of them representing the moral involvement dimension of the commitment-to-school-district construct, and two representing the same dimension but of the commitment-to-school construct. The fourth factor included two items, one of them representing the moral involvement dimension of the commitment-to-school-district construct, the other representing the same dimension but of the commitment-to-school construct. This result clearly showed that the three items representing the moral involvement dimension were the reason for overlap of the two commitment foci, and they definitely could lower the discriminant validity between the two constructs. Therefore, it was decided to omit the three items of moral involvement of the two constructs and each of them should use the six items representing the affiliation and identification dimensions. The reliability for each of the six item scales was high: .85 for commitment to the local unit and .92 for commitment to the school district.

In the next step, confirmatory factor analysis using LISREL VIII (Joreskog & Sorbom, 1993) was applied to test the discriminant validity of the two commitment foci. The two-factor model placed the 12 indicators of commitment to the school district and commitment to the local unit on separate latent factors. This model was compared with a one-factor model where all the 12 indicators were forced into a single latent factor. The findings revealed that the two-factor model fitted the data better than the one-factor model. As the two models were nested models, a chi-square difference test (Bollen, 1989) was applied to compare them. This test showed that the restrictions added to the alternative one-factor model significantly reduced the fit of this model compared with the two-factor model (chi-square $= 166.64$; $p \leq .001$). All the above findings suggested that despite the relatively high correlation between them $r = .58$; $p \leq .001$) the two commitments represented different constructs.

A further test for discriminant validity was the correlations between the two commitment forms and nonwork determinants, mainly perceived organizational response to nonwork, which were tested in that study. A t-test for the significance of the difference between the correlations of each commitment to the three organizational response variables was performed. The correlation between commitment to the school district and integration response $r = .30$) was found significantly higher ($t = 2.74$; $p \leq .05$) than that between commitment to the local unit and integration response $r = .11$). Also, a significantly ($t = 2.83$; $p \leq .05$) higher correlation was found between commitment to the school district and the respect response $r = .18$) and commitment to the local unit and the respect response $r = .33$). No significant difference was found for the relation between commitment to the school district and separation $r = -.25$) and commitment to the local unit and separation $r = -.17$), although the direction of this correlation was as expected. The regression analysis provides additional support for the difference in the relation between each of the commitment foci and the nonwork domain. Cohen (1997b) also found that the level of commitment to the local unit was significantly higher than commitment to the school district. These findings, together with the result of the confirmatory factor analysis, supported the notion that the two commitment foci represented different entities.

The conclusion from Cohen's (1993a) proposed matrix form is that despite some evidence for concept redundancy it emerged as an effective way of measuring multiple forms of commitment. First, it obliged the respondents to evaluate and indicate their attitudes to commitment forms simultaneously, as they did in the workplace. Second, it avoided the long questionnaires required when the commitment items are split across the questionnaire. The findings demonstrated that the proposed commitment measures revealed acceptable psychometric properties of reliabilities, means, and standard deviations. They also overcame some of the difficulties in the commonly used commitment scales (Morrow, 1983). They had the same definitions and items for all of the commitment forms and eschewed unlike definitions that may cause difficulties when conclusions are generalized by comparison of results from the commitment scales; they avoided overlapping with items relating to more than one facet of commitment. Also, the items of the measures did not overlap antecedents and outcomes; they demonstrated good predictive validity for the outcomes examined in that study.

Blau's et al.'s (1993) General Index of Commitment

Blau and his associates (1993) also took up Morrow's (1983) recommendation for establishing valid work commitment scales and followed what Morrow termed a two-step process. According to this process in the first step redundancy of measures within each work commitment facet should be minimized. In the second step, redundancy between work commitment facet measures should be reduced. For their first step, Blau and his colleagues (1993) selected several scales for each commitment focus. These were four career facet scales (Gould, 1979; Greenhaus, 1971, 1973; Sekaran, 1982, 1986 scale; and Blau, 1985, 1988), two work value scales (Kanunugo's 1982 work involvement scale; Blood's 1969 scale), one organizational commitment scale (Meyer & Allen's 1984 affective commitment scale), and one job facet scale (Kanungo's 1982 job involvement scale). First items were administered twice to a sample of part-time MBA students. Next, exploratory factor analysis was used to test for redundancy of work commitment facet measures.

A question at this stage is whether Blau and his associates actually followed Morrow's (1983) recommendation for the first step in their use of several scales for a given commitment focus and only one scale for another commitment focus. The answer to this question is not entirely positive. They did not explain why there was no consistency in the number of scales used for each commitment form. Why were some commitment scales over-represented (e.g., career commitment) and others under-represented (e.g., organizational commitment)? This created a situation where the raw data for the factor analysis had more items representing one commitment focus and fewer items representing another. By factor analyzing many items from one form and fewer from another, one ends up with a solution that includes more items for one commitment focus than for the other. Arguably, in the first step Morrow intended the use of only one established scale for each commitment form, not several.

Another question concerns the conceptual justification for including a scale of career salience (Greenhaus, 1971, 1973) and of career commitment (Blau,

1985, 1988) in the same group of items portraying career commitment. Each of these scales has a different conceptualization, so they should seemingly not be presented together. By using several commitment scales together, as Blau and his associates did, one might reinforce concept redundancy or even create it, as a result of mixing items from different scales of the same commitment form, each of which stands for a different conceptual framework.

As mentioned previously, Blau et al. (1993) conducted exploratory factor analysis on the 59 commitment items with a sample of MBA students twice: at time one and seven weeks later at time two. The results in the two analyses were similar, indicating stability of the findings. The findings of the factor analysis at the first step showed a meaningful four-factor solution representing four commitment forms. The fifth factor was not interpretable and was omitted. The first factor included 11 items of career commitment, the second 1 seven items of job commitment, the third 1 seven items of work values and the fourth, six items of organizational commitment. The result, with 31 work commitment items loaded on four factors, is presented in Fig. 4.3. Many items, eleven altogether, are seen to represent career commitment. This is not surprising, considering that most of the original 59 items included items from career commitment scales. Another problem is that Blau and associates' (1993) resulting work commitment scale contains only six of Meyer and Allen's items (1984) established organizational commitment scale, and only seven of the original ten items of Kanungo's (1982) established job involvement scale. No conceptual justification or obvious reason can be given for omitting items from an established and valid scale.

The resulting 31 items were subjected to confirmatory factor analysis on a different sample, namely, full-time registered nurses. An acceptable fit of the data to the four a priori facets resulted. The chi-square to degrees of freedom ratio was 1.97, goodness of fit was .92, adjusted goodness of fit was .90, and the root mean square residual was .06. All the items factor loading were significant. In summary, the results indicated that occupational commitment, job involvement, value of work, and organizational commitment were distinct work commitment facets.

In a later study presented as a continuation and operationalization of Morrow's notion of a general work commitment scale, Blau and Ryan (1997) developed a scale for work values deemed to fit better into the general work commitment scale. This study replicated the methodology used for the general work commitment scale in Blau et al.'s (1993) study. A variety of items, 25 in all representing different scales of work values, were analyzed. An exploratory factor analysis yielded an 18-item multi-dimensional scale; presented in Appendix A. Blau and Ryan (1977) suggested a shorter version of 12 items, also presented in Appendix A. Blau and Ryan concluded that the 12-item, shorter version of work ethic could be combined

Item content	Factors			
	1	2	3	4
1. If could, would go into a different occupation	.64	—	—	—
2. Can see self in occupation for many years	.67	—	—	—
3. Occupation choice is a good decision	.59	—	—	—
4. If could, would not choose occupation	.62	—	—	—
5. No money need, still continue in occupation	.49	—	—	—
6. Sometimes dissatisfied with occupation	.71	—	—	—
7. Like occupation too well to give up	.78	—	—	—
8. Education/training not for occupation	.55	—	—	—
9. Have ideal occupation for life work	.79	—	—	—
10. Wish chosen different occupation	.48	—	—	—
11. Disappointed that entered occupation	.74	—	—	—
12. Most important things involve job	—	.66	—	—
13. Job only small part of who I am	—	.61	—	—
14. Live, eat, and breathe my job	—	.75	—	—
15. Most interests centered around my job	—	.63	—	—
16. Most personal life goals are job-oriented	—	.54	—	—
17. Job is very central to my existence	—	.58	—	—
18. Like to be absorbed in job most of time	—	.70	—	—
19. Hard work makes self a better person	—	—	.80	—
20. Wasting time a bad as wasting money	—	—	.46	—
21. Person's worth is how well does work	—	—	.56	—
22. Better to have more responsible work	—	—	.52	—
23. People should get involved in work	—	—	.71	—
24. Work should be central to life	—	—	.75	—
25. Life goals should be work-oriented	—	—	.77	—
26. Don't feel like belong to organization	—	—	—	.57
27. Not emotionally attached to organization				
27. Not emotionally attached to organization	—	—	—	.57
28. Organization has personal meaning to me	—	—	—	.60
29. Do not feel like part of organization	—	—	—	.59
30. Glad to spend rest of days with organization	—	—	—	.73
31. Organization's problems are mine too	—	—	—	.74

FIG. 4.3. Blau et al.'s (1993) scale of multiple commitments. Factor 1 = occupational commitment; factor 2 = job involvement; factor 3 = Protestant work ethic; factor 4 = organizational commitment. From Blau, G., Paul, A., & St. John, N. (1993). On developing a general index of work commitment. Journal of Vocational Behavior, 42, 298–314 (p. 309). Copyright © by Academic Press. Reprinted with permission.

with a 10-item job involvement scale (Kanungo, 1982), the three 8-item measures of affective, continuance, and normative organizational commitment scales (Meyer & Allen, 1990) and the 11 or 12 items of the career commitment scale of Blau et al. (1993) or of Carson and Bedeian (1994). Such a combination would create, according to Blau and Ryan, a general index of work commitment with a reasonable length of 57 to 58 items.

Contrary to what might be thought, Blau and Ryan's (1997) work in fact abandoned the basic idea presented by Blau et al. (1993). Blau and Ryan neglected the main findings and conclusions of Blau et al.'s study (1993) and shifted to a different, indeed a better, interpretation of Morrow's two steps of developing a general scale of work commitment. A better interpretation of Morrow's suggestion is that existing established and valid scales of only one form for each commitment should be used first. Only later should one examine how the separate scales fit together when combined into a general scale. By concluding that their proposed work value scale should be integrated and tested with other established work commitment scales in their full and complete forms, Blau and Ryan (1997) seem to move to a different, more correct interpretation of Morrow's idea. However, their (1997) proposed work value scale has its own problems, being the result of a combination of different measures of work values, and therefore, contaminated with concept redundancy.

Despite its limitations, some of the methodology and steps used by Blau et al.'s (1993) study are recommended. For example, the procedure of first performing an exploratory factor analysis and then a confirmatory one; and using different samples for each step. But, I believe that Blau et al.'s (1993) work illustrates that the best way to develop a valid index for work commitment depends more on within-commitment concept redundancy. The key is to develop valid, reliable, and nonredundant scales for each commitment separately to underpin and participate in the development of a general scale of work commitment.

Reichers's (1985) Organizational Focus Approach

Reichers's (1985) approach seems to have attracted much attention in multiple commitment research. When mentioning the earlier work of Morrow (1983), Reichers posited a significantly different argument, namely, that an advanced approach to multiple commitments may represent a natural development of the construct that has also characterized other ideas in the field. Reichers offered two examples of an advanced approach for such development; the job satisfaction construct, also proposed by Morrow (1983, 1993) as the raw model for multiple commitments, and the organizational climate construct. Reichers, like Morrow (1983), evidently regarded the JDI of Smith et al. (1969) as the goal that multiple commitments should seek to emulate. However while Morrow did not clarify how to accomplish this, Reichers (1985) presented a detailed conceptual model also encompassing ideas for measuring the proposed multiple commitment construct.

The starting point, or even the focus of Reicher's (1985) approach was the organization: "It is the central thesis of this paper that organizational commitment can be accurately understood as a collection of multiple commitments to various groups that comprise the organization" (Reichers, 1985; p. 469). Reichers argued that for many employees "the organization is an abstraction represented in reality by groups and individuals (e.g., co-workers, supervisors, and customers) who collectively constitute the organization. Organizations should be viewed as composites of coalitions and constituencies, each of which espouses a unique set of goals and values that may be in conflict with the goals and values of other organizational groups. To specify the foci of multiple commitments, one must specify the various groups that are relevant to an organization, or the organization's set role. The question, 'What is it that employees are committed to?' can be answered in a way that reflects the coalitional aspects of organizations." According to Reichers (1985), not only are organizations coalitional entities, employees of organizations are themselves of the multiple sets of goals and values that different coalitions espouse.

Reichers's (1985) model is presented in Fig. 4.4, which shows the multiple commitments individuals experience. Reichers noted commitments to top managers, co-workers, clients, and customers and also to the union and the community as relevant in the proposed conceptual framework. The dotted line in the figure around the organization, the author explained, indicated the permeability of organizational boundaries. Arrows connecting the central self with various constituencies indicated that the self was, in part, composed of its identifications with various groups. These are the commitments, sometimes termed *attachments* or *linkages*. The shorter arrows could represent commitments that are relatively closer, psychologically, to the individual. The undifferentiated space inside the dotted line could be thought of as global organizational commitment.

Multiple commitments, according to Reichers (1985), could be measured by interviews with organization members for their perceptions of relevant constituencies. The OCQ measure of organizational commitment could perhaps be adapted to reflect identification with the goals of these specific groups, and the score of these multiple commitments could be correlated with global commitment in the usual way. Thus, the relation between multiple commitment and organizational commitment could be assessed. Reichers (1985) suggested that an even more accurate assessment of an individual's commitments might be obtained by means of a *forced-*

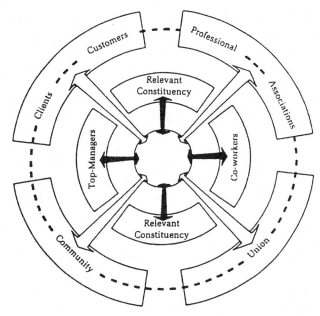

FIG. 4.4.   Reicher's (1985) model of organizational commitment. From Reichers, A. E. (1985). A review and reconceptualization of organizational commitment. Academy of Management Review, 10, 465–476 (p. 472). Reprinted with permission of the Academy of Management. Permission conveyed through Copyright Clearance Center, Inc.

choice response format, whereby the choices represent two conflicting goals held by two different constituencies. Every relevant constituency could be paired with every other, and respondents could be asked to endorse one goal over another for a series of items. This approach closely approximates the actual situation that individuals in an organization face when committed to constituencies that espouse conflicting goals, and thus may be a more realistic approach than earlier global conceptions.

Reichers (1985) argued that the problem of concept redundancy characteristic of organizational commitment might diminish if commitment was conceptualized and measured as a multifaceted construct possessing multiple foci. Global organizational commitment demonstrated a disturbingly high statistical overlap of concepts such as job involvement, job attachment, and career satisfaction. Specific commitments to particular goal orientations might arguably demonstrate less redundancy with other concepts than was the case for measures of global commitment in the past.

According to Reichers (1985), this multiple commitment approach strongly suggested that the commitment experienced by one individual might differ markedly from that experienced by another. One individual's "organizational commitment" may be primarily a function of the perception that the organization is dedicated to high quality products at a reasonable price; another person's commitment may largely depend on the individual's belief that the organization espouses humanistic values regarding employees. A global measure of organizational commitment might reveal both employees to be equally committed to the organization yet the focus of their two commitments is entirely different. A multiple commitment approach could aid in organizational diagnosis and intervention procedures that could pinpoint the strength, presence, or absence of particular commitments.

In short, Reichers (1985) presented an interesting view of multiple commitments. However, concentration on organizational commitment as the conceptual core of this approach was both an advantage and disadvantage of this approach. It was an advantage because it set out some guidelines of a conceptual framework for which commitments relevant in the workplace should be studied. According to Reichers, these were commitments relevant to the organizational setting. The idea that the organization is not a single whole entity is also interesting and deserves further attention in future research.

The disadvantage of Reichers's approach, however, is its profound conceptual limitation. It neglected several commitment forms, some fundamental to the understanding of multiple commitments. It made no mention of job involvement, work values, or even such a commitment form that has evidently grown in importance over the years as occupational commitment. Can we really understand commitment in the workplace without these forms? I doubt it. More and more arguments, some discussed set forth in earlier chapters, postulate that occupational commitment may perhaps replace organizational commitment as the leading commitment in the workplace (Meyer & Allen, 1997; Morrow, 1993). This limitation is undoubtedly so fundamental a deficiency in Reichers's conceptualization as to prevent us from adopting it as the conceptual framework for multiple commitment research.

Reichers's (1985) work did capture attention in commitment research, and a number of studies pursued some of her ideas (Becker, 1992). However, very few works attempted to apply Reichers's model as it stood. One of the few works to test this model again empirically was Reichers (1986). The main expectation of that study was that global organizational commitment might be largely a function of commitment to management's goals and values. One of Reichers's findings of current relevance was that of the four relevant constituencies examined in the study, namely, top management, funding agencies, professionalism, and clients, only commitment to top management's goals and values was also associated with organizational commitment measured by Porter et al.'s (1974) scale. This finding supported the earlier expectation of that research. However, the absence of any relation between the other three constituencies and organizational commitment was somewhat troubling, considering the expectations in Reichers's (1985) earlier conceptualization that the commitments to the different constituencies should be related to global commitment.

Another question regarding Reicher's operationalization is whether the OCQ is the appropriate measure for global commitment. Porter et al.'s (1974) scale was not designed or defined as a scale for global commitment, and it is questionable whether it should be interpreted and operationalized as such. It would have been better to develop and design a specific definition and measurement for global commitment and for the other constituencies.

Becker's (1992) Model of Foci and Bases of Commitment

Becker's (1992) model can be perceived as an elaboration of Reichers's (1985), the improvement being Becker's awareness that Reichers concentrated mainly on defining the possible foci of commitment from the organizational point of view. Becker's basic contention was that in addition to a definition of the foci of commitment, the process of commitment had to be determined. He argued that multidimensionality of commitment characterized not only the foci but also the process and motives of commitment, or as he termed them, the *bases of commitment*. Becker's model can be characterized as a dual multidimensional model of commitment highlighting not only in the foci, but also the process or bases of commitment.

According to Becker (1992), interest in distinguishing the contributions of the foci and bases of commitment contrasts markedly with the conventional view of commitment evinced by Porter et al.'s (1974) approach. Becker defined the latter approach as *unidimensional* because its measure of commitment assessed commitment along a single line. Becker is certainly correct, but he did not mention the more common approach to organizational commitment, that of Meyer and Allen (1991), which is multidimensional and examines the bases of commitment.

As for the foci of commitment Becker (1992) accepted Reichers's typology based on research on reference groups and role theory indicating that many organization members are aware of and committed to multiple sets of goals and values. Foci possibly relevant for many employees are co-workers, superiors, subordinates, customers, and other groups and individuals who collectively constitute the organization. Becker argued that commitment may not be a zero-sum game; employees can have a high degree of commitment to several foci at the same time.

From this argument, Becker (1992) adopted O'Reilly and Chatman's (1986) approach as the foundation for defining the bases of commitment. Note that O'Reilly and Chateman developed their approach for the organizational commitment focus, not for any other. They advanced three dimensions as possible bases for commitment. These are *Compliance*, when people adopt attitudes and behaviors in order to obtain specific rewards or to avoid specific punishments; *Identification*, when people adopt attitudes and behaviors in order to be associated with another person or group in a satisfying, self-defining relationship; and *internalization*, when one adopts attitudes and behaviors because their content is congruent with one's value system. Becker (1992) argued that for some people, identification with the work group could be central to their attachment to the workplace whereas for others, internalization of their supervisor's values might be critical. A multiple commitment approach could aid in organizational diagnosis and intervention procedures to pinpoint the strength, presence, or absence of particular commitments.

In short, Becker's approach can be viewed conceptually as a two-dimensional matrix as presented in Fig. 4.5. The columns represent the bases of commitment and the rows its foci. The measurement of this approach was explained in Becker's (1992) study. He first diagnosed the foci of commitment through individual interviews with 15 employees that included open questions such as, "If I followed you around on a typical day, who would I see you talking to and working with?" Based on the frequency of mention of particular foci, Becker selected the following for this particular research: the organization, its top management, immediate supervisors, and immediate work groups. Commitment to the organization was measured by the shorter version of Porter et al.'s scale (1974) and commitment to the other foci was measured by one item asking respondents, "How attached are you to the following people and groups?" (Top management, supervisor, and work group). Responses were given on a 7-point scale ranging from "not at all" to "completely."

The bases of commitment were measured by 17 items designed to assess compliance, identification, and internalization based on O'Reilly and Chatman (1986) and on modifications added by Becker (1972). These items were written for each of the foci, including the organization. An option of "not applicable" was given to each focus to prevent the respondent from answering 17 questions on a nonrelevant focus. Finally, from a series of factor analyses,

Focus of commitment	Nature of commitment		
	Compliance	Identification	Internalization
Organization			
Top management			
Unit			
Unit manager			
Work team			
Team leader			

FIG. 4.5.   Becker's (1992) model of multidimensional conceptualization of commitment.

Becker developed eight scales assessing the bases of commitment. These were: identification and internalization with respect to organization, supervisor, and work group; normative commitment to top management; and overall compliance, without regard to foci. Note that normative commitment represented a combined scale of identification and internalization, which were highly correlated. This is an indication that O'Reilly and Chatman's three-dimension conceptualization was not supported by the data.

Becker (1992) tested his measures and hypotheses with a sample of employees of a military supply company. The findings indicated multicollinearity problems between the foci and bases of commitment. Some of the reported intercorrelations were .78, .74, and .70, and some correlations were above .60. This is an indication of the concept redundancy problem. Another potential problem in Becker's operationalization was its being too specific to the sample. The foci of commitment to be examined were decided on the basis of the sample, and the scales of bases of commitment to be used were decided from the factor-analyses findings. Also, the use of 1-item measurement of foci of commitments other than the organization seems somewhat too simplistic and problematic. Yet, a further problem was the concepts used for bases of commitment. Here, Becker adopted an approach that cannot be defined as established, and he modified it in a way that one cannot be sure is applicable to other settings. An immediate question is why not use a much more established conceptualization of bases of commitment such as Meyer and Allen's (1991)? In addition, Becker's conceptualization was afflicted by all the problems besetting Reichers's (1985) approach. Namely, it left out important commitment foci such as work values, job involvement, and occupational commitment. These foci were not included in Reichers's conceptualization, and naturally not in Becker's.

The findings of Becker's study showed that foci and bases of commitment predicted satisfaction and intent to quit but not prosocial organizational behavior. In many of the dependent variables it was the Porter et al. (1974) scale that predicted much of the variance of these variables. All of these showed average predictive validity of Becker's commitment scales.

In two later studies Becker and his associates (1995, 1996) used the same conceptualization and measurement procedures to examine the relation between commitment forms and attitudinal and behavioral outcomes. In the first, Becker, Randall, and Riegel (1995) examined employees of a fast food restaurant chain. To identify meaningful foci of commitment, interviews, similar to those in the first study, were conducted with 16 employees. From the frequency of their mention in the interviews, the three following foci were selected for the study: the organization, the restaurant management, and nonmanagerial employees. To measure normative commitment to the organization the shorter version of the OCQ was applied. The 17 items from

Becker's (1992) earlier study were used to measure the bases of commitment to each of the other foci, the sole difference being that the titles of the foci were changed to those pertinent to the current investigation.

From a series of factor analyses, four scales assessing commitment were developed: normative commitment to the organization, which was measured by the shorter version of Porter et al.'s (1974) scale, normative commitment to restaurant management, normative commitment to nonmanagerial employees, and overall compliance with regard to foci. The findings of this study, particularly the intercorrelations among the commitment scales, indicated acceptable discriminant validity. The tested commitment foci were found to predict tardiness and altruism, and more than one focus proved significant in the relationship to the outcomes. However, note the difference between the early conceptualization of Becker (1992) and this research in terms of the tested commitment foci, particularly the bases of commitment. In the later study, the internalization and identification bases were normative commitment and there was only one compliance basis. Such changes in the foci tested make it quite difficult to generalize the findings and compare them in the studies.

In their third study, Becker and his associates (1996) used similar conceptualization and measurement to test the relation with performance in a sample of university employees. Two differences from the two earlier studies are worth mentioning. First, in the latest study only two bases of commitment were used, namely, internalization and identification. The compliance dimension was not tested in it, but it was tested in the two previous studies. Second, Porter et al.'s (1974) scale was not applied in the latest study, and overall commitment was measured by summing the organizational identification and internalization items. Porter et al.'s measure was tested in the two previous studies.

Becker et al.'s (1996) findings revealed very high intercorrelations among the different commitment measures. Some of the correlations were above .90, some above .80, and some above .70; very few were below .60. Becker and his colleagues used confirmatory factor analysis to demonstrate that employees distinguished foci from bases of commitment. But the intercorrelations were very high, indicating a severe concept redundancy problem in the conceptualization or the operationalization of commitment foci, or both. Some of Becker's concepts predicted performance although the amount of variance predicted by the commitment variables did not exceed 4%.

Becker's (1992) and Becker and his associates' (1995, 1996) studies marked some advance in multiple commitment research. First, they pointed out the need for a multidimensional perspective on commitment, showing that it could increase the prediction of important attitudes and behaviors in the workplace. Second, they suggested the possibility of dual multidimensionality of multiple commitments, namely different foci, but also different processes or bases of commitment. Becker's also contributed through his attempt to operationalize and test conceptual frameworks on multiple commitments, thereby guiding researchers toward improvements in both conceptualizations and empirical examinations. Yet, the main problem in Becker's approach seems to be the distinction among the bases of commitment. Too little conceptual justification is evident to argue that these bases according to O'Reilly and Chatman's (1986) conceptualization represent different dimensions. The data firmly rejected the distinction among the bases of commitment as conceptualized by Becker.

Meyer and Allen's (1997) Dual-Multidimensional Conceptualization

The next and more recent conceptualization naturally also advanced the notion of dual multidimensionality in commitment. Meyer and Allen (1997) acknowledged the contributions of Reichers (1985), Becker (1992), and Becker and his associates (1996), and concluded that although the multiple-constituency framework had not been tested extensively, preliminary evidence indicated some value in measuring commitments to more specific foci within the organization. They argued, however, that existing evidence did not negate the value of measuring organizational commitment at a global level. They agreed with Becker's conceptualization that commitment could be considered multidimensional in both its forms and focus, and held that these two approaches to developing a multidimensional framework were not incompatible. They proposed their own two-dimensional matrix, with the different forms of commitment listed along one axis and the different foci along the other. This matrix is presented in Fig. 4.6. The various cells within this matrix reflect the nature of commitment an employee has to each individual constituency of relevance to him or her. These authors stated that one should not use this matrix to classify employees. Rather, each employee's commitment profile would reflect varying degrees of different forms of commitment to each of the different constituencies.

The top row in Fig. 4.6 reflects the commitment model described by Meyer and Allen (1991). The first column reflects Reichers's (1985) multiple constituency approach and some of Becker's (1992) operationalization of this conceptualization. Accordingly, commitment is described as an affective attachment that can be felt to varying degrees for specific constituencies within and perhaps beyond the organization. There is however, a major difference between Meyer and Allen's model and Becker's (1992). Instead of O'Reilly and Chatman's (1986) conceptualization of the bases of commitment (e.g., identification, internalization, and compliance), Meyer and Al-

	Nature of commitment		
Focus of commitment	Compliance	Identification	Internalization
Organization			
Top management			
Unit			
Unit manager			
Work team			
Team leader			

FIG. 4.6.   Meyer and Allen's (1997) model of multidimensional conceptualization of commitment. From Meyer, P. J., & Allen, J. N. (1997). *Commitment in the Workplace: Theory, Research, and Application* (p. 21). Copyright © by Sage Publications. Reprinted with permission.

len proposed their own conceptualization of affective, continuance, and normative commitment to the organization. They did not explain why they held their three dimensions superior to those of O'Reilly and Chatman (1986) used by Becker. Instead, they defined the matrix they presented as an expansion of their organizational commitment model to include multiple components of commitment. They argued that with their model it should be possible to measure the different forms of commitment to each of the various constituencies and to enter a value into each cell in the matrix to reflect an employee's multidimensional commitment profile.

Meyer and Allen (1997) were aware that the matrix they presented created a complex multidimensional model of commitment that became virtually impossible to test or use in its entirety. They did not advocate such use for their model but presented it to underline the complex multidimensional nature of commitment within the workplace. They also sought to raise researchers' awareness that in trying to understand how employees' commitment develops and relates to behavior, they must frame their research questions more precisely than in the past. In particular, the relevant commitment should be examined in relation to the relevant work outcome. For example, behavior of direct benefit (or detriment) to a work team might be related more strongly to employees' commitment to the team or team leader than to the organization as a whole.

No attempt has been made at an empirical test of Meyer and Allen's (1991) entire model although a conceptual elaboration of this approach was advanced by Meyer and Herscovitch (2001). A few attempts were made to test parts of it. Meyer, Allen, and Smith (1993) extended the three-dimensional model of organizational commitment to occupational commitment. Conceptually, they argued that although all three forms of commitment might be related to an individual's likelihood of remaining in an occupation, the nature of the person's involvement in it might be quite different depending on which form of commitment was predominant. They explained that a person affectively committed to the occupation might be more likely than someone not attached to keep up with developments in the occupation, to join and be active in relevant associations, and so on. The same might be true of individuals with a strong normative commitment to the occupation. In contrast, individuals possessing a strong continuance commitment might be less inclined than those who remain for other reasons to involve themselves in occupational activities besides those required for continuing membership.

The idea behind the occupational commitment scales was to apply the three-dimensional scales of organizational commitment to occupational commitment by simply changing the word "organization" to the name of the relevant occupation. A very thorough analysis, and methodological procedures based on several samples, at first yielded six items for each dimension of occupational and organizational commitment. Meyer and Allen's (1991) original scales contained eight items, and two were omitted from each scale because of redundancy problems. The intercorrelations among the six dimensions (i.e., three for organizational commitment and three for occupational commitment) revealed some multicollinearity problems. Two correlations were above .70 (normative with affective commitment to the organization and continuance commitment to the organization with continuance commitment to the occupation) and one was above .60 (normative commitment to the occupation with normative commitment to the organization). Results of confirmatory factor analysis supported the distinctions among the six dimensions. The pattern of the correlations between the scales and their dimensions and a variety of work-related correlates indicated some differences in the pattern of the correlations that supported the discriminant validity of the scales. But a thorough examination of the correlations did not reveal strong differences, that is, they revealed some similarities in the pattern and magnitude of the correlations.

Meyer et al. (1993) concluded that the procedures used to develop occupational commitment measures could be easily applied to develop multifaceted measures of commitment to other entities. However, the findings of their attempt to extend their organizational commitment scales to occupational commitment were inconclusive. In addition to some multicollinearity problems, one could ask what would happen to the items if the scale were extended to other entities. That is, if two items were omitted from each of the six 8-item scales because of overlap problems. This means that the original conceptualization and operationalization of Meyer and Allen (1991) was not entirely applicable to multiple commitment research. This happened in the case of two foci, the organization and the occupation. One may wonder what would happen if this conceptualization were applied to other entities. How many more items, and which, would be omitted if these measurements were applied, say, to union commitment?

Note too, that with the omission of two items from each of the six dimensions the scales contained 36 items; with another entity they would amount to 54 items, and with yet another, to 72. This might result in too long a questionnaire to measure commitment to four foci. In addition, Meyer and Allen's (1991) conceptualization of organizational commitment still struggled with measurement problems, particularly regarding the continuance commitment dimension. In short, Meyer et al.'s attempt to apply their organizational commitment typology to occupational commitment demonstrated only some of the complexities and problems associated with applying their approach to multiple commitments.

Two other attempts to apply Meyer and Allen's conceptualization were studies that were crosscultural in nature. Clugston, Howell, and Dorfman (2000) applied the three components of commitment (affective, continuance, and normative) to three foci of commitment: the organization, the supervisor, and the workgroup. Altogether, nine commitment forms were examined in their study. The findings showed that the 9-factor model was superior to alternative 3-factor models. However the somewhat low fit indices of the 9-factor model caused them to modify this model by dropping certain items which cross-loaded among commitment latent variables and demonstrated significant correlated error with other latent constructs. The differential relations between the 9-factor model and four dimensions of culture led them to conclude that Meyer and Allen's commitment scales were adaptable to cover multiple foci.

Vandenberghe et al. (2001) examined ten commitment forms using Allen and Meyer's scales in a sample of employees working for the translation department of the European Commission. They examined affective and normative commitment to the organization, occupation, work group and Europe and continuance commitment to the organization and the occupation. Using six items for each focus, their findings showed that both continuance and normative commitment to the organization and the occupation were undistinguishable empirically. They decided to form one scale for continuance commitment to the organization and occupation and one scale for normative commitment to the organization and occupation. This finding and the solution adopted demonstrates some of the potential problems associated with applying the Meyer and Allen's typology. But it should also be noted that the final solution of 8 commitment foci, that was tested among 12 nationalities and controlled for cultural differences, showed that the multiple commitments model was valid and reliable across cultures and that the measurement properties were culturally robust.

Hunt and Morgan's (1994) Global
Organizational Commitment Model

Hunt and Morgan (1994) used Becker's research and model as the starting point for their work. Basically, they questioned the conceptual framework presented by Becker, and in an interesting re-analysis of Becker's data they presented two alternative conceptual models. In particular they questioned the conceptual role of what Becker (1992) termed *global organizational commitment* in his framework. Was global organizational commitment another construct equal in importance to the other constituencies proposed by Becker, such as top management, work team, and clients? Becker's (1992) conceptualization seems to follow this model. In this case all commitment constituencies, global commitment together with the others, should be related equally to work outcomes.

Hunt and Morgan (1994) however, advanced an alternative model where global organizational commitment was a key mediating variable among the different commitment foci. They argued that various constituencies to which an employee might be committed constituted organizations, including top management, supervisors, work groups, occupations, departments, divisions, and unions; studies generally showed significant, positive relations between commitment to these constituencies and global organizational commitment. The meta-analyses findings presented in earlier chapters of this volume, on the relation between organizational commitment and other commitment foci such as job, occupation, work values, and the union, strongly support this contention.

Hunt and Morgan (1994) concluded that these findings were precisely what the congruence model of organizations would suggest. In this theory the components of organizations would be consistent or congruent and substantial consistency would exist between most organizations' overall values and those of their components. Therefore, given the prominent role shared values played in both the development of corporate culture and the development of all forms of commitment, consistency specific commitments should contribute to global organizational commitment. Hunt and Morgan significantly noted that although commitment to such entities as an individual's church might conflict with global organizational commitment, they did not address such commitments because they were external to the individual's work organization. In summary, Hunt and Morgan's (1994) model argued that global organizational commitment directly influenced organizational outcomes, and that constituency specific commitments affected important outcomes only because they influenced global organizational commitment. That is, global organizational commitment was a key mediating concept in the

relation between constituency specific commitments and work outcomes. Their model is presented in Fig. 4.7.

Hunt and Morgan's (1994) finding strongly supported the mediating
model, suggesting that the mediating role of global organizational commitment becomes stronger as the focus of a constituency specific commitment
becomes more closely associated with an organization. For example, the
path from commitment to supervisor to global organizational commitment
was .131, and from commitment to top management to global organizational commitment it was .364, whereas from commitment to work group to
global organizational commitment it was low and not significant. Hunt and
Morgan contended that this finding had important implications for multiple
commitment research because it emphasized the value of analyzing other
constituency specific commitments, such as commitment to department,
functional area, or division to determine if the relation consistently

Based on their findings, these authors advanced the idea of what they
termed a *hybrid conceptualization* of organizational commitment. This is a
modification of the two conceptualizations presented and tested in their research: global organizational commitment as a mediating variable or as one of
many other correlates of outcomes. On the grounds of role theory's principles
of line of authority and conceptual distance, they suggested a hybrid model
that offered two guiding tenets. The first concerned the relations between the

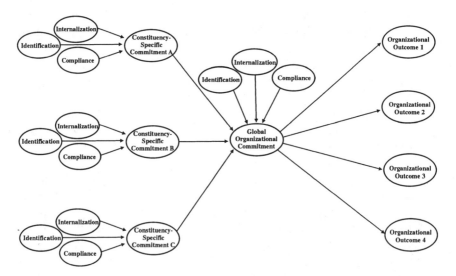

FIG. 4.7.   Hunt and Morgan's (1994) model of multiple commitments. From Hunt, S. D, &
Morgan, R. M. (1994). Commitment: One of many commitments or key mediating construct?
Academy of Management Journal, 37(6), 1568–1587. Reproduced with permission of the Acad-
emy of Management. Permission conveyed through Copyright Clearance Center, Inc.

constituency specific commitments and global organizational commitment. As the conceptual distance between a constituency and what a given employee views as the organization expands, the contribution of that constituency to global organizational commitment decreases. Hence, for many employees their work groups are not closely associated with their own views of what their organization is, which explains the researchers' findings that work group commitment had no significant effect on commitment to an organization as a whole. Similarly, Hunt and Morgan (1994) proposed that employees' commitments to clients, unions, and other constituencies conceptually distant from the employing organizations themselves would probably make little contribution to employees' global commitment in most cases.

The second tenet concerned the links between constituency specific commitments and specific outcomes. Accordingly, direct links between commitment foci and outcomes are expected when outcomes are closely associated with benefitting or harming a particular constituency. For example, an outcome such as service friendliness in a retailing or public service agency setting would be more closely associated with commitment to clients than commitment to work group. Therefore, future studies should not only investigate the relation between various constituency specific commitments and global organizational commitment, but should also examine some of those commitments' direct effects on some outcomes, where such effects are grounded in theory.

Hunt and Morgan (1994) concluded that because the hybrid model may be superior to the two models presented in their research, a finer grained theory, going beyond the two tenets they presented, was needed. A more detailed theory would further guide the development of a hybrid conceptualization that explicates the roles of other foci of commitment, would be closely tied to specific commitment outcomes and would address the possible mediating and moderating effects of other organizational variables.

One attempt to apply Hunt and Morgan's (1994) approach was made by Boshoff and Mels (2000). They compared a similar mediating model proposed by Hunt and Morgan to a direct model. Their findings suggested that neither model surpassed the other in explaining intentions to resign. However the authors argued that their findings could not be compared with those of Hunt and Morgan because the latter considered only commitments that were part of the organization. Boshoff and Mels examined professional commitment, job involvement, and supervisor commitment as the exogenous variables. The inclusion of the above first two commitments was not in accord with Hunt and Morgan's theory, which is why Boshoff and Mels's study did not fully examine Hunt and Morgan's theory.

In short, Hunt and Morgan (1994) seem to have simplified and clarified Becker's (1992) and also Reichers's (1985) notion of multiple commitments. Their main conceptual argument, one that is very important in the context of this 1volume, was that Becker's and Reichers's approaches did not extend to multiple commitment. The boundary of their approaches was organizational commitment. The other constituencies they referred to, such as top management or unit manager, were simply components of organizational commitment. Some of these components were related to organizational commitment more strongly than other components. They could contribute to the understanding of organizational commitment by informing researchers which of these components of the organization meant more to employees, and by their being affected, levels of organizational commitment could be changed. These components were interrelated and some of them could be related to other possible commitments in the workplace such as occupational commitment.

However, what Becker (1992) termed *global organizational commitment* was organizational commitment. The other constituencies, such as top management and unit managers, were not multiple commitments but components of organizational commitment. The distance idea advanced by Hunt and Morgan (1994) provided additional support for this contention. A constituency that is distant from the organization in the employees' view represents separate commitment foci and not a component of organizational commitment such as the top or middle management. The findings regarding the absence of a relation between group commitment and global organizational commitment supports the contention that group commitment is a form of commitment and is not a component of organizational commitment. One of Reichers's (1986) findings that is pertinent here was that out of the four relevant constituencies examined in the study, namely, top management, funding agencies, professionalism, and clients, only commitment to top management's goals and values was associated with global organizational commitment. This finding strongly supports Hunt and Morgan's contention and findings. Their model and findings put multiple commitment research into proper perspective again, and can prevent further misconceptions of what multiple commitments is.

CONCLUSIONS AND SUGGESTIONS
FOR FUTURE RESEARCH

This chapter described some of the important studies on multiple commitments. Directly or indirectly these dealt with one of the important issues of multiple commitment, namely, the components and boundaries of this concept and the conceptual or methodological justifications for embracing various commitment forms within them. A summary of the approaches and their main characteristics is presented in Table 4.1.

TABLE 4.1
Summary of Typologies of Commitment Forms

Typology	Orientation	Commitment Foci That are Included	Goals of Typology	Main Characteristics	Main Advantages	Main Limitations
Morrow's (1983, 1993) model	Methodological	Affective organizational commitment, continuance organizational commitment, work ethic, career commitment, and job involvement	Developments of a commitment index analogous to the Job Descriptive Index (Smith, Kendall, Hulin, 1969) reflecting different foci	Morrow did not elaborate on how exactly to develop a multiple commitment scale that would parallel the Job Descriptive Index	Such an index would allow for the formation of commitment profiles, allowing managers and others to pinpoint what forms of work commitment are less than optimal	An attempt to develop a multiple commitment scale similar to the Job Descriptive Index might result in scales that are too simplistic and trivial, disregarding the conceptual framework and essence of each commitment
Cohen' (1993) matrix approach	Methodological	Organizational commitment, occupation commitment, job commitment, and union commitment	Developing an effective way of measuring multiple forms of commitment	The 9 items are organized in matrix form. The vertical portion includes nine items that are phrased in general form, are the horizontal axis listed the types of work commitment (occupation, organization, etc). The respondents answer the same questions for each of the types of commitment	It obliged the respondents to evaluate their commitment attitudes simultaneously, as they did in the workplace. It avoids long questionnaires. It avoids overlapping with items relating to more than one facet of commitment	Results of factor analyses and the high correlations between some of the measures showed concept redundancy, especially between the occupation and job foci

continued on next page

TABLE 4.1 (continued)

Typology	Orientation	Commitment Foci That are Included	Goals of Typology	Main Characteristics	Main Advantages	Main Limitations
Blau and his associates (1993)	Methodological	Four career facet scales (Gould, 1979; Greenhaus, 1971, 1973; Sekaran, 1982, 1986; and Blau, 1985, 1988), two work value scales (Kanungo, 1982; Blood's 1969), one organizational commitment scale (Meyer & Allen, 1984), and one job facet scale (Kanungo, 1982)	To develop a multiple commitment scale following Morrow's (1983) two-step process. First, redundancy of measures within each work commitment facet should be minimized; second, redundancy between work commitment facet measures should be reduced	The study resulted in a 31 multiple commitment items that represent specific constructs of occupational commitment: job involvement, value of work, and organizational commitment. All were shown to be distinct work commitment facets	The methodology and steps used by Blau et al.'s (1993) study are recommended. For example, the procedure of first performing an exploratory factor analysis and then a confirmatory one, and using different samples for each step	There was no consistency in the number of scales used for each commitment form. Why were some commitment scales over-represented and others under-represented? As a result the final scale includes more items for one commitment focus than for the other
Reichers's (1985) organizational focus approach	Conceptual	Foci of organizational commitment such as top managers, co-workers, clients and customers, and also the union and the community are all relevant in the proposed conceptual framework	To present an organizationally oriented approach to multiple commitment. Reichers, like Morrow (1983), regarded the Job Descriptive Index of Smith et al. (1969) as the goal that multiple commitments should seek to emulate constructs	The central thesis is that organizational commitment can be accurately understood as a collection of multiple commitments to various groups that comprise the organization. To specify the foci of multiple commitments, one must specify the various groups that are relevant to all	Reichers set out guidelines of a conceptual framework for which commitments relevant in the workplace should be studied. These were commitments relevant to the organizational setting. The idea that the organization is not a single whole entity is also interesting	This approach neglected several commitment forms, some of them fundamental to the understanding of multiple commitments such as occupational commitment, job involvement, and work values

continued on next page

Becker's (1992) model of foci and bases of commitment	Conceptual and methodological	The model adopts the same foci of commitment suggested by Reichers. Accordingly relevant commitment foci are global organizational commitment and specific foci such as co-workers, superiors, subordinates, customers, and other groups and individuals who collectively constitute the organization	To advance a multiple commitment approach that could aid in organizational diagnosis and intervention procedures and pinpoint the strength, presence, or absence of particular commitments	Becker's model is an elaboration of Reichers' model. Becker argued that the multidimensionality of commitment characterized not only the foci but also the process and motives of commitment, namely, the bases of commitment	First, it showed that a multidimensional perspective on commitment could increase the prediction of important attitudes and behaviors in the workplace. Second, it operationalizes and test conceptual frameworks on multiple commitments, thereby guiding researchers toward improvements in both conceptualizations and empirical examinations	First, it did not include important commitment forms such as job involvement and occupational commitment. Second, it endured severe problems of concept redundancy. Third, the measures were different from one study to the next and lead to generalizability problems. Fourth, the distinction among the bases of commitment is problematic
Meyer and Allen's (1997) dual-multi-dimensional conceptual-ization	Conceptual and methodological	The model adopts the same foci of commitment suggested by Reichers. In addition it argues that the model can be elaborated and applied to other commitment forms such as the occupation, the union and so forth	To raise researchers' awareness that in trying to understand how employees' commitment develops and relates to behavior, they must frame their research questions more precisely than in the past. In particular, the relevant commitment should be examined in relation to the relevant work outcome	The approach is an expansion of their organizational commitment model to include multiple components of commitment. They proposed their own two-dimensional matrix, with the different forms of commitment listed along one axis and the different foci along the other	The model underlines the complex multidimensional nature of commitment within the workplace. As such each employee's commitment profile reflects varying degrees of different forms of commitment to each of the different constituencies	The model does not explain why the three dimensions of affective, continuance, and normative commitment is superior to those used by Becker. The matrix they presented created a complex multidimensional model that is virtually impossible to test or use in its entirety

111

TABLE 4.1 (continued)

Typology	Orientation	Commitment Foci That are Included	Goals of Typology	Main Characteristics	Main Advantages	Main Limitations
Hunt and Morgan's (1994) global organizational commitment model	Conceptual and methodological	The model adopts the same foci of commitment suggested by Becker. Accordingly relevant commitment foci are the global organizational commitment and its specific foci such as co-workers, superiors, subordinates, customers, and other groups who constitute the organization	Hunt and Morgan questioned the conceptual framework presented by Becker, and in particular what Becker termed global organizational commitment, and in an interesting re-analysis of Becker's data they presented an alternative conceptual model	Global organizational commitment is a key-mediating concept in the relationship between constituency specific commitments and work outcomes. That is, constituency specific commitments such as co-workers, superiors, subordinates, and customers, affect important outcomes only because they influence global organizational commitment	The model simplifies and clarifies Becker and Reichers's notion of multiple commitments. The basic argument is that the approaches of Becker and Reichers were not of multiple commitments. The boundary of these approaches was organizational commitment. The other constituencies they referred to, such as top management or unit manager, were simply components of organizational commitment	The model is based on secondary data analysis, Becker's data. It could be that the theory development was affected by the data at hand. There is a need to re-examine the theory based on new and original data

Morrow (1993) suggested that some forms of commitment can be defined as universal, relevant to all employees, and should always be tested in multiple commitment research (e.g., continuance organizational commitment, affective organizational commitment, job involvement, work ethic, and occupational commitment). One main problem in Morrow's suggestion is that the continuance organizational commitment does not fit within the multiple commitment framework, as research evidence showed. However, the above problem can be solved quite easily. Another form, such as group commitment or union commitment, can replace that of the continuance organizational commitment, or alternatively, what Morrow (1993) termed *universal forms of commitment* can include only four forms.

In Cohen's (1993) approach, the result of the factor analyses and the high correlations between some of the measures showed concept redundancy, especially between the occupation and job foci. The same problem was found in previous factor analyses of commitment scales (Morrow & McElroy, 1986; Morrow & Wirth, 1989), and also with the use of content analysis as the methodology for assessing discriminant validity (Morrow et al. 1991). Some of the redundancy in the latter study can be attributed to the matrix form of the measures, which might have caused some priming and consistency artifacts. Therefore, Cohen (1993a) suggested that some revisions in the measures should be considered in future research. In such a revision, problematic items would, in particular, be those composing the moral involvement dimension, which emerged as the main reason for redundancy in Cohen's (1997b) second study. The general formulation of the items would merit more attention too. From the factor analysis results in the first study, respondents apparently had problems in applying some items (e.g., items 1 and 4) to the job commitment foci.

Yet, for all the problems of Cohen's (1993a, 1997b) studies, we may note the good predictive validity of the commitment forms in the first study and the differential relations of commitment forms to nonwork determinants in the second. Indeed, one of the main reasons for the study of multiple commitments is the view that it can predict outcomes better than each commitment form separately. In summary, Cohen's (1993a) findings provide sufficiently good predictive validity and discriminant validity to consider this approach in future research.

As for Blau et al.'s (1993) approach, I believe that it should be perceived as an interesting methodological attempt, albeit not highly successful at this stage. A major limitation is that their approach has no conceptual or theoretical foundation. The original intention of this approach was methodological, but the absence of a conceptual framework was perhaps one of the reasons for some of the problems outlined above. A firm theoretical approach would probably have prevented the development of a scale for one commitment form based on items taken from different scales of that commitment form, each with a different conceptual basis.

The main contribution of Reichers's (1985) approach seems to be the idea that organizational commitment can be better understood by the development of a multidimensional view of it. Her conceptualization should be perceived as similar to Meyer and Allen's (1991). Whereas those authors presented a multidimensional view of the motives of commitment (affective, continuance and normative), Reichers presented a multidimensional view of the foci of organizational commitment. But Reichers's conceptualization is not enough for a grasp of the concept of commitment in the work place.

Becker's (1992) approach was an interesting attempt to conceptualize and measure multiple commitments. Its major limitations, as evident in the findings of the research that tested it, were at least three. First, it did not include important commitment forms such as job involvement and occupational commitment. Second, it suffered severe problems of concept redundancy. This problem was also mentioned by Hunt and Morgan (1994), who reanalyzed Becker's (1992) data and commented that some of the correlations Becker reported indicated multicollinearity. All the problematic correlations, according to Hunt and Morgan, involved an internalization or identification scale and its corresponding target of commitment. Third, the measures used by Becker and his associates were different from one study to the next. In all the studies based on Becker's approach the measures were changed to a greater or lesser degree, depending on the sample and the data. This raises an immediate question: How much generalizability can we expect from findings based on different measures? Researchers must choose whether we should aim to develop a measure that can be generalized across samples or ad hoc measures of commitment.

Meyer and Allen's (1997) approach seems to an interesting yet impractical way of measuring multiple commitments. For example, a survey applying the model advanced by Meyer and Allen (see Fig. 4.6) would include 8×18 items (eight items per dimension of commitment multiplied by the number of cells in the mode), namely 144 items. Very few researchers will use 144 items to measure six commitment foci. In addition, from Becker's experience regarding of the existence of multicollinearity and concept redundancy among the commitment measures (Becker, 1992; Becker et al., 1996), there is a good reason to believe that these problems will appear even more forcefully in any attempt empirically to test Meyer and Allen's suggested model. Finally, Hunt and Morgan's (1994) approach seems to have simplified and clarified Becker's (1992) and also Reichers's (1985) notion of multiple commitment. Their approach provides the conceptual basis for the model advanced later in this volume.

The main impression from the approaches presented here is that there is much confusion on this issue. One source of it is the foci of commitments. In selecting the commitment forms for examination in a particular study one should keep in mind the argument of Randall, Fedor, and Longenecker (1990) and of Reilly and Orsak (1991) that careful choice of an appropriate commitment is often neglected, creating a mismatch between research question and assessment instrument. Therefore, Reilly and Orsak (1991) suggested that different forms of commitment might best characterize different occupations.

Another problem with the definitions of the boundary of multiple commitments is the multidimensionality of each focus of commitment and the ambiguity that can result from presenting components of one form as separate and independent forms of commitment. As can be seen from the foregoing, some approaches are unidimensional (Cohen, 1993a; Blau, 1993) and some are multidimensional (Becker, 1992; Meyer & Allen, 1997; Hunt & Morgan, 1994). The idea advanced by Becker (1992) on the bases of commitment added much greater complexity into the notion of multiple commitments. It is my contention that this complexity is unnecessary. First, there is not enough empirical justification to support the multidimensionality of the bases of commitment advanced by Becker, namely internalization, identification, and compliance. As mentioned previously, the data to date have pointed to many problems with this conceptualization. An examination of the alternative dimensionality advanced by Meyer and Allen (1997), namely, affective, continuance, and normative bases does not alter the above conclusion. The continuance dimension is problematic, and too little empirical and conceptual evidence exists on normative commitment to consider it a valid and distinct dimension of organizational commitment. In fact, the conceptual differences between affective and normative commitment are not clear enough. Jaros (1997) and Ko et al. (1997) pointed to a high degree of conceptual overlap of affective and normative commitment.

Briefly, the evidence we have so far does not support the notion of adding another dimension to the complex concept of multiple commitments. Moreover, Morrow (1983, 1993) and Blau (1993, 1997) correctly argued that what we should look for is a parsimonious way to measure and test multiple commitments. A two-dimensional conceptualization and operationalization of multiple commitments would make the examination of multiple commitments too complex for measurement, analysis, and interpretation of findings. Indeed, such an approach would make multiple commitment research almost impossible.

The belief expressed here is that the approach advanced in earlier chapters is the correct one. It followed what Morrow (1983) termed a *two-step* process. First, redundancy of measures within each work commitment facet should be minimized; second, redundancy between work commitment facet measures should be reduced. That is, researchers should apply valid and established scales to each commitment form. Each scale should be based on a strong affective orientation. The scales should not be too complex or too long. This is what we should aim for. The most reliable and valid findings on commitment were found when commitment was defined as a uni-dimensional attitude. Meyer and Allen's scale of affective organizational commitment, Kanungo's job involvement and work involvement scales, and Gordon's loyalty dimension of union commitment scale should form the basis for an appropriate measurement of multiple commitments. When valid and reliable unidimensional scales are developed for occupational commitment, work values, and group commitment there will be a pool of scales for measuring different combinations of multiple commitments.

Suggested Model for Multiple Commitments

On the basis of the limitations and advantages of the approaches reviewed here, this volume introduces a model that attempts to overcome the limitations and better represent the notion of multiple commitments. The proposed model is presented in Fig. 4.8. According to this approach the basic commitment foci should still be the organization, job, occupation, work values, union, or work group. In the model, these are termed *global organizational commitment* or *global occupational commitment,* but basically they represent organizational commitment or occupational commitment per se. As can be seen from the model in Fig. 4.8, each of the commitment foci, termed *global commitments,* has its own constituency specific commitments. These constituencies are related to their specific commitment focus such that they can affect levels of that commitment. For example, in the case of organizational commitment, possible constituencies include aspects or dimensions of the organization such as management, clients, and supervision. These dimensions are related to the global organizational commitment and can affect its magnitude.

The suggested approach argues that each commitment is unidimensional and represents a global attitude to the relevant object of commitment. This approach follows the evidence set forth above that there is not enough empirical support for the multidimensionality of any given commitment form, particularly organizational commitment. It also follows McCaul, Hinsz, and McCaul (1995), who used Fishbein and Ajzen's (1975) theory of reasoned action to propose that attitudes are distinct from beliefs and intentions, and should be assessed differently. According to Fishbein and Ajzen's (1975) theory, beliefs about some object (e.g., an organization) influence attitudes about this object and these attitudes can influence intentions to behave in some manner relevant to that object. From this theory, McCaul et al. (1974) proposed that organizational commitment may be defined as a global atti-

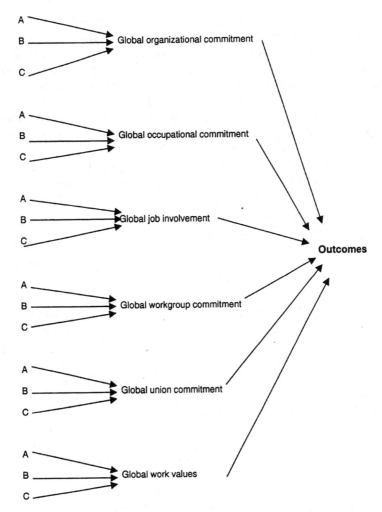

FIG. 4.8. A global model of multiple commitments.

tude that employees have toward the organization: an affective and evaluative reaction to it. In their research they contrasted an attitudinal measure to Porter et al.'s scale of organizational commitment. They also included measures of value acceptance, intentions to stay with the organization, and willingness to exert effort on behalf of the organization. Their data supported their basic argument. The brief semantic-differential attitude measure used in their study correlated highly with Porter et al.'s scale of organizational commitment in both time intervals.

McCaul et al. (1995) argued that viewing organizational commitment as an employee's global attitude to the organization can eliminate the conceptual confusion that stems from including beliefs and intentions in a multi component measure. Accordingly, different types of commitment measures measure different attitudes. For example, the continuance organizational commitment dimension of Meyer and Allen (1984) measures the attitude to staying with the organization but not organizational commitment. The social psychological approach to the attitude-behavior relation recommends differentiating an employee's global attitude to the organization from his or her intentions to behave in particular ways regarding the organization.

According to McCaul et al. (1995), considering organizational commitment a global attitude rather than a fractionated construct has additional implications for the consequences that should be predicted by organizational commitment. Accordingly, if one wants to predict staying with the organization, one should assess the attitude relevant to that behavior, that is, attitude to staying with the organization. Furthermore, if one wants to predict a variety of global behaviors (e.g., behaving positively with regard to the organization), the global attitude to the organization should be measured.

McCaul et al. (1995) concluded, and this conclusion is adopted here, that such an attitudinal approach could be applied to other forms of commitment. Beliefs about the value of belonging to a particular union or profession may lead to affective responses, attitudes that in turn may predict intentions to stay in the union or profession. That is, each commitment form should strive to represent a unidimensional attitude that measures only attitude to the relevant object of commitment.

Study of the relations between global commitment and its specific constituencies is not an examination of multiple commitments. It is more an internal analysis of each commitment. In the case of organizational commitment, the relations between organizational commitment and its constituencies are just a more specific analysis of organizational commitment. In fact, the proposed constituencies of each commitment form can be perceived as another category of determinants of this commitment. In the case of organizational commitment the literature advanced personal characteristics, role-related characteristics, structural characteristics, and work experiences as the main determinants of that commitment. Specific commitment constituencies to organizational commitment such as commitment to top management, unit, or unit management can become another category of organizational commitment determinants. Reichers (1985) and particularly Hunt and Morgan (1984) provide a good conceptual justification for considering these specific commitments as determinants of organizational commitment.

The same analysis can be performed on occupational commitment or union commitment. In the case of the former, one can look for specific commitment constituencies that are relevant to occupational commitment. Professional or occupational associations provide a good example of such a constituency. Different dimensions of professionals' behaviors and attitudes as represented by the existing scales of professionalism are another example for constituencies of professional commitment. Career or career salience can provide another relevant constituency. All these probably are related to occupational commitment but should be considered a determinant of occupational commitment.

In the case of union commitment, we can look for specific constituencies such as other structural levels of the union than the one investigated. If one examines commitment to the local unit, commitment to other levels such as main office, occupational union, or unionization in general might become relevant constituencies in the sense that they are related to and affect the commitment to the local union. As for job commitment or job involvement, different aspects of the job can provide the basis for developing constituencies for this focus. For example, the job characteristic model of Hackman and Oldham (1975) includes the following dimensions: skill variety, task identity, task significance, autonomy, and feedback can provide one basis for constituencies; the Job Diagnostic Survey of Smith, Kendall, and Hullin (1969) that contains five separately subscales, namely, type of work, pay, promotion opportunities, supervision, and co-workers can provide another perspective for constituencies.

The proposed model opens the door to much conceptual, methodological, and empirical work on commitment. The conceptual work should concentrate on detecting specific constituencies for each commitment focus, defining them, and proposing a conceptual framework for their relations to their relevant global commitment. One should consider the possibility that some constituencies might be related to more than one global commitment. For example, commitment to top management is probably related to global organizational commitment, but it also might be related to group commitment or union commitment.

Although some work on global organizational commitment-specific constituencies was done by Reichers (1985, 1986), Becker (1992), Becker and his associates (1995, 1996), and McElroy, Morrow, and Laczniak (2001), much more work is needed for the other global commitments, such as the occupation, the job, or the union. Methodological work is needed on measuring the specific commitment constituencies. Becker (1992) measured organizational commitment constituencies by one item. It is suggested that multi-item scales be developed and tested for commitment to specific constituencies. Empirical work is needed to examine the validity of the measures that to developed and the nature of the relation between specific global commitment and commitment to its constituencies.

Finally, as can be seen in Fig. 4.8, the relationship of each commitment-specific constituency and global commitment to possible outcomes should be explored. Hunt and Morgan's (1994) model should provide an interesting conceptual framework for such examinations. The idea is that the global commitment of each focus mediates the relation between its constituencies and work outcomes. Hunt and Morgan's findings provided empirical support for this model in the case of organizational commitment. Other constituencies and other outcomes should be tested for organizational commitment. Similar models should be proposed and tested for other commitment foci, for example, the relation between occupational commitment constituencies and work outcomes mediated by occupational commitment. Considering the somewhat disappointing findings regarding the relation between specific commitment forms and outcomes, a stronger relation may be found if commitment foci are examined as mediators in the relation between their commitment constituencies and outcomes. All these provide a rich and stimulating research agenda on multiple commitment.

5

The Interrelationship
Among Commitment Forms

The previous chapter dealt with typologies of multiple commitments that attempted to capture the meaning and essence of the concept. Assuming that the ambiguity surrounded this concept is partially resolved, an equally important aspect is the interrelations among forms of commitment. Morrow (1993) argued that whether each commitment is independent or some are antecedents and consequences of others is a major unanswered question impeding understanding of work commitment. The interrelations among these forms is important because they can affect the way these commitments relate to work outcomes (Mueller et al., 1992). The reason is that one needs to know more about the ordering of the commitment foci before proposing models dealing with the ordering of their effect on work outcomes. Morrow, for example (1993), stated that the nature of interrelations among forms of work commitment needs to be illuminated as soon as possible because evidence that one form of work commitment can moderate relations involving other forms is beginning to accumulate (Hunt & Morgan, 1994; Witt, 1993). The goal, Morrow (1993) suggested, should be a work commitment scale that would make possible formulation of commitment profiles, testing their relations with organizational outcomes (Becker & Billings, 1993), thus allowing managers to pinpoint what forms of work commitment are less than optimal (Morrow, 1993).

Nevertheless, few studies have investigated the differences among forms of work commitment or tried to explore the relations among them. Few conceptual and empirical attempts have been made to advance and test models of the interrelations among commitment forms. As mentioned previously, a reason for this is that most studies of work commitment have been methodological and not conceptual so little progress has been made in understanding the conceptual relations among different commitment forms. From the scant research on this issue, two main models seem to exist. The first is Morrow's (1993), the second is Randall and Cote's (1991). These models are presented in this chapter together with the empirical findings regarding their validity.

Morrow's Model

Morrow (1993) proposed two ways to advance work commitment research. First, as mentioned in the chapter, she suggested that among all foci of work commitment, five are basic in the sense that they are relevant to the maximal number of employees; she termed these universal forms of work commitment. These forms are affective commitment to the organization, continuance commitment to the organization, work ethic endorsement, career commitment, and job involvement. Second, Morrow (1993) proposed a conceptual model regarding how these forms are related to each other. Morrow suggested that one way to think about the interrelations among the five commitment forms is to locate each within a series of five concentric circles, with work ethic innermost followed successively by career commitment, continuance organizational commitment, affective organizational commitment, and job involvement in the outermost circle. The concentric circle model facilitates thinking about the composition of a given employee's work commitments. Morrow argued that no assumptions can be made regarding the size of each circle or the size of the entire model. A high level of one form of work commitment does not imply that less commitment must exist elsewhere: One does not have a fixed amount of loyalty to distribute among objects.

According to Morrow, commitment forms are positioned in this manner to reflect the idea that inner circles are more dispositional, cultural, and cohort-based in nature and therefore, relatively stable over time. The outer circles are thought to be more situationally determined, and therefore more subject to change and influence. Morrow argued that inner circles impact outer "Work ethic endorsement, as an illustration, would be expected to exhibit a stronger relationship with career commitment than affective organizational commitment, controlling for other factors" (Morrow, 1993, p. 163). Although Morrow mentioned specifically that a given commitment focus will most affect the next circle outside it, the quotation just mentioned allows the possibility that it will also affect the circle two stages away, but not as strongly as it affects the adjacent one. Morrow's model is shown in Fig. 5.1. In it, job involvement is the endogenous variable and the two forms of organizational

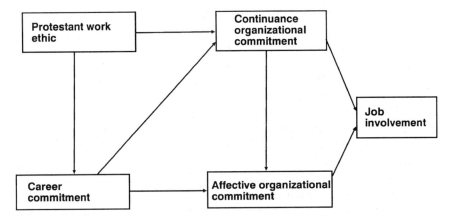

FIG. 5.1.   Morrow's model of the interrelationships among commitment forms. From Cohen, A. (1999). Relationships among five forms of commitment: An empirical examination. *Journal of Organizational Behavior, 20,* 285–308. Copyright © by John Wiley & Sons Limited. Reproduced with permission.

commitment are the variables that mediate the relations between the Protestant work ethic (PWE) and career commitment, these being the exogenous variables, and job involvement being the endogenous variable.

Morrow's (1993) model concentrates on the positioning of and conceptual differences between commitment forms in the inner and outer circles. It does not explain why or how each affects the other. This chapter elaborates on these issues from previous conceptual and empirical research. The logic of Morrow's model seems similar to other models proposed in other research (e.g. Blau et al., 1993; Gregerson, 1993; Yoon, Baker, & Ko, 1994; Mueller & Lawler, 1999; Johnson, 1999). According to Yoon et al. (1994), the mechanism that leads to stronger commitment to proximal targets is stronger interpersonal attachment among the members in such targets. They defined *personal attachment* as the degree of affective personal relations an individual has with other members in her or his immediate work unit, and based their arguments on Lawler's (1992) theory of attachment attributed mainly to nested subgroups. This theory or principle of proximal rules explains why Lawler, 1992, said "actors develop stronger affective ties to subgroups within a social system rather than to the social system, to local communities rather than to states, to work organization, and so forth" Lawler, 1992, (p. 334). Interpersonal attachment produces a stronger commitment to subgroups than to the larger group, because the credit for positive affect from interpersonal bonds is likely to be attributed to the proximal subgroups, whereas the blame for negative affects is likely to be attributed to the large group (Lawler, 1992). This logic can explain why one develops a stronger personal attachment to one's job than to one's career. One can develop a stronger attachment to the job, a proximal target in one's immediate work unit, than to one's career, which is a much more distant target.

Gregerson's (1993) and Mueller and Lawler's (1999) argument is based primarily on the idea that proximal variables exert the most significant influence on employees' actions because proximity provides more opportunities for exchange relations. Mueller and Lawler (1999) focused on the nested nature of organizational units. The general principle they proposed is that given the nesting of one unit within another, employees' commitment to a particular organizational unit in the structure are be affected primarily by the work conditions created and controlled by that particular unit. Commitment to the most proximate unit is influenced especially by work conditions, because day-to-day experiences in the local unit exert the strongest effects on positive emotions, and positive emotions produce commitment primarily to this more proximate unit.

According to Gregerson, individuals can come to identify strongly with and become significantly attached to proximal and potentially influential foci. For example, the logic of proximity suggests that when employees have frequent contact with customers and these interactions are perceived positively in general, they could develop a commitment to the customer. In contrast, the logic of proximity suggests lower levels of commitment to top management because top managers are a relatively distant commitment target with whom nonmanagement employees have infrequent contact. Gregerson's (1993) argument can easily be applied to the interrelations among the commitment forms and seems to provide another explanation for the way the commitment foci are positioned in Morrow's model. The most proximal to the employee, namely job involvement, is the endogenous variable, and the most distant, namely PWE, is the exogenous variable. Blau et al. (1993) proposed a slightly different approach and conceptualized the distinctions among the different forms of work commitment as being on a time line. Job involvement and organizational commitment would seem to have a more immediate focus, whereas occupational commitment is intermediate and value of work is the most long-term.

In brief, Morrow's model can be best understood as relying on proximity and time line. PWE is a dispositional variable characterized by a belief in the importance of hard work (Mirels & Garrett, 1971) and is assumed to be a relatively fixed attribute throughout an individual's life course (Morrow, 1983). As a general work value orientation learned early in the socialization processes (Shamir, 1986), PWE is the most stable commitment form because it is less affected by characteristics of the work setting. PWE is also the least proximal variable among the five commitment foci because it is not related specifically to any concrete characteristic in the workplace. Thus,

PWE very logically represents the exogenous variable in Morrow's model. According to Morrow, PWE should affect career commitment. The logic of time line and proximity support such a relation. Career commitment, defined as one's attitude toward one's profession or vocation (Blau, 1985), represents a more immediate and proximal construct than PWE. Whereas PWE reflects general values about work, career commitment represents a more specific, narrow focus, namely, one's own career or vocation.

How can PWE affect career commitment? Furnham (1990) applies Holland's (1973) theory according to which different types of people have different interests, competencies, and dispositions. They tend to surround themselves with people and situations congruent with their interests, capabilities, and outlook. People tend to search for environments that will let them exercise their skills, abilities, and personality. For example, Mirels and Garrett (1971) found that those with high PWE scores preferred conventional, realistic occupations and disliked those that were social or artistic. Accordingly, people with high PWE search for and work in careers that fit their personality and are more attached to them. The higher their level of PWE the more attached are to the vocation they choose. Similarly, a person with low PWE, in an occupation that values high PWE is expected to have low occupational commitment. Because occupational commitment is a function of a perceived fit between the individual and the occupation, low PWE simply does not fit into an occupational setting that values high PWE. The poor fit should manifest, therefore, in low attachment to the occupation.

The time line and proximity arguments lead one to expect a relation between career commitment and a more immediate, concrete, and proximal commitment focus, the organization. The literature provides conceptual as well as empirical support for a causal relation between the two variables. Witt (1993) argued that among some employees, a specialized occupation may lead to limited opportunities for employment elsewhere, so leaving the organization may be a less viable alternative for them than for others. A second explanation also proposed by Witt is based on Schneider's (1983) attraction-selection-attrition (ASA) framework, which states that people select themselves into and out of organizations. In other words, people seek the organization that fits them. In the ASA framework, individuals highly committed to their occupation may have carefully selected an organization as an appropriate workplace. Hence, they may be highly committed to the organization. Possibly less occupationally committed employees may have taken positions with organizations of convenience.

Another explanation for this relation was provided by Vandenberg and Scarpello (1994), who argued that organizational commitment depends in part on a perceived match or congruence between a person's own values and those espoused by the organization. Given that occupational values and expectations characterize a personal value system, the commitment of occupational members to the organization depends in part on their realizing their occupational values and expectations within that employment setting. Then too, occupationally committed individuals tend to seek employment (i.e., self-select) in settings that encourage them to behave according to the occupational value system. Thus, there is an even greater chance that an individuals' values fit those of the organization. Similarly, a person with low occupational commitment in an organization who values that occupation would be expected to have low organizational commitment. Individuals are cognizant of the resources most valued by the organization and how well their own attitudes, abilities, skills, and feelings fit. Because organizational commitment is a function of a perceived fit between the individual and the organization, a low psychological attachment to an occupation simply does not fit an employment setting that values the occupation. The poor fit should be manifested, therefore, in low attachment to the organization. Vandenberg and Scarpello (1994) reported a positive causal relation between occupational commitment and organizational commitment in a sample of MIS professionals.

None of the foregoing distinguishes continuance and affective commitment. Morrow's model includes two forms of organizational commitment proposed by Meyer and Allen (1984). Conceptually, their distinction between the two dimensions paralleled the distinction between the attitudinal approach of Porter and his colleagues (1974) and the side bet calculative approach of Becker (1960). The first dimension was termed *affective commitment* and was defined as "positive feelings of identification with, attachment to, and involvement in, the work organization (Meyer & Allen, 1984, p. 375). The second was termed *continuance commitment* defined as "the extent to which employees feel committed to their organizations by virtue of the costs that they feel are associated with leaving (e.g., investments or lack of attractive alternatives)" (Meyer & Allen, 1984, p. 375). McGee and Ford (1987) in their factor analysis found that the continuance commitment scale is a two-dimensional construct. One subdimension represents the personal sacrifices that would result from leaving the organization, and was termed *personal sacrifices*. The other, "low alternatives," represents the role of available employment alternatives in the decision to remain on one's organization. Research findings have supported the two-dimensional structure of the continuance commitment construct (Hackett, Bycio, & Hausdorf, 1994; Somers, 1993).

According to Morrow, career commitment should affect continuance commitment first. Based on the time line, there is conceptual support, for presenting continuance commitment before affective commitment. Continuance commitment develops as a result of lack of alternative employment opportunities and an accumulation of side bets, that is, investments that increase the costs associated with leaving the organization. These need time to accumulate before they can influence one's decision. On a time line, therefore, continuance commitment takes longer to develop and is less situationally determined than is affective commitment, that can develop immediately (Lee, Ashford, Walsh, & Mowday, 1992; Mowday et al., 1982). What needs further clarification is how career commitment will affects continuance commitment. Witt (1993) stated that among some employees, a specialized occupation may lead to limited alternative opportunities. Because continuance commitment develops partly as result of such "low alternatives," occupational commitment is related to continuance commitment more strongly than to affective commitment.

Although placing the continuance commitment in an inner cycle was clarified earlier, the causal relation between continuance and affective commitment was explained by McGee and Ford (1987) and Meyer, Allen, and Gellatly (1990). They stated that the accumulated investments that bind an individual to an organization can lead, through self-justification or dissonance reduction, to an affective attachment to the organization. That is, the binding properties of high personal investments are thought to be translated into a greater degree of affective attachment to the organization to blunt the disagreeable reality that one might be stuck with as a result of the high costs associated with exit. Partial support for this relation was provided by Meyer et al. (1990), who found that respondents who indicated that it would be costly to leave the organization reported feeling more affective attachment to it. Somers's (1993) findings of a positive relation between the sacrifice component of continuance commitment and affective commitment also supported this relation. Interestingly, Somers did not find a significant relation between affective commitment and the "low alternatives" component of continuance commitment. Somers's findings are important because unlike Meyer et al., who also found a causal relation between affective and continuance commitment, Somers found a significant relation only between continuance commitment and affective commitment.

The outer circle in Morrow's model is job involvement. Here the time line and the proximity rationale strongly support the placing of this construct as the endogenous variable. Kanungo (1982) viewed *job involvement* as a cognitive or belief state of psychological identification with one's job. This identification depends on the salience of one's needs (extrinsic and intrinsic) and the perceptions one has about the job's need-satisfying potentialities. Of all forms of commitment, the job is the closest, most immediate, tangible, and concrete focus. Job involvement was found to be affected by work situation variables (Morrow, 1993). Therefore, changes in the work setting have an immediate effect on job involvement. How does affective commitment affect job involvement? Witt's (1993) explanation of how occupational commitment affects organizational commitment is relevant here too. Witt relates three forms of commitment, namely, occupational, organizational, and job involvement, and explains the causal interrelations in the same order as in Morrow's model. First, a specialized occupation may lead to limited opportunities for employment elsewhere, so that leaving the organization may not be a viable alternative. Hence, employees with few alternative employment opportunities (high continuance commitment) develop affective attachment to the organization (high affective commitment) and positive attitudes to any job assignment they receive there (high job involvement). The ASA framework outlined earlier argues that because the occupationally committed employees may have selected their organization carefully, hence, may be more concerned with the long term, initial work assignments and the fairness of current work assignments may be less salient for them. That is, employees with high occupational commitment have high organizational commitment because they have selected an organization that fits their occupational needs. They become highly involved in their job to justify their prior occupational and organizational selection, either because their high affective organizational commitment compensates for an unfavorable job assignment or because they have no employment alternatives.

The Randall and Cote (1991) Model

Randall and Cote's (1991) approach is presented in Fig. 5.2, and is seen to differ from Morrow's (1993). It postulates that job involvement influences both organizational commitment and career salience directly and strongly. It affects organizational commitment because situational factors have been identified as potentially the most important set of antecedents of organizational commitment. Of these, job involvement in particular exerts a powerful influence on commitment to the organization. Job involvement was also found to predict career salience because it fosters job challenge, which in turn leads to career identification. Job involvement was strongly affected by the PWE, which has a key role in influencing an employee's affective responses in the workplace, and it was affected to a lesser extent by work group attachment. Randall and Cote's (1991) findings showed that their model did not fit the data well. They offered three possible reasons: first, there is random measurement error that cannot be accurately modeled. Second, the measures may be flawed, Third, and most important, the suboptimal fit of the model may show that relations are other than as specified or that important constructs were omitted from the model.

The main difference between the models of Randall and Cote and of Morrow is the role of job involvement, the endogenous variable according to Morrow and an important mediator according to Randall and Cote.

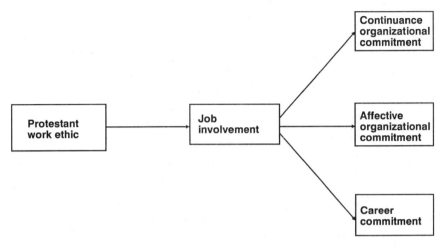

FIG. 5.2.   Randall and Cote's model of the interrelationships among commitment forms.
From Cohen, A. (1999). Relationships among five forms of commitment: An empirical ex-
amination. *Journal of Organizational behavior, 20*, 285–308. Copyright © John Wiley & Sons
Limited. Reproduced with permission.

Hence their approach is applied here and tested against Morrow's model.
The model based on their approach is presented in Fig. 5.1b. Although
Randall and Cote do not provide sufficient justification for what they
termed the *pivotal role of job involvement*, this chapter attempts to clarify and
justify their argument.

Clearly, Randall and Cote (1991) do not utilize the time line and the proximity arguments that influenced Morrow's model. Instead they apply a strong
situational approach. Accordingly, experiences in the work setting as represented at the level of job involvement, determine affective reactions to other
constituents in the workplace. As in Morrow's (1993) model, PWE is the exogenous variable. But in Randall and Cote's model, PWE affects job involvement instead of career commitment, as in Morrow's. Schnake (1991)
explained that people with a strong work ethic tend to have contempt for idle-
ness and self-indulgence. Such employees are likely to make sure that they put
in a fair day's effort and believe that work is its own reward. People with a
strong work ethic may be motivated to apply more effort, to continue to do so
even when bored or fatigued, and to accept responsibility for their work. They
may feel a moral obligation to perform the task to the best of their abilities.
Such people may also feel guilty when they believe they are not working as
hard as they should. Thus, they are more likely to be job involved than persons
with lower levels of PWE. Shamir (1986) argued that the PWE scale measures
the importance of work in a more abstract and remote way than the job involvement scale. Its items contain references to society and to moral judg-

ment. By contrast, some job involvement scale items refer to the respondent himself or herself and tend to focus on potential satisfactions to be derived from the work role. It is therefore reasonable to expect that positive attitudes to work in general leads to positive attitudes to the specific job. People who value the work role highly demonstrate that in their attitude to the job. According to Shamir, it would seem that commitment to the job, which is based on the individual meaning of the job, has a stronger influence on organizational commitment or occupational commitment. This argument accords with Randall and Cote's model.

How does job involvement mediate the relation among PWE, occupational commitment, and the two forms of organizational commitment? Witt (1993), suggesting that employees given unsatisfactory work assignments may develop unfavorable and durable attitudes to the organization, argued that the reactions to one's work assignments may be salient in the commitment decision. Witt's results were consistent with previous findings showing that early work experiences contribute to later commitment (Pierce & Dunham, 1987). He concluded that one's work experiences and attitudes are an important factor in later job attitudes. This supports the notion of job involvement as a mediator in work commitment interrelations. Job involvement is strongly affected by, and can be perceived as a reflection of, work experiences. The more positive these experiences, the higher the job involvement. Higher job involvement will lead to positive attitudes toward one's organization and career.

By inference, Randall and Cote (1991) seem to conceptualized job involvement as a mediator based on social exchange theory, namely, that given certain conditions people seek to reciprocate those who benefit them. Employees who are involved in their job have positive work experiences that are attributed to the organization or their career. To the extent that positive experiences are attributed to the efforts of organizational officials, these are reciprocated with increased commitment to the persons who caused them. Thus, it can be expected that attribution to organizational officials of unfavorable job assignments result in lower job involvement, possibly reducing psychological attachment to the organization (affective commitment). If the job experiences in a given organization are not positive, the sacrifices associated with leaving the organization are defined as lower, and reduce continuance commitment. Finally, one highly involved in a job will also attribute it to the occupation and reciprocate with high occupational commitment. Alternatively, negative work experiences may lead to second thoughts about one's occupational decision, reducing occupational commitment.

The difference between Morrow's (1993) and Randall and Cote's (1991) models constitutes an important reason to test and compare them. Although there are probably other potential models, these two are justified conceptually and present the best alternatives to be tested and compared. Another issue addressed is the continuance commitment form. As mentioned previously, earlier research has clearly shown that continuance commitment has two dimensions, "personal sacrifices" and "low alternatives." Morrow (1993) mentioned it but did not consider it in developing the work commitment model. Possibly the relations among the commitment foci differ depending on the kind of continuance commitment scale the model includes. Therefore, Morrow's and Randall and Cote's models should be tested not only with the full scale of continuance commitment but also with each of its dimensions.

Few studies have examined and compared theses above models. The few studies that examined and tested them empirically (Cohen, 1999a; 2000; Freund, 2000) provided valuable findings, which are presented next.

Research Findings

Study 1.   Cohen (1999a) compared Morrow's model with an earlier one proposed and tested by Randall and Cote (1991) who tested slightly different forms of commitment. These were PWE, career commitment, organizational commitment, work group attachment, and job involvement. They included only one form of organizational commitment, namely, affective, and instead of the continuance organizational commitment in Morrow's model they took the work group attachment form. Four forms of commitment, namely, affective organizational commitment, PWE, career commitment, and job involvement, were tested in both models. The participants in the study were 238 nurses from two hospitals in Western Canada.

As for the measures used in that study, two measures of organizational commitment were collected: the two eight-item scales of affective and continuance commitment of Meyer and Allen (1984). The two dimensions of the continuance commitment scale, "high sacrifices" and "low alternatives," were also analyzed. Career commitment was measured by the eight-item measure developed by Blau (1985). Job involvement (10 items) was measured by the measure developed by Kanungo (1979, 1982). This measure was selected as it overcomes the problem of the Lodhal and Kejner (1965) measure, which failed to distinguish the particular job from the generalized work context. The PWE was measured by ten items from the 19-item scale developed by Mirels and Garrett (1971). Items negatively phrased or seeming to overlap, mainly those touching on work commitment and job involvement, were excluded. The idea was to concentrate on items which, as stated by Shamir (1986), measured the importance of work in a more abstract and remote way than does the job involvement scale, with items containing references to society and to moral judgment. Items that focused on potential satisfactions with the work role similarly to job involve-ment (e.g., "I feel uneasy when there is little work for me to do") were omitted. The scales applied in this research were mentioned by Morrow (1993) as the most commonly used, reliable, valid work commitment scales. Each also stated to have strong discriminant validity in its relationship to other work commitment forms. The selection of the scales well matched Morrow's conceptualization.

The two models regarding the interrelations among the five commitment forms were assessed by path analysis using LISREL VIII (Joreskog & Sorbom, 1993). The models were evaluated by the two-stage approach to structural equation modeling suggested by Anderson and Gerbing (1988). This approach entails comparing the goodness-of-fit indices of a sequence of nested models. This step begins with changing the name of the measure-ment model to the *fully saturated path* model, because specification of all pos-sible inter-factor correlations in a factor analytic model is identical to specification of all possible paths in a structural equation model. Accord-ingly, the chi-square statistic and the goodness-of-fit characteristics of the measurement model become key standards, with which those values for the theoretical path model can be compared. The two competing models of this research were compared with the measurement model.

Because the models compared are nested models, a chi-square difference test (df; Bollen, 1989) was applied to compare the models. The statistic for this test is calculated as the difference in the usual chi-square estimators for the restricted and unrestricted models, with df equal to their difference in df. The specific hypothesis tested by this statistic is whether the restrictions added during the creation of the restricted model significantly reduce the fit compared with the fit attainable with all the model restrictions incorporated in the basic model. The basic model is the saturated one in the structural models, and the hypothesized one in the CFA. The saturated model in-cludes all the theoretical paths of all models. These models (unrestricted models) are then compared with each of the alternative models (restricted models). A significant chi-square indicates that the constraints imposed on the restricted models reduce their fit in comparison with the saturated or the hypothesized models. Note that Morrow's and Randall and Cote's mod-els are not nested because they are not identical models (Bollen, 1989). They are not compared with each other but each is compared with the mea-surement/saturated model.

The LISREL program calculates a *modification index* for every fixed pa-rameter in a model. The *modification index* reflects the minimum reduction in the chi-square statistics if the parameter is changed from fixed to free. The two models tested were revised on the basis of these modification in-dexes. The revised models are compared with the measurement model and with their original model. Breckler (1990) and Cudeck and Browne (1983) argued that cross-validation should be conducted whenever an initial model is modified on the basis of the data. That is, the modified model should be assessed by means of different data. Otherwise, the model should be cautiously interpreted.

Results of descriptive statistics, reliabilities, and the intercorrelations among research variables show acceptable reliabilities of the measures of this study, with somewhat low reliability ($r = .69$) of the continuance organizational commitment scale. Following previous research (Hackett et al., 1994; McGee & Ford, 1987; Somers, 1993) the continuance commitment scale was divided into two: "high sacrifices" and "low alternatives." However, the reliabilities of the four-item scales were very low (.54 and .60, respectively). Reliability analysis shows that omitting two items, one from each scale, improves reliability. Thus, for each of the two subscales, a three-item scale was formed with a reliability of .60 for "high sacrifices" and .65 for "low alternatives." These reliabilities are still low, but are higher than those found by Somers (1993) and in a sample of nurses (.57 and .59, respectively). Three-item scales for the two dimensions of continuance commitment were applied in most research (Dunham, Grube, & Castaneda, 1994; Hackett et al., 1994; McGee & Ford, 1987; Somers, 1993).

The correlations of the two subscales with work commitment constructs support their distinction. For example, "high sacrifices" had positive significant relations with affective organizational commitment ($r = .193$, p < .01), career commitment ($r = .130$, p < .05), and job involvement ($r = .159$, p < .01), whereas "high sacrifices" had negative relations with affective organizational commitment ($r = -.201$, p < .001) and career commitment ($r = -.272$, P < .001). The differential relations of the two subscales of continuance commitment with work commitment constructs explain the nonsignificant relations of the full scale with the same constructs. The correlations among the work commitment scales show that the affective commitment dimension had the highest correlation with other commitments such as job involvement ($r = .527$) and career commitment ($r = .483$). The PWE had a nonsignificant relationship with the two forms of organizational commitment and significant but weak correlations with career commitment ($r = .112$) and job involvement ($r = .272$). The correlations indicate a pattern where strong intercorrelations exist among affective organizational commitment, job involvement, and career commitment; and weak relations between PWE and continuance organizational commitment and the other three forms.

Path analysis. Table 5.1 shows the fit indexes for the models tested. Each of the models was tested four times: with the full continuance commitment

Table 5.1
Overall Fit Indexes for the Work Commitment Models

Model/Description	df	x^2	x^2/df	Model Comparison	Δx^2	RNI	RFI	NFI	TLI	CFI	RMSEA
With full scale of continuance commitment											
1. Measurement model	80	141.00***	1.76			0.95	0.85	0.89	0.93	0.95	0.059
2. Morrow's model	83	170.84***	2.06	1 vs. 2	29.84***	0.92	0.83	0.86	0.90	0.92	0.069
3. Morrow's revised model	85	160.25***	1.89	1 vs. 3	19.25**	0.93	0.84	0.87	0.92	0.93	0.063
4. Randall and Cote's model	86	162.86***	1.89	1 vs. 4	21.25**	0.93	0.84	0.87	0.92	0.93	0.064
5. Randall and Cote's revised model	84	148.44***	1.77	1 vs. 5	7.44	0.94	0.85	0.88	0.93	0.94	0.059
With full scale of continuance commitment (item level)											
1. Measurement model	125	261.71***	2.09			0.90	0.79	0.83	0.88	0.90	0.070
2. Morrow's model	128	291.57***	2.28	1 vs. 2	29.85***	0.88	0.77	0.81	0.86	0.88	0.076
3. Morrow's revised model	130	273.86***	2.11	1 vs. 3	12.15*	0.89	0.79	0.82	0.88	0.89	0.071
4. Randall and Cote's model	131	276.47***	2.11	1 vs. 4	14.76*	0.89	0.79	0.82	0.88	0.89	0.070

Model/Description	df	x^2	x^2/df	Model Comparison	$\triangle x^2$	RNI	RFI	NFI	TLI	CFI	RMSEA
With "personal sacrifices" as representing continuance commitment											
1. Measurement model	80	138.16***	1.73			0.95	0.86	0.89	0.93	0.95	0.057
2. Morrow's model	83	168.59***	2.03	1 vs. 2	30.43***	0.93	0.83	0.87	0.91	0.93	0.068
3. Morrow's revised model	85	151.57***	1.78	1 vs. 3	13.41*	0.94	0.85	0.88	0.93	0.94	0.060
4. Randall and Cote's model	86	154.11***	1.79	1 vs. 4	15.95*	0.94	0.85	0.88	0.93	0.94	0.060
5. Randall and Cote's revised model	84	148.52***	1.77	1 vs. 5	10.36*	0.95	0.85	0.88	0.93	0.95	0.059
With "low alternatives" as representing continuance commitment											
1. Measurement model	80	125.42***	1.56			0.96	0.90	0.90	0.95	0.96	0.051
2. Morrow's model	83	156.04***	1.88	1 vs. 2	30.62***	0.94	0.84	0.88	0.92	0.94	0.063
3. Morrow's revised model	85	153.13***	1.80	1 vs. 3	27.71***	0.94	0.85	0.88	0.93	0.94	0.060
4. Randall and Cote's model	86	155.65***	1.81	1 vs. 4	30.23***	0.94	0.85	0.88	0.93	0.94	0.061
5. Randall and Cote's revised model	84	137.22***	1.63	1 vs. 5	11.8*	0.95	0.86	0.89	0.94	0.95	0.054

*$p < .05$**$p < .01$***$p < .001$

From Cohen, A. (1999). Relationships among five forms of commitment: An empirical examination. *Journal of Organizational Behavior, 20,* 285–308. Copyright © by John Wiley and Sons Limited. Reproduced with permission.

scale using the three-indicators approach, with the same full scale using the item approach, with the "personal sacrifices" dimension, and with the "low alternatives" dimension. Table 5.1 shows that in the four analyses Morrow's model did not fit the data well. This was demonstrated in the fit indexes, which are lower than in the measurement model and all the other models, and mainly in the results of the chi-square test. As Table 5.1 shows, this test consistently yielded a high and significant chi-square value in the comparison between Morrow's model and the saturated/measurement model, demonstrating that the constraints imposed by the paths representing Morrow's model worsen the fit with the data. In addition, Table 5.2, which presents the structural coefficients for the model, shows that only three paths in the models were significant: from PWE to career commitment, career commitment to affective organizational commitment, and affective organizational commitment to job involvement. Application of each of the two dimensions of continuance commitment instead of the full scale, yielded one more significant path—PWE to continuance organizational commitment.

The results in Table 5.1 show that the Randall and Cote's (1991) model fits the data better than the Morrow's. This is demonstrated in a lower chi-square difference in a comparison of this model with the saturated one in all analyses except that using "low alternatives" as representing continuance commitment. Also, the fit indexes of the Randall and Cote model are better than those of Morrow's model. Three of the four path coefficients in Randall and Cote's model are significant. The only path is that from job involvement to continuance organizational commitment. This path becomes significant when the "low alternatives" dimension represents continuance commitment. A noteworthy finding is that the structural coefficients in Table 5.2 show that in general each dimension of continuance commitment relates differently to the relevant commitment foci. For example, career commitment has a significant negative relation with the full scale of continuance commitment (–.23), a positive and nonsignificant relation with the "personal sacrifices" dimension (.10), and a high negative relation with the "low alternative" dimension (–.36). The same pattern can be found in all the paths that involve continuance commitment.

However, although the findings show a better fit of Randall and Cote's (1991) model than of Morrow's they indicate that none of the models has a good fit with the data. Therefore, the two models were revised on the basis of the modification indexes. In Morrow's (1993) model the modification indexes showed that the model would be significantly improved if the following paths were included: from job involvement to affective organizational commitment; from job involvement to career commitment; from career commitment to job involvement; and from PWE to job involvement. The modification indexes in Randall and Cote's model showed a reduction in the size of chi-square if two paths are included: a path from career commitment to affective organizational commitment and a path from career commitment to continuance organizational commitment. Modification indexes also suggested paths from affective and continuance commitment to career commitment, which were not tested because paths are not allowed to go backward.

On the basis of these indexes the models were revised as presented in Figs. 5.3 and 5.4. Table 5.1 shows that the revised models fit the data significantly better that the original ones. Morrow's (1993) revised model shows in general a better fit with the data than the original one. Note that when "low alternatives" was used as representing continuance commitment Morrow's revised model showed hardly any improvement in its fit compared with the original model. A good indication of the improvement in Morrow's revised model is provided by the path coefficients presented in Table 5.2. All the paths except job involvement to continuance commitment are significant in Morrow's revised model. Moreover, even that problematic path is significant when "low alternatives" represents continuance commitment in Morrow's revised model.

The revised Randall and Cote (1991) model fits the data very well, as demonstrated in a nonsignificant chi-square when compared with the measurement/saturated model. Even in the two other analyses, where each of the continuance commitment dimensions was analyzed separately, the chi-square was quite low, although significant, at the .05 level. The fit indexes of the revised Randall and Cote model were similar to those of the measurement model and better than Morrow's original and revised models. Morrow's

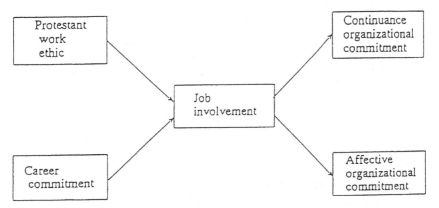

FIG. 5.3. Morrow's revised model of the interrelationships among commitment forms. From Cohen, A. (1999). Relationships among five forms of commitment: An empirical examination. *Journal of Organizational behavior,* 20, 285–308. Copyright © John Wiley & Sons Limited. Reproduced with permission.

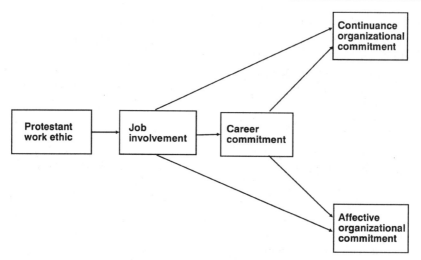

FIG. 5.4.   Randall and Cote's revised model of the interrelationships among commitment forms. From Cohen, A. (1999). Relationships among five forms of commitment: An empirical examination. *Journal of Organizational behavior, 20,* 285–308. Copyright © John Wiley & Sons Limited. Reproduced with permission.

revised model differed greatly from the original one and therefore was not compared with it as a nested model. However, the revised Randall and Cote model was the same as the original but with the addition of two paths. As a nested unconstrained model, it was compared with the original nonrevised model. The significant chi-square in three out of the four analyses (except for the model using "personal sacrifices" as representing continuance commitment) showed that the constraints imposed on the nonrevised model worsen its fit and therefore support the usefulness of the revised Randall and Cote model. Most of the paths in the revised model are significant except for two paths that include continuance commitment: from job involvement to continuance commitment, and in two cases that from career commitment to continuance commitment. In the revised models, as in the nonrevised, the structural coefficients are related in general differently to each dimension of continuance commitment, as seen in Table 5.2.

In summary, the findings of the commitment models show that Morrow's (1993) model was not supported by the data and that Randall and Cote's (1991) model fitted the data much better. The best fit with the data was found in a revised model of Randall and Cote. The findings also show that the models operated differently in terms of their fit and the structural coefficients, depending whether the full continuance commitment scale or each of its dimensions was used.

Table 5.2
Structural Coefficients for Research Models

Parameters for Proposed Models	Morrow's model[1]	Morrow's model with "personal sacrifices"	Morrow's model with "low alternatives"	Randall & Cote's model	Randall & Cote's model with "personal sacrifices"	Randall & Cote's model with "low alternatives"
Path coeffiecients						
Protestant work ethic-Career commitment	.09 (.09)	.09	.09			
Protestant work ethic-Job involvement				.28* (.28*)	.28*	.28*
Protestant work ethic-Continuance organizational commitment	.15 (.09)	.00	.21*			
Career commitment-Continuance organizational commitment	−.23* (−.09)	.10	−.36*			
Career commitment-Affective organizational commitment	.62* (.60*)	.58*	.59*			
Continuance organizational commitment-Affective organizational commitment	.14 (.10)	.17*	−.03			
Continuance organizational commitment-Job involvement	.00 (−.04)	−.07	.04			
Affective organizational commitment-Job involvent	.73* (.73*)	.74*	.74*			
Job involvement-Continuance organizational commitment				.00 (.01)	.13	−.19*
Job involvement-Affective organizational commitment				.71* (.71*)	.71*	.71*
Job involvement-Career commitment				.61* (.61*)	.62*	.62*

continued on next page

139

TABLE 5.2 (continued)

Parameters for Proposed Models	Morrow's model[1]	Morrow's model with "personal sacrifices"	Morrow's model with "low alternatives"	Randall & Cote's model	Randall & Cote's model with "personal sacrifices"	Randall & Cote's model with "low alternatives"
Path coeffiecients						
Parameters for Revised Models						
Path coefficients						
Protestant work ethic-Job involvement	.26* (.26*)	.26*	.25*	.30* (.30*)	.30*	.30*
Career commitment-Job involvement	.60* (.60*)	.60*	.61*			
Career commitment-Continuance organizational commitment				−.35* (−.13)	.05	−.41*
Career commitment-Affective organizational commitment				.23* (.23*)	.23*	.24*
Job involvement-Career commitment				.58* (.58*)	.58*	.58*
Job involvement-Continuance organizational commitment	−.01 (.01)	.13	−.19*	.21 (.09)	.09	.10
Job involvement-Affective organizational commitment	.70* (.70*)	.71*	.71*	.54* (.53*)	.53*	.52

[1]The numbers in parentheses are the path coefficients based on analyzing continuance commitment at the item level.

*p < .05

From Cohen, A. (1999). Relationships among five forms of commitment: An empirical examination. *Journal of Organizational Behavior, 20,* 285–308. Copyright © by John Wiley and Sons Limited. Reproduced with permission.

Because Cohen's (1999a) study was, in essence, the first to test those in-terrelations among commitment forms it was clear that the findings should be replicated in other samples and work settings. Consistent results across different settings are important in this regard to support the discriminant validity of these forms and the nature of their interrelations. Vandenberg and Scarpello (1994) argued that some settings may value an occupation more or less than others, and the strength of the occupational/organiza-tional commitment relation may vary as a function of setting. Future studies need to identify the moderating characteristics of the setting and how they influence this relation.

Study 2.   Following this recommendation, Freund (2000) performed a replication of Cohen's (1999a) study. In this replication the two models ex-amined by Cohen were re-examined in a different sample. This sample con-sisted of 122 employees of a public service organization in Israel. The major strength in Freund's research was the longitudinal design of this study. Spe-cifically, the data were collected at three points of time with approximately a six-month gap between the data administrations. This allowed an examina-tion of the stability of the models across time. Most of the scales in Freund's study were similar to those in Cohen's (1999a), except for the PWE scale. Freund used Blood's (1969) four-item scale of Protestant ethic. However, the reliabilities for this scale were below .60 in all three administrations so it was decided to test the models without this scale. Another difference be-tween Freund's study and Cohen's is that Freund's model included paths from the commitment forms defined as consequences in the two models to variables representing withdrawal cognitions like thinking of quitting, search intentions, and turnover intentions.

Freund tested the models in both regression analyses, which examined parts of each model, and by structural equations modeling with LISREL. Freund's findings supported Randall and Cote's model and not Morrow's in all three administrations of the data. The regression analyses supported Randall and Cote's model more strongly than it did Morrow's. The fit in-dexes in Randall and Cote's model were higher than in Morrow's in all ad-ministrations. The path coefficients also provided stronger support for Randall and Cote's model. In summary, despite the limitation of Freund's study due to the omission of PWE the findings furnished important support for Randall and Cote's model considering that very little research has exam-ined and compared the two models.

The strength of Freund's study is its longitudinal design. Table 5.3 sets out the intercorrelations among commitment foci and between these foci and the three variables representing withdrawal cognitions. These data are important considering that interrelations among commitment

TABLE 5.3
Intercorrelations Among Commitment Forms and Withdrawal Cognitions
in Three Time Lags

		JI			OC			PWE		
		T1	T2	T3	T1	T2	T3	T1	T2	T3
JI	T1	1.000								
	T2	.679**	1.000							
	T3	.587**	.807**	1.000						
OC	T1	.638**	.463**	.431**	1.000					
	T2	.469**	.628**	.567**	.688**	1.000				
	T3	.394**	.533**	.686**	.562**	.699**	1.000			
PWE	T1	.352**	.193*	.199*	.405**	.251**	.236*	1.000		
	T2	.289**	.413**	.372**	.134	.211*	.235*	.463**	1.000	
	T3	.242**	.343**	.415**	.174	.285**	.379**	.463**	.537**	1.000
AOC	T1	.558**	.415**	.419**	.623**	.497**	.491**	.353**	.105	.270**
	T2	.390**	.489**	.532**	.446**	.609**	.558**	.234*	.202*	.442**
	T3	.358**	.388**	.609**	.386**	.487**	.753**	.194*	.175	.416**
COC	T1	-.049	-.082	.080	-.055	-.148	.037	.237**	.025	.126
	T2	-.119	-.112	-.026	-.123	-.190*	-.012	.090	-.014	.092
	T3	-.036	-.031	.078	.017	-.015	.073	.144	.024	.076
SI	T1	-.117	-.208*	-.110	-.086	-.163	.016	.050	-.138	-.147
	T2	-.072	-.165	-.092	-.161	-.159	-.021	.075	-.002	.033
	T3	-.155	-.125	-.119	-.043	-.079	.030	-.028	-.080	-.155
TI	T1	-.411**	-.236*	-.242**	-.636**	-.454**	-.383**	-.232*	-.122	-.028
	T2	-.272**	-.378**	-.351**	-.406**	-.622**	-.480**	-.203*	-.215*	-.183*
	T3	-168	-.296**	-.419**	-.344**	-.448**	-.559**	-.154	-.134	-.207*
TOQ	T1	.072	-.020	-.058	.089	-.050	-.002	.063	.086	-.133
	T2	.029	.037	.040	.100	.198**	.171	.189*	.121	.168
	T3	-.091	-.006	.123	.073	.178	.191*	.136	.113	.068

N = 203 in Time 1, 153 in Time 2, and 122 in Time 3. JI = Job Involvement OC = Occupational Commitment AOC = Affective Organizational Commitment COC = Continuance Organizational Commitment SI = Search Intentions TI = Turnover Intentions TOQ = Thinking of Quitting

Note: From: Freund, A. (1999). *Multiple commitments to work factors: A longitudinal study examining the effects of turnover in the Israeli public sector* Unpublished doctoral dissertation, University of Haifa, Haifa, Israel. Copyright © 1999. Reprinted with permission of the author

		AOC			COC			SI		
		T1	T2	T3	T1	T2	T3	T1	T2	T3
JI	T1									
	T2									
	T3									
OC	T1									
	T2									
	T3									
PWE	T1									
	T2									
	T3									
AOC	T1	1.000								
	T2	.717**	1.000							
	T3	.587**	.727**	1.000						
COC	T1	.105	.097	.221*	1.000					
	T2	.082	.150	.222*	.694**	1.000				
	T3	.157	.191*	.303**	.635**	.627**	1.000			
SI	T1	.144	.048	.120	.559**	.503**	.401**	1.000		
	T2	.100	.056	.147	.499**	.665**	.433**	.656**	1.000	
	T3	.049	-.045	.083	.330**	.478**	.350**	.538**	.674**	1.000
TI	T1	-.517**	-.381**	-.312**	.002	.027	-.073	-.050	.054	-.109
	T2	-.439**	-.598**	-.476**	-.071	-.099	-.131	-.101	-.059	-.092
	T3	-.350**	-.490**	-.616**	-.132	-.153	-.23-*	-.003	.026	-.119
TOQ	T1	.132	-.041	.029	-.083	.149	.094	.137	.145	.284**
	T2	.132	.186*	.194*	.119	.191*	.149	.083	.144	.104
	T3	.083	.136	.220*	.081	.194*	.077	.125	.099	.168

continued on next page

foi in three time frames have hardly been researched. The findings in Table 5.3 show that the relation between a given commitment focus and another were the strongest at time 1. But the correlation between a given commitment form measured at time 1 and any other commitment form measured at times 2 or 3 was weaker. For example, the correlation between job involvement and occupational commitment at time 1 is .638; between job involvement at time 1 and occupational commitment time at 2 it is .469, and between job involvement at time 1 and occupational

TABLE 5.3 (continued)							
		TI			TOQ		
		T1	T2	T3	T1	T2	T3
JI	T1						
	T2						
	T3						
OC	T1						
	T2						
	T3						
PWE	T1						
	T2						
	T3						
AOC	T1						
	T2						
	T3						
COC	T1						
	T2						
	T3						
SI	T1						
	T2						
	T3						
TI	T1	1.000					
	T2	.590**	1.000				
	T3	.522**	.653**	1.000			
TOQ	T1	-.293**	-.126	.087	1.000		
	T2	-.261**	-.394**	-.325**	.540**	1.000	
	T3	-.137	-.364**	-.441**	.379**	.470**	1.000

commitment at time 3 it is .394. This pattern is consistent across most of the relations displaye in the table. Although this pattern of relationship is not unusual among attitudinal variables, it is important to note that it exists among commitment forms also.

In short, despite its limitations Freund's (2000) study provided additional support to Cohen's findings. More longitudinal designs are needed in commitment research to impart greater insight into the relations among commitment foci.

Study 3.   Cohen (2000) conducted another test of Randall and Cote's and Morrow's models in a setting consisting of Israeli nurses. In Cohen's (2000) study the following commitment forms were tested: affective organizational commitment, job involvement, career commitment, work involvement, and group commitment. The construct of work involvement represented the work ethic measures, because PWE is a multidimensional construct entailing the importance of work and also a rejection of leisure and excess money (Morrow, 1993). To use this three-dimensional construct with the other commitment foci would have unnecessarily complicated the models and analysis. Work involvement is a unidimensional construct, and therefore is a more appropriate scale to apply with other commitment foci as representing work values.

Other differences between Cohen's (2000) more recent study and the earlier one (Cohen, 1999a) are as follows: First, in the later one the continuance organizational commitment scale of Meyer and Allen (1984) was omitted. As described previously and in chapters 2 and 3, this form is problematic both in itself and in its relations with other commitment forms and work attitudes. Cohen decided to replace it by group commitment, which is a new concept in multiple commitment research (Morrow, 1993). As a result, Morrow's and Randall and Cote's models includedthe same four forms of commitment: PWE, job involvement, organizational commitment, and occupational commitment. But they differed in one commitment form: in Morrow's model the fifth commitment focus was another organizational commitment form, calculative organizational commitment, in addition to the affective one proposed by both Morrow and Randall and Cote. In Randall and Cote's model, group commitment was the fifth commitment form. Because the only way to make a meaningful comparison between the models was for both to have the same commitment foci, it was decided to use Randall and Cote's commitment foci and adjust Morrow's model to these forms. Thus, group commitment replaced calculative organizational commitment. As noted next in the description of Morrow's model, the differences between the models in a particular commitment form should not have affected the comparison. The two models differed in their conceptual arguments as to the interrelations among the forms, not in whether any particular commitment focus should or should not be included in them.

Secondly, Cohen's later study examined not only the interrelations among commitment forms but also those between commitment forms and work outcomes such as turnover intentions, actual turnover, and absenteeism. Again, this should not have affected the findings on the validity of the two models.

Randall and Cote's (1991) model in its current form is presented in Fig. 5.5. This model was explained above, but because of the changes from the previous model in two of the commitment forms some of the interrelations differ from the previous model and therefore need to be clarified. In this model (Fig. 5.5), work involvement and work group commitment are the ex-

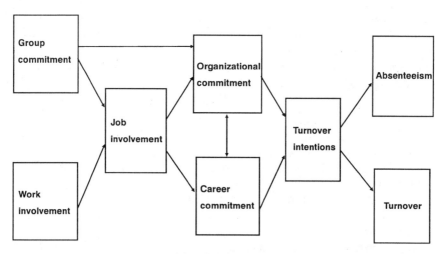

FIG. 5.5.   Randall and Cote's model with work outcomes. From Cohen, A. (2000). *The rela-tionship between commitment forms and work outcomes: A comparison of three models.* Copyright © 2002 by Sage Publications. Reprinted with permission.

ogenous variables that affect job involvement. The rationale for the relation between work involvement and job involvement is similar to that for PWE and job involvement. In the later study work involvement replaced PWE, but the conceptual arguments outlined in the earlier study (Cohen, 1999a) and described previously are relevant for both concepts representing work values (Morrow, 1993). In Randall and Cote's model, group commitment too is related to job involvement. The rationale for such a relation is the importance of the work group in forming an employee's orientation to work. For example, Lodhal and Kejner (1965) found that job involvement was correlated with the number of people contacted per day on the job and the need to work closely with others. According to Randall and Cote, group commitment is also related to organizational commitment in accordance with social involvement theory (Kanter, 1968). The social bond exerts an important environmental influence on organizational commitment. Leaving the organization means leaving significant others. Because socially involved individuals may be reluctant to break social ties, they may choose to remain in an organization. The mediation role of job involvement in the relation between both work involvement and group commitment and organizational commitment and career commitment was presented earlier, and has there is no need for restatement.

Morrow's model is presented in Fig. 5.6. The rationale for the relations in that model was explained with Fig. 5.5, but the role of group commitment has to be elaborated here, as it was not examined in the earlier model.

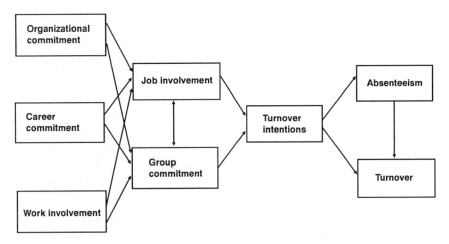

FIG. 5.6.   Morrow's model with work outcomes. From Cohen, A. (2000). *The relationship between commitment forms and work outcomes: A comparison of three models.* Copyright © 2002 by Sage Publications. Reprinted with permission.

Making group commitment the second dependent variable has a rationale similar to that for job involvement. *Group commitment*, like job involvement, can also be perceived in Morrow's terms as a close, immediate, tangible, and concrete focus. The juxtaposition of group commitment and job involvement is supported by the arguments raised by Yoon et al. (1994). Interpersonal attachment produces a stronger commitment to subgroups than to the larger group because the credit for positive affect from interpersonal bonds is likely to be attributed to the proximal subgroups, whereas the blame for negative affects is likely to be attributed to the large group (Lawler, 1992). This logic shows that one develops stronger personal attachment to one's group than to one's career or work because the group is a proximal target in one's immediate work unit, and career, work, and even the organization, for example, are more distant targets.

Cohen (2000) tested these models in a sample of 283 nurses from three small hospitals in Israel. Organizational commitment was measured by the shorter nine-item version of the OCQ (Porter, Steers, Mowday, & Boulian, 1974). Occupational commitment was measured by the 8-item measure developed by Blau (1985). Job involvement (10 items) and work involvement (6 items) were measured by the scales developed by Kanungo (1979, 1982). Group commitment was measured by the six-item measure developed by Randall and Cote (1991). All work commitment constructs were measured on a five-point scale (1 = strongly disagree, to 5 = strongly agree). As in the previous study, the models for the interrelations among the five commitment forms were assessed by path analysis using LISREL VIII (Joreskog & Sorbom, 1993). Results showed acceptable reliabilities of the measures of this study. The correlations among the work commitment scales showed that the job involvement dimension had the highest correlation with other commitments such as work involvement ($r = .67$) and occupational commitment ($r = .57$).

As can be seen in Table 5.4, Randall and Cote's (1991) models fitted the data slightly better than Morrow's. This is demonstrated in the lower chi-square of the two Randall and Cote models. The fit indexes of Randall and Cote's models are also slightly better than those of Morrow. Her model was only partially supported by the path coefficient presented in Table 5.5. This model expected a mediated effect of two commitment foci: job involvement and group commitment. Job involvement was found to mediate the relationship, as expected and was related to the three exogenous variables work involvement (.34), organizational commitment (.28), and occupational commitment (.49). It was also related to one of the outcome variables, turnover intentions. The findings, however, did not support the inclusion of group commitment as one of the mediators. Only one exogenous variable, organizational commitment (.31), was related to group commitment. Moreover, group commitment was not related to any of the outcome variables.

The path coefficients seem to support Randall and Cote's (1991) model more than Morrow's. The weaknesses of the latter were that one of the mediator variables, group commitment, did not mediate, and the model had fewer significant than nonsignificant paths. Randall and Cote's model overcame these problems. It evinced two mediation processes, both supported by the data. First, job involvement mediated the relation of group commitment and work involvement with occupational commitment and organizational commitment. All of the four-path coefficients were significant: from group commitment to job involvement (.29) and from work involvement to job involvement (.61), and from job involvement to occupational commitment (.74) and organizational commitment (.63). Second, organizational commitment and occupational commitment mediated the relation between the other commitment foci and work outcomes; both had a significant relation with turnover intentions (−.20 with occupational commitment and −.46 with organizational commitment). The only non-significant path was between group commitment and organizational commitment. Finally, a notable finding is that in both models most of the paths involving group commitment were not significant.

Study 4.   Hackett, Lapierre, & Hausdorf (2001) replicated Cohen's (2000) research by examining Randall and Cote's (1991) model and the re-

TABLE 5.4

Overall fit indices for the work commitment models

Model/Description	df	x^2	x^2/df	Model comparison	Δx^2	AGFI	RFI	NFI	TLI	CFI	RMSEA
1. Measurement/Saturated model	144	323.32***	2.25			0.85	0.86	0.90	0.92	0.94	0.067
2. Morrow's model	157	386.25***	2.46	1 vs. 2	62.93***	0.84	0.85	0.88	0.91	0.92	0.072
3. Randall and Cote's model	160	358.44***	2.24	1 vs. 3	35.12**	0.85	0.86	0.88	0.92	0.93	0.066

*p < .05 **p < .01 ***p < .001

From Aaron Cohen, "The relationship between commitment forms and work outcomes: A comparison of three models," *Human Relations, 53*, p. 406.

TABLE 5.5
Structural coefficients for research models

Parameters	Direct model	Morrow's model	Randall & Cote's model
Path coefficients			
Work involvement–Career commitment			
Work involvement–Job involvement		.34*	.61*
Work involvement–Organizational commitment			
Work involvement–Group commitment		.01	
Work involvement–Turnover intentions	.29*		
Work involvement–Absenteeism			
Work involvement–Turnover			
Organizational commitment–Job involvement		.28*	
Organizational commitment–Group commitment		.30*	
Organizational commitment–Turnover intentions	–.49*		–.46*
Organizational commitment–Absenteeism			
Organizational commitment–Turnover			
Career commitment–Job involvement		.49*	
Career commitment–Group commitment		.1	
Career commitment–Organizational commitment			.55
Career commitment–Turnover intentions	–.14		–.20*
Career commitment–Absenteeism			
Career commitment–Turnover			
Job involvement–Organizational commitment			.63*
Job involvement–Career commitment			.74*
Job involvement–Group commitment		.44	
Job involvement–Turnover intentions	–.20	–.45*	
Job involvement–Absenteeism			
Job involvement–Turnover			
Group commitment–Job involvement			.29*
Group commitment–Organizational commitment			.11
Group commitment–Turnover intentions	–.04	–.11	
Group commitment–Absenteeism			
Group commitment–Turnover			
Turnover intentions–Absenteeism	.06	.06	.05
Turnover intentions–Turnover	.14*	.13*	.13*
Absenteeism–Turnover	–.08	–.08	–.08

*p < .05

From: Aaron Cohen, "The relationship between commitment forms and work outcomes: A comparison of three models," *Human Relations, 53*, pp. 408–409.

lation of commitment foci to withdrawal cognitions from the organization and the occupation. The model Hackett also is presented in Fig. 5.7. The main difference between their model and Cohen's one is that their model did not test group commitment and thus included four commitment forms (work involvement, job involvement, organizational commitment, and occupational commitment). Another difference is in the outcomes tested. Whereas Cohen tested behavioral outcomes in addition to the attitudinal ones, Hackett et al. tested two attitudinal outcomes, intention to leave the occupation and the organization. Their sample included 852 part-time and full-time Ontario nurses and their commitment measures were quite similar to those applied by Cohen (2000). It should be noted that unlike Cohen, who tested his model using structural equation modeling, Hackett et al. used a regression analysis.

The findings strongly supported the model. That is, intentions to withdraw from the organization and the occupation were both directly influenced by organizational commitment and occupational commitment, respectively. Organizational commitment and occupational commitment were both directly influenced by job involvement, which was influenced by work involvement. Hackett et al.'s findings strongly supported the mediating role of job involvement that mediated the relation between work involvement and organizational commitment and between work involvement and occupational commitment. They concluded that the model they have tested offers incremental empirical evidence for Randall and Cote's (1991) theoretical model. They mentioned that because their model did not include group commitment their results offer only partial support for Randall and Cote's model. It should be mentioned that because Randall

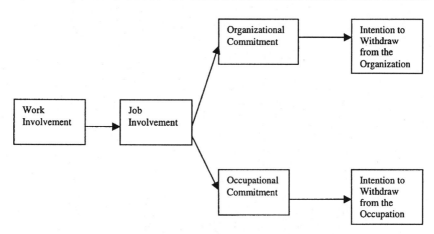

FIG. 5.7.   Hackett et al.'s model. From Hackett et al. (2001). Understanding the links between work commitment constructs. *Journal of Vocational Behavior, 58*, 395.

and Cote's model was supported by a regression analysis used by Hackett et al., not only by structural equation modeling used by Cohen, both Cohen's works (1999, 2000) strengthen the empirical support for Randall and Cote's model.

Study 5.   Carmeli and Freund (2001) provide another testing of the Randall and Cote's model. They however applied Morrow's (1993) five universal forms of commitment (affective organization, continuance organization, career, job involvement and PWE). Their model is presented in Fig. 5.8 and as can be seen, provides another testing of the Randall and Cote's model, albeit with some differences in comparison to the original model or previous testing. First, group commitment is not included here. Second the outcomes here are job satisfaction and subjective job performance. But as can be seen in Fig. 5.8, the main rationale of Randall and Cote's model is demonstrated in the one tested by Carmeli and Freund (2001). The sample consisted of 183 lawyers working in private firms in Israel. The response rate was somewhat low, 17.8% and the commitment measures used in this study are similar to those applied by Cohen (1999, 2000).

The findings based on path analysis (LISREL VIII) supported in general the Randall and Cote's (1991) model. All the paths were significant except for the one from job involvement to continuance organizational commitment. This path was not significant in Cohen's (1999) study too, and shows the problems associated with including continuance commitment in a multiple commitments model. Job involvement was again demonstrated as a mediator between PWE and organizational and career commitment. The three commitment forms, career, affective organizational commitment, and

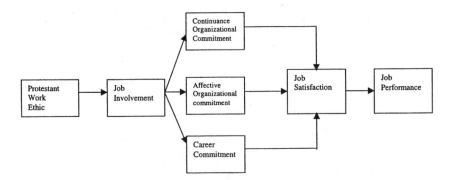

FIG. 5.8.   Carmeli and Freund's model. From Carmeli, A., & Freund, A. (2001). *Five universal forms of work commitment, job satisfaction, and job performance: An empirical assessment.*Paper presented at the Annual Academy of Management Meetings, OB Division, Washington, DC. Copyright © 2001. Reprinted with permission.

continuance organizational commitment were related to job satisfaction that was in turn related to subjective job performance.

Conclusions

The studies surveyed in this chapter gave no empirical support to Morrow's model regarding the interrelations among the commitment foci. The main reason for this nonsupport is the role of job involvement in the first study (Cohen, 1999a) and the role of job involvement and group commitment in the second (Cohen, 2000). Morrow suggested that job involvement was more situation-affected than any other commitment form, and therefore, was the endogenous variable. The data of the first study (Cohen, 1999a) strongly rule out this argument. They poorly fitted with Morrow's model regardless of the continuance commitment dimensions applied, the modification indexes all indicated that the model would improve its fit if job involvement were not an endogenous variable, and substantial improvement was effected in the revised model when job involvement was placed as a mediator.

Job involvement is possibly not a situationally dependent variable, as Morrow (1993) argued. From other research, Blau and Boal (1989) argued that job involvement is a more stable work attitude than is organizational commitment in the sense that job involvement may be more difficult to change. They argued that several behavioral scientists (e.g., Lodhal, 1964; Siegal, 1969) noted that individual differences in job involvement can be traced to orientations toward work early in the person's socialization process, such as early school experiences. Longitudinal research designs are needed to deal with the issue of which commitment focus is more stable than others. Such designs are needed also to test the possibility suggested by Morrow (1993) of reciprocal causation over time among the commitment foci. Future research should also test Morrow's model without group commitment, which was found to have a poor relation with all other commitment foci that were tested.

The findings described here strongly support Randall and Cote's (1991) argument that job involvement seems to be a key mediating variable in the interrelations among work commitment constructs. The fit indexes for Randall and Cote's model in both studies and the fit indices of the revised model in the second study support this conclusion. The proximity and time line explanations regarding the commitment foci interrelations seem not to have empirical support. Instead, the notion of exchange was supported as the main rationale for the mediating role of job involvement. That is, commitment foci that represent cultural and socialization effects such as PWE affect job involvement. However, its relation with the other commitment foci, in particular the two organizational commitment forms, is affected by the kind and type of exchange relation developed in the work setting. Employees who are highly involved in their job have more positive work experiences, attributed to organizational officials or their career decision, and reciprocate with higher commitment to these foci.

Several specific conclusions regarding particular commitment forms are worth noting. These comments should be considered in future research-examining models of commitment forms. The conclusions are in regard to three forms: continuance organizational commitment, group commitment, and career commitment.

Continuance Organizational Commitment

Cohen's (1999a) findings also show that the models operate differently in terms of their fit and the structural coefficients depending on whether the full continuance commitment scale or each of its dimension is used. The question of which two dimensions best represent continuance commitment is important because it has to be decided which dimension of continuance organizational commitment should be included as the universal form. The results described in this chapter do not facilitate such a decision. The discriminant analysis findings showed a better fit with the "low sacrifices" dimension. The structural models showed that the Randall and Cote (1991) model had the best fit with the "personal sacrifices" dimension of continuance commitment. As for the revised models, Morrow's (1993) revised model was shown to fit best with the "personal sacrifices" dimension, whereas Randall and Cote's revised model fitted best with the full scale of continuance commitment. Clearly, future research must resolve this issue.

Conceptually, "personal sacrifices" fits better into the universal forms of work commitment because the "low alternatives" dimension seems to represent cognitions of withdrawal from the workplace, which is more an outcome variable than a commitment focus. The correlations showing that "low alternatives" is related to variables that are turnover correlates, such as tenure, years in the occupation, and job satisfaction (Cotton & Tuttle, 1986) partially support this contention. The concept of continuance commitment as presented by Meyer and Allen (1984) is based on Becker's (1960) conceptualization. Becker suggested that commitment to a course of action develops as one makes side bets that would be lost if the action discontinued. These side-bets represent potential costs of leaving the organization. The "personal sacrifices" dimension seems to capture Becker's idea of potential costs more than does the "low alternatives" one, as reflected in "It would not be too costly for me to leave my organization in the near future." The inclusion of the "personal sacrifices" dimension and not the "low alternatives" one can ease the difficulty of the other four commitment foci all representing affective or cognitive components of attitudes, although the continuance commitment dimension has a behavioral intent or cognitive emphasis.

Brief and Roberson (1989) showed that each of the attitude components may have differential determinants and consequences. Omitting the strongest behavioral intention component from the continuance commitment dimension increases consistency among the commitment forms in representing all the same attitudinal components. Before any of the dimensions is used, however, items have to be added to the three-item scale ordinarily used to increase its reliability for integration with the other forms of commitment (Somers, 1993).

Career Commitment

These findings seem to substantiate the notion that in work commitment models, organizational commitment is an endogenous variable, PWE an exogenous variable, and job involvement mediates this relation. On the assumption that these conclusions are confirmed in future research, the role of career commitment needs to be settled. Findings from the Randall and Cote (1991) model and the two revised models suggest two options. First, career commitment is an endogenous variable in the interrelations together with the two forms of organizational commitment, as suggested by Randall and Cote (1991) and presented in Fig. 5.3. Second, career commitment mediates the relationship between job involvement and organizational commitment, as the revised model (Fig. 5.4) shows. Future research and theoretical work should resolve this issue. Such research is also needed to validate the revised models, which should be tested with new data before any firm conclusions about them are made.

Group Commitment

The findings question the usefulness of group commitment as one of the commitment foci in terms of the relationship with work outcomes. This was demonstrated by the few significant paths of this focus with any other commitment foci and by the nonsignificant relation of this focus with any of the work outcomes. This finding was consistent across all the models tested. The group commitment focus was included by Randall and Cote (1991) but not by Morrow (1993). Even in Randall and Cote's study, the relation of group commitment with other commitment foci was modest or nonsignificant. Randall and Cote raised some doubts about the need to include group commitment as one of the commitment foci in a work commitment model. They suggested that group commitment is related to organizational commitment only when work-group and organizational goals are compatible.

The findings, together with those of Randall and Cote (1991), suggest that in what Morrow termed a *universal model of commitment forms*, group commitment is not an essential focus. The findings here strengthen such a conclusion because they were collected from a sample of nurses, for whom the work group is an essential component of the work setting. One cannot argue that the reason for the weak place of group commitment is that this focus is not relevant in this particular work setting. Such an argument could perhaps have been advanced in Randall and Cote's study, where the data were collected from staff at a large university. An interesting dilemma for future research and theoretical developments is which commitment focus should replace group commitment? Is it continuance organizational commitment, as Morrow suggested, is it another form of commitment, or is four commitment foci enough for a universal model of commitments?

Briefly, the main conclusion of the this research is that the idea of examining how commitment foci are related to each other, and whether and how some commitment forms are determinants or consequences of other forms, received empirical support in Cohen's studies (1999a, 2000) and in later studies (Hackett et al., 2001; Carmeli & Freund, 2001). These studies clearly showed that Randall and Cote's earlier model (Randall & Cote, 1991) or their revised one (Cohen, 1999a) provides the best characterization of the interrelations among commitment forms. In these interrelations the role of job involvement as mediator is essential. This perhaps explains the modest relation between job involvement and work outcomes (Brown, 1996). Job involvement does not relate directly to outcomes but is related to commitment foci such as the organization and career, and these two forms are related to outcomes. Commitment foci are related to each other in two possible ways. First, job involvement mediates the relation between forms of commitment across all settings. In this case, the models that were supported in Cohen's studies are supported in any examination of commitment foci and their relation to outcomes. The second possible way, however, which is discussed in chapter 6, is that different models will be required for different outcomes. That is, the interrelations among commitment foci differ depending on the outcome examined. Job involvement mediates the relation among commitment foci in the case of turnover, and another commitment focus might mediate this relation in the case of another outcome, such as organizational citizenship behavior. These questions should be examined in future research.

Several other steps are desirable in future research to establish the validity of Randall and Cote's (1991) model. First, the findings presented in this chapter should be replicated in other samples and work settings. Consistent results across different settings are important to support the discriminant validity of these forms' and the nature of their interrelations. Vandenberg and Scarpello (1994) argued that some settings may value an occupation more or less than others, and the strength of the occupational/organizational commitment relation may vary as a function of setting. Future studies need to identify the moderating characteristics of the setting and how they influence this relation. The fact that Randall and Cote's model was supported in two different cultures, Canadian and Israeli, might indicate that the model is unaffected by culture. However, much more research is needed to support this argument.

An important related issue is the measures for the different constructs. The research presented here apply measures that are extensively used in commitment research. But measures different from the constructs applied in these studies should also be tested. Such research assists in determining whether the findings were affected by the way commitment foci were measured. If the findings prove consistent across different measures of commitment, this strengthens the conceptual conclusion of the superiority of Randall and Cote's model. Most of the research that examined the interrelations among commitment forms has applied cross-sectional design. More research is needed that will use longitudinal designs. Such a design enables a more accurate testing of the direction of the relations among commitment foci. For example, it enables a more precise testing of whether it is job involvement (measured in time 1) that affect organizational commitment (measured in time 2), or perhaps the direction of the relation is the opposite; organizational commitment, measured in time 1, affect job involvement, measured in time 2. In addition, understanding how commitment foci develop and highlighting the factors related to tenure that cause changes in commitment would help managers optimize the commitment of their employees (Beck & Wilson, 2001). Some important suggestions for performing longitudinal research on multiple commitments were advanced by Beck and Wilson (2001).

IV

Trends in Multiple Commitment Research

6

Commitment Forms and Work Outcomes

The importance of this topic rests on the argument that work commitment cannot be established as a valuable concept unless it can be verified as one that affects major work outcomes in the work environment. That is, continued interest in multiple commitments depends on whether commitments predict employees' behavior in the workplace. Moreover, a stronger expectation is that in a multiple commitment model, more than one commitment will be related to outcomes. This is an important justification for studying multiple commitments rather than only one. In fact, a reason for the interest in the relation between multiple commitments and outcomes is the disappointing results obtained in terms of the relation between commitment forms examined separately and outcomes. Despite constant concern about the limited conceptual frame used to study work-related commitment, most studies have included only one form of commitment (Somers & Birnbaum, 1998).

The very moderate relation between commitment forms examined separately and outcomes was powerfully demonstrated in meta-analyses that summarized these relations. Mathieu and Zajac (1990) who examined organizational commitment (OC) reported a corrected correlation of $r = .13$ (based on 10 samples) of this form with job performance measured by other ratings, and of $r = .05$ (based on 6 samples) with job performance measured by output measures. The corrected correlation was with attendance (23 samples) $r = .10$, lateness $r = .12$, and turnover (26 samples) $r = -.28$. Griffeth, Hom, and Gaertner (2000) reported a corrected correlation of $-.27$ of OC with turnover, similar to the result of Mathieu and Zajac, but based on 67 samples. These are not strong relations, and this holds particularly for turnover, which is considered the main outcome that should be predicted by OC (Mowday et al., 1982).

Several additional meta-analyses tested the relation of OC, with outcomes controlled by several methodological and conceptual moderators such as the measurement of commitment (Cohen, 1993d; Mathieu & Zajac, 1990; Griffeth et al., 2000), age and tenure (Cohen, 1991; Cohen, 1993d), or type of occupation (Cohen & Hudecek, 1993). They found somewhat stronger relations between OC and some outcomes. Note also that the relations between OC and attitudinal outcomes, such as withdrawal cognitions were higher than between commitment and behavioral outcomes, for example, $r = -.41$ with intention to leave (36 samples) and $r = -.48$ with intentions to search (five samples). However, the relatively low correlations with the behavioral outcomes led Randall (1990) even to question the usefulness of examining OC.

The findings are not much different in the relation between other commitment forms and outcomes. A thorough meta-analysis by Brown (1996) on the relation between job involvement and correlates revealed more problematic relations between this form and outcomes, for example, a corrected correlation of $r = .09$ with overall performance (25 samples) and $r = .04$ (4 samples out of 25) with objective measures of per- formance; and a corrected correlation of $r = -.14$ with absenteeism (17 samples) and $r = -.13$ with turnover (based on 11 samples). A similar corrected correlation with turnover ($r = -.12$) was found by Griffeth et al. (2000) based on 16 samples. Here too, the corrected correlations with attitudinal outcomes were higher, $r = .25$ (7 samples) with effort and $r = -.31$ (23 samples) with turnover intentions, but they were lower than those between OC and attitudinal outcomes.

Lee et al. (2000), in their meta-analysis, also reported relatively low correlations between occupational commitment and outcomes. The corrected correlation with turnover was $r = -.21$ (8 samples), with supervisor rated performance $r = .22$ (5 samples). As in the case of OC and job involvement, the corrected correlations were higher with attitudinal outcomes. The correlations were $r = -.62$ with occupational turnover intentions (18 samples) and $r = -.30$ with organizational turnover intentions (27 samples). To date no meta-analysis has been performed for the other commitment forms, but the reported correlations between other commitment forms such as PWE and group commitment with outcomes were not much different from those just mentioned.

The data exemplify the problem faced by commitment scholars, namely, weak relations between each separate commitment focus and work outcomes. It is not easy to justify research on work attitudes that do not predict behaviors that, according to theory, they are expected to predict. This has led some researchers to consider the possibility that examining the relation between multiple commitments and outcomes improves the prediction of behaviors at work by commitment forms. Several explanations were advanced to support this contention. Wiener and Vardi (1980) asserted that because individuals in a work setting simultaneously experience varying degrees of commitment to several aspects of working life (e.g., the employing organization, the job or task, personal career), work outcomes may be better understood as a function of all such commitment types rather than of one or another separately. They argued that because different objects of commitment forms represent distinct attitudes, different effects on behavioral outcomes could be expected. Steers and Rhodes (1978) contended that work outcomes such as absenteeism could be understood as a result of conflict among commitments. When employees are committed to factors other than the organization inside or outside the work environment they experience less internal pressure to go to work.

Proposed linkages between commitment and outcomes were initially driven by the properties ascribed to each form of work related commitment. That is, one of the hypothesized benefits of being committed at work (job, career, and/or organization) is improved job performance (Somers & Birnbaum, 1998). The logic or theory as to why commitment forms should be related to outcomes follows the exchange approach. Employees who experienced positive exchanges with the organization, job, or the work group reciprocate with higher levels of commitment, which moves them to contribute to the organization in other ways, such as lower turnover, absenteeism, or better performance. This logic can be attached to the rationale for examining multiple commitments.

This indicates that commitment forms are a useful indicator of the quality of individuals' experiences in their work roles. Nonetheless, not much research has empirically examined the joint effect of commitment forms on work outcomes (Mowday et al., 1982; Cohen, 1999a). As mentioned previously this is surprising because the main justification for continuing research on multiple commitment should be its effect on work outcomes. Moreover, it should be demonstrated that a multivariate approach to commitment could predict work outcomes better than each commitment could do separately (Cohen, 1993a). This has been examined quite rarely.

Studies that examined multiple commitments in their relations to outcomes can be categorized into two groups. The first is studies that used a direct approach to the relation between commitment forms and outcomes. That is, several commitments were tested in their relation to outcomes, often by means of statistical analyses with multiple variables, particularly multiple regressions. The second and more recent and complex approach proposes and tests models dealing with the interrelations among commitment forms and the way these relations affect work outcomes. The usual method is path analysis. The presentation and analysis here of research on the commitment-outcomes relation follows this categorization.

Direct Approach

The direct approach relies on the testing of several commitment forms in their relation to work outcomes. No assumptions are made of any mediation or moderation processes among commitment foci. This approach assumes that several commitment forms should be related to work outcomes for the reasons listed earlier. In most of the cases this approach examined the relationship among three or more forms of commitment together, and one or more work outcomes, each taken separately. Much of the knowledge acquired so far on the relation between multiple commitments and outcomes is based on this approach. Because most research on separate commitment forms has been on OC, this form is naturally included in almost any study that examined the commitment forms-outcomes relation. However, by advancing the notion of multiple commitments researchers expected that commitment foci other than OC would also explain some variations in work outcomes (Wiener & Vardi, 1980). In fact, research demonstrated the effect of other commitment forms such as job involvement (Blau & Boal, 1989) and career or occupational commitment (Wiener & Vardi, 1980) on outcomes. Therefore, most of the literature regarding multiple commitments has traditionally included some or all of the three forms of commitment: organization, job, and occupation.

Later research covered other forms of commitment, including those rarely examined in the context of multiple commitments. PWE and work involvement represent work values, and these have been very rarely examined in the context of the commitment-outcomes relationship, although indications for such a relation exist. Work ethic measures, for example, were found to be important moderators between situational factors such as job characteristics and work reactions (Morrow, 1983). The essence of PWE is the belief that hard work is intrinsically good, as an end in itself. One's personal worth and moral stature are to be gauged by willingness to work hard (Morrow, 1983). This leads one to expect a positive linkage between PWE and performance measures. Kanungo (1979, 1982) developed the concept of work involvement, that emphasized the difference between this construct and job involvement on the one hand and Protestant work ethic on the other hand. Work involvement is also expected to be related to outcomes.

Other commitment foci that have rarely been examined for their relation to outcomes as part of the multiple commitment concepts are group commitment and union commitment. Becker (1992) adopted Reichers's (1985) view of the importance of group commitment, and in an empirical examination, found some interesting correlations between group commitment and various measures of performance. Becker's work is one of the few to test group commitment in relation to outcomes, and it showed a promising relation.

As for union commitment, Gordon, Philpot, Burt, Thompson, and Spiller (1980) argued that the ability of union locals to attain their goals is generally based on the loyalty of members. In this sense, commitment is part of the very fabric of the union. Martin (1986) examined propensity to strike and confirmed the usefulness of the commitment concept in explaining strike support. He based this conclusion on his findings that variables that other studies had found to be related to commitment were significantly associated with a willingness to strike in support of the union. Other studies also found meaningful relations between union commitment and perceived union effectiveness (Liebowitz, 1983), union participation (Fullagar & Barling, 1989; Thacker, Fields, & Barclay, 1990); union militancy (Black, 1983), and union grievance-filing behavior (Dalton & Todor, 1981).

Conceptual Framework. Three conceptual frameworks were advanced to explain the type of relation between commitment forms and outcomes. The most common framework argued that commitment forms would be related differently to various outcomes. This approach argues that the type of work-related commitment under consideration might have some bearing on how commitment might direct behavior in organizations (Somers & Birnbaum, 1998; Shore, Newton, & Thornton, 1990; Siders et al., 2001). As different objects of work commitment represent distinct attitudes, differential effects on behavioral outcomes can be expected. Therefore, researchers should attempt to match the focus of their independent variable with the focus of their work outcome variable (Becker, 1992).

Given that the object of OC is the employing organization, the most likely behavior to be affected by this commitment is organization-oriented behavior such as turnover intentions, actual turnover (Mowday et al., 1982), absenteeism, and organizational citizenship behavior, particularly the compliance dimension. Similarly, the most likely behavior to be affected by job involvement is task-oriented behaviors such as organizational citizenship behavior and performance. Job involvement is also expected to have a stronger relation with absenteeism than with OC, in keeping with previous empirical evidence (Blau, 1986). Behaviors that are expected to be related to occupational commitment are occupation or career-oriented behavior such as withdrawal cognitions and actual withdrawal from the occupation. One should note in that regard there is some support in the literature for commitments affecting behaviors that are not directly related to the focus of that given commitment. Alutto and Belasco (1974) for example, found negative relations between OC and attitudinal militancy among teachers and nurses. Dalton and Todor (1982) found that grievance-filing behavior was more a function of a negative relation with OC than of a positive relation with union commitment.

An important argument related to this approach is that the relation between commitment forms and work outcomes is not direct, but is mediated by behavioral intentions. Although this assumption has its roots in the literature that examined the relation between commitment forms and outcomes separately, it also seems to affect research on the multiple commitment-outcomes relation. This tendency arises from strong evidence that the relationship between attitudes—commitment foci in our case, and behaviors, turnover and absenteeism in our case—is not direct. Mobley (1977) and Mobley, Griffeth, Hand, and Meglino (1979) suggested a linear process model where an individual's low work attitudes cause thoughts of quitting an organization, leading to intention to search for other employment, which causes the formation of an intention to leave or stay, and finally, quitting. Research has generally supported the perspective that employees engage in a hierarchically ordered sequence of withdrawal, where declining attitudes (e.g., commitment, turnover intentions) precede temporary withdrawal (absenteeism), and these episodes foreshadow permanent withdrawal (actual turnover; Farrell & Petersen, 1984; Parasuraman, 1982; Rosse, 1988).

Cohen (1998; 1999b) advanced another explanation for the differential relation between commitment forms and outcomes. This is that one way to conceptualize the distinction among commitment forms, as suggested by Blau et al. (1993), is on a timeline. Job involvement and OC have a more immediate focus, occupational commitment is intermediate, and PWE and work involvement are the longest term. To expand this distinction, the organization, job, and occupation provide more specific, definite, and concrete foci in terms of their relation to the immediate work setting. PWE and work involvement are more abstract and general in terms of their relations to the work setting. PWE and work involvement should have some effect on work outcomes. People who believe in hard work and in the value of work would be expected to demonstrate it in their behavior at work. However, because the foci of these commitments are more general as compared with the organization, job, and occupation foci their effect is expected to be weaker than these commitments.

An interesting and fruitful explanation, the third one, was advanced by Vandenberg and Scarpello (1994) who argued that some settings may value an occupation more or less than others, and the strength of the occupational or organizational commitment relation may vary as a function of setting. There is a need to identify the moderating characteristics of the setting and how they influence this relation. If one is more strongly committed to the occupation than to the organization, it is expected that this commitment is related to outcomes stronger than OC. Another employee may be more firmly committed to the organization than to the occupation; here it is expected that OC affects her or his behavior (Somers & Birnbaum, 1998) more strongly than does occupational commitment.

Research Findings on the Direct-Relationship Approach

Table 6.1 presents a summary of the findings of research that examined the relation between commitment forms and outcomes. As can be seen in the table, Wiener and Vardi's (1980) study was one of the first to test the relation between multiple commitments and outcomes. Considering that their scales predicted effort and attachment in their samples, and more than one form was related to these variables in most of the cases, Wiener and Vardi (1980) seem to have successfully demonstrated the utility of applying multiple commitments to predict outcomes. Their research provided the basis for many studies on the relation between multiple commitments and outcomes. Yet, some of the findings can be attributed to the commitment scales applied in that research, obsolete scales that have hardly been used in other commitment research.

Cohen in three studies (1993a, 1998, 1999b) followed Wiener and Vardi's research and tested the relationship between commitment forms and outcomes. As Table 6.1 shows, Cohen found divergent relations between commitment forms and outcomes, a result that supports the findings of Wiener and Vardi (1980). Cohen's studies demonstrated the usefulness of occupational and career commitments as important predictors among commitment measures and the usefulness of multiple commitments as a predictor of union effectiveness, thus supporting Martin's (1986) argument regarding the usefulness of the commitment concept in predicting union effectiveness.

It must be stated that Cohen's first two studies (1993a, 1998) had their own limitations, the main one being that most of the outcomes examined in them were not actual behaviors but were intentions of behaviors. Moreover, absenteeism in the later study (Cohen, 1998) was measured by a self-report measure that did not cover different types of absenteeism as earlier research proposed (Mathieu & Kohler, 1990). The design could have been firmer, with actual turnover and performance being measured in addition to the three withdrawal intentions and perceived performance. The strong relation between withdrawal intentions and actual turnover (Steel & Ovalle, 1984) decreases the impact of not measuring actual turnover.

In the later study, Cohen (1999b) examined the relation between commitment forms and attitudinal and behavioral outcomes. The commitment scales in this study were already established. Organizational commitment was measured by the shorter nine-item version of the OCQ (Porter et al., 1974). Career commitment was measured by the eight-item measure devel-

TABLE 6.1

Relationship Between Commitment Forms and Outcomes

Studies	Sample	Commitment Forms that Were Examined	Outcomes that Were Examined	Main Findings	Magnitude of Relationship
Wiener & Vardi (1980)	56 insurance sales agent in three insurance companies in a Midwestern city	Job commitment, calculative organizational commitment, normative organizational commitment, career commitment	Effort, attachment, performance and satisfaction from work (JDI)	Job commitment was related to effort and calculative organizational commitment was related to attachment. One or two commitment forms were related to various forms of satisfaction. Job commitment and career commitment (negatively) were related to performance	R-square was .21 for effort, .24 for attachment, and .17 (not significance) for performance. It ranged between .27 to .13 for the various satisfaction scales
Wiener & Vardi (1980)	85 staff professionals employed at the headquarters of a chemical-manufacturing firm	Job commitment, calculative organizational commitment, normative organizational commitment, career commitment	Effort, attachment, and satisfaction from work (JDI)	Job commitment and two scales of organizational commitment were related to effort and attachment. One or two commitment forms were related to various forms of satisfaction	R-square was .34 for effort and attachment and ranged between .19 to .01 for the various satisfactions scales
Cohen (1993)	129 white-collar employees from across Israel (e.g., engineers, practical engineers, technicians, administrative personnel)	Organizational commitment, occupational commitment, job commitment, union commitment	Organization, job, and occupation withdrawal intention, union activity, union militancy, and union success	Organizational and occupational commitment were related to organizational withdrawal intention. Job and occupational commitment were related to job withdrawal intentions. Job commitment was related to occupational withdrawal intentions. Union commitment was the strongest predictor of union activity, union militancy, and union success. In addition, job commitment positively affected union activity, and occupational commitment negatively affected union success	R-square was .10 for job withdrawal intentions, .24 for occupation withdrawal intentions, and .36 for organization withdrawal intentions. R-square was .20 for union activity, .13 for union militancy, and .11 for union success

Study	Sample	Commitment forms	Outcomes	Findings	Results
Cohen (1998)	238 nurses from two hospitals in Western Canada	Organizational commitment, job involvement, Occupational commitment, work involvement, Protestant work ethic	Intentions to leave the organization, job, occupation, absenteeism, perceived performance, job-induced tension	Organizational and occupational commitment were related to intentions to leave the organization. The above two together with Protestant work ethic (negatively) were related to intentions to leave the job. Occupational commitment was related to intentions to leave the occupation. Organizational commitment and job involvement (positively) were related to absenteeism. Job involvement (positively) and occupational commitment were related to job-induced tension. None was related to perceived performance	R-square was .30 for intentions to leave the organization, .27 for intentions to leave the job, and .38 for intentions to leave the occupation. R-square was .04 for absenteeism and .06 for job induced tension
Cohen (1999b)	283 nurses at three hospitals in northern Israel	Organizational commitment, job involvement, Occupational commitment, work involvement, Protestant work ethic	Actual turnover, intentions to leave the organization, job, occupation, absenteeism frequency, absenteeism duration, Organizational citizenship behavior (OCB), life satisfaction	Occupational commitment was related to actual turnover. Occupational and organizational commitment were related to turnover intentions from the organization and the job. Occupational commitment and work involvement (positively) were related to intentions to leave the occupation. Work involvement was related to absence frequency and organizational commitment to absence duration. All forms except group commitment were related to OCB and all forms except work involvement were related to life satisfaction	R-square was .04 for the two measures of absenteeism. It ranged between .30 to .50 for the three turnover intention scales. R-square was .29 for OCB and .12 for life satisfaction. For actual turnover logistic regression showed that the percentage of cases correctly predicted was 92.8%
Somers & Birnbaum (1998)	109 hospital employees drawn from a university teaching hospital located in the southeastern US	Job commitment, career commitment, and organizational commitment	Supervisor-rated task proficiency, extra role performance, disciplinary actions in each employees' file	Career commitment (positively) and job commitment (negatively) were related to task proficiency. Job commitment was the only predictor of extra-role behavior. None of the commitment forms were related to disciplinary actions	R-square was .08 for task proficiency and extra-role behavior. R-square was .03 (not significance) for disciplinary actions

continued on next page

169

TABLE 6.1 (continued)

Studies	Sample	Commitment Forms that Were Examined	Outcomes that Were Examined	Main Findings	Magnitude of Relationship
McElroy, Morrow, Power and Iqbal (1993)	166 insurance agents attending continuing education seminars in a US rural Midwestern state	Job involvement, professional commitment, and community commitment	Intention to remain in profession and performance as measured by self-reported income	ANCOVA results showed that job involvement and professional commitment were related to intention to stay in the profession. Only professional commitment was related to performance. An interaction of job involvement and community commitment was also related to performance	Job involvement and professional commitment explained each 3.4% of intention to remain in profession. Professional commitment explained 19.2% of performance and the interaction of job involvement and community commitment explained 3.7% of performance
Gregeren (1993)	290 non-management employees from health care professions and administrative services from two hospitals	Organizational commitment, Commitment to supervisor, commitment to top management, commitment to co-workers, commitment to customers	Extra role behavior	Organizational commitment and commitment to supervisor were related to extra role behavior for employees with 2-8 years of tenure (advancement career stage); commitment to supervisor and commitment to top management (negatively) were related to extra role-behavior foe employees with 8+ years of tenure (Maintenance career stage). None of the commitments were related to extra role behavior for employees with less than 2 years of tenure (establishment career stage)	Commitment forms explained 21% of the variance for employees with 2-8 years of tenure. They explained 11% of the variance for employees with 8+ years of tenure
Becker (1992)	440 employees of a military supply company who respondent to two waves of the survey	Commitment to immediate supervisors, commitment to top management, commitment to immediate work-groups, organizational commitment	Intent to quit, prosocial organizational behavior	Organizational commitment separately, and the other foci of commitment as a block were related to intent to quit. Organizational commitment separately, and the other foci of commitment as a block were related to overall prosocial behavior and to its dimensions such as altruism, conscientiousness, and idleness	R-square was .42 for intent to quit, .17 for overall prosocial behavior. It was .15 for altruism, .12 for conscientiousness, and .18 for idleness

Study	Sample	Commitment variables	Outcome	Results	Variance explained
Chang (1999)	227 researchers working for 8 business or economic research institutes in Korea	Continuance organizational commitment, affective organizational commitment, career commitment	Turnover intentions	All three commitments showed significant negative effects on turnover intention. A significant interaction effect was detected between career and affective commitment on turnover but not between career and continuance commitment	R-square for the equation of the three commitments was .53. R-square for the significant interaction was .05
Becker, Randall, & Riegel (1995)	112 crew members, supervisors, and assistant managers of 16 restaurants of the same fast-service chain in Seattle, Washington	Normative commitment to the organization, normative commitment to restaurant management, normative commitment to non-managerial employees, and overall compliance without regard to foci	Altruism, tardiness, intent to altruism, intent to punctuality	Employees normative commitment was related to intent-altruism ($p < .10$); Organization-normative was related to intent-punctuality; Store management-normative, and employees-normative was related to altruism; Employees-normative and compliance was related to tardiness	Commitment variables explained about 11% of intent-altruism, 12% of intent-punctuality, 10% of altruism, and 14% of tardiness. The explained variance above was over and above the variance explained by demographic variables
Boshoff & Mels (2000)	382 chartered accountants, teachers and office administrative personnel	Organizational commitment, professional commitment, supervisor commitment, job involvement	Intentions to resign	Results of path analysis showed that the path coefficients from organizational (–.40) and professional (–.43) commitment to intentions to resign were significant and in the predicted direction. The two other paths were not significant	The four commitments model explained 56.2% of the variation in intentions to resign
Becker, Billings, Eveleth, & Gilbert (1996)	281 members of the May 1993 graduating class of a large Northwestern university	Supervisor-related identification, supervisor-related internalization, organizational identification, and organizational internalization	Job performance	Supervisor-related internalization and organizational internalization (negatively) were related to job performance	Commitment variables explained 4% of the variance over and above the variance explained by control variables (age, gender, tenure, and impression management). The overall explained variance was 6%

continued on next page

TABLE 6.1 *(continued)*

Studies	Sample	Commitment Forms that Were Examined	Outcomes that Were Examined	Main Findings	Magnitude of Relationship
Desrochers & Dahir (2000)	210 employees working in 17 firms in western US and members in one of 10 professional/vocational categories	Organizational commitment, professional commitment and career advancement motivation	Turnover intentions	With job satisfaction as control variable that has a significant coefficient, organizational commitment and career advancement motivation were also significantly related to turnover intentions. Professional commitment was not related to turnover intentions	All variables including job satisfaction explained 46% of the variance of turnover intentions
Bashaw & Grant (1994)	560 industrial salespeople from 16 companies operating primarily in the Southeastern US	Organizational commitment, job commitment and career commitment	Performance (self-reported) and propensity to leave	Career commitment and job commitment were positively related to performance. Organizational commitment was not related to it. Organizational commitment (negatively) and career commitment (positively) were related to propensity to leave. Job commitment was not related to it	Career and job commitment explained 4% of performance variance; Organizational and career commitment explained 48% of the variance of propensity to leave
Vandenberghe, Stinglhamber, Benstein & Delhaise (2001)	580 employees pertained to 12 European nationalities working for the translation department of the European Commission in Brussels	Affective and normative commitments to the organization, the occupation, the work group, and Europe; continuance commitment to the organization and the occupation	Intent to quit the European Commission	Intent to quit was explained by organizational as well as nonorganizational commitment components. Among the significant relationships, those involving affective bonds were dominant. The continuance commitment component toward the organization and occupation was significantly related to intent to quit across all cultural dimensions. No normative commitment components were related to intent to quit	Path analysis model that allowed all paths from commitment foci to be freely estimated explained 47% of the variance in intent to quit The constrained model, which specified no influence from nonorganizational components explained 41%

Siders, George, & Dharwadkar (2001)	328 sales executives employed in four sales organizations in the orthopedic implant industry	Attitudinal commitment to the organization, supervisor, and customer	Sales volume, growth rate, new accounts, product breadth, and market share	Commitment to organization and supervisor were both related to sales volume. Commitment to organization was related to product breadth (negatively) and commitment to the supervisor to growth rate and new accounts. Commitment to customer was related to product breadth and marker share	Commitment to organization and supervisor explained both 32% of sales volume. Commitment to the organization explained 1% of product breadth. Commitment to supervisor explained 10% and 19% of growth rate and new accounts respectively. Commitment to supervisor explained 4% and 17% of product breadth and market share

oped by Blau (1985). Job involvement (10 items) and work involvement (6 items) were measured by the scales developed by Kanungo (1979, 1982). Group commitment was measured by the six-item measure developed by Randall and Cote (1991). The findings clearly showed that commitment forms better predicted attitudinal outcomes such as turnover intentions, organizational citizenship behavior, and life satisfaction than did behavioral outcomes such as turnover and absenteeism. Cohen's (1999b) results, presented in Table 6.1, also showed that in the case of the attitudinal outcomes more than one commitment form predicted each of these attitudes. The expectation fulfilled in earlier studies, that each commitment form would be related to the relevant outcome variable, was partially fulfilled by Cohen's (1999b) data. The negative relation of OC to absence duration and its strong positive relation to citizenship behavior supported the logic of this expectation. Note the pattern of the relation between the outcomes and work involvement. Work involvement increased absence frequency and intentions to leave the occupation and decreased organizational citizenship behavior. This finding contradicted the expected favorable relation between commitment forms and outcomes.

A different group of studies on the relation between multiple commitments and outcomes, also shown in Table 6.1, was that conducted by Becker (1992). This research however, examined constituencies of OC for their relationship to work outcomes. As described in earlier chapters, Becker relied on Reichers's (1985) approach, which defined multiple commitments as components of OC. Therefore, it is hard to generalize from Becker's findings to those presented earlier on the relation between commitment forms and outcomes. Becker's (1992) first study illustrates this point. In his analysis, Becker tested the relation of OC, other foci of commitment, and bases of commitment to work outcomes such as organizational citizenship behavior and turnover intentions. Examined were OC, based on Porter et al.'s scale, commitment to top management, supervisor, and work group. The last three commitment foci were measured by one item.

Clearly, these foci, and the way some of them were measured, are not what this volume defines as multiple commitments. The problem is that commitments to the other foci were measured by one item per focus. Moreover, Becker (1992) presented the contribution of the foci of commitment as a group and not as the contribution of each focus. The same applied to the bases of commitment. This presentation does not permit an evaluation of the effect of each focus of commitment on outcomes. Becker's main finding is thus quite general in terms of multiple commitment. Other foci of commitment, as well as bases of commitment, contribute to the understanding of organizational citizenship behavior and turnover intentions. We do not know which of the foci of commitment or bases of commitment affect outcomes more than the others—or if they do at all.

In another study, Becker et al. (1995) examined the relationship between commitment forms, defined slightly differently from the formulation in the earlier work (Becker, 1992), and altruism, a dimension of organizational citizenship behavior, and tardiness. In a later study using the same conceptual framework, Becker et al. (1996) examined the relation of foci and bases of commitment to performance as measured by the evaluation of the immediate supervisor. Several items measured the commitments to the organization and to the immediate supervisor (the two forms that were tested). In addition, the reported analysis was more detailed and allowed evaluation of the contribution of specific commitments. A good, clear design and presentation of Reichers's approach was performed by Gregersen (1993) (see Table 6.6) who tested the relation of multiple commitments, for example, to organization, supervisor, top management, co-workers, and customers with extra-role behavior. Organizational commitment was measured by Porter et al.'s scale. The other foci were measured by modifications of that scale, mainly by the substitution of the word "organization" by the names of the other foci as relevant.

Siders et al. (2001) followed Beckers, approach and examined the relation between commitment to the organization, the supervisor, and the customer and a set of objective performance measures such as sales volume, growth rate, and product breadth (see Table 6.1). This is perhaps one of the best implementations of Becker's work in terms of the relation between commitment foci and outcomes because of two reasons. The first reason is because objective performance measures were used; the second is because multiple items were used to measure each of the aforementioned commitments. The findings were also promising in terms of the variance explained by commitment foci, 32% of the variance of sales volume were explained, for example, by commitments to the organization and the supervisor

Becker's (1992) and Becker's et al.'s (1996) findings, as presented in Table 6.1, are interesting, but their contribution to the understanding of commitment foci-outcomes relation is limited. The problems of this approach presented by Reichers were reviewed thoroughly in earlier chapters and there is no need to repeat them. These problems are relevant to the findings regarding the relation between commitment forms as defined by Becker and outcomes. The main conclusion that can be reached from the work of Becker and his associates is that dimensions of OC, or constituencies of OC, are related to work outcomes. But we do not know what the relative contribution of these constituencies is, compared with constituencies of other commitment foci such as the occupation, or with multiple commitments as conceptualized and defined here.

An interesting and fruitful demonstration of the direct approach was advanced by Bishop et al. (2000), who used structural equation modeling to test the effect of two commitment forms, organizational and group commitment, on outcomes such as intent to quit, job performance, and organizational citizenship behavior. Their findings were encouraging and showed that each commitment had its unique and relatively strong effect on these outcomes. As the authors themselves concluded, more such research on the same and other commitment forms are needed to enrich the data on commitment-outcomes relation and to improve our understanding on this relation.

The findings also supported the usefulness of distinguishing different types of turnover based on the finding that commitment foci have differential relations with various forms of withdrawal intentions. Krausz, Koslowsky, Shalom, and Elyakim (1995) argued that traditional research focusing on turnover intentions out of the organization has ignored two additional turnover criteria: within-organizational turnover from one unit to another and turnover from the employee's profession. However, employees may want to continue in their current organization, albeit in a different job (Wiener & Vardi, 1980). Employees may also consider leaving their existing occupation to begin a second (new) career in a different occupation. This type of consideration is no doubt affected by the attachment the employees have developed to their occupation during their career. The findings presented in Table 6.1 support the usefulness of distinguishing the three types of turnover intentions.

The foregoing accords with earlier findings (Gardner, 1992; Reilly & Orsak, 1991) that occupational commitment is an important form of commitment and should be included in future research. Note the strong relation between occupational commitment and intention to leave the organization, occupation, and job, and the fact that occupational commitment was an important predictor in many of findings presented in Table 6.1. From the data presented, it seems that for professional employees such as nurses, the key commitment forms in respect of their attitudes and behaviors are the occupational and organizational foci. This finding is consistent with previous conceptualizations by Gouldner (1958); it also supports Gardner's (1992) conclusion, based on the strong relation between occupational commitment and outcomes, that enhancing occupational commitment produces benefits for both individuals and their employing organizations. Professionals should be encouraged through incentives to participate in professional activities and to be involved in career planning.

In short, these findings showed the usefulness and the potential of commitment forms in predicting valuable outcomes. Yet one finding to emerge is that commitment forms are more effective in predicting attitudes than behaviors. In all the attitudinal outcomes examined, several forms of commitment were clearly found to be firmly related to outcome variables rather than to one form of commitment. Thus, it is useful to examine the relation of a variety of commitment forms instead of concentrating on only one. Based on the findings, the main value of commitment lies in predicting turnover intentions. It is more limited in predicting other work outcomes such as actual turnover performance and absenteeism. The probable reason is the distinct evidence showing that the relationship between attitudes—commitment foci in our case, and behaviors, turnover and absenteeism in our case—is not direct. Research has generally supported the view that employees engage in a hierarchically ordered sequence of withdrawal, where declining attitudes (e.g., commitment, turnover intentions) precede temporary withdrawal (absenteeism) and these episodes foreshadow permanent withdrawal (actual turnover; Parasuraman, 1982; Farrell & Petersen, 1984; Rosse, 1988).

Indirect Approach

The research surveyed in the previous section assumed a direct relation between multiple commitments and multiple work outcomes, so researchers have tested hypotheses on the relative magnitude of the effect of commitment foci on outcomes. Little research has attempted to propose and test alternative conceptualizations. The weak and inconsistent linkage between commitment forms and outcomes might largely stem from a lack of understanding of how work commitment constructs interrelate. Models of the interrelations among commitment foci and their relation to outcomes may improve the disappointing relations found between commitment forms and outcomes such as tardiness (Randall & Cote, 1991). Morrow (1993) argued in that regard that a major question impeding understanding of work commitment is whether each commitment focus is independent, or whether some are antecedents and consequences of others. The nature of interrelations among forms of commitment had to be discovered without delay because evidence that one form of work commitment could moderate relations involving other forms was beginning to accumulate (Hunt & Morgan, 1994; Witt, 1993).

Yet very little research has tested whether and how given proposed interrelations among commitment foci are related to work outcomes. Only two works probing the interrelations among commitment constructs and their relation to outcomes have been conducted so far, namely, that by Hunt and Morgan (1994) and by Cohen (2000). Cohen presented and compared three models regarding the relation between commitment forms and outcomes. He tested models originally advanced by other researchers such as Morrow (1993) and Randall and Cote (1991) for the interrelations among forms of commitment. Cohen's contribution was to further develop these models to examine how the interrelations among commitment forms are related to outcomes. These models are described in the following section.

Hunt and Morgan's (1994) Model

Hunt and Morgan's (1994) model, shown in Fig. 4.7, stems from their approach as described in chapter 5. Global organizational commitment directly influences outcomes, and constituency specific commitments, such as commitment to top management and commitment to supervisor, influence outcomes only by virtue of their impact on global commitment. As can be seen in Fig. 4.7, global organizational commitment is a key mediating construct. The basic rationale for this model is that various constituencies to which an employee might be committed are top management, supervisors, work groups, and unions. Studies have generally shown significant, positive relations between commitment to these constituencies and global organizational commitment. These findings are precisely what the congruence model of organizations would suggest, namely, that the components of organizations will be consistent, or congruent. Substantial consistency is evident between most organizations' overall values and those of their components. Therefore, given the prominent role of shared values in both the development of corporate culture and the development of all forms of commitment, constituency specific commitments should contribute to global organizational commitment. According to this model, constituency specific commitments affect outcomes only because they influence global OC.

Hunt and Morgan's findings showed that the mediating role of global OC became stronger as the focus of a constituency specific commitment became more closely associated with an organization. Also, a positive relation was demonstrated by the path coefficients between global OC and dimensions of extra-role behaviors such as altruism (.21; $p \leq .001$), conscientiousness (.14; $p \leq .01$), and nonidleness (.28; $p \leq .001$); and a negative path was found between global OC and intent to quit (-.69; $p \leq .001$). Hunt and Morgan (1994) concluded that their findings needed to be replicated with outcome variables such as tardiness, attendance, and performance measures.

One should note however, that at root these authors examined the relation between OC and outcomes. As explained in chapter 5, global organizational commitment is simply OC, so from the perspective of this book what was tested was an indirect model of the relation between constituencies of OC and its outcomes. Organizational commitment is a construct that mediates this relation. Hunt and Morgan (1994) indicated a need to explore the role of other foci of commitment in their relation to outcomes. The main contribution of their work is their indication of the possibility that the relation between commitment and outcomes is not direct and their encouragement of researchers farther to test this direction. More work is needed to test how constituencies of other commitment forms, such as occupation, are related to outcomes and whether and how the specific commitment form mediates this relation.

Cohen's (2000) Study

Cohen's (2000) study differed significantly from Hunt and Morgan's (1994). Cohen proposed and tested three models on the relation between commitment forms and outcomes, differing chiefly in how they postulated the interrelations among commitment foci. In each model, Cohen tested five commitment forms in their relation to outcomes (organization, job, occupation, work, and the group) and examined which of them mediated this relation. The first model relied on the traditional approach that each commitment focus is directly related to outcomes. It assumed no interrelations among commitment foci. This model followed the one tested by Wiener and Vardi (1980), with the addition of group commitment and work involvement. No mediating process was proposed among the commitment foci. Organizational commitment was expected to be strongly related to turnover intentions, actual turnover, and absenteeism. Job involvement was also expected to be related to the above outcomes, and perhaps to have a stronger relation with absenteeism than OC, in keeping with previous empirical evidence (Blau, 1986). Occupational commitment was likewise expected to have a strong relationship to the outcome variable because of the nature of this sample, nurses, who were expected to identify strongly with their occupation. The expectation then, was that this commitment focus would be related to the outcomes perhaps even more strongly than would job involvement. The other work commitment foci, group commitment and work involvement, were also expected to be related to the three outcomes but not as strongly as would job involvement and occupational and organizational commitment.

Morrow's (1993) Model

According to this model, presented in Fig. 5.1, job involvement and group commitment should mediate the relation between the other commitment foci and work outcomes. In the relationship between job involvement and work outcomes a cognitive state of identification with the job, based on perceptions of its potential for satisfying salient psychological needs, is expected to precede and then trigger motivational processes that influence motivation and effort, and ultimately performance, absenteeism, and turnover (Brown, 1996). According to Brown, this implies that some work behaviors are more proximally related to job involvement, whereas others like absenteeism and turnover, are more distally related. Brown (1996) argued that this implies further that more proximal outcomes of job involvement mediate indirect relations with more distal outcomes. This argument accords with the suggestion of a path from job involvement to turnover intentions, not a path directly to absenteeism and performance. The path from job involvement to turnover intentions follows the progressive withdrawal process and is very relevant to this model. This path is supported by Brown's (1996) meta-analysis findings of stronger correlations between job involvement and turnover intentions ($r = -.31$) than between job involvement and actual turnover ($r = -.13$) or absenteeism ($r = -.14$).

Hardly any theory or findings exist on the relation between group commitment and work outcomes. Becker's (1960) side bet theory provides some rationale for expecting such a relation. Becker suggested that commitment to a course of action develops as one make side bets, which are lost if the action discontinues. These side bets represent potential costs of leaving the organization. Leaving a work group to which one feels attached represents such a cost. Therefore, one tends not to leave the organization so as not to leave one's work group. A negative relation between group commitment and turnover is thus expected. It is also logical to expect that an employee who is highly committed to the work group tends more not to disrupt the work of the group because she or he likes the company of the members of the group. Finally, the two moderators, job involvement and group commitment, are expected to correlate with one other.

Randall and Cote's (1991) Model

In Randall and Cote's (1991) model presented in Fig. 5.2, occupational commitment and OC were the two dependent variables in the interrelations of work commitment constructs. The logical conclusion of this model is that they mediate the relation between the other three commitment foci (i.e., work commitment, group commitment, and job involvement) and work outcomes. The literature strongly supports the relation between OC and turnover (Mowday et al., 1982; Mathieu & Zajac, 1990; Cohen, 1991; Cohen, 1993d; Cohen & Hudecek, 1993). By definition, highly committed employees want to remain with the organization (Mowday et al., 1982). Therefore, a strong relationship should be expected between OC and turnover intentions and actual turnover.

Strong evidence also exists that occupational commitment is also related to work outcomes. One explanation of the usefulness of occupational commitment in predicting an individual's decision to remain with or leave an organization—or the intention to do so—is offered by Jauch, Osborn, and Terpening (1980) and Bedeian, Kemery, and Pizzolatto (1991). They suggest that an individual's attachment to a specific organization may result from identification with that organization, and also from identification with either a specific career or a particular set of peers. If individuals are committed to a specific career but not a specific organization or peer group, these orientations may be comparatively unimportant in predicting either turnover or turnover intentions as long as the organization provides career opportunities. Also, Price and Mueller (1981) argued that stated intentions of leaving a job or an occupational field are an expression of an emotional response to work or the profession.

Occupational commitment was found to be an important determinant of nurses' turnover, stronger than were other work-related commitments such as the organization and work (Mueller et al., 1992). Gardner (1992) emphasized the importance of occupational commitment in nursing because it relates to the attraction of nursing as a lifelong occupational choice and valued career option. Gardner's findings showed that occupational commitment is important for nurses' performance in the first year on a new job and for turnover. Finally, the two mediators in Randall and Cote's model, OC and occupational commitment, are expected to correlate on grounds of strong evidence that these two commitments are related (Morrow, 1993). However, no causal relation is expected between the two mediators.

Progressive Withdrawal Process. The models tested adopted the view of a progressive withdrawal process. The need for this approach arose from strong evidence that the relationship between attitudes—commitment foci in our case, and behaviors, turnover and absenteeism in our case—is not direct. Mobley (1977) and Mobley, Griffeth, Hand, and Meglino (1979) suggested a linear process model where an individual's low work attitudes cause thoughts of quitting an organization, leading to intention to search for other employment, which causes the formation of an intention to leave or stay, and finally quitting. Research has generally supported the perspective that employees engage in a hierarchically ordered sequence of withdrawal, where declining attitudes (e.g., commitment, turnover intentions) precede temporary withdrawal (absenteeism), and these episodes foreshadow permanent withdrawal (actual turnover; Farrell & Petersen, 1984; Parasuraman, 1982; Rosse, 1988).

Cohen (2000) tested the idea of a progressive withdrawal process by the paths from all commitment foci to turnover intentions. The notion that turnover intentions mediate the relation between commitment and turnover was strongly supported by research (Lee & Mowday, 1987; Jaros, Jermier, Kohler, & Sinsich, 1993). Parasuraman (1989), in a study of turnover among staff nurses also asserted that intentions play a key mediating role between attitudes and turnover and are the immediate determinant of actual turnover. The next two paths, also in harmony with the logic of the progression of the withdrawal process, are from turnover intentions to actual turnover and to absenteeism.

The testing of both behaviors in the same model is supported by several writings. First, Rosse, and Hulin (1985) argued that there is sufficient evidence to conclude that job attitudes underlie a spectrum of withdrawal or adaptive behaviors. Gupta and Jenkins (1991) contended that examination of absenteeism and turnover individually suffers from criterion contamination and criterion deficiency in that both absenteeism and turnover encompass voluntary and involuntary behaviors, in that the two behaviors might serve as alternatives depending on organizational and other constraints. The final path in the linear withdrawal process model is from absenteeism to turnover. Mitra, Jenkins, and Gupta's (1992) meta-analysis supported the progressive course of the withdrawal process model, particularly the positive effect of absenteeism on turnover.

Findings of Empirical Testing of the Models. Cohen (2000) examined the models presented previously in a sample of 283 nurses working in three small hospitals in Israel. The models were assessed by path analysis using LISREL VIII (Joreskog & Sorbom, 1993). Randall and Cote's (1991) models were found to fit the data slightly better. This is demonstrated in the lower chi-square of the two Randall and Cote models. The fit indices of Randall and Cote's models are also slightly better than are those of Morrow's models. An important, consistent finding is that in all the models tested, those with the progression withdrawal process better fit the data better than those without it. This finding was consistent across all three sets of models tested here. In terms of the path coefficients (presented in Table 5.5) the findings are more complex and less conclusive than those regarding the fit indices. The direct model had only three significant paths out of the eight hypothesized; from work involvement to turnover intentions (.29), from OC to turnover intentions (−.49), and from turnover intentions to actual turnover (.14). Morrow's model was only partially supported by the path coefficient. This model expected a mediated effect of two commitment foci: job involvement and group commitment. Job involvement was found to mediate the relationship, as expected. It was related to the three exogenous variables, work involvement (.34), organizational commitment (.28), and occupational commitment (.49). It was also related to one of the outcome variables, turnover intentions, and thereby supported the progressive withdrawal process model. The findings however, did not support the inclusion of group commitment as one of the mediators. Only one exogenous variable, organizational commitment (.31) was related to group commitment. Moreover, group commitment was not related to any of the outcome variables.

The path coefficients seem to support Randall and Cote's (1991) model more than did the direct model or Morrow's (1993) model. The weakness of the direct model was path coefficients, which contradicted the hypothesis (work involvement to work outcome relations) and low ratio of significant paths compared with nonsignificant. The weaknesses of Morrow's model were that one of the mediator variables, group commitment, did not mediate, hence the model had few significant paths in comparison with nonsignificant ones. Randall and Cote's model overcame these problems, indicating two mediation processes, both supported by the data. First, job involvement mediated the relation of group commitment and work involvement to occupational commitment and organizational commitment. All four-path coefficients were significant: from group commitment to job involvement (.29) and work involvement to job involvement (.61), and from job involvement to occupational commitment (.74) and organizational commitment (.63). Second, organizational commitment and occupational commitment mediated the relation between the other commitment foci and work outcomes. In the progressive withdrawal process model, both had a significant relation with turnover intentions (−.20 with occupational commitment and −.46 with organizational commitment). The only path that was not significant was between group commitment and organizational commitment.

In summary, the strength of Randall and Cote's model derives from the firm support its anticipated path coefficients received from the data. All three mediation processes suggested by the model were supported: Job involvement mediated the interrelations among commitment foci; occupational commitment and OC mediated the relation between commitment foci and turnover intentions; and turnover intentions mediated the relation of OC and occupational commitment to actual turnover

Conclusions and Future Directions

The research in this chapter demonstrated some of the potential of multiple commitments to predict outcomes. Yet, it seems that to date the amount of variation in work outcomes explained by commitment forms is not as high as we expected it to be. This can be attributed to several causes. First, research into commitment forms-outcome relations does not propose or use a solid conceptual framework for the relation between commitment forms and outcome variables. Second, it does not examine the possibility that commitment forms interact in their effect on outcome variables. Mathieu and Kohler (1990) emphasized the need for more research into interaction effects to advance our understanding beyond what has been gained from examining strictly linear relations. Somers (1995) conducted such research about the relation between different dimensions of organizational commitment and outcomes.

These factors may be the cause of the relatively low variations of outcomes explained by relations with commitment forms. The main question is what should be done in future research to increase the predictive power of commitment forms? Following are several recommendations and considerations for future research on the commitment forms-outcomes relation.

A.   There is strong evidence that the relation between attitudes—commitment foci in our case, and behaviors, such as turnover and absenteeism in our case—is not direct. Mobley (1977) and Mobley, Griffeth, Hand, and Meglino (1979) suggested a linear process model where an individual's low work attitudes cause thoughts of quitting an organization, leading to intention to search for other employment, which causes the formation of an intention to leave or stay, and finally, quitting. The notion that turnover intentions mediate the relation between commitment and turnover was strongly supported by research (Lee & Mowday, 1987; Jaros, Jermier, Kohler, & Sinsich, 1993). Parasuraman (1989) in a study of turnover among staff nurses also asserted that intentions play a key mediating role between attitudes and turnover and are the immediate determinant of actual turnover. There is evidence that this process is relevant for more than one behavior. First, Rosse and Hulin (1985) argued that there is sufficient evidence attesting that job attitudes underlie a spectrum of withdrawal or adaptive behaviors. Gupta and Jenkins (1991) contended that examination of absenteeism and turnover individually suffers from criterion contamination and criterion deficiency in that both absenteeism and turnover encompass voluntary and involuntary behaviors, and in that the two behaviors might serve as alternatives depending on organizational and other constraints. Jaros et al. (1993) tested several causal models of the relation between commitment (organizational commitment) and turnover. Commitment was found to affect turnover only indirectly, through withdrawal intentions. That is, a change in an individual's level of commitment affected the formation of an overall tendency to withdraw from, or stay with, an organization. This tendency affected actual turnover.

Wiener and Vardi (1980) and Somers and Birnbaum (1998) advanced the idea that mediators are present in the relation between multiple commitments and job performance. Commitment was thought to influence job performance through two elements, effort and attachment. *Effort* is the motivational component that impels one to action on behalf of the organization, for example, because of immersion in work. This explanation argued that commitment has an effort-driven motivational component. This component was strongly emphasized by Mowday et al. (1982). The second element, *attachment*, suggests that commitment directs behavior. The argument presented by Somers and Birnbaum (1998) is described as follows. The properties that define each form of work-related commitment provide some clues as to why individuals remain attached to some entity (e.g., organization, career), that in turn gives some indication of one's preferred work behaviors (i.e., those which support the organization, advance one's career, etc.).

Commitment therefore, can be viewed as directing behavior toward preferred tasks. This explanation provides some indication of why commitment forms produce only moderate relations with outcomes. According to this explanation, future models of the relation between commitment and outcomes should compare direct versus mediating models to examine which of the two better fits the data, namely, if the relation between commitment forms and outcomes is direct or mediated by behavioral intentions such as the progressive withdrawal process.

B. A way to increase the predictive power of commitment forms stems from McCaul et al.'s (1995) argument, presented previously in the volume. They hold that viewing OC as an employee's global attitude toward the organization can eliminate the conceptual confusion arising from the inclusion of beliefs and intentions in a multicomponent measure. Accordingly, different types of commitment measures measure different attitudes. For example, Meyer and Allen's (1984) continuance organizational commitment dimension measures attitudes to staying with the organization, but not OC. The social psychological approach to the attitude-behavior relation recommends differentiating between an employee's global attitude toward the organization and their intentions to behave in particular ways toward the organization.

This argument has important implications for the consequences that should be predicted by OC. If one wants to predict staying with the organization, one should assess the attitude relevant to that behavior, namely, the attitude to staying with the organization. Furthermore, if one wants to predict a variety of global behaviors (e.g., behaving positively with regard to the organization), one should measure the global attitude to the organization. McCaul et al. (1995) stated that the relative strength of the relation between OC and organizational effectiveness might vary depending on the behaviors to which the employees were committed, such as commitment to stay in the organization or commitment to work in support of organizational objectives. Their findings provided some support for the mediating roles of the two behavioral commitments in the relation between OC and organizational effectiveness.

McCaul et al. (1995) concluded that such an attitudinal approach could be applied to other forms of commitment. Beliefs about the value of belonging to a particular union or profession may lead to affective responses, namely, attitudes that in turn may predict intentions to stay in the union or profession. That is, each commitment form should strive to represent a unidimensional attitude that measures only the relevant object of commitment. The main argument of this approach is that the construct validity of commitment forms should be improved first, and only then can better prediction of outcomes by commitments be expected. The cause of the low predictive validity is not only the problems in the match between the attitudes and the behaviors they are supposed to predict. It is also that commitment forms are too widely defined and too widely operationalized, so they cannot predict far more specific and focused behaviors. This situation should be improved in future research.

C. Another way to increase the predictive power of commitment forms is to consider the possibility that specific commitment forms are more valuable in one setting and less in another. The commitment forms tested for their relation to outcomes might not have been the relevant forms in the setting where they were tested. For example, Vandenberg and Scarpello (1994) argued that some settings may value an occupation more or less than do other settings, and the strength of the occupational/organizational commitment relation may vary as a function of setting. They concluded that future research should identify the moderating characteristics of the setting, which might influence the commitment-outcome relation. This, of course, is one good reason to study multiple commitments and their relation to outcomes. Whether this or that commitment form is more valuable in a given setting, an examination of all commitment forms in some way guarantees that the possible moderating effect of the setting is controlled.

D. More research is needed to consider the possibility that commitment forms are interrelated, and if some commitment forms are determinants or consequences of others. This possibility was raised by Randall and Cote (1991), Cohen (1999a), and Vandenberg and Scarpello (1994). In this case the appropriate test is by a causal model that examines both the interrelations among commitment forms and their relation to given outcomes. There may be different models for different outcomes. In one model, a given commitment form is the determinant of another form, and in another model, designed for a different outcome, the order is changed. In addition, research should also test for interactive effects among work commitment foci in affecting work outcomes. Little research has examined interactions among commitment foci. Some conceptual and empirical work on interactions among commitment foci in relation to absenteeism and turnover was performed regarding organizational commitment and job involvement (Blau, 1986; Blau & Boal, 1987, 1989; Mathieu & Kohler, 1990). More conceptual and empirical work is needed on interactions among other constellations of commitment including three-level interactions.

E. Somers and Birnbaum (1998) suggested that multidimensional models of both commitment and job performance, for example, are desirable. From their findings they suggested that commitment variables affective in nature might direct behavior toward task proficiency, whereas commitment with foci tied more closely to work values might influence altruistic behavior in organizations. They concluded that further testing of the above propositions was needed, involving the study of patterns of commitment across multiple, distinct facets of performance.

F.   Another recommendation is to examine a larger variety of commitment forms in their relation to outcomes. Morrow and McElroy (1993) argued that one of the limitations of commitment research is that occupation/career foci are not included enough in such studies. The above previously mentioned findings showed that occupational commitment is an important form of commitment and should be included more in future research. From the findings presented earlier, for professional employees, the key commitment forms affecting their attitudes and behaviors seem to be the occupation and the organization foci. This finding is consistent with previous conceptualizations by Gouldner (1957, 1958) and Sheldon (1971).

G.   Although the findings emphasized the importance of occupational commitment as predictor of outcome variables, they elicited many questions about the usefulness of job involvement. Job involvement had no effect on withdrawal intentions and had negative impacts on the other outcome variables to which it was related. It increased absenteeism and job-induced tension, and decreased life satisfaction and nonwork participation. Although the lack of effect on withdrawal intentions was explained as resulting from the inclusion of occupational commitment, other findings about job involvement deserve more attention in future research. The finding that employees with higher job involvement were less satisfied with their lives and participated less in nonwork activities supports the workaholic concept as one of the negative consequences of high job involvement (Cherrington, 1989). In the context of multiple commitments, high job involvement is therefore not necessarily a desirable attitude. This finding has important practical implications. Because there is no support for the assumption that increasing all commitment forms leads to desirable attitudes and behaviors, organizations should be selective in their training programs aimed at increasing commitment forms. Enhancing OC, and if possible occupational commitment, should result in positive attitudes and behaviors of employees from the organization's viewpoint. So far as organizations can affect job involvement, one might question whether there is any value in increasing it. Again, future research is needed on this matter.

H.   Another recommendation is based on Gregersen's (1993) and Cohen's (1991, 1993b; 1993d) conclusions. They argued that career stage might moderate the relation between commitment form and outcomes. According to Gregersen (1993) career, as well as socialization literature, suggests that the first and second years of tenure in an organization are transition times, when individuals try to become effective in their work roles and its formal demands, and become acquainted with potential commitment targets within the workplace. During this period, career and socialization theorists would suggest, individuals need a certain amount of time to become proficient in their roles and familiar with the values and goals of various stakeholders within the organization. In consequence, we would not expect to find particularly strong commitments to specific foci during this stage of socialization. After completing the newcomer or establishment stage (in terms of organization tenure and experience), individuals have usually established themselves in their respective work roles and have had the opportunity to develop stronger attachments to specific foci. Future research should further examine the moderating effect of career stage.

l.   Finally, scholars of commitment should also consider the possibility that alternative theories exist, positing that commitment forms do not necessarily have a strong positive effect, or any effect, on outcomes. Committed employees may not necessarily be effective employees. For example, the literature on job involvement raised the issue of the negative consequences of over involvement for both the individual and the organization (Rabinowitz & Hall, 1977). The term workaholic was suggested for this phenomenon of employees who are over involved in their job or work. *Workaholics* were characterized as obsessive, unable to relax, dishonest, and self-centered, and therefore, as employees who may perform poorly and create conflicts with co-workers (Scott, Moore, & Miceli, 1997). Although it is debated somewhat whether job and work involvement are determinants or outcomes of over involvement or over commitment (Scott et al., 1997), this phenomenon needs further examination (Morrow, 1993).

The literature also indicates possible negative outcomes of high levels of OC. According to Randall (1987), several potential negative consequences for the organization arise from employees with high levels of commitment. Young executives who are blindly devoted to their employer might waste their talents and energies in jobs they do not enjoy, and this would be unprofitable for company and society. That is, the firm may attract individuals who are strongly attached to the organization, but are not suited to an organizations needs.

Mowday et al. (1982) argued that high levels of commitment might also result in lower levels of creativity and adaptation in organization. Too much commitment also can reduce an organization's flexibility. It may result in too much trust in past policies and procedures and the entrenchment of traditional practices (Randall, 1987). Individuals who are totally committed to the organization may not be able to carry out alternative lines of action. Excessive devotion by employees to the organization may burden it with "true believers." Over-zealous behavior on the part of these employees can create problems for the employer, irritate other employees, or antagonize people outside the organization. Finally, Randall (1987) argued that one of the most significant but unrecognized consequences of high levels of commitment is that highly committed employees may be more willing to perform illegal or unethical behavior on behalf of the organization. Often if there is a conflict, highly committed employees put corporate dictates above their own personal ethical or societal dictates. The conflict between the "local" and the "cosmopolitan" (Gouldner, 1957) points to the negative consequences of being committed to the occupation or the profession. This supports Randall's (1987) argument that the commonly assumed linear relation between commitment and desirable consequences should be questioned.

7

Profiles of Commitments

One of the main goals of commitment research should be a work commitment scale that would make formulation of commitment profiles possible, testing their relations to organizational outcomes (Becker & Billings, 1993; Morrow, 1993). This would allow managers to pinpoint forms of work commitment that are less than optimal (Morrow, 1993). Profiles reflecting the foci of commitment could aid in organizational diagnosis and intervention procedures, which could identify the strength, presence, or absence of particular commitments (Reichers, 1985). Profiles based on the motives for commitment could differentiate employees who are likely to remain but contribute little. All these above exemplify potential contributions of research on commitment profiles. Yet, despite the potential theoretical and practical importance of commitment profiles, work to date has scarcely developed specific patterns of commitment or empirically examined the usefulness of such patterns (Becker & Billings, 1993).

The main current of studies on commitment profiles has used two forms of commitment to portray the profiles. Different combinations based on the magnitude of these commitments produce two to four profiles in most cases. Another important characteristic of this current of research is the attempt by some studies to relate these profiles, conceptually and empirically, to outcomes, antecedents, or both. The central conceptualizations of commitment profiles are reviewed next. Two are fairly obsolete and were advanced before the current of research on multiple commitments in the work place had started. These are the concepts of *local versus cosmopolitan* and *dual versus unilateral commitment to union and employer*. Others are more up to date, and have been influenced by commitment theory and research. These in-

clude studies that examined the mutual effect and profiles of job involvement and organizational commitment and the work of Becker (1992),
which developed the profiles using multiple commitment research as the basis for the conceptual framework.

This chapter first presents the more obsolete conceptualizations of commitment profiles. Characteristic of these approaches is the notion of hidden
conflict between identities or commitments, namely a conflict between the
organization and the occupation or profession in the local-cosmopolitan
conceptualization, and a conflict between the union and the company in
the dual versus unilateral commitment to union and company. The more
current approaches to commitment profiles follow.

Local Versus Cosmopolitan Typology

One of the oldest conceptualizations concerning profiles of commitment,
albeit not directly, was advanced by Gouldner (1957, 1958). Since its introduction, the cosmopolitan-local distinction has been applied to several professions in a variety of settings such as faculty in universities, scientists in
nonacademic work settings, police chiefs in large cities, and military personnel. The variety of applications clearly demonstrates that the cosmopolitan-
local construct is well recognized in the organizational literature (Larwood,
Wright, Desrochers, & Dahir, 1998). This construct describes hidden roles
or identities among professionals in work organizations. Manifest roles of a
group in an organization are the expectations of that group, which are universally shared and relevant to a given context. Latent roles are the inter-
nalized shared expectations, which although not always deemed relevant at
face value, are predicted to affect an individual's attitudes and behavior.
The two most widely recognized roles are the local and the cosmopolitan,
first advanced by Gouldner (1957, 1958). *Locals* are individuals who are primarily identified with and committed to the institution in which they work.
They have strong loyalty to their employing organization and low identification with their profession. They use internal organizational groups as their
reference, and are more committed to their employing company. By contrast, *cosmopolitans* are committed to maintaining the skills and values of the
profession to which they belong and have high identification with their professional qualifications. They tend to use external groups as their reference,
so they are more committed to profession or specialty.

Wide diversity exists in the conceptualization and measurement of this
concept. One approach is to develop specific scales for the cosmopolitan-
local concept, following Gouldner (1957, 1958). Another, which is closer to
the theme of this volume, is to examine the professional versus organizational commitments of employees. The two approaches are discussed in the
following section.

Cosmopolitan Versus Local: Traditional Approach.   Gouldner's (1957, 1958) basic idea was a single cosmopolitan-local continuum of role orientations. Gouldner identified three variables specifying a person's position on this continuum: commitment to the professional skills and values, organizational loyalty, and reference-group orientation. Gouldner regarded these variables as so highly associated that they form a single dimension: Cosmopolitans are high on professional commitment, low on organizational commitment, and externally oriented; locals are low on professional commitment, high on organizational commitment, and internally oriented.

Several studies attempted to conceptualize and operationalize the cosmopolitan-local constructs after the early work of Gouldner (1957, 1958). Efforts simultaneously to define latent roles and to determine their applicability resulted in ambiguous and inconsistent conclusions on the dimensionality (e.g., unipolar vs. bipolar) of the cosmopolitan and local latent role constructs (Larwood et al., 1998). These studies did not use the concept of commitment but concentrated on developing specific scales for cosmopolitan and local (Abrahamson, 1965; Ben David, 1958; Blau & Scott, 1962; Goldberg, Baker, & Rubenstein, 1965; Raelin, 1989; Ritti, 1968). Some distinguished the cosmopolitan construct from the local construct by the former being multidimensional and the latter being bipolar and unidimensional. Grimes and Berger (1970) in their review found empirical evidence indicating that the simplistic bipolar conceptualization of the construct should not be used. Moreover, they argued that in its current state of development, the cosmopolitan-local construct was merely an appealing label reified by researchers neglecting the problems inherent in substantive classification models. They recommended that the practice of using cosmopolitan-local as a variable to differentiate organization members be abandoned, but that development research on the construct itself be pursued.

Their recommendation was taken up in later research, for example, the studies of Raelin (1989) and Wright and Larwood (1997). The latter developed two scales, one to measure the construct of local and the other of cosmopolitan, in keeping with Gouldner's (1957) conceptualization. Their scale showed acceptable psychometric properties and was applied by Larwood et al. (1998), who tested its relationship with work outcomes. Some research suggested that there could be up to six statistically independent latent role orientations (Berger & Grimes, 1973; Tuma & Grimes, 1981). Tuma and Grimes (1981) for example, described five possible models of the cosmopolitan-local concept. They argued from their data that role orientations had at least five conceptually distinct dimensions: professional commitment, commitment to organizational goals, organizational immobility, external orientation, and concern with advancement.

Cosmopolitan Versus Local: Commitment Approach.   The more common elaboration of Gouldner's original scheme was a two-dimensional model. One dimension refers to professional commitment representing the cosmopolitan orientation, and the other refers to organizational commitment, representing the local orientation. Early literature based on this approach assumed an inherent conflict between professional and organizational goals (Sheldon, 1971). The traditional professional–bureaucratic conflict argument assumed that the structural characteristics of the nonprofessional workplace were responsible for professional–bureaucratic conflict and were critical in affecting professionals' commitment to their chosen occupation (Wallace, 1993; 1995b). Accordingly, professional commitment should have a negative association with organizational commitment because the professional value system was believed to emphasize values such as professional autonomy, conformity to professional standards and ethics, collegial authority, and client orientation and loyalty (Tuma & Grimes, 1981). By contrast, the bureaucratic value system was said to emphasize hierarchical authority and control and organizational loyalty.

Some research supported the above contention. Sheldon (1971) found in a sample of scientists and engineers, that professionals with high commitment to the profession tended not to be committed to the organization and that the profession increasingly provided a reference group which competed with the organization over loyalty. Promotion to a higher position did not counteract the effects of increased professional commitment for all personnel. Sorensen and Sorensen (1974) argued that because professionals operated in a combined professional and bureaucratic organizational setting, their orientation and behavior were likely to be affected by the contrast in these two types of orientations. Their findings with a sample of accountants supported this contention.

However, other research (Dolen & Shultz, 1998; Tuma & Grimes, 1981; Aranya, Pollock, & Amernic, 1981; Wallace, 1993) contradicted the conflict assumption and pointed to the existence of an alternative approach suggesting that professional and organizational memberships were not necessarily incompatible. This alternative approach was advanced by several explanations. Hall (1968) argued that conflict occurs within a professional group or within an organization only to the degree that specific aspects of bureaucratization or professionalization vary enough to conflict with other specific aspects. The implication is that, in some cases, equilibrium may exist between the levels of professionalization and bureaucratization in the sense that a particular level of professionalization may require a certain level of bureaucratization to maintain social control. Hall concluded that the assumption of inherent conflict between the professional group and the employing organization appears to be unwarranted. Thornton (1970) also argued that professional and organizational commitment could be compatible under certain conditions. Generally, the extent to which the organizational professional experiences and perceives an organizational situation as reaffirming and exemplifying certain principles of professionalism determines the compatibility of the two commitments.

Later research elaborated the above arguments. Aranya and Ferris (1984) contended that the notion of organizational–professional conflict partly stemmed from the use of control systems in organizations. The professional's behavior was presumably dictated by a code of ethics established and monitored by an external collegial peer group, but this behavior may also be controlled by directives issued by an employing organization. So long as the organization-directed behavior was consistent with that specified by the ethical code, conflict should not arise. They posited that organizational–professional conflict was low when both commitments were high. The conflict was high when both commitments were low, and was moderate when one of the two commitments was high and the other low. Aranya and Ferris's (1984) findings showed partial support for their contention.

Lachman and Aranya (1986a) argued that conflict between commitment to the profession and to the organization was not inherent, and none need exist if the individual's professional work expectations and goals were met by the employing organization (Lachman & Aranya, 1986a, 1986b; Wallace, 1995a). If that were the case, the two may prove consistent with each other, or even interdependent. More specifically, if the workplace were part of the professional community, provided professional career opportunities, and allowed for professional autonomy, it might alleviate the potential for professional–bureaucratic conflict. A bureaucratic workplace of that sort would reward professional behavior and provide incentives in keeping with the professional value system (Wallace, 1995a). As a result, although conflict may remain, it would be considerably less between professional and organizational goals. The implication was that we might expect a positive association between professional and organizational commitment (Wallace, 1993; 1995a). Later research substantiated the arguments made by these studies. It showed that employees could display high organizational and occupational commitment, low organizational and occupational commitment, or high commitment in one of them and low commitment in the other (Friedlander, 1981; Lachman & Aranya, 1986a; Lewick, 1981; Rotondi, 1980; Wallace, 1993, 1995a, 1995b).

As for an empirical test of these identities by the commitment approach, research usually examined the correlation between the two constructs, organizational and occupational or professional commitments, and/or examined their correlates. The most important research in terms of the relation between the two commitments is three meta-analyses of this relation. Wallace (1993) found a corrected correlation of .452 in 25 samples. Moderator analysis of this relationship revealed that the relation was stronger for managers and supervisors (corrected $r = .469$ in five samples) than for professional staff (corrected $r = .287$ in three samples). It also revealed a stronger relation for occupations defined as high in their level of professionalization, such as accountants, nurses, and so on (corrected $r = .505$ in 16 samples), than for those defined as low (corrected $r = .321$ in nine samples). Although Wallace recommended further research to investigate the factors responsible for the variation displayed by the moderator analysis, the fact that all correlations were positive dispels the notion of conflict between the two identities.

In another meta-analysis Lee et al. (2000) found a corrected correlation of .45 between occupational commitment and affective organizational commitment in 49 samples. In their moderator analysis, Lee et al. found that the corrected correlation for professionals working in professional organizations was .484 in 21 samples, for professionals working in bureaucratic organizations it was .202 (four samples) and for nonprofessionals it was .448 (ten samples). An interesting finding here is the lower relationship between the two commitments for professionals working in nonprofessional organizations. This indicated that professionals in a less professional setting were less attached to the organization than professionals in a professional setting, probably because these organizations were less responsive to their needs.

Another interesting meta-analysis examined, among other things, the relation between the two commitments and the concept of organizational–professional conflict (Brierley & Cowton, 2000). This meta-analysis was performed for accountants' samples and found low and negative corrected correlation between organizational commitment and organizational–professional conflict (corrected $r = -.14$ for six samples). Low and negative corrected correlation was also found for the relation between professional commitment and organizational–professional conflict (corrected $r = -.19$ for six samples). These relations showed that high organizational and professional commitments were related to lower organizational–professional conflict. Altogether, the findings from the three meta-analyses contradicted any conclusion indicating conflict between cosmopolitan and local orientations; this was evident from the high correlations in the main analysis and the positive, relatively high correlations in any combination of the moderator analysis. It was also evident from the negative, albeit low, relation between the two commitments and organizational–professional conflict.

Occupational/Professional Commitment and Correlates

An important research question that has not received enough attention is the relationship between the two commitments and their determinants and outcomes. Table 7.1 shows main findings of this research. In order to support the existence of conflict between the two commitments one would expect strong differences in the direction and magnitude of the relationship between given correlates and each of the two commitments. As can be seen in Table 7.1, in some of the studies there were modest differences in the magnitude of the relation between organizational commitment, professional commitment and some of the correlates that were examined in relation to them. The pattern of these differences was well characterized by Meyer et al. (1993). In their study they defined both commitments as multidimensional constructs each of which includes the affective, continuance, and normative component. The authors summarized their findings in the argument that in general the correlations observed for occupational commitment were similar to, and often lower in magnitude than, the correlations obtained for organizational commitment. This seems to be the dominant pattern of the relationship between the two commitments and correlates. This finding does not support the notion of conflict between the two commitments.

An important line of research tried to relate the concept of cosmopolitan-local to outcomes such as academic publications or research productivity (Jauch, Glueck & Osborn, 1978; Tuma & Grimes, 1981); perceived or actual job performance (Darden et al., 1989; Meyer et al., 1993); turnover intentions (Aranya & Ferris, 1984; Brierley, 1996; Aranya, Lachman, & Amernic, 1982; Lachman & Aranya, 1986); or actual turnover (Vandenberg & Scarpello, 1994); absence, and tardiness (Meyer et al., 1993). The pattern of the findings here is similar to that found for the correlates of the two commitments, namely lower magnitude in the relation between occupational commitment and outcomes than between organizational commitment and outcomes. Again, this does not support the existence of conflict between the two commitments. Some of the findings are interesting in terms of the magnitude of the relation and call for more research on this issue.

Dual Versus Unilateral Commitment to Union and Employer: Union and Organizational Commitment

This profile, alongside many aspects of unionization, attracted the attention of scholars almost half a century ago, with the rise of unionism in the United States in the early 1950s. One of the concerns at that time was that unionization, and consequently commitment to the union, would result in diminished loyalty to the employer. This concern started a series of studies on the concept of *dual commitment*, namely commitment to both the organization and the union. Specifically, *dual commitment* refers to a worker's positive or negative attachment to both a union and an employing organization. Uni-

TABLE 7.1
Relationship Between Professional/Occupational and Organizational Commitment and Correlates/Determinants and Outcomes

Studies	Sample	Professional/Occupational Commitment (PC)			Organizational Commitment (OC)		
		Correlates/Determinants That Were Examined	Outcomes That Were Examined	Main Findings	Correlates/Determinants That Were Examined	Outcomes That Were Examined	Main Findings
Aranya, Pollock, & Amernic (1981)	1206 Chartered Accountants selected randomly from all over Canada	Organizational commitment, professional-organizational conflict, satisfaction with rewards, organizational level		PC, professional-organizational conflict (negatively), and satisfaction with income were related to professional commitment. R-square was .23		Professional commitment	OC together with other variables (professional-organizational conflict, satisfaction with rewards) was related to professional commitment
Aranya, Lachman, & Amernic (1982)	1206 Chartered Accountants selected randomly from all over Canada		Intentions to leave the organization	PC was related to organizational commitment (path analysis) that was related to turnover intentions	Need deprivation, professional commitment	Intentions to leave the organization	OC was affected by professional commitment and need deprivation and affect job satisfaction and intentions to leave the organization
Jauch, Glueck, & Osborn (1978)	84 researchers in the basic sciences at a large Midwestern university		Academic research productivity measured by objective (research productivity) and subjective (self-assessment) measures	PC contributed unique variance in objective productivity (r square = .05). It did not explain any variance of the subjective productivity measure		Academic research productivity measured by objective (research productivity) and subjective (self-assessment) measures	OC did not provide any significance proportions of unique variance in both objective and subjective measures of productivity

continued on next page

TABLE 7.1   (continued)

Studies	Sample	Professional/Occupational Commitment (PC)				Organizational Commitment (OC)		
		Correlates/Determinants That Were Examined	Outcomes That Were Examined	Main Findings		Correlates/Determinants That Were Examined	Outcomes That Were Examined	Main Findings
Tuma & Grimes (1981)	393 full-time faculty and administrators at a large, research-oriented university	A large list of demographic and work experiences variables such as gender, alumni, PhD, worked at other university, years in present rank, being tenured, working in a professional school, and so on	A large list of academic activities including publications	PC was related to number of publications, having a national professional office, % of time spent writing for nonacademic audience (negatively), and being female		A large list of demographic and work experiences variables such as No. of publications, No. of meetings attended, No. of students known well, % of time spent on teaching, research, and so on	A large list of academic activities including publications	OC was related to being a full professor, having been an administrator, % of time spent on administrative tasks, not belonging to AAUP; % of time spent on teaching (negatively), being in a professional school
Aranya & Ferris (1984)	1206 Canadian, and 810 US certified public accountants		Perceived organizational-professional conflict	The correlation coefficient between organizational-professional conflict and the interaction of OC and PC was r = −.57. That is high OC and PC is related to lower conflict			Perceived organizational-professional conflict	The correlation coefficient between organizational-professional conflict and the interaction of OC and PC was r = −.57. That is high OC and PC is related to lower conflict

Study	Sample	Variables	Findings	Variables	Outcomes	Findings
Lachman & Aranya (1986)	810 certified accountants in California	Job satisfaction, organizational commitment, realization of expectation, turnover intentions	Path analysis showed that PC was positively related to OC and realization of expectation. In the group of partners and sole practitioners it was related to job satisfaction	PC and realization of expectations	Intentions to leave the organization	Path analysis showed that PC and realization of expectations affected OC. OC affected job satisfaction and intentions to leave the organization (negatively)
Darden, Hampton, & Howdell (1989)	261 retail salespersons from a traditional Midwestern department store chain	Parent SES, work values, role conflict, role clarity, supervisory style, perceived rewards	Career commitment was strongly affected by supervisory style, perceived rewards, and role clarity that explained over 65% of the variance. Career commitment was also related to job performance and job satisfaction	Parents SES, work values, role conflict, role clarity, supervisory style, perceived rewards	Perceived job performance, job satisfaction	OC was strongly affected by supervisory style, perceived rewards, and role clarity that explained over 65% of the variance. OC was also related to job performance and job satisfaction
Meyer, Allen, & Smith (1993)	603 registered nurses randomly chosen from the membership of the College of Nurses of Ontario	Age, years in nursing, employment status, clinical area of choice, geographic area of choice, job satisfaction, sense of obligation	PC was related to many of the correlates and outcomes such as age, tardiness, absence, use of time, voice, loyalty and neglect. Regressions showed that it make a significant, albeit small, contribution to the prediction of outcomes even when OC was controlled	Age, years in nursing, employment status, clinical area of choice, geographic area of choice, job satisfaction, sense of obligation	Leave occupation, leave organization, professional activity, absence, objective and subjective performance, use of time, voice, loyalty, neglect, tardiness	OC was related to many of the correlates and outcomes such as age, job satisfaction, leave intentions, tardiness, performance, voice, loyalty, neglect, absence, use of time, helping others

continued on next page

TABLE 7.1 (continued)

Studies	Sample	Professional/Occupational Commitment (PC)			Organizational Commitment (OC)		
		Correlates/ Determinants That Were Examined	Outcomes That Were Examined	Main Findings	Correlates/ Determinants That Were Examined	Outcomes That Were Examined	Main Findings
Vanbenberg & Scarpello (1994)	100 MIS professionals randomly selected from 455 working in a multinational software, research and development firm located in the Southeast US		Turnover intentions, job search, turnover behavior	There is a causal priority from PC to OC; a significant positive influence of PC on OC; OC causally affect turnover intentions and behavior; PC possesses a meaningful role in process models of turnover	A large list of demographic and work experiences variables such as No. of publications, No. of meetings attended, No. of students known well, percentage of time spent on teaching, research, and so on	Turnover intentions, job search, turnover behavior	There is a causal priority from PC to OC; a significant positive influence of PC on OC; OC causally affect turnover intentions and behavior; PC possesses a meaningful role in process models of turnover

Brierley (1996)	191 chartered accountants in the United Kingdom	Job satisfaction	Organizational turnover intentions, professional turnover intentions	PC was related to organizational turnover intentions (r = –.26), professional turnover intentions (r = –.39), and to job satisfaction (r = .38)		OC was related to organizational turnover intentions (r = –.43), professional turnover intentions (–.31), and job satisfaction (r = .49)
Wallace (1995b)	583 lawyers working in private practice in law firms (professional organizations) and 147 lawyers employed in government and private corporations (nonprofessional organizations)	Participation, legitimacy, fairness, autonomy, formalization, promotions, specialization, task variety, and control variables such as education, gender, work motivation and labor market		Participation (negative), coworker support and work motivation explained 25% of the variance for lawyers in nonprofessional organizations. Legitimacy, autonomy, formalization, specialization, task variety and work motivation explained 31% for lawyers in professional organizations	Participation, legitimacy, fairness, autonomy, formalization, promotions, specialization, task variety, and control variables such as education, gender, work motivation and labor market	Legitimacy, autonomy, and specialization explained 49% of the variance for lawyers in nonprofessional organizations. Legitimacy, fairness, autonomy, promotions, task variety, and coworker support explained 47% of the variance for lawyers in professional organizations

lateral commitment describes a positive attachment to a union or to an employer, but not to both (Stagner & Rosen, 1965). The studies on this concept concentrated on the relation between commitment to the employer/organization and commitment to the union (Dean, 1954; Derber et al. 1953, 1954; Gotlieb & Kerr, 1950; Purcell, 1954; Stagner, 1954, 1956, 1961). Some found that employees could be committed to both the union and the organization, whereas a smaller number found that employees who were loyal to either the union or the employer were not loyal to the other entity (Purcell, 1954; Stagner & Rosen, 1965). Involvement with one side, particularly holding a formal position in it, drew employees away from the other. However, the main findings of these studies was that dual commitment was a common phenomenon, and that being a committed member of the union did not necessarily mean that an employee would be hostile to the organization, and vice versa. From the viewpoint of this volume, this research in the 1950s was perhaps the earliest to apply a multiple commitment approach, although it encompassed only two forms, union commitment and organizational commitment.

In subsequent years, these works were criticized (Angle & Perry, 1986; Fucami & Larson, 1984; Gordon et al., 1980), mainly because of their methodological limitations. Criticism centered on the measurement problems of the two commitment scales, which in most of these studies were measured by use of one item and not by more valid and reliable instruments. This hampered the possibility of generalizing meaningful conclusions from these studies. Another criticism was that the studies did not develop an adequate conceptual framework for explaining the relationship between the two commitment foci. However, after this extensive research on union commitment in the 1950s and 1960s, interest in it fell steeply. But renewed attention was drawn back to the concept of dual commitment in the 1980s, firstly owing to the expanding research on organizational commitment. This stimulated researchers to examine commitment to other foci as well, including union commitment. The start of this revival was the work of Gordon, et al. (1980), who developed a new approach and scales for defining and measuring union commitment. The union commitment approach and operationalization have been closely reviewed in previous chapters. Here it may noted that dual commitment to union and organization was examined by the application of more valid and reliable scales to the two concepts.

Several conceptual frameworks exist for the concept of dual commitment, three of them set out by Magenau, Martin, and Peterson (1988). The first is based on the notion of conflict, which postulates difficulty in maintaining simultaneous commitments to organizations in conflict with one another. Dual commitment is possible when relations between union and management are positive, but the presence of strong conflict tends to push workers toward unilateral commitment to one side or the other. The literature (Strauss, 1977; Tannenbaum, 1965) suggested that union activists or high union participators had a high stake in their employment. Therefore, some forms of union participation may carry stronger potential for such conflict to occur than other forms.

This conflict will create a situation of the union as opposed to the employer. This was demonstrated in early findings that examined the concept of dual versus unilateral commitment to union and employer (Dean, 1954; Stagner, 1954, 1961). Those studies showed that union stewards tended to develop higher levels of commitment to the union and lower levels of commitment to the employer. This contrasted with managers, who tended to develop higher levels of commitment to employers and lower levels of commitment to the union. Support for this finding was found in the work of Magenau, et al. (1988), who found that among union stewards levels of unilateral commitment to the union (high levels of union commitment and low levels of organizational commitment) were much higher than among the rank and file. Walker and Lawler (1979) and Martin (1981) also found empirical support for this notion of conflict. Employees with high levels of organizational commitment eschewed joining militant unions, which might have put their personal welfare at risk.

The second explanation for dual commitment is based on Stagner's (1956) early work, which described dual commitment as a phenomenon arising from people's tendency to perceive their work situation as a unit rather than as sharply differentiating the union role from the management role. According to Magenau et al. (1988), that explanation implies that conditions such as high job satisfaction and positive union–management relations should lead to dual commitment if they are attributable to the joint actions of the two parties. Accordingly, *unilateral commitment* appeared to be the rule among people more deeply involved with one side than with the other. A similar explanation of dual commitment is the frustration-aggression theory, mentioned by Klandermans (1986a). This approach sees trade union participation as a reaction to frustration, dissatisfaction, or alienation in the work situation. People and organization are defined as systems striving for equilibrium. If the equilibrium is disturbed, they attempt to restore it. At the heart of this approach is the belief that unions are symptoms of employees' incomplete integration into the company. This framework has also been applied to trade unions as organizations to explain nonparticipation and member turnover due to frustration, dissatisfaction with, and alienation from the union organization.

A third explanation is based on the exchange theory, which is the common approach to the understanding of the mechanism of multiple commitment in general and organizational commitment in particular. According to this explanation, if an organization serves as a vehicle for the use of an individual's abilities and satisfies his or her needs, the person reciprocates by commitment to the organization. If an organization fails to serve as such a vehicle, commitment to it is low. On the one hand dual commitment then, should be related to a combination of variables reflecting a perception of a satisfying exchange relationship with both union and employer. On the other hand, unilateral union commitment should be related to a combination of the same variables reflecting perception of a satisfying relation with the union and a less satisfying relationship with the employer. *Unilateral employer commitment*, the opposite of unilateral union commitment, should be related to a reverse set of conditions to those present for unilateral union commitment.

Identification of Dual Commitment

Gordon and Ladd (1990) and Bemmels (1995) pointed out two approaches to identifying dual commitment: the taxonomic and the dimensional. The *taxonomy* classifies individual union members into taxons based on self-reports about organizational commitment and union commitment. Subsequent steps in taxonomic research customarily involve the identification of other characteristics of the union members in a taxon, thereby providing a richer description of those individuals and more definite standards for classification. Accordingly, individuals are the units of analysis in the taxonomic approach (Gordon & Ladd, 1990). The dimensional approach focuses on an organizational phenomenon rather than on individual differences. Instead of individuals being classified into categories determined by their relative union and organizational commitment, *dual commitment* is evinced from the pattern of scores across individuals presumed to constitute a meaningful institutional entity. Specifically, the dimensional approach determines whether a linear relation exists between union commitment and organizational commitment within a sample representing a particular organization. The existence of dual commitment is established through tests addressing the magnitude of the correlation between measures of union commitment and organizational commitment. A significant, positive correlation between the two commitments documents the existence of dual commitment; that is, in a given organizational unit, individuals' conviction about their company tends to match their convictions about their union.

A third approach not mentioned previously, is the formulation of a specific scale for dual commitment. Angle and Perry (1986) for example, who developed a five-item scale for dual commitment applied such an approach. Their findings in a sample of rank-and-file employees of municipal bus companies showed that their dual commitment scale was positively and significantly related to both union commitment ($r = .40$) and organizational commitment ($r = .48$). However, this approach does not accord with the notion of commitment as do the two previous approaches. Moreover very little research has applied it to the study of dual commitment.

Findings Based on the Taxonomic Approach

Works on the concept of dual commitment using the taxonomic approach classified individuals into four quadrants and formed four-dimensional profiles of the concept. In most cases they formed high and low commitment groups by crosstabulating employer and union commitment measures, dichotomized into values greater than, smaller than, or equal to the scale midpoints. Generally, the cutoff scores for establishing the quadrants were the mean, median, or midpoints on the organizational and union scales (Bemmels, 1995). These cutoff scores were used to form a consistent definition of high and low commitment, which would be applied across all groups. This midpoint was in some cases the average and in others the median. This formed a four-dimensional classification of employees: those high in both commitments, those low in both commitments, and those low in one and high in the other. This line of research frequently combined the design and analysis of the profiles with discriminant analysis that determined the variables that best discriminate the groups of the profiles.

A summary of these works is presented in Table 7.2. The findings presented in the table yield an important conclusion regarding the percentages of classification of employees' commitments. Concern for unilateral commitment to either union or company was apparently less realistic than was expected in earlier literature, and the concept of dual commitment is not a zero-sum game (Thacker & Rosen, 1986). Yet some exceptions to this general conclusion should be mentioned. An interesting finding in this regard is that of Beauvais, Scholl, and Cooper (1991) who found in a sample of unionized faculty at an American university that the percentage of employees in the dual commitment category was greater after contract settlement than at the start of negotiations. This finding demonstrated the usefulness of longitudinal design in examining dual commitment. Sverke and Sjoberg (1994) found that despite Swedish management's tradition of recognizing the union's role, simultaneous commitment to both company and union was lower in Sweden than in North American countries, suggesting a conflict between union and management roles. These findings call for more crosscultural studies on dual commitment.

As for the determinants of dual or unilateral commitment, an important conclusion based on the findings presented in Table 7.2 is that unique organizational and union experiences and attitudes determined the patterns of commitment (Fullagar & Barling, 1991). Variables related to both dual and unilateral commitment were likely to be positive characteristics of the work

TABLE 7.2

Findings of Research on Dual Commitment to Union and Organization

Studies	Sample	Classification of Employees' Commitments in Percentages	Variables That Discriminate Between the Two Commitments		Determinants of the Two Commitments	
			High vs. Low Dual Commitment	Unilateral Commitment to Union vs. Unilateral Commitment to Organization	Union commitment	Organizational Commitment
Thacker & Rosen (1986)	601 nonmanagement employees in a large Midwestern public utility located in the US	Unilateral commitment to union—15.8% Unilateral commitment to organization—23.7% High dual commitment—49.6% Low dual commitment—10.8%	Participation in union activities and autonomy	Participation in union activities and autonomy		
Martin, Magenau, & Peterson (1986)	192 union stewards in a 10,000-member local union representing employees in one bargaining unit of a supermarket chain in a Midwestern state	Unilateral commitment to union—52.1% Unilateral commitment to organization—6.3% High dual commitment—29.7% Low dual commitment—12.0%	Union decision making, employment mobility, influence on employer, female, and skill trade	Skill trade, work place size, union activities, union decision making, supervisor support, and income from employer	Employment mobility, use grievance to punish, union activities, union decision making, work place size	Tenure, employment mobility, supervisor support, promotion opportunities, influence on employer, work place size
Magenau, Martin, & Peterson (1988)	218 stewards of a local union in a Midwestern state attending the union's annual steward's conferences in 1982	Unilateral commitment to union—40.8% Unilateral commitment to organization—7.3% High dual commitment—44.5% Low dual commitment—7.3%	Use grievance to punish, union-management relations, union decision making, job satisfaction	Union activities, integrative bargaining, union management relations, union decision making, influence on employer, job satisfaction, unit size		

Magenau, Martin, & Peterson (1988)	268 stewards of a local union in a Midwestern state attending the union's annual steward's conferences in 1983	Unilateral commitment to union—43.3% Unilateral commitment to organization—8.6% High dual commitment—35.1% Low dual commitment—13.1%	Employment mobility, union-management relations, union decision making, job satisfaction	Union activities, union management relations, union decision making, influence on employer, promotional opportunities, supervisor support, job satisfaction	
Magenau, Martin, & Peterson (1988)	225 rank-and-file union members of a local union in a Midwestern state surveyed in 1981	Unilateral commitment to union—20.4% Unilateral commitment to organization—28.0% High dual commitment—12.4% Low dual commitment—39.1%	Integrative bargaining, union-management relations, union decision making, influence on employer, job satisfaction	Union activities, union decision making, promotion opportunities, job satisfaction	
Magenau, Martin, & Peterson (1988)	104 rank-and-file union members of a local union in a Midwestern state surveyed in 1982	Unilateral commitment to union—13.5% Unilateral commitment to organization—34.6% High dual commitment—10.6% Low dual commitment—41.3%	Union decision making, steward effectiveness	Union decision making, promotion opportunities, supervisor support, job satisfaction	
Beauvais, Scholl, & Cooper (1991)	146 faculty members of a medium sized 4-year university in the Northeast US who were surveyed early in 1987	Unilateral commitment to union—26% Unilateral commitment to organization—27% High dual commitment—25% Low dual commitment—22%			Internal and external pay equity, salary group

continued on next page

TABLE 7.2 (continued)

Studies	Sample	Variables That Discriminate Between the Two Commitments			Determinants of the Two Commitments	
		Classification of Employees' Commitments in Percentages	High vs. Low Dual Commitment	Unilateral Commitment to Union vs. Unilateral Commitment to Organization	Union commitment	Organizational Commitment
Sherer & Morishima (1989)	579 unionized airline employees				Layoff experience, gender, internal pay comparison, union post, labor management program, job influence, information source: management/union	Tenure, wage, gender, market wage, external pay comparison, tier, labor management program, job influence, information source: management/union
Fullagar & Barling (1991)	426 members of two unions: an academic staff union and a support staff union, employed on a full-time basis by one of two large universities in Ontario.	Unilateral commitment to union—32.9% (47.0%)[1] Unilateral commitment to organization—50.7% (26.9) High dual commitment —50.9% (46.7%) Low dual commitment —34.1% (28.0)		Extrinsic and intrinsic job satisfaction, role conflict, role ambiguity, supervisor support, union attitudes, union-management relations, union instrumentality, union involvement		

Bemmels (1995)	1459 shop stewards in 15 unions in Canada.	Unilateral commitment to union—30.1% Unilateral commitment to organization—20.2% High dual commitment—30.4% Low dual commitment—19.3%	Supervisor's consideration, satisfaction with the grievance procedure, union-management relations, age, gender	Supervisor's consideration, supervisor's initiating structure, union-management relations, gender, steward training program	Supervisor's consideration, supervisor's initiating structure, satisfaction with the grievance procedure, gender, education, experience, steward training	Supervisor's consideration, supervisor's initiating structure, satisfaction with the grievance procedure, union-management relations, age
Sverke & Sjoberg (1994)	257 members of a Swedish public sector white-collar local union	Unilateral commitment to union—17% Unilateral commitment to organization—23% High dual commitment—28% Low dual commitment—32%		Informal union socialization, union instrumentality, local union leader responsiveness. Company tenure, autonomy, occupational prestige, local union leader responsiveness.		
Fucami & Larson (1984)	114 full-time male employees in the transportation department of a large metropolitan unionized newspaper in an Eastern city			Social involvement. Company tenure, job scope, job stress		
Barling, Wade, & Fullagar (1990)	100 full-time teaching staff and counselors of a community college in south-western Ontario			Company tenure. Work satisfaction, organizational climate, job involvement		

continued on next page

TABLE 7.2 (continued)

Studies	Sample	Classification of Employees' Commitments in Percentages	Variables That Discriminate Between the Two Commitments		Determinants of the Two Commitments	
			High vs. Low Dual Commitment	Unilateral Commitment to Union vs. Unilateral Commitment to Organization	Union commitment	Organizational Commitment
Angle & Perry (1986)	1057 rank-and-file employees in 22 separate municipal bus companies in the Western US. 89% of them were bus drivers		Labor-management relationship climate, and an interaction of this variable with union participation			
Johnson & Johnson (1992)	234 male members of a local union of a national tire and rubber manufacturing company operating in a Midwestern state			Union satisfaction and steward support. Company tenure, union satisfaction, job satisfaction, job involvement, job equity, and supervisor support		
Johnson & Johnson (1995)	252 female clerical employees at Iowa State University. The sample includes members and nonmembers of Local 96		Age, organizational tenure, union membership	Education, organizational tenure, union membership	Union membership	
Wallace (1995)	583 law firm lawyers practicing in a large metropolitan city in Western Canada	Legitimacy, fairness, autonomy, promotion, task variety, coworker support		Legitimacy, autonomy, formalization, specialization, task variety, coworker support, work motivation		

Wallace (1995)	147 corporate and government lawyers practicing in a large metropolitan city in Western Canada	Legitimacy, autonomy, promotions, specialization	Participation, coworker support, work motivation	
Carson & Carson (1998)	75 nursing department employees in a small rural hospital in a Southeastern state	Organizational citizenship behavior	Emotional intelligence, self-awareness, mood regulation, empathic response, internal motivation, organizational citizenship behavior	
Darden, Hampton & Howell (1989)	261 retail salespeople from a traditional Midwestern department store chain	Rewards, supervisory style, role conflict, role clarity, job performance, job satisfaction	Rewards, supervisory style, role conflict, role clarity, job performance, job satisfaction	Parental SES, role clarity, job performance, job satisfaction
Bishop, Scott, & Burroughs (2000)	380 production employees from an automotive outsource manufacturing plant in the Southern USA	Stronger correlation with perceived organizational support and weaker with perceived team support		Stronger correlation with perceived team support and weaker with perceived organizational support

continued on next page

TABLE 7.2 (continued)

Studies	Sample	Variables That Discriminate Between the Two Commitments			Determinants of the Two Commitments	
		Classification of Employees' Commitments in Percentages	High vs. Low Dual Commitment	Unilateral Commitment to Union vs. Unilateral Commitment to Organization	Union commitment	Organizational Commitment
Mueller & Lawler (1999)	838 classroom teachers in the third largest public school system in the USA that includes 600 elementary and secondary schools	Promotional opportunities, distributive justice, supervisory support, inadequate resources, role ambiguity, routinization, negative affectivity, race (white), job satisfaction		Promotional opportunities, distributive justice, role ambiguity, negative affectivity, routinization, race (white), teaching experience, job satisfaction		
Mueller, Finley, Iverson, & Price (1999)	838 classroom teachers in the third largest public school system in the USA that includes 600 elementary and secondary schools	Years as a teacher, positive affectivity, teachers/students ratio, attendance rate, percentage on welfare, secondary school, percentage of student quality, resource inadequacy, autonomy, coworker support		Years as a teacher, positive affectivity, perception of student quality, resource inadequacy, and coworker support		
Cohen (1999a)	238 nurses from two hospitals in Western Canada	Children, age, tenure, years in occupation, perceived performance, job satisfaction	Gender, tenure, job satisfaction	Children, perceived performance, job satisfaction, life satisfaction, job tension	Job tension	

Bashaw & Grant (1994)	560 industrial salespeople from 16 companies operating primarily in the Southeastern US	Education	None	Marital status, *age*		
Morrow, McElroy, & Blum, (1988)	2200 employees of a department of transportation in a Midwestern state in a variety of job categories	Tenure, position (supervisor vs. nonsupervisor)	Tenure, position, gender			

[1]The subjects were divided to two groups based on the median split of scores: the high organizational loyalty one (not in parentheses) and the high union loyalty one (in parentheses)

Underlined variables represent negative relationship with the relevant commitment focus.

situation attributable to one of the parties, but not to the other. Variables related only to dual commitment were positive characteristics of labor relations attributable to both parties, and variables related only to unilateral commitment appeared to be adversarial thinking and behavior (Magenau & Martin, 1984). The findings also emphasized the importance of the structural variables in determining classification into unilateral union or organizational commitment, and the importance of the participation in union or organizational decision-making variable in determining one's being of high or of low dual commitment (Martin, Magenau, & Peterson, 1986).

All the findings above seem to indicate that workers will be committed to both union and management where a positive work situation exists. Also, if workers are dually committed they seem more likely to accept and be supportive of problem-solving approaches to collective bargaining. The findings suggest that a positive relation between management and union, and positive management practices, will not undermine workers' commitment to the union. Similarly, positive practices by the union do not undermine workers' support for the employer. At least in well-established relations, it does not appear that conflict is necessary for the union to obtain the commitment of the rank and file.

Findings Based on the Dimensional Approach

As mentioned above, this approach is based on examining the correlations between the two commitment forms. The accumulated data on this issue led to three meta-analyses on the relation between the two variables. These meta-analyses themselves yielded detailed data on the relation between the two constructs and on the existence of dual commitment based on the dimensional approach. Such data are decidedly more valuable than any quantitative review on the relation between the two commitments.

Reed, Young and McHugh (1994) based their meta-analysis on 76 samples involving a total of 15,699 respondents. They found a mean corrected correlation of .42, which supported the notion of the existence of dual commitment. Reed et al. found that in countries defined as characterized by a consensual approach to industrial relations such as Japan and Sweden the relation between the two variables was stronger than in countries characterized as having adversarial relations, such as the U.S. and Canada. Bamberger et al. (1999) found a corrected correlation of .36 in 41 samples involving a total of 17,935 respondents. Johnson et al.'s (1999) meta-analysis was based on 31 samples with 84 independent correlations involving 22,012 unionized employees in seven countries. The corrected correlation between the two commitments was .37. The correlations found in the last two meta-analyses are slightly lower than the findings of Reed et al., but they lead to the same conclusion regarding the existence of dual commitment.

Johnson et al. (1999) tested three moderators in their analysis: white-collar versus blue-collar employment, crosscultural work values, and type of commitment measures. The corrected correlation for blue-collar employees was .22, whereas the average effect size for white-collar employees included zero, and indicated that the estimate of the correlation between the two commitments was zero for the white-collar employee sample. As for the crosscultural work values, the findings indicated quite interestingly that dual commitment was higher for workers influenced by non-Western work values than for those influenced by Western work values. The results of the moderator analysis for the type of commitment measure revealed a non-significant difference in the estimate of the correlation between company and union commitment for the subgroup of measures. This finding does not support the moderating influence of difference in types of commitment measures used to operationalize the attitudinal constructs.

These findings based on the dimensional approach generally support the notion of the existence of dual commitment. The relatively high and positive corrected correlation between the two variables across the three meta-analyses strongly supports this conclusion. However, it should be treated with caution considering the limitations of the dimensional approach mentioned by Gordon and Ladd (1990). The use of meta-analysis that corrects the effect size for sampling and measurement errors overcomes some of these limitations, but not all. In addition, more moderators in this relation have to be sought. The finding of Johnson et al. (1999) that no significant relationship exists for white-collar employees provides an indication that for some groups or some settings the relationship might not be characterized by high dual commitment. Therefore, more research is needed to examine other moderators in the relation between the two commitments. For example, Fullagar, Barling, and Christie (1991) found that the relation between the two commitments was significantly greater for members of a protective union than of an aggressive union, suggesting that union type moderates dual commitment. Conlon and Gallagher (1987) found that union membership status also moderated the relationship between the two commitments. For example, the correlation between the two commitments was significantly higher for nonmembers who had been members and had left the union ($r = .48; p < .001$) than for union members ($r = .14; p < .05$) or for people who had never been members ($r = .08$; n.s.).

Determinants and Outcomes of Dual Commitment

Naturally, an important aspect of the concept of dual versus unilateral commitment is its relationship with determinants and outcomes. Knowledge of the relation with determinants is important for understanding the causes of being dually or unilaterally committed. Technically, many researchers used what is termed the *parallel models approach* (Fukami & Larson, 1984), where organization and union commitment are each regressed on a set of independent variables to identify common predictors of both union and organizational commitment, which are then considered predictors of dual commitment. Dissimilarity in the determinants might indicate that the two commitments are related to different processes, and this provides stronger support for the existence of unilateral commitment.

A summary of the findings of this research is presented in Table 7.2. Fukami and Larson's (1984) findings that variables related to organizational commitment were not related to union commitment supports the notion that the two commitments represent divergent models. Barling, Wade, and Fullagar (1990), who replicated Fukami and Larson's (1984) study, obtained similar findings together with Johnson and Johnson (1992) and Magenau et al. (1988) who, in four samples of rank and file and stewards, found few common predictors of commitment to union and organization.

The findings of Sherer and Morishima (1989) and Bemmels (1995) showed more variety in the pattern of the relation between the determinants and each of the two commitments. Sherer and Morishima found that some variables were related positively to one commitment form and negatively to the other. For example, wage was related positively to organizational commitment and negatively to union commitment. This finding is interesting, indicating that lower paid workers are more likely to be committed to a union and less likely to be committed to an organization. According to Sherer and Morishima (1989), this suggests that although the union is the vehicle for gaining more benefits, the company is viewed as the provider of the benefits. Sherer and Morishima suggested that whereas work-related variables are usually related to organizational commitment and not to union commitment, variables that represent other settings such as external market and industrial relations can be related to both commitments.

Bemmels (1995) found that two styles of leadership behaviors, consideration and initiative structure, were related to both commitments but the signs were opposite and supported this conclusion. Consideration had a positive relation with employer commitment but a negative relation with union commitment. The variable structure had a negative relation with employer commitment but a positive relation with union commitment.

Outcomes of Dual Commitment

Dual commitment research has focused on identifying the presence of dual commitment through the taxonomic and dimensional approaches. However, dual commitment alone is not important. Its importance is based on the desirable behaviors and organizational outcomes that are allegedly a consequence of dual commitment. The importance of dual commitment as a unique construct must also be established by being shown to offer unique predictive power to explain behaviors or organizational outcomes beyond the separate effects of union commitment and organizational commitment (Bemmels, 1995). Yet, little research has examined the relationship between dual commitment and outcomes or between union and organizational commitment and outcomes. The few studies that examined this relationship reached interesting findings that call for more research on this issue.

In their sample of members of two Canadian unions, Fullagar and Barling (1991) found unique consequences for both union and organizational commitment. Their findings showed that union commitment was related only to union-related consequences such as positive attitudes to unionism, greater involvement in union activities, and more positive perceptions of the union–management relation. Similarly, high organizational commitment was related to greater intrinsic and extrinsic job satisfaction, increasing job involvement, reducing both role ambiguity and conflict, and fostering stronger perceptions of co-worker and supervisor support. From the findings, which showed unique consequences for both union and organizational commitment, and no interactions between the two commitments, the authors concluded that there are divergent models of organizational and union commitment.

Bemmels (1995) examined the predictive power of dual commitment by regression models, which included union commitment, organizational commitment, and an interaction between union and organizational commitment. These variables were related to six outcomes: three of them were the measures of the stewards' behavior patterns relating to grievance filing and processing, and three of the dependent variables were the outcome measures relating to the grievance procedure. Each regression model also included a measure of the labor–management relations climate, since it had been argued that dual commitment may be little more than a surrogate for a good labor relations climate.

The findings showed that union and organizational commitment were statistically significant in all of the regressions except two of the outcome measures, namely, the proportion of the grievances resolved by year's end and the union success rate. These significant results further attest to the importance of employer and union commitment as constructs to be included in models explaining behaviors and organizational outcomes. The estimate for the employer commitment and union commitment interaction was statistically significant in two of the models, the stewards' frequency of informal grievance resolution and the proportion of grievances resolved by year's end. In both models, the estimated coefficient for the interaction was positive, indicating that dual commitment was associated with more frequent informal resolution of grievances and a greater proportion of grievances resolved at the end of the year. The findings also showed that commitment to either the employer or to the union was associated with more frequent, informal grievance resolution, but dual commitment was associated with an even stronger frequency of informal grievance resolution beyond the combined main effects of union commitment and organizational commitment. The results also showed that commitment to the union or to the organization had no effect on the proportion of grievances resolved, but those stewards with dual commitment did have a greater proportion of grievances resolved by the end of the year.

Job Involvement and Organizational Commitment

Another interesting conceptual framework for commitment profiles was that by Blau and Boal (1987). Their starting point was the attempt to improve the prediction of valuable outcomes, such as absenteeism and turnover, by commitment forms, job involvement, and organizational commitment. They argued that instead of examining the relation between organizational commitment and job involvement separately with turnover and absenteeism, use of the two attitudes jointly (in an interaction) might increase their predictive power. Accordingly, specific interactive combinations of job involvement and organizational commitment levels help predict particular types of turnover and absence behaviors. Blau and Boal argued that workers with high levels of both job involvement and organizational commitment should be the most motivated because they are attracted by both the job and the organization.

Blau and Boal (1987) proposed a conceptual framework using four combinations of high and low levels of job involvement and organizational commitment to predict withdrawal and absenteeism. Employees of each of the four types responded to different organizational and personal cues when deciding whether to quit or to be absent; and they did the same when they chose the meanings that they attributed to their withdrawal. The first cell contained employees with high levels of job involvement and organizational commitment. Because work was important to their self-image, they were expected to put a high level of personal task-related effort into their jobs. In addition, because these individuals strongly identified with the organization and its goals, they were expected to display a high level of group-maintenance effort to help maintain the organization. The individuals in this cell represented the most valuable members to an organization, termed by Blau and Boal institutionalized stars. For institutionalized stars to quit, they would need to (a) be unhappy or disillusioned with the organization (disillusionment could occur because of goal displacement or a change in the organizational culture or climate), (b) be dissatisfied with their work, (c) feel under-rewarded. The nonlikelihood of co-occurrence of all three conditions led to the expectation that institutionalized stars generally did not actively seek other positions, although they would be sought after. Regarding absenteeism, institutionalized stars would make the greater effort to be present at work due to their high levels of job involvement and organizational commitment.

The second cell contained individuals with a high level of lob involvement and a low level of organizational commitment. Although work was important to them, they did not identify with the organization or its goals. Therefore, these individuals would invest a higher level of individual task-related effort, but would not show much group maintenance-related effort. Blau and Boal (1987) termed these individuals the *lone wolves* of an organization. The authors thought that Gouldner's (1958) definition of "cosmopolitans" had much in common with individuals in this cell. Because lone wolves were not bound to the organization, they would seek to leave voluntarily if better task-related opportunities arose elsewhere. With their combination of high job involvement and low organizational commitment, *lone wolves* believed in maximizing their work opportunities. Such individuals were more willing to violate the organization's absenteeism policy; personal and organizational goals conflicted because of the importance of their work agenda. Accordingly, a positive relation between absence and turnover was expected for lone wolves.

The third cell contained individuals who exhibited a low level of job involvement and a high level of organizational commitment. Their work was not personally important but they identified strongly with the organization and its goals. Therefore, such individuals did not exert much individual task-related effort, but focused instead on group maintenance-related effort. They were termed *corporate citizens* by Blau and Boal (1987). Gouldner's (1958) definition of "locals" had much in common with the individuals in this cell. Corporate citizens were likely to conform to the organization and fulfill their prescribed roles or behavioral expectations. They were not expected to leave voluntarily. They were less likely to violate illegitimately the organization's absenteeism rules because they identified with the organization.

The fourth cell contained individuals exhibiting low levels of job involvement and organizational commitment. Work was not viewed as important to the self-image of these employees so they did not exert a high level of task-related effort. Furthermore, because they did not strongly identify with the organization, these employees exerted the bare minimum of effort (task- and group-related) to get by. The individuals in this cell represented the least valued members in an organization. Blau and Boal (1987) labeled them *apathetic employees*. Their attachment or compliance with organizational expectations and norms arose from calculative judgements. They would be most sensitive to feelings of reward satisfaction and to the availability of other opportunities in decisions to withdraw. From the organization's perspective, if apathetic employees left voluntarily such turnover would be functional, especially if they were replaced by individuals who belonged to the other cells. Concerning absenteeism, apathetic employees were expected to take maximal advantage of any company policy that did not penalize the practice. However, whether their lack of attachment resulted in high rates of absenteeism or turnover depended on the constraints on each behavior, for example, labor market conditions that limited job opportunities.

Several studies tested this conceptual framework, and their findings are presented in Table 7.3. As can be seen from the data presented in the table, the main focus of the studies was to test the effect of the two commitments and of their interaction on work behaviors and attitudes. Although some of the research provided partial support for Blau and Boal's (1987) conceptualization, some research evinced no support. Huselid and Day (1991) for example, found that models estimated with ordinary regressions replicated the findings of Blau and Boal (1989). However, identical models estimated with logistic regressions provided no support for a commitment-involvement interaction. They concluded that the disparity in the results cast serious doubt on the empirical support for Blau and Boal's (1987) hypotheses. Keller (1997) examined the relationship between the two commitments and job-performance measures. Whereas job involvement was found related to each of the performance measures, no significant effect of the job involvement-organizational commitment interaction appeared on any of the performance measures. Keller suggested that perhaps Blau and Boal's conceptualization, which aimed to predict turnover and absenteeism, should remain within the limit of these two behaviors and not attempt to predict other behaviors.

Becker and Billing's (1993) Profiles of Commitment

Becker and Billing's (1993) model differs from the models shown previously. Although all those were based on clear conceptual frameworks advanced first and tested later, Becker and Billings extracted their profiles from data analysis. Using data collected earlier (Becker, 1992) they applied a statistical technique, cluster analysis, which generated the profiles. Eight variables applied in Becker's (1992) early conceptualization were the input for the cluster analysis: organization-related identification, organization-related internalization, supervisor-related identification, supervisor-related internalization, work-group related identification, work-group related internalization, normative commitment to top management, and overall compliance.

TABLE 7.3

Findings of research on the relationship between job involvement (JI) and organizational commitment (OC) with outcomes and/or correlates.

Studies	Sample	Outcomes and/or correlates of JI and OC	Method of analysis	Main findings	Magnitude of relationship
Blau (1986)	82 registered staff nurses at a large hospital located in a Midwestern city	Unexcused tardiness and unexcused absence	Hierarchical regression that includes JI, OC, and their interaction	For unexcused tardiness OC and an interaction of OC × JI were significantly related to it. For unexcused absence only the interaction of OC × JI was significantly related to it	For tardiness the full model explained 13% of the variance, 8% of it was added by the interaction. For absence, the full model explained 10% of the variance, 7% of it was added by the interaction
Blau & Boal (1989)	129 college graduates insurance personnel, of a company headquartered in a large Eastern city, working at various field offices around the US	Job withdrawal cognitions and actual turnover	High and low JI and OC categories were created using a median split on the two variables. Analysis of variance (ANCOVA) was performed	The JI by OC interaction significantly accounts for additional turnover variance beyond the covariance of sex, marital status, and tenure and the JI and OC main effects. Job withdrawal cognitions did not mediate the above relationship	Not reported
Mathieu & Kohler (1990)	193 transit bus operators from a large public authority in the Midwest	Four types of absence frequency: illness, personal, family obligations, transportation problems, and total absence	Moderated regression analysis that includes JI, OC, in the first step and the interaction of JI by OC in the second step	The direct effects of OC and JI were nonsignificant as related to any of the absence indices. The interaction term accounted for a significant additional variance only for personal absences. The interaction was significant for transportation absences but not the overall equation	The explained variance for all the equations, including the interactions, ranged between .01 to .05. Only the equation for personal absences was significant

continued on next page

TABLE 7.3 (continued)

Studies	Sample	Outcomes and/or correlates of JI and OC	Method of analysis	Main findings	Magnitude of relationship
Huselid & Day (1991)	138 third-level supervisors of a nationwide home-products retailing firm, headquartered in the Midwestern US	Actual turnover and several control variables such as age, gender, job tenure, job performance, met expectations, education, pay equity, etc.	Both ordinary regressions and logistic regressions evaluated research models. Continuance organizational commitment was also examined in addition to the attitudinal one	The ordinary regressions showed considerable support for the existence of attitudinal OC × JI interaction, as well as significant coefficients for attitudinal OC and JI (but not for continuance OC). The logistic regression procedure found none of the main effect or interaction terms to be significant	The explained variance for the ordinary regressions was r = .12 when JI, attitudinal OC, and their interaction is included in the model. The addition of continuance OC and its interaction with JI did not contribute significance variance
Martin & Hafer (1995)	108 full-time and 372 part-time telemarketing sales agents employed in eight locations of a major national telemarketing firm	Turnover intentions and several control variables such as employment status (part-time or full-time), gender and tenure	Moderated regression analysis that includes control variables in the first step, JI and OC in the second step and the interaction of JI by OC in the third step	OC and JI were significantly related to turnover intentions for both full-time and part-time employees. The interaction was significant only for full-time employees	The model for full-time employees explained 57% of the variance (1% was explained by the interaction). The model for part-time employees explained 54% of the variance (3% were explained by the interaction)
Keller (1997)	532 scientists and engineers of four corporate R & D organizations from the chemicals, energy, electronics, and scientific instruments industries	Measures of job performance such as supervisory performance ratings, number of patents obtained, number of publications	Moderated regression analyses	JI was significantly related to each of the three performance measures. OC and the interaction of OC by JI were not related to any of the performance measures	JI explained 9% of the variance of supervisory ratings, 7% of the variance of number of patents, and 10% of the variance of number of publications

McElroy, Morrow, Crum & Dooley (1995)	644 railroad employees such as shop crafts, train crews, clerks, and maintenance employees	Five dimensions of job satisfaction (i.e., work, promotion, supervisor, co-workers, pay) and eight dimensions of perceptions of climate (structure, rewards, warmth, support, identify, safety, and stress)	Analyses of covariance for JI and OC on each of the 13 dependent variables, controlling for tenure and job classification/union grouping	JI and OC were independently related to most of the attitudes. However, when the interaction effect in all the 13 attitudes was not statistically significant effects for the job involvement-organizational commitment interaction term	JI accounted for 1%–7% of the variance of the dependent variables. OC accounted for 2%–21% of the variance of the dependent variables.
Morrow, EmElroy, & Blum (1988)	2200 employees of a department of transportation in a Midwestern state in a variety of job categories	Tenure, position (supervisor vs. nonsupervisor)	Tenure, position, gender		

223

The cluster analysis produced four clusters, each representing a different profile. Cluster 1 included 46.1% of the total sample (440 employees). This profile of commitment involved relatively high commitment to top management and the organization, but relatively low commitment to the supervisor and work group. Becker and Billings (1993) labeled this cluster *globally committed*, because commitment for this group was directed toward the organization in general and top management, which perhaps best represented the interests of the organization in general. Cluster 2 included 25.1% of the sample, whose profile involved high levels of commitment to all four foci. This cluster was called the committed. Cluster 3 included 18.7% of the sample, whose commitment was universally low, regardless of foci. It was called the uncommitted. Finally, cluster 4 included 10.1% of the employees, whose profile involved low commitment to top management and the organization but high commitment to the supervisor and work group. This cluster was labeled the locally committed, because commitment for this group was directed at foci with which employees interacted regularly.

Having established the four profiles Becker, and Billings (1993) next tested hypotheses on the relation between them and correlates and outcomes. First, the findings showed that older workers, more educated workers, and workers with greater job tenure tended to be among the *committed* or the *locally committed*. The *committed* proved to have the highest overall satisfaction, the *uncommitted* the lowest. The *committed* more often engaged in prosocial organizational behavior than did the *uncommitted* and the *globally committed* but did not differ significantly from the *locally committed*. The *uncommitted* had the lowest level of overall prosocial organizational behavior. The *globally committed* had an overall level of prosocial organizational behavior between the *committed* and the *uncommitted*, but the *locally committed* were not significantly lower than the *committed*. The *globally* and *locally committed* did not differ significantly in prosocial organizational behavior.

As for turnover intentions, the *committed* were shown to have the lowest intent-to-quit, and the *uncommitted* the highest. The *globally committed* and *locally committed* had intent-to-quit levels between these two extremes, but not significantly different from each other. Also, the *locally committed* were more likely to be in teams than either the *uncommitted* or the *globally committed*. The *committed* were similarly more likely to be in teams than either the *uncommitted* or the *globally committed*. Differences in proportions between the *locally committed* and the *committed* were not significant.

Conclusions and Directions for Future Research

Four major attempts to develop and advance profiles of commitment have been presented. Two had their roots in the early literature of 1950s, namely the local-cosmopolitan profile and the dual commitment to union and employer; two of them, those of Boal and Blau (1987) and of Becker and Billings (1993), are relatively new and were influenced by the development of multiple commitment research. An important characteristic of the two earlier profiles is that they are based on the notion of conflict, or role conflict between two identities, profession and organization in one case and union and employer in the other. The notion of conflict between identities is not an important characteristic in the two later profiles. However, the four conceptualizations of these profiles seem similar in that they all include, overtly or covertly, some version of the local versus cosmopolitan profile. This strongly intimates that any future developments of commitment profiles should include the conflict between the organization and foci outside the organization, namely, the cosmopolitan-local-profile.

The cosmopolitan-local profile is one that has attracted much attention from researchers. However, it seems that more work is needed on this construct to increase its importance and value. First, the literature is still unclear regarding the approaches that can best conceptualize and operationalize this construct. Some use the commitment approach that is more relevant to the theme of this volume, and some attempt to develop measures specific to the concept of local and specific to the concept of cosmopolitan. So far, the commitment approach seems to have produced more valid and reliable instruments demonstrated in using the commitment scales, as against a variety of quite problematic scales for the cosmopolitan-local construct. Therefore, it is suggested that the commitment approach leads research on this construct. Second, far more conceptualization is needed regarding the profiles themselves. Until now the dominant conceptualization has been two-dimensional. However, more than two dimensions may be possible here. For example, an employee can be high on both commitments, low on both of them, high in one and low in the other. This means a four-dimensional profile. Yet, there is very little conceptual work on the meaning of these dimensions. Third, too little work has been done on the relation between the construct and its determinants and outcomes. It is difficult to determine the value of this concept without demonstrating its relationship to behaviors at work. Meyer et al.'s (1993) work is important in this regard because it examined the added contribution of occupational commitment to organizational commitment in predicting of a set of work outcomes. These authors found that occupational commitment increased the prediction of outcomes in addition to the prediction of organizational commitment. Many more such studies are needed to substantiate this important finding.

The profile of union versus organizational commitment is one of the more interesting profiles. The evidence accumulated so far demonstrates some interesting findings. However, the work on dual commitment suffers from some limitations. Gordon and Ladd (1990) pointed out many of them; some are methodological and some conceptual. A foremost limitation they mentioned is that the empirical work on the concept is not theory driven. More work is needed, for example, on the theoretical meaning of each of the four possible profiles derived from classifying employees according to high or low in each of the two commitments. What is the meaning of being dually committed to both union and management? What kind of behaviors and attitudes are expected from employees who are dually committed, and why? Gordon and Ladd (1990) also indicated some serious measurement problems that need to be addressed by future research. For example, what is the best cutoff point in the taxonomic approach? Use of the Pearson correlation in the dimensional approach also causes some problems, associated with the limitations of the Pearson correlation coefficient. These authors concluded that these fundamental issues needed to be resolved; otherwise research on dual commitment seemed pointless.

The model advanced by Blau and Boal (1987) regarding the job involvement-organizational commitment interaction provided an interesting conceptualization of commitment profiles. An advantage of this model is that it was designed better to predict work outcomes, one of the most important goals in commitment research. Yet, research evidence showed some limitations of this model. First, the variance accounted for by the two commitments, and particularly their interaction, was low in most cases. This showed the practical limitation of this conceptualization. Also, the rejection of Blau and Boal's conceptualization by replications of the findings that supported this model using more appropriate statistical techniques deserves attention in future research.

Blau and Boal's (1987) conceptualization in terms of multiple commitment research is limited mainly in that it focuses only on two commitment forms. The absence of other commitment forms might have some conceptual implications, and is perhaps a reason for the modest empirical support for the model. The main problem here is that this conceptualization concentrates on job involvement, not on occupational commitment. For professional employees, commitment to the occupation arguably exerts a strong effect on work outcomes, possibly even stronger than does job involvement.

Moreover, some of the arguments used in Blau and Boal's conceptualization (1987) seem more apt for occupational commitment than for job involvement. This holds particularly for two of the types they describe. The first is the lone wolves, namely, those with high job involvement and low organizational commitment. As noted, Blau and Boal (1987) stated that Gouldner's (1957, 1958) cosmopolitans shared much with their lone wolves. In fact, cosmopolitans, even as this definition was cited and used by

Blau and Boal (1987, p. 295), has far more in common with occupational commitment than with job involvement. Blau and Boal's description of the lone wolves is more appropriate for employees with high occupational commitment and low organizational commitment. The same argument holds regarding Blau and Boal's *corporate citizens*, those with high organizational commitment and low job involvement: They applied Gouldner's (1957, 1958) definition of locals to their corporate citizens' behavioral and attitudinal patterns. They also made use of Sheldon's (1971) study in their conceptualization. However, locals or corporate citizens can be better defined as employees with low occupational commitment rather than low job involvement. Blau and Boal's (1987) description, together with those of Gouldner (1957, 1958) and Sheldon (1971), are more appropriate for employees with high or low occupational commitment than with high or low job involvement. This is because Gouldner and Sheldon, in their conceptualizations, referred to the occupational values rather than to the job. All this leads to the conclusion that occupational commitment should not be ignored in any conceptualization of the effect of commitment forms on outcome variables.

Cohen's (1998) findings for example, did not support the conceptualization of a job involvement or organizational commitment interaction proposed by Blau and Boal (1987). Earlier research produced mixed results regarding this interaction, and Cohen's study tended to confirm the position (Huselid & Day, 1991) that Blau and Boal's (1987) hypotheses enjoyed little support. But Huselid and Day's (1991) lack of support resulted from their use of logistic regressions instead of the linear models used by Blau and Boal (1989). Cohen's (1998) conclusion however, was based on a conceptual argument that the effect of occupational commitment was stronger than the proposed job involvement or organizational commitment interaction. Occupational commitment was not tested together with job involvement and organizational commitment in previous research that examined this interaction effect. Cohen's findings support the argument presented earlier that occupational commitment expressed strong effects on attitudes and behaviors of professional employees. The inclusion of occupational commitment together with other commitment forms is argued to be the main reason for the lack of support for the organization or job interaction. Thus, in the broad context of commitment little empirical support exists for the job involvement or organizational commitment interaction.

Becker and Billing's (1993) profiles suffer from the limitation noted above of Reichers's approach to multiple commitments: The profiles do not acknowledge commitment foci such as the occupation or the job and are based on patterns of organizational commitment. In addition, one may criticize the development of profiles based on data analysis rather than a conceptual framework. However, as Becker and Billings (1993) concluded, their main contribution was to demonstrate that commitment profiles should be considered part of the explanation of commitment-related phenomena such as turnover, performance, and extra-role behaviors.

In short, much more work is needed on commitment profiles. This need is exemplified by the limited contribution of these profiles in accounting for variance in work outcomes. Few attempts to do so were made in the local-cosmopolitan and the dual commitment to union and employer profiles. The results to date show some potential for explaining some outcomes, but a great deal more research is needed on the relation between these profiles and outcomes. Blau and Boal's (1987) job involvement or organizational commitment profile was specifically designed for better prediction of behaviors such as turnover and absenteeism, and the studies based on this profile applied the appropriate techniques to examine this relation. Still, the variance accounted for in work outcomes is relatively low, rarely exceeding .05. The single study on Becker and Billing's (1993) profile bars us from reaching any conclusions.

However, the potential benefits of developing commitment profiles were described earlier, and they are important. Commitment profiles can assist organizations in both selection and maintenance of human resource functions. If organizations know which profiles are more beneficial for them they can integrate some of this knowledge into their selection criteria. Also, they can include and increase the relevant commitments through their training programs. Conceptually, developing profiles of commitment can increase our understanding of similarities and differences between commitment forms. They can also promote greater comprehension of the relation between commitment forms and outcomes. As Becker and Billings (1993) argued, because the identification of relevant constructs is an essential element of theory development, the investigation of commitment profiles should be regarded as laying the groundwork for further conceptual and empirical work.

8

Commitment Forms and Nonwork Domains

Few studies have examined the influence of the family and other nonwork domains on work behavior and particularly on commitment. Organizational researchers and management studies have mostly ignored the influence of families and focused instead almost exclusively on job and economic factors to predict performance and commitment (Orthner & Pittman, 1986). As a result the work and nonwork relation has attracted much speculation but has produced little in the way of concrete results. Despite some research and debate on the issue, the relation between work and other aspects of our lives is still not well understood (Near, Rice, & Hunt, 1980; Perlow, 1998). This is quite true for the relation between nonwork domains and commitment in the workplace. This relation has rarely been examined and in fact has been neglected by commitment scholars. They have focused on work-related variables as determinants of commitment forms and overlooked the possible effects of extra-work factors on this relation.

A reason why researchers should focus on the impact of extra-work variables on work-related attitudes such as commitment is that family, financial security, and household factors play an important role in explaining work-related outcomes. The justification for evaluating the effects of family and household variables on various commitment domains lies in the premise that just as workplace factors affect extra-work life, so do family and household factors influence organizational and career commitments. The impact of family and household factors on commitment domains is emphasized as an especially salient issue for working women with families. This is because research suggests what many have long suspected: Married professional women, because they still carry the burden of household responsibilities, have more role obligations than do their male counterparts, and may be more likely to experience inter-role conflict than do married professional men. Household factors such as the willingness of the family to share household chores, the capacity of the family to plan and solve problems, and the level of marital satisfaction may be expected to affect the professional woman's capacity to commit her to various foci in the workplace (Steffy & Jones, 1988).

Some indirect attention to the notion that commitment in the workplace might be related to nonwork domains was mentioned in early research on the work and nonwork relation. This research emphasized the need for further empirical explorations of how the nonwork domain is related to behavior and attitudes in the workplace (Goldthorpe, Lockwood, Bechhofer, & Platt, 1968, 1969, 1971; Blauner, 1964, 1969). Some of this research (Goldthorpe et al., 1968) predicted that in the future workers would emphasize their nonwork needs at the expense of their commitment to their employer. This argument has rarely been tested empirically.

In later research, the sociological perspective on work involvement has been offered as a reminder that individuals in modern industrial societies are engaged in multiple social roles (Champoux, 1981). Followers of this perspective argued that the task for future research for both the sociologist and psychologist is to understand why, and to what degree, individuals become involved in one role rather than another (Perlow, 1998, 1999; Shaffer, Harrison, Matthew, Gilley, & Luk, 2001). Furthermore, because it is clear that the work role is not acted out in a social vacuum, greater use of extra work variables should be made in work and organizational research (Champoux, 1981; Perlow, 1998). This contention demonstrates the usefulness of commitment in both work and nonwork domains as a concept that can assist us in understanding how individuals cope with multiple and sometimes conflicting roles inside and outside the work setting.

A demonstration of the above contention can be found in the early studies regarding work as a central life interest (Dubin, 1956; Orzack, 1963; Kornhauser, 1965). The concept of work as a central life interest examines the importance of the work role compared with other roles, particularly nonwork roles. A problem in this line of investigation is concept redundancy because items that represent work and nonwork domains are included in the same scale that measures this concept, impeding evaluation of how one domain is related to or affected by the other (Morrow, 1983). Yet, the aforementioned studies were perhaps the first attempt to deal empirically with the relation between one form of commitment and nonwork domains.

Although these arguments emphasize the usefulness of commitment as an important concept in the relation between work and nonwork, early research on the relation between commitment and nonwork was sparse and most of it dealt with this relation indirectly. As a result, a meager conceptual framework was advanced for this relation and little research examined it empirically. Only in later years was attention renewed in nonwork domains, in the context of commitment. Mathieu and Kohler (1990) and Cohen (1993a) for example, argued in this respect that the relations between a variety of commitment forms and nonwork domains needed to be examined. Later research indeed paid more attention to the relation between several commitment forms and nonwork domains (Cohen, 1995, 1997b).

Conceptual Framework

Although no specific framework has been developed for the relation between commitment forms and nonwork domains, the common conceptual framework for nonwork domains is also relevant for the relation between commitment forms and nonwork. This has been demonstrated in the fact that most research on the relation between commitment forms and nonwork domains applied this framework. This common theory shaped three competing models of this relation (Champoux, 1981; Randall, 1988) based on a role theory that permits examination of the importance of, and effort devoted to, multiple roles (Randall, 1988). The same people typically engage in distinct institutional spheres (e.g., the family, the work organization), where each of these spheres bears a set of expectations of appropriate behavior. Individuals may need to manage potentially competing expectations from a variety of work and nonwork spheres.

   The *spillover* or the *expansion* model states that the nature of one's work experiences carry over into the nonwork domain and affect attitudes and behaviors therein. Hence, an individual's degree of involvement at work is be directly related to his or her degree of involvement in social roles outside the workplace. The functioning of the spillover model can be understood in terms of generalization of beliefs, attitudes, and values learned in one setting to another. The *compensatory* or the *scarcity* models state that workers who experience a sense of deprivation at work compensate for it in their choice of nonwork activities. This model suggests that individuals who are not involved in their work seek involvement outside work. An individual holding a job that does not permit him or her to be creative compensates by choosing creative nonwork activities. The third model can be termed the *segregation model*, and it suggests that no relation exist between one's work and one's nonwork domain. The institutions of work are entirely segregated, physically, temporally and functionally, from the various social institutions in the nonwork sphere. Each institution makes separate and virtually independent value and behavioral demands on the individual. By the segregation model, work involvement could safely be studied with no concern for nonwork roles. From the empirical literature, Champoux (1981) concluded that the evidence so far did not allow any conclusion about which model was the most valid, so the conditions under which an individual would follow any of the three models could not be described with certainty.

Research on the relation between commitment forms and nonwork domains is far from conclusive regarding the nature of the relation between commitment and extra-work domains. Randall (1987) suggested that the relation between commitment and the nonwork domain should be negative, following the compensatory model. Accordingly, Randall posited a zero-sum relation between commitment and other aspects of an individual's life; for example, she proposed that high levels of organizational commitment would result in stress and tension in an individual's personal life. Romzek (1989) advanced an alternative approach, arguing that this trade-off reasoning reflected a subtle but significant misunderstanding of the concept of commitment as psychological attachment. Unlike time, the competing claimant was not finite. High levels of psychological attachments to a work organization did not necessarily mean lack of psychological energy to sustain commitment. According to Romzek (1989), this tendency to link a high level of absorption in work with psychological attachment to a work organization may be the source of the discrepancy between the propositions of Randall (1987) and of Romzek (1989). Psychological attachment to a work organization is not the same as high absorption, or workaholism, both of which presume a preoccupation with the focal role. Employees with high levels of organizational commitment have strong psychological attachment to their work organizations, but are not necessarily exclusively or excessively absorbed in their jobs, nor are they necessarily workaholics. Employees with high levels of organizational involvement can also sustain high levels of psychological attachment to their families, their social organizations, and so on.

Research Findings

Specific Forms of Commitment and Nonwork Domains.   As mentioned above not much research has been done on the relation between foci of commitment and nonwork domains; in fact, research on the impact of extra-work factors on work and nonwork commitments is virtually nonexistent (Steffy & Jones, 1988). Most studies have concentrated on the relation between organizational commitment and nonwork domains (Randall, 1988; Romzek, 1989; Wiley, 1987; Kirchmeyer, 1992). Fewer studies examined the relation between commitment forms other than organizational. The main findings of these studies are presented in Table 8.1. The findings showed that commitment forms, particularly organizational commitment, are related to a variety of aspects that represent nonwork domains. Domains

TABLE 8.1

Findings of Research on the Relationship Between Commitment Forms and Nonwork Domains

Studies	Sample	Commitment Form/s Examined	Aspects of Nonwork Domains Examined	Main Findings	Magnitude of Relationship
Randall (1989)	455 classified staff personnel at a large Western US university	Organizational commitment	A set of questions dealing with the effort and importance of seven non-work activities such as hobbies, friends, political parties, family, and so on	Weak correlations were found between some of the nonwork activities and commitment: importance of political organizations, religious organizations, family, other jobs, effort to other jobs, political organizations, and friends	The correlations ranged between r = .09 to r = .20. The correlations for effort and importance of other jobs were the highest (r = −.19; r = −.20 respectively) but were negative
Romzek (1989)	334 full-time public employees from three federal offices, three state agencies, and three local governments in Kansas and Missouri	Organizational involvement	Nonwork satisfaction, family involvement	Organizational involvement at time one and family involvement at time two affected nonwork satisfaction positively	The variables, organizational involvement, family involvement and age as a control variable accounted for 11% of the variance of nonwork satisfaction
Wiley (1987)	191 MBA and graduate students enrolled in evening classes at a large Southeastern university	Organizational commitment and job involvement	Job/person conflict, role overload, job/family conflict, and family/job conflict	A negative effect of job/person conflict and a positive effect of job/family conflict on organizational commitment; a positive effect of job/family conflict and a negative effect of family/job conflict on job involvement	The models accounted for 13% of the variance of organizational commitment and 21% of the variance of job involvement
Gray (1989)	249 female nursing personnel working at a large hospital in an urban Florida community	Organizational commitment	Work interference with family life, family support	Work interference with family life, gender ideology, and children were related to organizational commitment. Other variables included in the regression such as family support education, training, marital status, race, were not significant	The variables in the regression model accounted for 16% of the variance of organizational commitment

continued on next page

TABLE 8.1 (continued)

Studies	Sample	Commitment Form/s Examined	Aspects of Nonwork Domains Examined	Main Findings	Magnitude of Relationship
Kirchmeyer (1992)	122 graduates of a business program in a Western Canadian university who occupy low- to middle-level management jobs	Organizational commitment	Time commitment to nonwork domain, and resource enrichment from nonwork domain	The hours spent in, and resources provided by, certain non-work activities contributed significantly to the prediction of organizational commitment after the effects of work-related correlates, including work involvement, were controlled	The two nonwork domain variables added 5% to 13% to the regression equations. The total variance accounted for in these regression equations ranged between .30–.41
Scandura & Lankau (1997)	160 matched male and female managers working in a variety of organizations in the US	Organizational commitment	Family responsibility, flexible work hours	Women who perceived their organizations offered flexible work hours reported higher organizational commitment (OC) than women who did not. Flexible work hours were not related to higher OC for those having family responsibilities	The MANOVA analysis showed a significant interaction effect for gender and flexible work hours and a significant effect for the interaction of family responsibility and flexible work hours
Loundsbury & Hoopes (1986)	92 females and 36 males who were drawn from 24 different organizations, and their jobs represented 43 different positions within these organizations	Organizational commitment and job involvement	Length of vacation and vacation satisfaction	The MANOVA results showed that job involvement measured as a central life interest decreased after a vacation Regression analysis showed that neither the length of vacation nor vacation satisfaction contributed uniquely to the prediction of post-vacation job involvement or organizational commitment	Neither length of vacation, nor vacation satisfaction explained accounted for a significant variance of postvacation job involvement or postvacation organizational commitment
Blegen, Mueller, Price (1988)	2070 all levels of hospital employees in five hospitals in the Rocky Mountain area	Organizational commitment	Kinship responsibility	Kinship responsibility has a positive but moderate correlation with organizational commitment. The correlation was higher for female than for male.	The total correlation was $r = .10$. The correlation was $r = .09$ for males and $r = .21$ for females

O'Driscoll, Ilgen, & Hildreth (1992)	120 persons residing in Lansing, Michigan, were randomly selected from the local telephone directory	Organizational commitment	Off-job satisfaction, off-the-job time demands, job and off-job interference, psychological strain	Path analysis showed that off-job-satisfaction had no direct influence on commitment, although it was linked with it indirectly via job satisfaction. Off-job interference and job time demands contributed significantly to variance in commitment	Zero order correlation of commitment with psychological strain was r = –.28. The correlations with all other nonwork variables were below .14
Aryee (1992)	354 married professional women employed in both public and private sectors in Singapore	Occupational commitment, spouse occupational commitment	Job-spouse conflict, job-parent conflict, and job-homemaker conflict	Higher levels of occupational commitment increased job-parent conflict. Spouse's occupational commitment was not related to job-parent conflict. Occupational commitment and spouse's occupational commitment were not related to job-spouse conflict or to job-homemaker conflict	Occupational commitment together with parental commitment explained 6% of the variance of job-parent conflict
Steffy & Jones (1988)	118 female and married registered nurses in a large psychiatric hospital located in the Northeast	Organizational commitment, career commitment, community commitment	Dual career planning/support, marital satisfaction, perceived satisfaction of problem solving in the marriage, household coping mechanisms	Career planning was related to organizational commitment. Marital satisfaction, career planning, coping behavior, dual career planning/support, and having relatives in vicinity were related to career commitment. Career planning and number of children were related to community commitment	The simple r-square (the value that would be obtained if only this predictor was used in the regression equation) for each of the variables that were related to the three commitment forms ranged between .51 to .83

continued on next page

TABLE 8.1 (continued)

Studies	Sample	Commitment Form/s Examined	Aspects of Nonwork Domains Examined	Main Findings	Magnitude of Relationship
Wallace (1997)	512 active members of the legal profession in a large, Metropolitan city in Western Canada. The sample was stratified by gender (51% males)	General commitment to work and professional commitment	Number of hours worked and work-to-non-work spillover	Path analysis showed that while commitment to work in general was positively related to hours worked, professional commitment was not. Neither work commitment form was related directly or indirectly with work-to-non-work spillover	The two commitment forms together explained significant unique variance in hours worked, 5%. They did not make a substantial incremental contribution to variation in work spillover
Orthner & Pittman (1986)	751 married air force members with less than ten years of service who resided on six air force bases	Job commitment	Perceived organizational support, and family support	Path analysis (LISREL) showed that perceived organizational support had direct and positive effects on family support and job commitment. A direct and positive effect was found for perceived family support on job commitment	Standardized parameter estimate between organizational support and job commitment was .62. Standardized parameter estimate between family support and job commitment was .32
Frone & Rice (1987)	141 nonteaching professional employees at a major public university in the Northeastern US	Job involvement	Two dimensions of work-family conflict: job spouse conflict, and job parent conflict, and family involvement	Moderated regression analysis showed that job-spouse conflict was positively related to job involvement among high spouse involved individuals but not among low spouse involved. Job involvement was positively related to job-parent conflict regardless of the level of parental involvement	10% of the variance in job-spouse conflict was explained by job involvement, spouse involvement (not significant) and their interaction that added 5%. Job involvement explained 10% of the variations in job-parent conflict
Frone, Russel & Cooper (1992)	631 employed adults residing in Erie County, New York. They were married or had children living at home	Job involvement	Family involvement, family-work conflict and work-family conflict	Path analysis showed that job involvement was not related to work-family conflict. Family involvement was positively and significantly related to family-work conflict	The path coefficient between family involvement and family-work conflict was .12

		Union commitment	Family commitment		
Aryee & Debrah (1997)	205 members of three branches of an industrial union and an enterprise union in Singapore			The two variables were not correlated	The correlation between union and family commitment was −.06 and not significant
Furnham & Rose (1987)	86 full time employees, students, housewives and retired. Most of them were employees	Protestant work ethic	Leisure ethic defined as seeing recreation as the main means to personal fulfillment	There was a negative correlation between Protestant work ethic and leisure ethic	The size of the correlation was $r = -.31$
Kirchmeyer (1995)	221 Canadian managers belonged to a national management association and were active in multiple domains	Organizational commitment	Nonwork involvement, nonwork hours, and three types of perceived organizational responses to nonwork: separation, integration, and respect	Regression analysis showed that nonwork involvement and nonwork hours were not related to organizational commitment. Two of the three types of organizational responses were related to commitment: separation negatively and respect positively	Separation, respect and integration entered to the regression equation in step 2 added 9% (significant) to the variance of organizational commitment
Mellor, Mathieu, Barnes-Farell, & Rogelberg, (2001)	Sample 1: 1252 employees at 16 communication companies and Sample 2: 470 employees in a variety of jobs and organizations	Affective and continuance organizational commitment	Relatives, spouse's relatives, children, marital status	Main effect findings showed that marital status was the only variable related to affective commitment and only in sample 2. Children and several interactions (marital status × relatives; children × relatives; children × spouse's relatives) were related to continuance commitment in both samples	The variance of affective and continuance commitment explained by research variables ranged between .00 to .07

are examined more intensively were different aspects of conflict between one's family role and one's work role. Individual and organizational coping strategies, with the resulting conflict between the roles, is aspect also examined in research, although not intensively as the foregoing. Less research examined the relation between commitment to objects in the work setting and commitment to objects in nonwork settings.

Noteworthy in the findings of all the above research is that the direction of the relationship is not consistent. In some research, aspects of nonwork domains decrease levels of commitment forms and in other research they increase them. This finding shows than none of the theories, the spillover or the compensatory models, can be defined as better characterizing the relation between commitment forms and nonwork domains. The relation seems to be more complex in the sense that different theories can be relevant for some aspects of nonwork domains but not for others. In other words, the nature of the nonwork domain in question seems to determine the nature of the relation between it and a given commitment focus. In short, the conflicting results in Table 8.1 demonstrate the need for further research, as well as conceptual development, in the nature of the relation between commitment foci and nonwork domains.

Multiple Commitment Approach

Few works examined multiple commitments and their relation with nonwork domains. In fact, only two studies examined this relation, applying a multiple commitment approach (Cohen, 1995, 1997b). Accordingly these should be viewed as exploratory, able to guide future research on the issue. The first study (Cohen, 1995) examined directly the relation between multiple commitments and aspects of nonwork domains. It contributed by examining the relationship between nonwork domains and several forms of work commitment simultaneously; by proposing and examining a conceptual classification of work commitment forms; and by examining the possibility of a complex interaction effect of nonwork to work domains. A major advantage of Cohen's work is the examination of five commitment forms simultaneously in their relation to nonwork domains. This had not been done by earlier research; most studies examined one form of commitment.

Cohen (1995) employed the following typology for testing this relation. The five foci of commitment examined in his research, such as organization, job, occupation, work, and Protestant work ethic (PWE) were divided into two categories: one comprised organization, job, and occupation, the other work and PWE. Cohen justified this classification by arguing that one way to conceptualize these distinctions among work commitment forms was, as suggested by Blau et al. (1993), on a time line. Job involvement and organizational commitment had a more immediate focus, occupational commitment was intermediate, and PWE and work involvement were seen as long term. In an expansion of this distinction, the organization, the job, and occupation were commitment foci related to the work setting more directly and closely than work involvement and PWE. Organization, job, and occupation were more specific, definite, and concrete foci in terms of their relationship with the immediate work setting. PWE and work involvement were more abstract and general. In keeping with this distinction, Cohen (1995) held that any effects of nonwork domains on work commitment would be more meaningful and explicit in terms of the effects on commitment to organization, job, and occupation (career) than the effects on abstract and long-term commitments, such as work in general and PWE. For example, more time devoted to the family might result in higher satisfaction with the family, as well as fewer work or family conflicts, and this should have a positive impact on one's behaviors and attitudes to the work setting. To theorize such an impact on work involvement or on PWE was difficult because the effect on these commitments seemed to be more long-term and indirect.

Cohen (1995) also examined the relation between personal and organizational responses to nonwork and commitment forms. As for personal responses, he argued that the type of personal strategy used to cope with the demands and responsibilities of multiple domains appeared to affect the experience of interdomain conflict (Hall, 1972; Kirchmeyer, 1993a). Successfully coping with multiple domains involved operating good personal organization and developing an appropriate attitude. Kirchmeyer (1993a) found that managers seemed to be most effectively helped to cope with a multitude of life domains by strategies aimed at altering their own attitudes as opposed to altering others', and by increasing their personal efficiency as opposed to decreasing their activity level or relying on others. Accordingly, it was expected that the way individuals coped with their nonwork domains would affect their commitment. Effectiveness in dealing with nonwork domains should result in fewer work or nonwork conflicts; this might prevent the development of negative attitudes to the work setting, which can be perceived as a possible cause of these conflicts. People who dealt more effectively with pressures from nonwork claimants were expected to be more committed to work foci than those who handled nonwork domains less effectively. However, the effect of individual coping strategies was expected to vary for different commitment forms. PWE and work involvement were attitudes reflecting personal beliefs less related to the immediate work setting. Accordingly, they were expected not to be strongly related to work commitment, but to variables representing other personal traits such as the ability to deal effectively with multiple pressures. Organizational and occupational commitment, together with job involvement, were attitudes related to the work setting, and would be related to variables closer to that setting, such as work commitment.

Cohen (1995) contended that of equal importance to the issue of personal coping strategies was the way organizations coped with work and nonwork issues. Kanter (1977) identified two opposing types of responses to work and nonwork issues adopted by employers. One response was based on the myth of separate work and nonwork worlds. Employers with this outlook expected employees to leave their nonwork lives at the office or factory door, and were concerned mainly with employees' work behaviors. The contrary type of response was termed *integration*. Here employers assumed responsibility not only for employees' work lives, but also for aspects of their nonwork lives. This response, aimed at closing the work and nonwork gap, could reduce the conflict between work and nonwork domains and should result in more favorable attitudes toward the organization (Bailyn, Fletcher, & Kolb, 1997; Kirchmeyer, 1993b).

The way in which the organization responded to its employees' nonwork domains was thus expected to affect their commitment. The greater the respect shown by the organization with regard to its employees' nonwork domains, the higher the resultant level of commitment from those employees. The effect of the organizational response was expected to be different for the different commitments. It would be stronger regarding the more work-specific commitments, such as the organization, job, and career, and was expected to have a weaker effect on the more general commitments, such as work and PWE. The logic for this differential effect stemmed from the argument proposed earlier that what the organization does will have a stronger effect on attitudes more related to the immediate work setting (e.g., commitment to the organization, job, and occupation) and less on more general work attitudes (e.g., work involvement and PWE). The more general commitments were not expected to be affected by any particular organizational policy, because they arose from the individual's value systems.

Cohen (1995) also advanced the possibility of interaction effects among commitment forms in their relation to nonwork domains. Whereas Randall (1988) examined the direct effect of the importance of outside ties and the effort invested in them on organizational commitment, Cohen argued that such an effect might not be direct but moderated by the organizational or individual responses to nonwork domains. The effect of nonwork domains on commitment forms might be stronger for employees who cope better with the nonwork domains than for those who cope with them less well. Putting more effort into nonwork domains increases the pressures on one's life and the potential for work and nonwork conflicts. For employees who cope better with the pressures from work and nonwork domains, more effort directed towards nonwork domains would lead to more positive effects of nonwork on work domains by reducing the pressures of more demands on their lives. For employees who do not cope effectively with pressures from their work and nonwork domains, more additional demands from nonwork domains would increase the pressures on them and might lead to negative attitudes to work. The proposed interaction effect was expected to be stronger for work involvement and PWE because of the expected stronger effect of personal coping strategies on these commitment foci.

The effect of nonwork domains upon work commitment might be stronger when the organization supported the nonwork domains of its employees. The logic was similar to that of personal coping strategies. Organizational support for nonwork issues (e.g., having employees assistance programs, providing Flexi time, and not being rigid about keeping certain hours) would reduce the pressures caused by an increasing role in nonwork domains, thus maintaining and even strengthening the effect of nonwork domain on work commitment. The opposite was expected when the organization was not supportive of its employees' nonwork domains. In this case, an increasing role in nonwork domains would cause more pressures on a workers' life and might lead to more work and nonwork conflicts, and as a result to negative work attitudes. This interaction effect was not expected to hold for work involvement and PWE because of the limited effects of organizational policies on these two commitments.

Finally, the use of two moderators for the relation between nonwork domains and work commitment raised the possibility of a joint effect of these moderators and thus a possibility of a three-way interaction effect. It was reasonable to expect that the interaction of nonwork domains and personal coping strategies would differ depending on the support of the organization for nonwork. That is, the nonwork domain and personal coping strategies would operate differently when the organization supported the nonwork domains of its employees from when it did not. One explanation is that in a supportive organization the effect of nonwork domains on work commitment is positive for employees who cope effectively with their nonwork domains. On one hand worker who values her or his nonwork domains, and uses effective coping strategies to prevent work and nonwork conflicts, responds by higher commitment when the organization supports his or her nonwork domains. On the other hand, a worker who values his or her nonwork domains, and uses effective coping strategies to prevent work and nonwork conflicts, but realizes that the organization is not supportive of his or her efforts and coping, reacts negatively toward the organization.

Cohen (1995) examined the expectations mentioned previously in a sample of 238 nurses from two hospitals, one mid-sized and one small, located in two medium-sized cities in Western Canada. To control for possible differences between the two hospitals, Cohen decided to use an indicator variable for the organization in the regression equations so that heterogeneity among the tested groups would be controlled. Two additional control variables were tenure and education. Organizational commitment was measured by the shorter nine-item version of the Organizational Commitment Questionnaire (OCQ; Porter et al., 1974). Career commitment was measured by the eight-item measure developed by Blau (1985). Job involvement (10 items) and work involvement (6 items) were measured by the scales developed by Kanungo (1979, 1982). PWE was measured by the 19-item scale developed by Mirels and Garrett (1971).

The main findings of Cohen's study are presented in Tables 8.1 and 8.2. Table 8.1 shows the correlation matrix among research variables and Table 2 the regression analyses of nonwork domain variables of commitment forms. The findings showed that nonwork domains affected all work commitment forms, particularly organizational commitment. Also, variables representing nonwork domains could affect forms of work commitment in different ways. For example, although organizational commitment was strongly related to one variable (e.g., organizational support for nonwork), job involvement was affected by a complex three-way interaction effect.

As mentioned previously Cohen's (1995) research employed a classification of work commitment forms that constituted the basis for the research hypotheses, and it received partial support by the findings. The findings showed a good match with the classification offered here in three commitment foci: organizational and occupational commitment, which represented the immediate short-term work-related commitments, and PWE, which represented the more general long-term commitment. The main problem of the classification can be seen in the findings regarding job and work involvement. Results of Table 8.2 showed more similarities than differences between these two commitment forms in both the correlation and the regression analyses. Kanungo (1982) developed and proposed these two measures based on the argument that, in this way, it would be possible conceptually to distinguish the two as representing two different contexts, that is, a specific or particular work context (job involvement) and a more generalized work context (work involvement). From the findings of Cohen's study, it is difficult to conclude that job and work involvement, in the way they are operationalized, represent two different contexts, and insufficient discriminant validity between the two is one explanation for the findings. Cohen concluded that future research should explore this issue further to find out whether this similarity occurs only regarding the relation of the two commitments with nonwork domains or with other variables also.

Cohen's (1995) findings tend to support the expansion or the spillover model to a work and nonwork relation. As Table 8.1 shows, most of the significant correlations between nonwork claimants and work commitment

TABLE 8.2

Descriptive statistics, reliabilities, and intercorrelations among research variables (reliabilities in parentheses)

	Mean	S.D.	1	2	3	4	5	6	7	8	9	10	11	12
1. Organization	.66	.47												
2. Tenure	10.41	7.34	.00											
3. Education	3.43	1.50	.06	-.21***										
4. Organizational commitment	38.88	8.19	-.13*	.16**	-.11*	(.83)								
5. Job involvement	32.84	8.25	-.16**	.14*	.02	.47***	(.79)							
6. Occupational commitment	36.99	9.31	-.10	-.02	.02	.47***	.57***	(.87)						
7. Work involvement	18.41	4.81	-.15**	.09	-.01	.39***	.64***	.40***	(.64)					
8. Protestant work ethic	71.88	12.55	-.04	-.04	-.12*	.16**	.38***	.25***	.44***	(.78)				
9. Effort to outside ties	20.09	3.82	-.06	.00	-.03	.22***	.03	.18*	.08	.03				
10. Importance of outside ties	22.99	3.88	-.07	.03	.07	.27***	.16**	.22**	.16**	.10	.69***			
11. Personal coping strategies	27.74	5.06	-.10	-.07	.13*	.22***	.02	.15*	.02	.06	.33***	.25***	(.75)	
12. Organizational support for nonwork	11.19	3.94	.16**	.04	.04	.26***	.14*	.19*	.13*	.06	-.13*	.09	.16**	(.73)

Note: N = 208–238 due to missing values. 1. 0 = organization 1; 1 = organization 2 *p ≤ .05 **p ≤ .01 ***p ≤ .001.

From Cohen, A. (1995). An examination of the relationship s between work commitment and nonwork domains, *Human Relations*, 48, 249.

Copyright © 2002 by Sage Publications. Reprinted with permission.

Table 8.3

Multiple Regression Analyses (Standardized Coefficients) of Nonwork Domains Variables (With Importance of Outside Ties) on Multiple Commitments.

	Organizational Commitment						Job Involvement						Occupational Commitment					
	Step 1	Step 2	Step 3	Step 4	Step 5	Step 6	Step 1	Step 2	Step 3	Step 4	Step 5	Step 6	Step 1	Step 2	Step 3	Step 4	Step 5	Step 6
Control Variables																		
Organization	-.13	-.13	-.13	-.13	-.13	-.13	-.16*	-.17*	-.17*	-.18*	-.18*	-.17*	-.10	-.10	-.10	-.10	-.11	-.10
Tenure	.14*	.12	.12	.12	.11	.11	.15*	.13	.13	.14	.14	.14*	-.02	-.04	-.04	-.03	-.04	-.03
Education	-.08	-.12	-.12	-.12	-.12	-.12	.06	.04	.04	.05	.05	.05	.02	-.01	-.01	-.00	-.00	-.00
Nonwork Domains Variables																		
Importance to outside ties	.21**	.21**	.21**	.22***	.22**	.14*	.14*	.14*	.14*	.13	.18*	.18*	.18*	.19*	.18*			
Personal coping strategies	.13	.13	.13	.13	.12		-.05	-.05	-.06	-.06	-.10	.06	.06	.05	.05	.03		
Organizational support for nonwork	.27***	.27***	.27***	.27***	.27***	.15*	.15*	.15*	.15*	.14	.20**	.20**	.20**	.20*	.19*			
Interactions																		
Importance to outside ties × Personal coping strategies			.02	.02	.01	.01			-.00	.01	.00	-.01			-.00	.00	-.00	-.01
Importance to outside ties × Organizational support for nonwork				-.01	-.01	-.02				-.06	-.06	-.08				-.06	-.06	-.07
Personal coping strategies × Organizational support for nonwork					.07	.07					.01	.01					.04	.04

Protestant Work Ethic and Work Involvement — hierarchical regression results

	Work Involvement						Protestant Work Ethic					
	Step 1	Step 2	Step 3	Step 4	Step 5	Step 6	Step 1	Step 2	Step 3	Step 4	Step 5	Step 6
Control Variables												
Organization	-.15*	-.17*	-.16*	-.16*	-.17*	-.16*	-.04	-.03	-.02	-.02	-.02	-.02
Tenure	.10	.08	.08	.08	.08	.08	-.06	-.07	-.05	-.06	-.06	-.07
Education	.02	.01	.00	.00	.00	.01	-.13	-.14	-.15*	-.16*	-.16*	-.16*
Nonwork Domains Variables												
Importance to outside ties	.14*	.14*	.14*	.15*	.14		.09	.09	.09	.11	.10	
Personal coping strategies	-.05	-.05	-.05	-.05	-.07		.03	.03	.05	.05	.05	
Organizational support for nonwork	.15*	.14*	.14*	.14	.13		.06	.04	.03	.02	.02	
Interactions												
Importance to outside ties × Personal coping strategies		-.03	-.03	-.04	-.05	-.16*		-.20**	-.21**	-.23**	-.23**	-.23**

Summary statistics

	Work Involvement						Protestant Work Ethic					
	Step 1	Step 2	Step 3	Step 4	Step 5	Step 6	Step 1	Step 2	Step 3	Step 4	Step 5	Step 6
Importance to outside ties × Personal coping strategies × Organizational support for nonwork						.02						.15*
R^2 (Adjusted)	.05(.03)	.22(.19)	.22(.19)	.22(.18)	.22(.18)	.22(.18)	.05(.03)	.09(.06)	.09(.05)	.09(.05)	.09(.05)	.09(.06)
F	3.13*	8.43***	7.21*	6.28***	5.72***	5.13***	3.05*	2.97**	2.29*	2.03*	2.23*	2.53*
ΔR^2	.17	.00	.00	.00	.04		.13	.00	.03	.06	.04	.01
F for ΔR^2	13.12***	1.20	.03	.00	2.80*		.68	.00	3.80*	6.25***	.96	.64

	Step 1	Step 2	Step 3	Step 4	Step 5	Step 6
Importance to outside ties × Personal coping strategies × Organizational support for nonwork						.08
R^2 (Adjusted)	.11(.06)	.01(.00)	.10(.07)	.10(.07)	.10(.06)	.11(.06)
F	2.29*	2.03*	0.66	3.48***	2.97**	2.67**
ΔR^2	.28					1.23

continued on next page

245

TABLE 8.3 (continued)

	Work Involvement						Protestant Work Ethic					
	Step 1	Step 2	Step 3	Step 4	Step 5	Step 6	Step 1	Step 2	Step 3	Step 4	Step 5	Step 6
Importance to outside ties × Organizational support for nonwork			-.00	-.00	-.01					.10	.10	.09
Personal coping strategies × Organizational support for nonwork				.03	.03					.10	.10	
Importance to outside ties × Personal coping strategies × Organizational support for nonwork					.08					.00		
R^2 (Adjusted)	.03(.02)	.07(.04)	.08(.04)	.08(.03)	.08(.03)	.08(.03)	.02(.00)	.03(.00)	.07(.04)	.08(.04)	.09(.05)	.09(.04)
F	2.07	2.47*	2.13*	1.86	1.67	1.61	1.16	1.12	2.07*	2.04*	2.02*	1.81
ΔR^2		.04	.00	.00	.00	.00		.01	.04	.01	.01	.00
F for ΔR^2		2.81*	.20	.00	.20	1.10		1.07	7.56**	1.73	1.81	.00

Note: N = 209–238 due to missing values 1. 0 = organization 1; 1 = organization 2 *$p \leq .05$ **$p \leq .01$ ***$p \leq .001$

From Cohen, A. An examination of the relationship s between work commitment and nonwork domains, *Human Relations*, 48, pp. 258–259.

Copyright © 2002 by Sage Publications. Reprinted with permission.

were positive. The variable importance of outside ties had a positive significant effect on all work commitment forms except PWE, where the effect was positive but not significant. The positive effect of organizational support for nonwork domains on all forms of work commitment also supported the expansion model. Thus, there seems to be no support for the argument that work commitment is immune from the influence of outside work claimants. However, the effect of nonwork domains on work commitment is more complex than simply direct, as was demonstrated in the interaction effect for two of the commitment forms.

The main variable affecting most of the forms of work commitment is the amount of support the organization is perceived to provide for nonwork domains (see Table 8.2). This finding shows the usefulness of this variable in explaining the employees' attitudes. Moreover, it has an important practical implication. Organizations can increase the positive attitudes of their employees by showing more respect for their nonwork domains. This finding is interesting in light of early research findings (Goldthorpe et al., 1968) that workers' participation in work-based clubs and societies at three firms where these facilities were provided was relatively low. The management of these three companies was disappointed, and interpreted the low participation rates as an indication of a problem of "attitudes to work." The employees in Goldthorpe and associates' research showed a separation response to the work and nonwork interface in the interviews; the organization produced an integration response, and the outcome was disappointment on both sides.

As can be seen in Table 8.2, Cohen's (1995) research showed that an intermediate response from the organization demonstrating respect and support for its employees' nonwork domains had a positive effect on their attitudes to work. So a good strategy for the organization would be to show such respect and to offer support for the nonwork needs of employees. This conclusion should be examined in future research comparing the effects of different organizational responses to the work and nonwork interface on employees' attitudes and behaviors at work. Moreover, these research findings regarding the weak effect of personal coping strategies on work commitment forms are also worth noting. How organizations act regarding their employees' nonwork domains, not employees' effective management of work and nonwork domains, can increase work commitment. This applies particularly to commitments to foci that are more important to the organization, such as the job, the occupation, and the organization.

Cohen's (1995) findings also revealed an interaction effect for PWE when the effect both of effort put into outside ties and of their importance was moderated by personal coping strategies. The interaction showed that for employees with high coping strategies, more effort devoted to outside ties led to higher PWE. For employees with low coping strategies, more effort given to outside ties led to lower PWE. The same interaction effect was anticipated for work involvement, but that was not supported by the data. The effect of effort devoted to and/or importance of outside ties was not moderated by organizational support for nonwork domains for any of the work commitment forms.

In addition, the findings revealed a three-way interaction effect for job involvement. The interaction pattern was as follows: When the organization was perceived as supporting nonwork domains, among employees with high coping strategies more effort directed to outside ties led to higher job involvement. But when the organization was perceived as not supporting its employees' nonwork domains, among those same employees with high coping strategies greater effort devoted to outside ties led to lower job involvement.

As Table 8.2 shows, the variance explained by nonwork domains was high for organizational commitment and lower for the other commitment forms examined in that research. But variables representing nonwork domains were significantly related to all commitment forms. This is important because work commitment forms are expected to be related mainly to personal and situational antecedents (Morrow, 1983). The fact that nonwork domain variables were related to all commitment forms suggests that nonwork domains should be included in future models of work commitment antecedents. The findings strengthen Kirchmeyer's (1992) conclusion that to truly understand the individual at work, not only must his or her work life be considered, but so must his or her life away from the workplace.

In another study performed by Cohen (1997b), the relation between commitment forms and nonwork domains was tested in a sample of 300 employees of a school district in Western Canada. As in the previous study, an important contribution of this one was the examination of the relation between nonwork domains and several commitment forms simultaneously. Another notable contribution was the distinction drawn between commitment to a specific organization for which one works (mostly schools in that study) and commitment to the school district, which is basically the head office for all the schools in that district. This distinction accorded with findings of Gregerson and Black (1992), who examined the relation of several antecedents of commitment to the parent company and to the local work unit. The difference is that Gregersen and Black examined the commitment of American expatriate managers to their parent company and to the local work unit on repatriation.

Cohen (1995) also examined the relation between the way individuals coped with work and nonwork issues and commitment. Randall (1988) found a positive relation between the effort devoted to nonwork domains and organizational commitment, and between the perceived importance of nonwork domains and organizational commitment. The relation between importance and commitment was stronger than that between effort and commitment. A possible reason is that the value people assign to nonwork domains has a stronger effect than does the actual effort because quite often, people are not able to fulfil their nonwork plans. Yet for many of them, nonwork domains might still be an important component of their life despite their inability to be more active in those domains. Therefore, Cohen's study used only the variable importance of nonwork, not the variable perceived effort devoted to nonwork. Perceived importance of nonwork domains was expected to be related to commitment forms. The contradictions and the inconsistencies in the results regarding the direction of the relation between commitment forms and perceived importance of nonwork domains (Randall, 1988) prevented the formulation of hypotheses on the direction of this relation.

As in the first research (Cohen, 1995), here too Cohen argued that the type of personal strategy used to cope with the demands and responsibilities of multiple domains appeared to affect the experience of interdomain conflict (Hall, 1972; Kirchmeyer, 1993a). Cohen expected here too that the way individuals coped with their nonwork domains would affect their commitment. Effectiveness in dealing with the work and nonwork interface should result in fewer work and nonwork conflicts and prevent negative attitudes to the work setting that could result from these conflicts. Therefore, employees who dealt more effectively with pressure from nonwork claims were expected to be more committed to work foci than individuals who were less effective in the way they handled nonwork domains.

Hall and Richter's (1988) findings on the work–family interface suggested that organizations should adopt a third type of response, which could be termed *respect*. Unlike the separation response, this third type entails acknowledging and valuing employees' nonwork lives. It aims not to close the work and nonwork gap, but to maintain (and respect) it. That is, rather than taking over nonwork responsibilities for employees, it provides employees with personal resources to fulfil such responsibilities themselves. Thus, the way in which the organization responds to its employees' nonwork domains is expected to affect their commitment forms. The greater the integration and the respect shown by the organization with regard to its employees' nonwork domains, the higher their commitment level. A greater separation type of response demonstrated by the organization lowers the level of the commitment forms.

As in the earlier study (Cohen, 1995), Cohen argued that the effect of the variables importance of nonwork and personal coping strategies, and of the three organizational response variables, on commitment forms might not be direct but a more complex interaction. The explanation for these interactions was described earlier. Finally, the use of three moderators in the relation between nonwork domains and commitment forms raised the possibility of a three-way interaction effect that was explained above.

Cohen (1997b) measured multiple commitments using a comprehensive definition and measurement of commitment forms proposed and tested by Cohen (1993a) in an attempt to overcome some methodological limitations in existing commitment measures. *Multiple commitments* were defined as an affective attachment to one or more of the objects of commitments (e.g., organization, occupation, and job). In keeping with Cohen (1993a), the list of items was organized in matrix form. The vertical portion of the matrix included the nine items that were phrased in general form, and the horizontal axis listed the types of commitment measured in this study (school, school district, occupation, and job).

The main findings of this study showed that the effect of nonwork domains on commitment forms was found to be both meaningful and complex. It was meaningful because nonwork domains affected all commitment forms examined in that study, particularly commitment to the school district. It was complex because variables representing nonwork domains affected forms of commitment not only directly. The effect of nonwork domains on the two foci of organizational commitment (i.e., commitment to the local unit and to the school district) was quite strong. A significant amount of the variance of organizational commitment, mainly of commitment to the school district ($R^2 = .25$), was explained by the nonwork domain variables. This finding is important in light of the fact that organizational commitment is expected to be affected mainly by work setting variables (Mowday et al., 1982). Thus, the findings did not support Randall's (1988) conclusion that organizational commitment is not related to nonwork domains.

The findings reported by Cohen (1997b) were part of a larger study that examined additional commitment forms. Next, more data than those presented in Cohen's report (1997b) are discussed, particularly concerning the relation between nonwork domains and additional commitment forms, such as job and occupation and nonwork. These additional findings support previous arguments about the need to apply a multidimensional approach to the concept of multiple commitments in general and organizational commitment in particular. Nonwork domain aspects were found to be related differently to different forms of commitment. Commitment to the school district and commitment to the occupation were found to be more strongly related to nonwork domains than were commitment to the local unit and to the job. Two comparisons are interesting in that regard. The first is between commitment to the school district and commitment to the local unit. The stronger relation of commitment to the school district to nonwork domain variables, and in particular to organizational responses to nonwork variables, showed that the commitment object responsible for the policy regarding nonwork domains are more strongly affected by these variables.

Moreover, the employees in this sample were committed to the local unit more than to the school district; however, they fully realized that the policy was determined in the head office, and this caused a strong effect of organizational response variables on commitment to the head office. The other interesting comparison is the stronger relation of nonwork domain variables with occupational commitment than with job commitment. This finding showed that job commitment was a function of personality and individual difference in regard to the specific work situation (Morrow, 1983) whereas career commitment was a function both of personal (e.g., coping strategies) and situational variables (organizational responses to nonwork). The findings of that study were consistent with previous findings regarding an impact on career commitment by situational factors such as the organizational context (Tuma & Grimes, 1981), and in regard to the effect of nonwork domains on career commitment (Greenhaus & Kopelman, 1981). The work and nonwork interface is more specific and less abstract in its relation with career foci than with job foci commitments.

As in the earlier study (Cohen, 1995), the findings here also showed the usefulness of organizational response variables in explaining commitment forms. Organizational responses seem to have a stronger effect on commitment forms than do the personal responses to nonwork such as the importance of nonwork domains and coping strategies. An important practical implication of this is that organizations can strengthen the positive attitudes of their employees by showing more respect for employees nonwork domains, as demonstrated in the positive effect of integration and respect on commitment to the school district. Alternately, organizations can weaken these attitudes by showing no concern for their employees' nonwork domain needs, as demonstrated in the negative effect of the separation response on occupational commitment and commitment to the school district. This finding goes against the weak effect of personal coping strategies on commitment forms. The way organizations react toward nonwork domains of their employees, rather than the management of the work and nonwork interface by employees, can increase commitment.

Cohen's (1995) findings also showed the existence of some interaction effects, although not all the expected interactions were found by the data. Still, the effect of nonwork domains on commitment forms was more complex than simply direct, as demonstrated in the interaction effects. The pattern of the interactions found in Cohen's study are interesting and important both conceptually and practically. A consistent interaction effect of importance of nonwork and respect was found for all of the four commitments examined in Cohen's research. The pattern of the interactions proved to be the same for all four interactions. For employees who perceived their nonwork domains as important, higher respect of nonwork from the organization increased all commitment forms. For employees who perceived their nonwork domains as unimportant, higher respect for nonwork by the organization had either no effect on commitment or a slightly negative effect.

The respectful response had no direct effect, and any effect it might have had was dependent on the importance of nonwork domains to the employee. Organizations should certainly notice that a respectful response might act to increase commitment only for those employees who value their nonwork domains and perceive them as important part of their lives. It did not affect, or might even decrease the level of commitment of employees who assign low importance to their nonwork domains. Before determining its responses to their employees' work and nonwork interface, organizations should first assemble some information about the importance of nonwork domains to their employees then apply their responses selectively, depending on the perceived importance of nonwork domains.

The interaction of importance of nonwork with the two other organizational response types was less consistent. When integration, not respect, was analyzed as the organizational response, an interaction appeared of importance of nonwork domains with integration, which was related to occupational commitment. For employees who perceived their nonwork domains as important, higher integration increased their occupational commitment. Another interaction was found when separation was analyzed as the organizational response: an interaction of coping strategies and importance of nonwork domains in their relation to job commitment. However, this interaction did not significantly add to the variance explained in the previous steps, and it is not discussed here. As for the three-way interaction, in all 12 regression analyses performed in this study not one a single three-way interaction effect was found.

Conclusions

The issue of nonwork domain and its relationship to multiple commitments is important because of its conceptual and practical implications. Conceptually, it can increase our understanding of the relationship between work and nonwork domains. Commitment forms represent important work values, so it is important to understand their relation to nonwork domains. Practically, aspects of nonwork domains are expected to increase commitment levels, which in turn should be related positively to valuable outcomes in the workplace. Career management, both through individual career planning and through household planning, may improve career commitment and, to a lesser degree, organizational commitment. Therefore, organizations might benefit from programs intended to aid employees, particularly female employees, in planning their careers and managing household activities that might interfere with work-related commitments (Steffy & Jones, 1988). Understanding these aspects can assist in finding ways positively to affect commitment forms. However, research on the relation between commitment forms and nonwork domains is still sparse. Some research exists on the relation between organizational commitment and nonwork domains, less on that between other commitment forms and nonwork domains, and hardly any on the relation between multiple forms of commitment and nonwork domains.

Conceptually, Cohen's (1995, 1997b) findings tended to support the extension of the spillover model to the work and nonwork relation. Most of the significant correlations between the nonwork domain variables and commitment foci were positive. The variable positive nonwork-to-work spillover had positive correlations with all commitment forms. Moreover, there were no significant correlations between negative nonwork-to-work spillover and any of the commitment forms. The variable importance of outside ties had a positive significant effect on three commitment forms. The positive effects of organizational support (e.g., integration and respect) for the nonwork domains and the negative effect of the separation response on forms of commitment also support the extension model. Thus, no support is apparent for the argument that commitment forms are immune to the influence of extra-work claims.

Romzek (1989) pointed out that the question of whether work affects the nonwork arena or vice versa was still unanswered. This question, as applied to the relation between multiple commitments and nonwork domains, concerns causality. Whereas the basic assumption described in the studies is that nonwork domains affect commitment, Romzek (1989) advanced the opposite rationale. According to Romzek, employee commitment affords individuals a chance to develop a sense of belonging and to fulfill the human need for meaningful work. When individuals feel committed to their work organizations they share the organizations' values. As a result, they feel good about themselves and what they do at work. In turn, these good feelings are expected to spill over into employees' nonwork lives. Orthner and Pittman (1986) held that there was evidently more potential reciprocity between work and family roles than what had been reported in the literature. Neither the family nor work is a closed system. Changes in one should influence the other; arguably, the organization undergoing the greater change in society nowadays is the family, not the corporation.

Most studies presented here examined the relation between nonwork determinants and commitment forms, and generally assumed that its direction was that nonwork domain concepts affected commitment forms. Few applied a longitudinal design. Their assumptions and conclusions therefore lack strong empirical support because the cross-sectional design does not allow the conclusion of a causal relation. All that we can conclude from this research is that the two concepts are related. Research is needed using the appropriate design that tests both directions, thereby allowing the testing of the direction of causality: is it commitment foci that affect nonwork domains or vice versa?

Another interesting future research agenda could be to explore the effect of the variables examined in Cohen's (1995, 1997b) research together with the effect of work setting variables. This will make possible the examination of whether the nonwork domain variables add to the effect of work setting variables, which are considered strong determinants of work commitment forms (Morrow, 1983). Generally, nonwork aspects should receive further attention to clarify the effect of nonwork to work domains on employees' attitudes and behaviors in general, and on work commitment in particular. Note finally, that Cohen's findings, derived from two occupational groups in female-dominated professions (teachers and nurses), are of limited generalizability and need to be replicated in other occupational groups.

Future research should also develop measures for commitments to nonwork domains and test their relation to commitment forms in the work setting. Such research should follow Morrow et al. (1983), who examined the relation of job involvement, professional commitment, and community commitment to job perceptions and job attitudes and work outcomes. Morrow (1993) mentioned community commitment, a focus examined by Steffy and Jones (1988). Other research examined concepts such as family commitment (Aryee & Debrah, 1997; Frone & Rice, 1987; Frone et al., 1992; Wang & Wildman, 1995). Morrow (1993) suggested that the negative relation found by Steffy and Jones (1988) between career and community commitment provided a strong rationale for examining this form of commitment and its relation to commitment in the workplace. Morrow argued that research on community commitment showed that extra-work variables may have an impact on work-related variables. For example, this relation suggests that commitment to one's career goals perhaps necessitates withdrawing from community interests. Alternatively, being committed to one's community could make it necessary to be less committed to one's career. Morrow argued that the utility of community commitment might be particularly salient for those jobs or occupations where long-standing ties within a community are useful (e.g., real estate and insurance agents, employment agency personnel). Other findings support Morrow's contention. For example, Frone and Rice (1987) found negative relation between job involvement and spouse involvement, and between job involvement and parent involvement.

In short, the concepts and findings here showed the usefulness and the importance of continuing research on the relation between commitment forms and nonwork domains. It seems that this area is only at the exploratory stage of its research. Much more work is needed here conceptually and empirically. Conceptually, there is a need to develop more specific explanations for the relation between commitment forms and nonwork domains. So far, research has relied on general theories of the relation between work and nonwork. The conflicting and ambiguous results on the relation between commitment and nonwork domains emphasize the need for more specific theories on the commitment and nonwork relation. These theories can either follow the line of reasoning developed by the more general theories on the work and nonwork relation or advance different explanations for commitment.

Empirically, much more work is needed on almost every aspect of the commitment and nonwork relation. Particularly, more research is required that will examine multiple commitments in their relation to nonwork. Although most research has concentrated on organizational commitment, it is important to simultaneously examine other commitment forms such as the occupation and the job. Such works allow comparisons of a differential relation between nonwork domains and different forms of commitment. Aspects of nonwork domains have justifiably received more attention by scholars and practitioners. There is a need for a stronger integration of the concept of multiple commitments in this line of research. The few findings collected so far showed that commitment could increase our understanding of how employees manage their lives in two different, but important, settings.

9

Multiple Commitments From a Crosscultural Perspective

Crosscultural aspects of commitment have long attracted the attention of scholars and practitioners. Even at the early stages of research on commitment, mainly organizational commitment (OC), considerable interest was shown in the concept of commitment in other cultures, particularly Japan. This interest can be attributed to several factors, some more practical in nature and some more conceptual. The practical arguments state that as multinational companies increase their direct investment overseas, especially in less developed and consequently less studied areas, they require more information concerning their local employees to implement effective types of interactions between the organization and the host country. The knowledge acquired thus far is based on American theories that work well for Western nations. Are they equally applicable in non-Western countries (Ronen & Shenkar, 1985)? With the increasing focus on international ventures and management, it is important that organizational researchers and practitioners comprehend intercultural similarities and differences, particularly because many psychological and managerial principles are culturally relative (Earley, 1989).

From a more theoretical point of view, crossnational research should be applied to any social theory to verify the generalizability of the relations and to demarcate the limits of the theory's applicability to diverse populations (Triandis & Vassiliou, 1972). Although cultural values potentially have an impact on a range of micro and macro organizational phenomena, Boyacigiller and Adler (1991) argued that most organization theories were "made-in-the-USA" and therefore influenced by the political, economic, and cultural context of the United States. Yet, few researchers have explicitly addressed the influence of American values on U.S.-based organizational science. Most organizational theories appear implicitly to assume universality. Even when the applicability of these theories to other cultures is tested, researchers usually select methods that are most acceptable according to American norms, thereby rendering results that are just as culturally conditional.

For organizational science to continue to develop, scholars should explicitly address cultural assumptions. Through this reflection, they can develop an appreciation of the cultural conditioning of organization theory. They can thereby become more cognizant of how American values underlie much of organization theory, and consequently render it constrained. Examining the cultural roots and assumptions is a necessary, but not sufficient, condition for beginning to uncover neglected, overemphasized, and overgeneralized aspects of organizational theory (Boyacigiller & Adler, 1991).

In short, cultures and management systems outside the United States need to be examined. Crossnational research obliges scholars to question the adequacy of their domestically derived models, thereby encouraging them to create theoretical and methodological approaches not predicated solely on single-culture (especially U.S.) assumptions (Boyacigiller & Adler, 1991; Hofstede's, 1980). To develop a more robust organizational science scholars should clearly state the cultural and geographical domain of their theories, otherwise, they inappropriately promulgate a universalistic view of organizational theory. Accordingly, they should also indicate the national and cultural characteristics of their sample so readers can recognize the potential limitations. This argument, relevant to many other concepts and theories, is likewise most apt for the study of multiple commitments.

As for commitment, the need for research that would test it in different cultures was strongly stated by Becker (1960), who asserted:

> For a complete understanding of a person's commitment we need ... an analysis of the system of values or, perhaps better, valuables with which bets can be made in the world he lives in ... In short, to understand commitment fully, we must discover the systems of value within which the mechanisms and processes described earlier operate. (p. 39)

But as in other fields in organizational behavior, the majority of commitment studies examined employees in Western societies. This is understandable given the social and economic sources of support for this kind of research in the West, yet, the international nature of business today and the widening cultural diversity of work forces in the most industrialized countries call for an understanding of workers not only of European descent.

Even rarer than commitment studies of non-Western societies are those that simultaneously examine workers from two cultures. If commitment research is to remain relevant, a substantially greater proportion of studies need to go beyond the purely domestic perspective (Adler, 1983; Kohn, 1989). Moreover Clugston, Howell, and Dorfman (2000) argued that differences in employees' commitment could be predicted on the basis of cultural dimensions even within a homogeneous work setting within one country. In an American sample they found that the conceptual framework of using cultural dimensions to predict foci and bases of organizational commitment was sensitive to variations also in an individual's cultural socialization. The above finding strengthens the importance of culture as a factor that can impact findings not only between cultures but also within one single culture.

This chapter reviews and evaluates the existing cross-cultural works on commitment. Many of them focused on one form of commitment. Because of the importance of this topic most of the studies are reviewed here, including those that examined only one commitment form. However, particular attention is given to studies that examined multiple commitments in a crosscultural setting.

Conceptual Framework for Commitment in a Crosscultural Setting

An important question regarding crosscultural research on commitment is its conceptual framework. The most studied commitment focus in general and in crosscultural research particularly is OC. Therefore it might be expected that a conceptual framework for examining commitment in a crosscultural setting would have been proposed for this focus. Yet, research on crosscultural differences in OC lacks an overarching theoretical framework to help explain why OC would be expected to vary across cultures (Randall, 1993). Guided by theory, commitment researchers would be able to predict the level of commitment over that range. As it is, our knowledge of the generalizability of observed relations and boundary conditions for theories of commitment remains limited.

Some consensus, however, has crystallized to the effect that the appropriate conceptual framework for understanding crosscultural differences in commitment is Hofstede's (1980) Value Survey Module (VSM). The VSM model is thought to be the most widely cited work on culture developed for the study of organizations (Erez & Earley, 1993). More importantly, it is considered the most popular measure of cultural values, holding great promise as a theoretical framework to guide crosscultural comparisons of organizational commitment (Clugston, Howell, & Dorfman, 2000; Kirkman & Shapiro, 2001; Randall, 1993) as well as commitment to other foci (Vandenberghe, Stinglhamber, Benstein, & Delhaise, 2001). The VSM identifies fundamental differences in the way people in various countries perceive and interpret their worlds. These different value structures have profound consequences for the validity of the transfer of theories and technologies from one country to another (Randall, 1993). With data from more than 40 countries, Hofstede (1980) developed an important overview consisting of four common dimensions, the most important in explaining differences between cultures. By means of the VSE a country's culture could be summarized across them. The four dimensions are *power distance, uncertainty avoidance, individualism/collectivism,* and *masculinity/femininity.*

Power distance refers to the extent members of a culture accept inequality and large differentials between those with power (supervisors) and those with little power. In high power distance countries such as the Philippines, Venezuela, and India, superiors and subordinates consider bypassing the boss insubordination; whereas in low power distance countries such as Israel and Denmark, employees expect to bypass the boss frequently to get their work done.

Uncertainty avoidance reflects the emphasis on ritual behavior, rules, and labor mobility within a culture. High uncertainty avoidance is found in countries that report high levels of stress. Lifetime employment is more common in high uncertainty-avoidance countries such as Japan, Portugal, and Greece; high job mobility more commonly occurs in low uncertainty avoidance countries such as Singapore, Hong Kong, and Denmark (Adler, 1991).

Individualism/collectivism reflects the extent to which individuals emphasize their own goals over those of their clan or group. Members who strive to achieve their own goals, who narrow family structures, and whose movement among groups is a function of self-interest, characterize individualistic cultures. Members who emphasize the needs of the group over self-interests and live in extended family structures, by contrast, characterize collectivist cultures. Determinism characterizes collectivist cultures, for instance Japan, where people believe that the will of the group should determine members' beliefs and behavior. Self-determination characterizes individualistic cultures, for instance the U.S., where individuals believe that each person should determine his or her beliefs and behaviors.

An essential attribute of collectivist society is that individuals subordinate their personal interests to the goals of their collective, or in-group, those with whom a person works and identifies. In-group membership is stable even when the in-group makes high demands on the individual. Individuals belonging to an in-group share common interest and seek collective outcomes or goals. A driving force within a collectivist culture is cooperation so as to attain group goals and safeguard group welfare (Earley, 1989). An individualistic culture emphasizes self-sufficiency and control, the pursuit of individual goals that may or may not be consistent with in-group goals, and membership of multiple in-groups. Individuals in an individualistic society often drop out of in-groups if membership becomes a burden or inhibits the attainment of individual goals. In an individualistic culture, people feel proud of their own accomplishments and derive satisfaction from performance based on their own achievements. Individuals in a collectivistic culture derive pleasure and satisfaction from group accomplishment (Earley, 1989).

Masculinity/femininity refers to societies that differentiate on the basis of activity and gender. For instance, a masculine culture emphasizes differences between genders, whereas in a feminine culture, gender differentiation is minimal. The centrality of work in a person's life is greater in a masculine than in a feminine culture and the general quality of life over work is emphasized more in a feminine culture (Erez & Earley, 1993). According to Hofstede's (1980) definitions, masculine societies define gender roles more rigidly than do feminine societies. For example, women may drive trucks or practice law and men may be ballet dancers or househusbands more easily in feminine societies. In Japan and Austria, people generally expect women to stay home and take care of children without working outside the home. In the U.S. women are encouraged to work and are given a certain amount of support for childcare in the form of maternity leave and daycare centers. In Sweden, women are expected to work; parents are given the option of paternity or maternity leave to take care of newborn children and of day-mothers to care for older children.

Individualism Versus Collectivism and Commitment.   Of the four dimensions, individualism versus collectivism seems to be the most common dimension used by researchers to understand the differences in commitment between the American culture and other cultures, or between any two or more cultures. Most of the rationale for the importance of this dimension to the understanding of commitment from a crosscultural perspective was advanced for research on OC. However, the logic advanced by scholars seems to be relevant to other commitment foci as well. A reason given to the importance of individualism/collectivism for crosscultural research on commitment is that many organizational theories, particularly North American ones, reflected an individualism bias (Boyacigiller & Adler, 1991). Most U.S. management theories are based on a self-interest motive that may not be appropriate for an intercultural model. For instance, the most prevalent work-motivation models, goal setting and expectancy theory, presume a self-interest motive. One can question the basic assumption that the self-interest motive fully explains individual and collective actions within organizational settings.

Organizational scientists who develop models of behavior need to consider the fundamental assumption of the self-interest motive, because its assertion can shape the nature of derived theories and principals (Earley, 1989). Earley (1989) found that collectivist beliefs are an important consideration in developing a culture-based model of group performance. The author concluded that an individual's motives are influenced by cultural background, and these motives play an important role in group-based work.

In addition, in countries where individualism dominates, individuals view their relation with the organization from a calculative perspective, whereas in collectivist societies, the ties between the individual and organization have a moral component. The concept of OC clearly carries much different connotations in collectivist societies than from those in individualistic societies. Employees with collectivist values commit to organizations primarily owing to their ties with managers, owners, and co-workers (collectivism), and far less owing to the job itself or the particular compensation scheme (individualistic incentives). Consonant with its individualistic orientation, the U.S. has the most executive search firms and one of the highest levels of managerial mobility in the world. Therefore, it is not surprising, although it is most unfortunate, that American theoretical structures fail to include a full range of explanations for organizational commitment and its lack (Allen, Miller, & Nath, 1988).

Furthermore, in countries that believe in collectivism the identity of groups is important. Membership of a group has certain associated well-defined expectations and modes of conduct. Subordinates in these cultures are supposed to maintain absolute loyalty and obedience to authority and to the group in the fulfillment of their obligations. In such countries, individuals can be ostracized for deviating from the norm. In addition to a collectivist attitude, existence of high power distance (which makes subordinates dependent on their supervisors), means that they must follow rules and procedures to obtain their supervisor's patronage and protection and to remain a member of the organization. In a culture where autocratic authority is the ideal image of a supervisor, enforcement of rules and procedures may have a weaker negative impact on the organizational commitment of subordinates (Agarwal, 1993). Therefore, in collectivist cultures one would expect high levels of organizational commitment, particularly normative organizational commitment.

In summary, most research that applied a conceptual framework in testing commitment across cultures used that of Hofstede. Examples are the studies of Agarwal (1993), Randall (1993), Cohen (1999b), and Parnell and Hatem (1999). This framework seems to be the best for explaining crosscultural differences, and it should be used more often. Particular attention should be paid to grasping which of the four dimensions can best explain crosscultural or crossnational differences. As was emphasized earlier, and as will become evident in the following sections, individualism/collectivism has received the most attention in commitment research.

Research on Commitment in Crosscultural Settings

Most research on intercultural differences regarding commitment has concentrated on OC. The rationale was that OC is a universal phenomenon, affecting management and lower-level employees. Comparison of workers' OC in different countries has attracted more attention of researchers (e.g., Lincoln & Kalleberg, 1985; Luthans, McCaul, & Dodd, 1985; Near, 1989). Other commitment forms tested in different cultures were usually union commitment and work involvement or work as a central interest. Few studies tested multiple commitments in a crosscultural setting. Accordingly, this chapter also describes findings on each commitment form in a crosscultural setting, on the basis of existing evidence. Because the theme of this volume is multiple commitments, it naturally elaborates on studies that have tested multiple commitments in this setting.

ORGANIZATIONAL COMMITMENT

Organizational Commitment in Japan

Most of the research on intercultural differences in respect of OC has concentrated on countries with vastly different societal cultures. Studies comparing the commitment of workers in different countries have mostly concentrated on American as against Japanese employees (e.g., Cole, 1979; Lincoln & Kalleberg, 1985; Luthans, McCaul, & Dodd, 1985; Near, 1989). Abegglen (1958), in a study of a large factory in Japan, highlighted the dissimilarity between Japanese and American social organization in the factory. The research showed the notion of lifetime commitment, namely, a worker's entering a firm directly from school and remaining there until retirement. According to Abegglen, Japanese organizations differ from the Western in the pattern of lifetime commitment, which is supported by Japanese beliefs in the firm as one family, in familial management, and in the seniority system. According to this much-cited study, lifetime commitment is the general rule in the large factories in Japan. Abegglen's work was a stimulus to research on commitment in Japan. The notion of Japanese employee with a high level of commitment to his or her employer, in contrast to the American employer who evinces lower commitment, and consequently higher levels of turnover, aroused researchers' curiosity as to the reasons for this difference. The cultural rationale provided by Abegglen added to the growing interest in the Japanese work setting.

Marsh and Mannari (1971, 1972, 1977) examined Abegglen's (1958) concept of lifetime commitment. In general, they disagreed with it. If Japanese employees remained in the same large firm by reason of lifetime commitment, those authors contended that this was due to the cumulative advantages of long service (status enhancement) rather than to loyalty to the company as such, which is considered separately from status enhancement. Japanese employees' reasons for staying in one firm were the same as those that tied Western employees to a firm (Marsh & Mannari, 1971). Marsh and Mannari also concluded that certain factors continued to operate to maintain and strengthen commitment to one firm, and the Japanese interfirm mobility rate in the immediate future was not likely to become as high as in the U.S. Nevertheless, Marsh and Mannari discerned indications that the well-entrenched Japanese paternalism was slowly but surely losing its viability and appeal to workers. Japanese industry was applying liberalization and rationalization first to technology, then to marketing, and it was likely to extend these policies and practices increasingly to personnel administration (Marsh & Mannari, 1972).

Marsh and Mannari (1977) reaffirmed that conclusion in an empirical study they conducted at an electrical goods company in Japan. Their data, derived from the first attempt to predict empirically from prior lifetime commitment norms and values, disconfirmed the lifetime commitment model. The conclusion that when turnover was low the lifetime commitment model was supported proved invalid. The model implied not simply that employees did not voluntarily leave their organization, but that they did not leave because of specific motivational factors: adherence to norms and values of lifetime commitment and loyalty to the company. Because the researchers' measures of these norms were not related to turnover, they concluded that in the restrictive sense the lifetime commitment model was not applicable.

Marsh and Mannari's (1977) findings were replicated in later research. Lincoln and Kalleberg (1985) tested the hypothesis that OC was higher among Japanese than American workers, and that this commitment gap may be an outcome of the greater prevalence of a "welfare corporatist" structure in Japanese firms. With data from a survey of over 8,000 employees in nearly 100 plants in Japan and in the U.S., they found that consistent with a theory of "corporatist" control, participatory work structures and employee services were more typical of Japanese plants, yet functioned in both countries to raise commitment. They concluded that their data provided no evidence of greater commitment in Japan. Near (1989) examined 7,000 Japanese and American production workers and found, contrary to the expectation, that the Japanese workers were less committed to their organization than were the American workers. Near concluded that many of the assumptions made about Japanese productivity and its bases required reexamination. Another interesting finding was that the amount of variance explained in OC for the Japanese sample was low, far lower, indeed than that for the American sample. Namely, no meaningful differences were found in the pattern of the relations observed in the two samples (in both, perceptions of job characteristics were related to commitment more than to structural or personal variables). But the variables explained a much lower percentage of the variance for the Japanese sample (10%) than for the American sample (31%). One explanation provided by Near was that the psychological notion of commitment did not apply to Japanese workers.

Luthans, McCaul, and Dodd (1985) compared overall levels of organizational commitment among samples of employees in three countries, the U.S., Japan, and Korea. The last, a country similar to, though in many ways different from Japan, was included for the purpose of comparison of two Asian countries. The Japanese and Korean employees, who showed no difference in levels of organizational commitment, were both found to be less organizationally committed than the American employees. A positive relation of organizational commitment with age and tenure was also found. These relations held across the countries as well. The authors concluded that their findings refuted the widespread belief that Japanese workers were more committed to the organization than their U.S. counterparts. Organizational commitment then, was not based on culture-specific norms and values.

The main conclusion of most research comparing commitment in Japan and the U.S. is that differences were not as profound as expected (Lincoln & Kalleberg, 1985; Luthans, Baack, & Taylor, 1987; Marsh & Mannari, 1971, 1972, 1977; Near, 1989). These findings ran counter to the myth of the committed Japanese employee, as against the less committed American. The contradiction between the myth and the evidence propelled some researchers to seek explanations. Besser (1993) reviewed and assessed the literature comparing commitment of American and Japanese employees, and noted an important contradiction in it. Whereas U.S. workers expressed higher levels of organizational commitment than did Japanese workers, the latter had lower rates of absenteeism, turnover, and tardiness than the former.

Besser (1993) attributed this contradiction to three possible factors. First, various aspects of the political and social contexts made turnover less likely in Japan than in the U.S., regardless of workers' attitudes. Turnover may not be a valid measure of commitment in comparisons between the U.S. and Japan. Second, the lower level of expressed commitment among Japanese workers may have reflected the greater duality of their economy. American workers were more likely than Japanese to work for a core organization with commitment enhancing features. Third, a comparison of attitudes and behaviors of Japanese and American workers in core organizations might still reveal a higher level of commitment among the American workers.

Besser (1993) pointed out that some studies suggested that even in core Japanese organizations, commitment was a complex attitude strongly influenced by the by the norms, sanctions, and pressures of the small group, family, and community rather than strong attitudes of commitment to the organization. Japanese culture was the stoic performance of duty to family, work group, and community, regardless of personal cost or gain. According to Besser, some research indicated that the importance of this value was declining. Yet, its residual impact may have explained the circumstances in which workers were not enthusiastic about their jobs or employers, but worked hard although grumbling to each other about the demands made on them. From the evidence he cited, Besser concluded that the committed behaviors of the Japanese work force were partially explained by the pressures of the work group, family, and community, rather than strong attitudes of commitment to the organization. Furthermore, the Japanese core organizations—the welfare corporatist companies—had probably evolved effective mechanisms for using employees' loyalty to these groups in order to achieve the organization's goals. If employees knew that tardiness, absence, and shoddy workmanship would negatively impact their immediate co-workers, they were likely to refrain from those behaviors, and informal group norms and sanctions may develop to encourage co-workers to comply with the rules.

The little research conducted so far on the relation between commitment and outcomes does not enable us to indicate which of these explanations, if any, is correct. Nor do we know if the contradiction observed by Besser (1993) figures in other crosscultural comparisons. Obviously, more crosscultural comparisons of the relation between commitment forms and work outcomes are necessary. Besser concluded that critical examination of the theoretical paradigm is definitely warranted when refinement of the survey instrument and replications continue to produce the same incongruity between survey results and behavioral indicators.

Organizational Commitment in Other Countries

Randall (1993) reviewed 27 OC studies across countries. Of these, 12 involved Canadian respondents, and Japan was the next most frequently explored country in organizational commitment research. Using Hofstede's (1980) framework, Randall compared the four value dimension scores assigned by Hofstede with the reported organizational commitment scores for the same countries. In terms of individualism/collectivism, the level of attitudinal commitment measured by the OCQ appeared from Randall's review to be lower in more collectivist countries (South Korea and Japan) than in some of the more individualistic countries (Canada). It was anticipated that countries such as Japan and South Korea, with some of the highest uncertainty avoidance scores, would reflect high organizational commitment levels. Yet studies in Canada, with a substantially lower uncertainty avoidance score, reported higher commitment levels among workers. Findings regarding the power distance dimension were generally consistent with expectations. Countries with lower power distance (notably Canada) reflected higher OC levels than countries with higher power distance (Japan and South Korea). Findings on the masculinity/femininity dimension were unclear. Although Japan had the highest masculinity score and South Korea had the lowest masculinity score among the countries studied, both had roughly equivalent commitment levels. Canada, with a high commitment level, had only a median level on the masculinity index.

Randall (1993) concluded that these findings were tentative due to the limited number of countries available for comparison. But Randall considered the findings on individualism/collectivism particularly interesting, as they were contrary to expectations. An important comment by Randall was that the assumption of total cultural homogeneity within a single nation, or within nations in a cluster, was questionable because linguistic, regional, tribal, ethnic, religious, social class, and caste difference within nations made a single value survey module score unrepresentative of a nation.

Studies of OC in cultures other than Japan, with or without comparison to the U.S., did not find a marked difference between the American employees' commitment and that of employees of any other given nationality. These studies are reviewed in Table 9.1. As can be seen in the table, out of the 18 studies that are reviewed, three concluded that culture had some impact on the relation between commitment and correlates. From their findings Palich, Hom, and Griffeth (1995) concluded that cultural relativists overstated the cultural boundedness of American theories and practices. They further concluded that the findings contradicted Hofstede's (1980) objections to standardization of management techniques. On the contrary, their results implied that American multinational enterprises could build parent company affiliation in European and Canadian managers by following established domestic practices, adjusting to cultural dynamics when desired outcomes did not ensue.

Sommer, Bae, and Luthans (1996) also concluded that their results were consistent with those found in American studies. Except for management style, all other antecedents drawn from the American literature had a significant relation with Koreans' organizational commitment. Sommer et al. concluded that popular constructs in the American management and

TABLE 9.1
Findings of Cross National/Cultural Research on Organizational Commitment

Studies	Countries That Were Examined/ Compared	Sample	Variables Examined in Relation to Organizational Commitment	Differences Found Between the Countries/Cultures	Magnitude of the Relationships	Cross National/Cultural Conclusions
Alvi & Ahmed (1987)	Male and female employees in Pakistan	1116 employed workers (971 male and 145 female) in various organizations	A variety of personal attributes (i.e., age, education etc.), exchange-based measures (i.e., job security, tenure etc.), psychological and other factors (i.e., job satisfaction, role conflict, authority etc.)	Variables from all three groups contributed to the explanation of commitment. Pakistani female workers appear to have greater organizational commitment than men	The variables explained 39% of the variance in the commitment for male and 52% for female	North American models and explanations also are relevant for a developing country like Pakistan
Putti, Aryee, & Kim Liang (1989)	Singapore	175 workers performing a variety of jobs in a subsidiary of an American multinational corporation	Six subscales of work values such as activity preference, pride in work, upward striving, and demographic and control variables such as gender, age, income and education and job level	Education and intrinsic work value scale that includes pride in work, activity preference, upward striving, and job involvement were the only variables related to commitment	The variance that was explained by the research model was 3%	Work values, which have been demonstrated to be related to commitment in Western societies also, hold true in the Asia context
Agarwal (1993)	India and U.S.	178 industrial salespersons in India; 184 industrial salespersons in the U.S.	Job codification, rule observation, role ambiguity, and role conflict	The U.S. sample reacted more negatively to organizational formalization (both job codification and rule observation) as compared to thew Indian sample	29% of the variance were accounted for in the U.S. sample and 24% in the India sample	Because of low power distance and high individualism U.S. sample may not be favorably disposed toward bureaucratic structure
Cohen & Gattiker (1992)	Canada and U.S.	306 Canadian employees from organizations in Western Canada; 157 Americans in organizations in Western U.S.	Demographic variables such as age, education, tenure, married, earnings, hierarchical level, and gender	Age, earnings, and gender had a greater effect on calculative commitment in Canada than in the U.S., while education had a significant effects upon calculative and value commitment in the U.S. only	R-square was quite low and ranged between .01–.06 for all commitment scales in both samples	A similarity in cultural expectations between Canada and the U.S. explains the lack of major differences between them

continued on next page

TABLE 9.1 (continued)

Studies	Countries That Were Examined/ Compared	Sample	Variables Examined in Relation to Organizational Commitment	Differences Found Between the Countries/Cultures	Magnitude of the Relationships	Cross National/Cultural Conclusions
Palich, Hom, & Griffeth (1995)	15 Europeans and Canadian affiliates of a U.S. multinational firm	1859 managers from Austria (44), Belgium (71) the Netherlands (75), Spain (66), Italy (224), England (371)	Job scope, individual extrinsic rewards, participative management, role clarity	In contrast to participation, job scope, role clarity, and extrinsic rewards were positively related to the European and Canadian managers' commitment to an American global corporation	The variables predicted the bulk (65%) of the commitment variance in their multinational sample	Sources of attachment to American multinationals generalized across their European and Canadian subsidiaries
Sommer, Bae, & Luthans (1996)	Korea	1192 employees from large Korean firms	Age, education, position, organization and job tenure, organization structure, size, management style, organization climate	Their findings showed a significant contribution of organizational structure, organizational size, and organizational climate. Management style did not have a significant effect	The control variables explained 9% of the variance. 42% were added by the organizational factors	The results are consistent with those in American studies. Variables from the American literature were related with the Koreans' commitment
Tjosvold, Sasaki, & Moy (1998)	Two Japanese organizations in Hong Kong	27 employees (17 female) from textile organization and 12 (4 female) from heavy machinery organization	Cooperative goals versus competitive or independent ones; open discussions of opposing views, coordination of work, work relationship, interaction behaviors, productivity	Social interaction (i.e., having cooperative goals and open discussions of opposing views), relationships, and productivity are important antecedents of employee commitment	The results of the structural equation analysis (goodness-of-fit index of .94) support the model	The theory of cooperation and competition is useful for understanding interdependence and interaction in Asian and America
Leung (1997)	Hong Kong	231 sales staff from 26 shops of retail chain specializing in casual apparel	General satisfaction, subjective and objective performance	Analysis at the shop level (n=26) showed that commitment was related to self-reported performance but not to objective performance. Commitment was also related to satisfaction	Correlation between commitment and subjective performance was .53; with general satisfaction, .84	Western findings (Ostroff, 1992) were replicated in a different culture

Parnell & Hatem (1999)	Members of the American Chamber of Commerce in Egypt	21 Egyptian, 39 American, and 47 top executives from other nationalities	Aspects of management styles such as high career aspirations, seek leadership roles, participate in decisions, seek participation from subordinates, have honesty and integrity, work effectively in groups	Differences were found between Egyptians and Americans. Participation and job satisfaction were negatively related to commitment in the Egyptian setting and positively in the American setting	Analysis of variance showed that the nationality of the top executives impacted their perceived management style	Culture impacts management style. Not every characteristic seen as desirable in one culture context is viewed likewise in another
Ko, Price & Mueller (1997)	South Korea, Seoul	278 employees of research institute and 589 employees of head office of an airline company	A long list (about 27) that includes a variety of determinants and outcomes of the three dimensions of commitment based on Meyer & Allen (1991) scales	Problems were found about the discriminant and construct validity of normative and continuance commitment. These problems were encountered in previous research in Western samples	The determinants were strongly related to affective and normative commitment but not to the continuance	The findings do not differ significantly from findings in Western societies. The problems of the scale are not affected by culture
Brewer & Ko (1995)	Australia	729 nurses from 4 teaching hospitals within the Sidney metropolitan area	Ten Variables such as identification, feeling about work, equity, trust, managerial strategy, participation, voice, investment, compliance, exit	Trust Identification and voice had the greatest influence on commitment	Trust ($r = .46$), identification ($r = .33$), and voice ($r = .32$) had the highest correlation with managerial strategy	The results confirmed findings from previous studies that a positive managerial strategy can generate greater organizational commitment
Agarwal, DeCarlo, & Vyas (1999)	India and U.S.	181 industrial salespersons in India; 184 industrial salespersons in the U.S.	Initiation of structure, consideration, role ambiguity, and role conflict	Initiation of structure was not related to organizational commitment in both cultures Consideration was positively related to organizational commitment in both cultures	36% of the variance were accounted for in the U.S. sample and 32% in the India one	American and Indian salespersons exhibit very similar responses toward leadership behaviors pertaining to consideration
Chen & Francesco (2000)	China	333 employees/managers from 36 service and manufacturing companies in Guangzhou and Shanghai	Demographic variables such as age, education, tenure, gender, position, control variables such as city and industry, and turnover intentions	Of the demographic variables only position was related to commitment. Commitment, its interaction with gender, and some demographic variables were related to turnover intentions	R-square was for commitment was quite low, .01. It was .51 for turnover intentions	Under the influence of traditional Chinese culture, Chinese employees behave differently than their western counterparts

continued on next page

· TABLE 9.1 (continued)

Studies	Countries That Were Examined/ Compared	Sample	Variables Examined in Relation to Organizational Commitment	Differences Found Between the Countries/Cultures	Magnitude of the Relationships	Cross National/Cultural Conclusions
Chang (1999)	Korea	227 researchers working for 8 business or economic research institutes in Korea	Age, position, education, tenure, promotion, training, supervisor's support, employment security, career commitment	Tenure, position and security predicted continuance commitment. Affective commitment was predicted by tenure, promotion, training, security and career commitment	R-square for continuance commitment was .19, and for affective commitment .52	Continuance commitment was not clearly operationalized with Koreans as it was with Americans
Harrison & Hubbard (1998)	Mexico	83 Mexican workers within a large division of a U.S. equipment manufacturing firm located in Monterry, Mexico	Gender, age, tenure, education, job satisfaction, organizational effectiveness, initial structure, consideration, participation in decision making	Regression analysis showed that three variables were related to commitment: age, job satisfaction and participation in decision making	Adjusted R-square was .44	Mexican employees are similar to their U.S. counterparts
Singh & Vinnicombe (2000)	Britain and Sweden	37 (16 matched pairs of male and female + 5 males) engineers from 3 high-tech organizations	Semi-structured interviews about the meaning of commitment via descriptions of role models of commitment and discussion of how they demonstrated commitment and perceived and evaluated it in others	In contrast to participation, job scope, role clarity, and extrinsic rewards were positively related to the European and Canadian managers' commitment to an American global corporation	The variables predicted the bulk (65%) of the commitment variance in their multinational sample	Sources of attachment to American multinationals generalized across their European and Canadian subsidiaries
Gregerssen & Black (1999)	Japanese expatriates	173 Japanese managerial expatriates from seven large Japanese multinational corporations	Tenure in overseas, time since return, culture novelty, tenure, work experience, career transfer loop, role discretion, role clarity, role conflict, pre return training, repatriation compensation, overseas adjustment and more	Perceived value of international experience (by the organization), overseas adjustment, and role discretion ($p \le .10$) were significantly related to organizational commitment	Adjusted R-square was .26. Total R-square was .32	The dual commitment of U.S. repatriates are not necessarily generalizable to Japanese managers during repatriation

Cheung (2000)	Taiwan	927 employees in eight high-technology companies in Hsinchu Science and Industry Park	Organizational support and demographic variables such as gender, age, education, marital status, number of children, organization and position tenure, job level, and company	Path analysis showed that the model that the reciprocal relationship between commitment and organizational support fitted the data the best. Age and job level, were also related to commitment	The path coefficient from commitment to support was .94. The coefficient from support to commitment .77	Exchange theory explains a large part of the Taiwanese employee's organizational commitment as well as that of Americans
Kalleberg & Mastekaasa (2001)	Norway	2910 employees who participated in the 1989 Norwegian Survey of Organizations and Employees and the 1993 follow up	Turnover, layoff, promotion, downward or lateral change in job, job rewards (well paid, secure, pleasant working conditions, interesting) and control variables such as gender, age, education, seniority, sector, job level, unionization, wage level, employment	When all variables were tested there is a no effect of promotions on commitment and a slightly stronger negative effect of downward/lateral job changes. Also quits have a small but significant effect on commitment whereas layoffs have a considerably stronger negative effect	R-square was .20 without the rewards variables and .29 including the rewards variables	Intra- and inter-organizational mobility lead to changes in organizational commitment. Quits has a positive effect on commitment and layoffs has a negative effect
Wong, Hui, Wong & Law (2001)	China	205 middle-level managers and technical workers in four joint ventures and locally owned enterprises in China	Rewards associated with employment, age, gender, tenure, and turnover intention	Age and rewards were related to organizational commitment. Commitment was negatively related to turnover intentions and positively to job satisfaction. Job satisfaction was not related to organizational commitment and turnover intentions	Structural equation modeling using LISREL 8 showed good fit of the model	Organizational commitment among Chinese employees has a much stronger effect on job satisfaction and turnover intention than results from studies conducted in the West
Wong, Hui, Wong & Law (2001)	Hong Kong	245 graduates of a major university in Hong Kong who responded to three surveys over two consecutive years	Job satisfaction, and turnover intentions measured in three time intervals, as was organizational commitment	The longitudinal data showed that commitment was negatively related to turnover intentions and positively to job satisfaction. Job satisfaction was not related to organizational commitment and turnover intentions	Structural equation modeling using LISREL 8 showed good fit of the model	Organizational commitment among Chinese employees has a much stronger effect on job satisfaction and turnover intention than results from studies conducted in the West

continued on next page

TABLE 9.1 (continued)

Studies	Countries That Were Examined/ Compared	Sample	Variables Examined in Relation to Organizational Commitment	Differences Found Between the Countries/Cultures	Magnitude of the Relationships	Cross National/Cultural Conclusions
Cecil, Pearson & Chong (1997)	Malaysia	286 full-time nursing staff of a large hospital	Five job dimensions: skill, identity, significance, job feedback, autonomy, and two interpersonal task attributes: feedback from others, dealing with others, and four cultural variables based on the Chinese Value System	The task content characteristics had a main effect on commitment. The interpersonal task attributes accounted for additional variance in commitment. The interactions among the task variables and the cultural accounted for additional variance in commitment	The task variables accounted for 17% of the variance of commitment, the interpersonal attributes added 2%; all other variables added 3%	The finding that content and interpersonal attributes were significant predictors of commitment is compatible with key propositions of Western literature

organizational behavior literature should not be automatically dismissed as culture-bound.

However, although few differences were found between the American and Asian culture, indications were that more marked differences exist between Western and Arab and Chinese cultures. Parnell and Hatem (1999), who compared American and Egyptian managers, used Hofstede's (1980) framework. This study found that the strong negative association between job satisfaction and loyalty in the Egyptian context ran counter to a large body of research demonstrating a positive relation in American managers. Parnell and Hatem argued that this anomaly may be indicative of job frustration in Egyptian workers, one which, to their credit, did not appear to lower their effort or loyalty. As such, Egyptian managers were viewed as hardworking and loyal. Parnell and Hatem (1999) argued that one possible explanation for this behavior might be found within the collectivist nature of Egyptian society, where loyalty to the organization is crucial. In a collectivist culture, an employer hires an individual who belongs to an in-group, and the employee generally acts according to the interest of this in-group, whether or not it coincides with his or her individual interest. The commonly held view that Egyptian managers are hardworking might emanate from the Islamic work ethic. Wong, Hui, Wong, and Law (2001) concluded, from their data collected in two samples in China and Hong Kong, that organizational commitment among Chinese employees has a much stronger effect on job satisfaction and turnover intentions than results from studies conducted in the West. Wong et al. contended that due to traditional Chinese values, employees' commitment toward the organization is an important attitude that organizations should try to cultivate.

Crosscultural Differences in Other Commitment Forms

As mentioned earlier, most research on crosscultural differences regarding commitment concentrated on OC. Some studies, however, examined other forms of commitment and probably encouraged the few crosscultural studies on multiple commitments. These studies have concentrated on two forms of commitment: work values like work centrality or the meaning of work, and union commitment.

Crosscultural Studies on Work Values. Agassi (1982), who compared level of commitment to employment between men and women in three countries (Israel, U.S., & Germany), found wide gaps between the level of commitment of men and women in the Israeli and German groups. That is, the women's level of commitment was lower than were the men's. However, American women's level of commitment to employment was found to be somewhat higher than that of American men.

Harpaz and his colleagues made several international comparisons of meaning of work and work centrality. Harpaz (1989) compared nonfinancial commitment (e.g., "Would you stop or continue working if there were no economic reasons to carry on working?") of employees in seven countries. In each country the majority was found to prefer to continue working even if it were no longer a financial necessity. The Japanese sample was ranked the highest in terms of nonfinancial commitment, the British and the West German the lowest. The American sample was ranked second, followed by Israel, the Netherlands, and Belgium. Harpaz (1989) concluded that the constituent element of the work ethic, represented by the value of wanting to work and hold a job, was still much in evidence in the labor force in Western industrialized countries.

Harpaz, Claes, Depolo, and Quintanilla (1992) examined the meaning of work of career starters in eight countries. They found that work was quite central in all participating countries, and differences between countries were small. France was found to be the leading country, followed by Portugal, England, Israel, then Spain and the Netherlands. Belgium was ranked seventh, ahead of Italy which was ranked eighth, and last. In a comparison of the two occupational groups in the study, in Belgium and England, machine operators were found to consider working significantly less important than did an office technology group; the opposite was true for Israel and France; for Italy, the Netherlands, Portugal, and Spain, no significant differences appeared between target groups.

In a later study, Harpaz (1998b) examined religious conviction in relation to the meaning of work through representative samples of the labor forces in Germany, Israel, and the Netherlands. Work centrality was found to be a significant predictor of religious conviction and had a positive relation with religious conviction in Germany, although this was not significant in the Netherlands. In Germany, and to some degree in the Netherlands, the more religious the individual, the greater the importance attributed to work. Workers in Germany and the Netherlands who were religious and had also received a religious education scored high on the work centrality index. In Israel, the opposite was true: the more religious the person, the less important was work centrality. This negative relation was explained by the fact that religious Jews may view work as less important than the practice of their religion, and may even perceive work as an interference with it. The absolute strength of work centrality was greater in Israel than in Germany or the Netherlands.

Harpaz and Fu (1997) compared work centrality and its determinants in Germany, Israel, Japan, and the U.S. Their findings showed that work centrality was relatively high in all four countries, the highest in Japan and the lowest in Germany. In all four countries, female employees consistently attributed less importance to work as a central role in their lives than did male employees. The traditional value placed on women to be more home-oriented still is dominant in these four countries. Education level was negatively associated with centrality of work in the three countries for which this variable entered the model (the exception being Germany). Expressive orientation and obligation were both positively associated with centrality of work in all four countries. Interpersonal relations in both Germany and the U.S., the only countries for which this parameter was available, had a negative impact on work centrality. Differences emerged in regard to income level, instrumental orientation, and the entitlement norm across the countries. In Japan and Israel, a higher income correlated with a higher value placed on work centrality; in Germany, the opposite was true. Entitlement impacted positively on work centrality in Israel, but the effect was negative in each of the three other countries. *Instrumental orientation* (attitude to the importance of making money as a work goal) had a negative effect on work centrality in Israel, Japan, and the United States; in Germany this effect was positive.

Crosscultural Research on Union Commitment. Barling, Fullagar, and Kelloway (1992) observed that union commitment had been subjected to much research in countries other than America, where Gordon et al. (1980) performed their original study; this was important because the predictors of union commitment could still differ across countries or contexts, even if no differences were evident in mean levels. For example, although union loyalty was predicted by job involvement for white collar workers, and by job alienation for blue-collar workers in South Africa (Fullagar & Barling, 1989), no such relations emerged in Canada (Barling, Wade, & Fullagar, 1990). Likewise, extrinsic job dissatisfaction had a direct effect on union loyalty among white collar workers in South Africa, but not in Canada. Also, whereas the four union commitment dimensions did not predict union turnover in America (Gordon et al. 1980), they did in Klanderman's (1989) Dutch sample.

Barling et al. (1992) contended that because these studies differed in numerous factors other than national origin, any conclusion that the predictors or levels of union commitment did not generalize across countries was premature. They concluded, in keeping with Thacker et al. (1990), that union commitment was influenced more by the proximal, microlevel work situation than the larger economic, political, and cultural systems. Nonetheless, they suggested that more research was needed to further clarify this issue.

In another study, Fullagar and Barling (1990) compared union commitment between Black and White members of a multiracial South African union. They found that for Black members, Marxist-related beliefs were strong predictors of union loyalty, whereas for White members, work ethic was the strong predictor. This finding supported the notion of "deprived" workers being more concerned with the political dimension of unionization than nondeprived workers. At the same time, union socialization and union instrumentality were found to have similar strong effects on the commitments of both Black and White members.

Cohen and Kirchmeyer (1994) surveyed 721 white collar union members from 18 manufacturing and public sector organizations in Israel. They found that the main differences between the East European immigrants and the native-born Israelis was that the immigrants held more supportive attitudes toward their unions, such as union commitment, and were more active in their unions' formal and informal activities. These differences support Spinrad's (1960) argument that minorities are more supportive of unions because of some form of deprivation inherent in their minority status and their greater responsiveness to unions' emphasis on collective efforts for improvement. An alternative and more culturally specific explanation of the supportive attitudes and behaviors of these immigrants can be derived from Fullagar and Barling's (1990) finding noted earlier. The Marxist ideology to which the East European immigrants were exposed in their countries of origin may have instilled in them an acceptance of collectivist groups, including unions.

In short, far more crossnational and crosscultural on commitment is needed before any firm conclusion can be drawn about the nature of differences among cultures if any. Few crosscultural comparisons exist about forms of commitment such as occupational or group commitment. Because of the ambiguous findings, there is a need to collect more crosscultural data on the other forms of commitment such as organizational and union commitment.

Multiple Commitments in Crosscultural Settings

Most of multiple commitment research in crosscultural settings has examined commitment forms in one setting. Little has examined and compared commitment forms across more than one nation or culture. Misra, Kanungo, Rosenstiel, and Stuhler (1985) examined job involvement and work involvement in West Germany and India and compared their findings with those of Kanungo (1982), collected in Canada. Misra et al.'s (1985) work was primarily methodological, aimed at testing the validity of Kanungo's scales of job and work involvement and their findings showed that in the three countries, the two constructs of job and work involvement appeared distinct and unidimensional. In all the three countries there was a stronger association between measures of job involvement and job satisfaction than there were between measures of work involvement and job satisfaction. Also, measures of job involvement were more strongly associated with the satisfaction of the most important rather than least important needs on the job, and extrinsically motivated individuals were as likely to be involved in their jobs as intrinsically motivated individuals, provided their present levels of job satisfaction were equal. The authors concluded that the above findings gave empirical support to the claim that the motivational formulation of involvement had pan-cultural validity and generalizability. In the three different countries hypotheses derived from the motivational formulation were consistently supported.

Chay and Aryee (1999) examined the effect of a careerist orientation on job involvement, organizational commitment, and turnover intentions in a sample of graduate employees in Singapore. They also examined the potential moderating influence of career growth opportunities on the relation between careerist orientation and the above commitment forms. Their findings showed that individuals high in careerist orientation were most likely to perceive an incompatibility between their interests and those of the employing organization, leading to a low level of job involvement and organizational commitment and high turnover intentions. They also found that career growth opportunities did not moderate the relation between careerist orientation and organizational commitment and job involvement. They concluded that the two commitment forms might have little or no relevance in the protean career era or under transactional psychological contracts. They also concluded that their findings appear to suggest that a careerist orientation may not be culture-bound. Employees in Singapore, much like their individualist American counterparts, seem to have developed an individualist, self-oriented (careerist) posture regarding of their careers.

Buchko, Weinzimmer, and Sergeyev (1997), in an interesting study examined, together with other variables, job involvement and organizational commitment of 180 managers and workers in a large Russian company. They compared their findings with those of studies done in the U.S., and concluded that strong support was evident of the applicability of American-based organizational commitment theory in Russian organizations. They based this conclusion on several findings. First, a strong correlation appeared between organizational commitment and job involvement in the Russian sample ($r = .75; p \leq .001$), similar to findings in the American samples. Second, Russian workers scored significantly higher than American workers on the job involvement scale. They suggested that these relations might occur because Russian workers had a high sense of pressure, creating high levels of job involvement. Therefore, because commitment to one's job correlated positively with commitment to one's organization, the correlation between job involvement and organizational commitment was very high for Russian workers. The comparison also showed that Russian organizational commitment was significantly lower than American organizational commitment.

These authors also found a moderate positive correlation between pay satisfaction and organizational commitment ($r = .28$; $p \leq .01$), suggesting that the more satisfied Russian workers were with wages, the more committed they were to the organization. Note that the relation between pay satisfaction and job involvement was not significant. Additionally, a significant positive relation was found to exist between co-worker satisfaction and organizational commitment and job involvement. This finding is consistent with the contention that Russians have high levels of work-group cohesion and loyalty, thus increasing co-worker satisfaction and creating a positive relation between this variable and organizational commitment. Their findings also showed positive and significant correlations between the two commitment forms with other dimensions of satisfaction such as supervisor, promotion, and work satisfaction. From their results these researchers concluded that American theories on commitment could be applied to Russian employees, but that their findings needed to be replicated and extended to improve their generalizability. A major limitation of the above study, despite the interesting data, is that it was based on correlation analysis and did not propose a stronger conceptual framework that could be tested by other and stronger analyses.

One of the more comprehensive studies of multiple commitments across cultures was performed by Vandenberghe et al. (2001), who examined multiple commitments using a sample of employees working for the translation department of the European Commission located in Brussels. Applying the Meyer and Allen's (1997) typology to multiple commitments, the survey questionnaire included measures of affective and normative commitments to the organization, the occupation, the work group and Europe; continuance commitment to the organization and the occupation and intent to quit. Participants (N-580) pertained to 12 European nationalities (Belgium, Denmark, England, Finland, France, Germany, Greece, Italy, Portugal, Spain, Sweden, and The Netherlands) and responded to a French or English version of the questionnaire. Moreover, the data was dichotomized according to the cultural framework of Hofstede.

The findings on commitment levels showed only two differences across cultural dimensions, which involve means on commitment variables. Employees from individualistic European countries displayed higher levels of continuance commitments to their organization and occupation, and employees from countries scoring high on the masculinity dimension exhibited stronger levels of affective commitment to Europe. The findings also showed that the variable turnover intention was explained by organizational as well as nonorganizational commitment components. Among the significant relations, those involving affective bonds were dominant. Between the two other forms of commitment components, only the continuance commitment component toward the organization and occupation was significantly related to intent to quit across the cultural dimensions. No normative commitment components were significantly related to intent to quit. The relations between commitment foci and intent to quit were consistent across cultural dimensions. This study is quite unique and innovative in terms of the large number of commitment foci that were examined and the number of cultures. However, one should note that all employees examined here worked at the same location in Brussels and the size of the sample for each nationality was quite small, ranging between 21 and 61.

In an interesting study, Darwish (2000) examined a culture rarely examined in commitment research, a sample of 474 employees from 30 organizations in five districts in the United Arab Emirates (UAE). The study examined the mediating role of organizational commitment in the relation between Islamic work ethic and attitudes toward organizational change. Organizational commitment was measured using the three dimensions (affective, continuance, and normative) of Meyer and Allen (1991). An important cultural aspect of this study was the use of a specific scale for Islamic work ethic (IWE) instead of the Protestant work ethic (PWE) scale applied in Western cultures. Path analysis results showed that Islamic work ethic directly and positively influenced various dimensions of both organizational commitment and attitudes toward organizational change. All three dimensions of organizational commitment were found to mediate the effects of IWE on both affective and behavioral tendency dimensions of attitudes toward organizational change.

The author concluded that that Western management theories related to the relations in question were valid in a non-Western environment. But there was a problem with this conclusion related to the sample. The author reported that 23.4% of their subjects were UAE nationals, 36.7% were Arab expatriates, 34.6% were Asians, and 5.1% were Westerners. Yet, Darwish (2000) analyzed the data without controlling the different subgroups in the sample, thereby perhaps missing potential crosscultural differences between Arabs and Asians, for example, not to mention Westerners. Such control or comparisons among the different groups must be performed before a firm conclusion on cultural similarity could be reached.

This control is exemplified in Cohen's (1999b) study of Arab and Jewish nurses, comparing different cultural groups in the same country, namely, Israel. This study sought to shed more light on some of the unanswered questions and contradictions raised by Besser (1993) and others regarding the conflicting findings in studies that examined commitment in Japan. Cohen argued that the demographic composition of Israel provided an opportunity to compare the work and nonwork relation of workers from two diverse cultures located in the same country. The population of Israel is segmented into a number of socially significant groupings. The deepest demarcation is national, between Israeli Jews and Israeli Arabs. This gap overlaps with that of religion, between Jews and Muslims, Christians, and Druzes. Almost all non-Jews are Arabs. Studies of Jewish men and women in Israeli work settings suggest that their attitudes and experiences are similar to those of Western Europe and North America (e.g., Toren, 1991; Yishai & Cohen, 1997). The Jewish culture in Israel can be considered more westernized in terms of work attitudes and values than the Arab culture (Ronen & Shenkar, 1985). Semyonov and Lewin-Epstein (1987) concluded, "As a whole, the non-Jewish minority group is lower in all aspects of socioeconomic status than the Jewish population ... (and) both occupational and residential segregation between Jews and Arabs are extreme." Both ethnic groups were examined simultaneously with the same scale instruments and the same behavioral indicators. Specifically, the outcomes of work and nonwork demands included subjective measures, namely, perceived organizational citizenship behavior, turnover intention, and life satisfaction, as well as objective measures, namely, turnover and absenteeism over the following year. In addition, hypotheses on differential effects of commitment forms on the outcomes across the two groups were developed and tested. Such a comparison of the different groups was missing in Darwish's (2000) study, and it could have strengthened any conclusion reached in that research.

Cohen (1996) argued that there were two reasons to expect higher commitment among Arabs than among Jews. The first was the setting, as just outlined. The data show almost undoubtedly that Arabs are a deprived minority. In terms of their occupational and organizational choices, they have far fewer opportunities than do the Jewish majority group. An Arab nurse who loses her or his job in one of the few Arab-populated hospitals has only one alternative: to work in one of the Jewish-populated hospitals. This is a major decision, and many are undoubtedly discouraged, expecting that in the latter establishment they probably will be more deprived than in their current workplace. One may, therefore, expect Arabs to be more committed to their organization, job, and occupation. They will also be more committed to their work group, knowing that this is a preferable setting for them than working as a minority in a Jewish-populated hospital.

Although this explanation does not support a difference in commitment to the work between Arabs and Jews, the cultural differences between the two groups do. Arabs represent a more traditional society than do the Jews. Among the Arabs, commitment is a complex attitude influenced by the norms, sanctions, and pressures of a small group, family, and community. Values among Arabs suggest particular views typical of more traditional societies, including preference for more personal ties to supervisors, acceptance of more paternalistic treatment, and a sense that power relationships should be hierarchical. These factors may influence Arabs' attitudes, resulting in greater commitment to the firm. The Jewish culture is thought to be more Western-oriented, hence more heterogeneous and focused on different values. In the present case, although the Jewish culture may have affected the Jewish nurses' attitudes, the effect was likely to be less obvious because this culture is not as homogeneous as the Arab culture. Cultural differences were expected to provide another reason for the higher levels of commitment forms tested here in Arabs than in Jews. These explanations should also be relevant to the outcome variables. Besser (1993) termed the outcome variables *indexes of behavioral commitment*. Following this line of argument, Arab nurses were also expected to demonstrate high, more favorable outcomes than were the Jewish nurses.

The main expectation of Cohen's (1997) study was that commitment forms would have a more favorable effect on outcomes for Arabs than for Jews. This expectation relied on the cultural differences between Arabs and Jews as demonstrated by means of Hofstede's (1980) framework. Cohen argued that the particular setting of the Arabs in Israel highlighted two of these as probable reasons to expect that commitment would have a more favorable effect on outcomes for Arabs than for Jews. The two were individualism/collectivism and uncertainty avoidance. With the first, Arab culture emphasizes collectivism much more than does Jewish culture. For example, in *The Arab Executive*, two thirds of all surveyed Arab executives thought employee loyalty was more important than efficiency (Muna, 1980). As members of a Western-oriented society, the Jewish nurses adopted the individualist orientation, which holds that each person should determine her or his beliefs and behavior. In societies oriented more to individualism, loyalty is less important than in societies oriented more to collectivism. Therefore commitment could be expected to have stronger and more favorable impact outcomes in the collectivism-oriented Arab culture than in the individualism-oriented Jewish one.

Concerning the second dimension, uncertainty avoidance (described earlier in this chapter), the Arabs in Israel, as a minority group are more threatened by ambiguous situations. Commitment is an attitude that should be more common in high uncertainty avoidance situations, like that of the Arabs in Israel. It can strongly assist in reducing uncertainties among the Arabs and make their behavior more predictable. For the minority Arab group threatened by ambiguous situations in their environment, commitment is an important attitude that provides internal stability. The Arab nurses examined here were employed in the economic enclave of minority owned hospitals. As stated above, their employment opportunities were limited. If they lost their job in the hospital they may be obliged to move to a different city and to work in a Jewish hospital where most of the employees are Jewish. This would not be favorable, as Arabs employed in Arab-owned businesses have been found to receive greater returns from education and to experience less job loss. The fear of losing their employment and the lack of employment alternatives is the main reason for the stronger commitment of the Arabs. Commitment among Jewish nurses is the result of the work set-ting and structure and the perceived exchange between the organization and its employees (Mowday et al., 1982). It would not operate as an uncer-tainty avoidance mechanism, as in the Arab culture. Although it was ex-pected to be related favorably to outcomes, the relation was not expected to be as strong as it was for the Arabs.

In the case of Japanese employees, the organization was deemed to en-hance its employees' commitment by offering permanent employment, in-ternal labor markets, quality circles, and company welfare programs. In the Arab case, their particular setting as a minority group magnifies the impor-tance of commitment and its effect on outcomes. Commitment would not only be higher for Arabs than for Jews, it would also have a more favorable effect on outcomes for Arabs than for Jews.

These expectations were tested in a survey of 283 nurses at three hospi-tals in Northern Israel. Two of the hospitals are located in areas populated by Arabs and virtually all their employees were Arabs. They are close geo-graphically, so the characteristics of their work forces were assumed to be alike. The third hospital was located in a Jewish area and employed predom-inantly Jewish workers. As for commitment measures, organizational com-mitment was measured by the shorter nine-item version of the Organizational Commitment Questionnaire (OCQ; Porter, Steers, Mowday, & Boulian, 1974). Career commitment was measured by the eight-item measure developed by Blau (1985). Job involvement (10 items) and work involvement (6 items) were measured by the scales developed by Kanungo (1979, 1982). Group commitment was measured by the six-item measure developed by Randall and Cote (1991).

The findings showed that levels of all commitment forms other than group commitment were higher for Arabs than for Jews: organizational commitment (4.01 versus 3.55), career commitment (4.03 versus 3.77), job involvement (3.63 versus 3.40), and work involvement (3.51 versus 2.96). Level of group commitment was also higher for Arab nurses than for Jewish nurses (3.64 versus 3.51), but here the difference was not significant.

The findings of the moderated regression analysis showed that the five commitment forms better predicted attitudinal outcomes such as turnover intentions, perceived organizational citizenship behavior (OCB), and life satisfaction than the behavioral outcomes such as turnover and absenteeism. Once the effects of these variables were controlled, ethnicity contributed significantly in the cases of absence frequency, absence duration, OCB, and life satisfaction. Being Arab meant higher absence frequency, lower absence duration, lower OCB, and lower life satisfaction. The effect of ethnicity was not significant for actual turnover or for the three forms of turnover intentions tested in the study (intention to leave the organization, the occupation, and the job). Also, 14 of the 40 interactions that tested the effect of each commitment interacting with the variable of being a minority (Arab vs. Jew) proved significant. Specifically, organizational commitment had a more favorable effect on absence duration with Arabs. Increase in organizational commitment resulted in a marked rise in absence duration with Jewish nurses. No such rise was found with the Arab nurses. Organizational commitment meant more OCB with both ethnic groups although it was less evident with Jews. Organizational commitment had also a more favorable effect on the three turnover intention variables with Arabs than with Jews. More organizational commitment decreased turnover intentions with the Arabs nurses more than with the Jewish nurses. The interaction term with work involvement contributed only to intentions to leave the occupation. The pattern of this interaction contradicted the expectation because it showed that work involvement had a more adverse effect on intentions to leave the occupation among the Arab nurses. That is, more work involvement increased Arab nurses' intentions to leave the occupation more than it did Jewish nurses' intentions to leave.

The interaction term with group commitment contributed to intentions to leave the organization, intentions to leave the job, and intentions to leave the occupation. Group commitment had a more favorable effect on intentions to leave the job with Arabs than with Jews. That is, it decreased Arab nurses' intentions to leave the job more than it did Jewish nurses' intentions to leave. But in the two other interactions, the effect of group commitment was not as expected. Group commitment had a more favorable effect on intentions to leave the organization and the occupation with Jewish than with Arab nurses.

The interaction term with job involvement contributed to intentions to leave the job and intentions to leave the occupation. The pattern of the interaction differed between the two turnover intention variables. Job involvement had a more favorable effect on intentions to leave the job with Jewish nurses and a more favorable effect on intentions to leave the occupation with Arab nurses. That is, increased job involvement decreased intentions to leave the job with the Jewish nurses and decreased intentions to leave the occupation with the Arab nurses. The interaction term with career commitment contributed to absenteeism duration, intentions to leave the organization, and intentions to leave the occupation. In all three interactions, career commitment had a more favorable effect on Arab than on Jewish nurses. With the Jewish nurses, career commitment increased absenteeism duration more than with the Arab nurses. It also increased the Jewish nurses' intentions to leave their organization and occupation.

In short, Cohen's (1997b) data showed that most interactions evinced more favorable effects of commitment forms on Arab nurses. The five interaction terms with organizational commitment and the three interaction terms with career commitment were consistent in that regard. Results were mixed for the interaction terms with group commitment and job involvement, and the only interaction term with work involvement contradicted the expectation. Another noteworthy pattern is that the two and only significant interactions found for the behavioral outcomes, namely the interactions for absence duration, supported expectations, organizational commitment and career commitment, had a more favorable effect on absence duration for Arab nurses than for Jewish nurses. Together, 10 of the 14 significant interactions supported the research expectation.

Cohen (1997b) concluded that his findings were more conclusive than those that examined the Japanese setting. They showed that the nature of the relation between commitment forms and outcomes clearly differed across the two ethnic groups, indicating culture to be an important moderator of the effects of commitment forms on work and nonwork-related outcomes. In general, Arab nurses were found more committed than Jewish nurses, and their commitment had more favorable effects on their behavior, especially attitudes at work. Therefore, social scientists must remain cautious about generalizing research findings on commitment in one culture to other cultural settings. The findings of Cohen's study also indicated the exercise of care with generalizations about the effects of commitment across different outcomes, particularly from the effects on perceptual outcomes to those on behavioral outcomes.

Conclusions and Suggestions for Future Research

Crosscultural research on multiple commitments is one of the most stimulating areas for future research, so it is quite disappointing that relatively few studies have examined this issue. Too little research has been devoted to examining separate commitments in a crosscultural setting, and as a result, not much can be found on multiple commitments. It is very difficult to produce meaningful conclusions and suggestions from the scant research available on the topic. Above all, more crosscultural and crossnational research on multiple commitments is needed. Research is required that not only tests multiple commitments but also compares their relation with determinants and outcomes across different cultures and nations.

Research on multiple commitments in cultures other than the U.S. is important. But more important is research that compares multiple commitments across cultures and nations. By applying the same research instruments on more than one culture, more meaningful conclusions can be reached regarding similarities and differences in commitment. Comparing the findings of one study conducted in one culture using a given commitment scale with the findings of another study in a different culture using a different scale cannot yield strong and valid conclusions. Some of the ambiguous conclusions on cultural differences and or similarities can be attributed to the differences in the scales or in the administration of the survey.

Future research should explore the meaning of commitment in different cultures and examine whether they share the same meaning of commitment in general, and separate commitment items in specific scales in particular. Arguably, that differences that do exist are hard to explain because cultural values, norms, and beliefs are so vastly different that certain commitment items used in the U.S. cannot be included in the survey instrument given to Japanese workers (Hanada, 1984). Near (1989) used the common Porter et al. (1974) commitment scale for comparing models of commitment between Japanese and American production workers, and found that Americans demonstrated higher levels of OC. From these findings, Near suggested that the Western conception of commitment might simply not apply to this other culture because "Western concepts and measures of commitment may not explain the sentiment that Japanese workers feel towards their organizations" (p. 294).

Most crosscultural research has concentrated on OC or work values. Some of it examined union commitment. There is little on other forms of commitment, for example, occupational commitment, group commitment, or job involvement across cultures. These are important commitment forms that need to be examined in a crosscultural setting. With the increasing emphasis on occupational commitment as an important focus, research is needed to compare the importance of this form across cultures. Group commitment is also a form that needs crosscultural research because it is related conceptually to one of the important characteristics of culture, namely, individualism/collectivism. More studies examining a variety of commitment foci such as the one by Vandenberghe et al. (2001) are essential for increasing our understanding on multiple commitments across cultures.

Another consideration for future research is the difference between crossnational and crosscultural research on commitment. Not much attention has been paid to this aspect. Most research has used a crossnational approach. But in a given nation, several different cultures can exist together, and analyzing them as one entity might lead to faulty conclusions. Cohen and Gattiker's (1992) data, for example, suggested a high degree of similarity between the U.S. and Canada, as suggested by other researchers (e.g., Griffeth, Hom, DeNisi, & Kirchner, 1985). In keeping with Becker's (1960) arguments, they concluded that similarities in cultural expectations between Canada and the U.S. and the value systems of subcultures "such as those associated with occupational groups" (p. 39), might explain the lack of major differences they discovered. Cohen and Gattiker's conclusion was supported by a study (Mathieu, Bruvold, & Ritchey, 2000) that compared the OCQ psychometric properties between French- and English-speaking Canadian salespersons and did not find meaningful differences between the French and the English version of the OCQ.

However, from Cohen and Gattiker's (1992) results and those of others such as Near (1989), or even Vandenberghe et al. (2001) it can be concluded that the Western conception of commitment seemed to apply only to similar cultures and not to different cultures such as those of Japan and India. Also, in an assessment of commitment even in cultures that are quite similar (e.g., Western countries, speaking the same language, sharing a large border, and engaging in free trade with each other), caution was warranted and differences in commitment had to be carefully interpreted. As crossnational similarities lend themselves to interpretation more readily than differences (Kohn, 1989), future research that compares similar cultures should disregarded the differences in the cultures and political and economic systems, and concentrate instead on social-structural universals (cf. Kohn, 1989). Such research should test crosscultural differences by comparing occupational groups (e.g., white collar workers, engineers, and teachers) in the U.S. and Canada for example, for crossnational similarities and/or differences in commitment measures.

As for comparisons of different cultures Cohen's (1999b) study showed significant differences between Arabs and Jews, two cultures, living in the same country, Israel. For example, all five interactions with organizational commitment indicated a more favorable effect on Arabs than on Jews. Both groups reported that occupational commitment was the form they were very highly committed to. Here too, Arab nurses were more committed than Jewish nurses, and the three significant interactions showed more favorable effects of this commitment on outcomes with Arabs than with Jews. This consistency in the findings for the Arab and Jewish data, compared with the ambiguity of the American and Japanese data, is an important issue that should be the concern of future crosscultural research on commitment forms. Several tentative explanations can be offered here, which should be tested in future research. One is that the theory applied to the American and Japanese data was not appropriate for that setting. The main expectation in that context was that the Japanese culture was more traditional than was the American, so Japanese employees would be more committed than American employees and this commitment would lead to more favorable outcomes. However, Besser (1993), argued that Japanese employees behaved more favorably at work because the Japanese core organizations had evolved effective mechanisms to encourage employees to meet the organizations' expectations, not because they harbored strong attitudes of commitment to the organization. Workers' cooperation in Japan was won through effective but subtle psychological and social pressures rather than through employees' personal commitment. This was Besser's (1993) explanation for the contradiction whereby the Japanese are less committed than the Americans but their behavior at work is more favorable than the Americans'.

The cultural explanation received stronger support in Cohen's (1999b) study. The more traditional culture of the Arab nurses, together with their setting as a minority group, made them more committed employees than the Jewish nurses. Moreover, their commitment affected their behavior more favorably than the Jewish nurses' commitment affected theirs. Accordingly, the theory applied in the Japanese and American case was not appropriate for the Jewish and Arab setting. Japanese culture is exposed intensively to American culture, and does not differ significantly, but cannot be defined as a traditional society. The same applies to the culture of the Jewish nurses who are part of a more Westernized society. Commitment is a more valuable attitude in more traditional societies, and the Arabs studied adhere to their traditional way of life more than do Americans, Japanese, or Jewish nurses in Israel. The Arab setting as a minority group, and undoubtedly a deprived one, operates only to increase the importance of commitment as a mechanism to assist them in coping with what some of them perceive as a hostile setting. Cohen (1999b) concluded that future research should seek data that allows testing of this explanation. It should also attempt to find context that allows some separation between culture and setting, namely, a cultural group that does not face the structural environmental constraints encountered by Arabs in Israel. Arabs in some Middle Eastern countries may constitute a good target population.

The cultural perspective received additional support from the work of Mueller, Finley, Iverson, and Price (1999), who found that the school racial composition of teachers and the school racial composition of students affected school commitment and career commitment of American teachers. Their findings showed that White schoolteachers reported higher organizational and career commitment in White teacher and White student dominated schools than White teachers in other racial composition configurations. There were no differences in commitment for Black teachers in schools with different racial compositions. The effect of the racial composition was much stronger on OC than career commitment. The authors concluded that individuals who are accustomed to being in the minority in society are not negatively affected by being in mismatched contexts. White teachers are. Black teachers seem to have adapted to the variety of racial contexts they find themselves in, whereas White teachers may experience some forms of culture shock when they find themselves in unfamiliar mismatched contexts when they are the minority.

Although Clugston et al.'s (2000) findings, that differences in employees' commitment could be predicted on the basis of cultural dimensions even within a homogeneous work setting within one country, Cohen's (1999b) and Mueller et al.'s (1999) findings lead to the conclusion that culture is much more than a difference between a country or a nation. This should guide future research on crosscultural aspects of multiple commitments. Therefore, researchers should be cautious in comparing countries without a more detailed description of their sample in terms of potential cultural differences. Similar cases can exist in other countries. If there is a potential for such differences, these should be explained and analyzed as control variables in the data analysis.

Future research then, should concentrate on developing concepts of commitment that accurately reflect the values and meanings of commitment of the particular culture in which the measure is to be applied. Several questions should be addressed. What degree of cultural similarity will permit use of measures of commitment based on the same concept of commitment? Can two different cultures even be compared? Can two different concepts of commitment (one for each culture) be used to compare employee levels of commitment? Moreover, how may these differences be interpreted? Answers to these questions can facilitate future cross national and crosscultural comparisons of the concepts of organizational commitment and work commitment in general.

V

Synthesis and Summary

10

Where do We Go From Here? Conclusions and Recommendations for Future Research

The concept of multiple commitments in the workplace has attracted the interest of scholars and practitioners particularly in recent years. Although early research on commitment focused on separate commitments, the tendency to view commitment as a more complex phenomenon is growing. It started by developing multidimensional perspectives on separate commitments, a trend demonstrated particularly in the case of organizational commitment in the works of Meyer and Allen (1991, 1997). It continued by developing a multidimensional perspective on the whole concept of commitment in the workplace (Morrow, 1993). This multidimensional view is justified conceptually. Multiple commitments seem to represent one's linkages to the work setting better than a single commitment separately. As argued throughout this volume, examining one commitment independently seems not to capture the notion of employees' commitment in the workplace.

In an era introducing major and rapid changes into almost every aspect of our lives, it is too simplistic to isolate one commitment and to assume that only this particular form is related to one's attitudes or behaviors. Moreover, in an economic and technological environment that compels many organizations to deal with problems such as decline and reduction in the workforce, the organization cannot be the main focus of commitment for all employees. Many may shift their commitment or divide it among other foci, such as to the occupation or the union. To fully understand commitment in the workplace we must assume that employees are committed to more than one form. Although we do not know which forms employees are committed to or the relative magnitude of these commitments, we do know which forms employees might be committed to, for example, the organization, occupation, job, workgroup, union, or work values, and we can concentrate on examining these forms.

The need for the multiple commitment approach has also increased as a result of the low predictive power of each commitment separately of valuable behaviors in the workplace such as performance, turnover, tardiness, and absenteeism. The assumption behind increased interest in multiple commitments is that several commitments predict behavior better than one can separately. This assumption has strong justification considering employees are committed to more than one form, and in different settings, different forms can have stronger effects on behavioral outcomes.

Consequently, interest in the multiple commitment approach has increased. Many of its arguments and findings have been described in this volume. The research presented here illuminated the potential of continuing the study of this concept. In the first stages of research on multiple commitments, researchers focused their attention on similarities and differences in commitment forms to avoid conceptual and measurement overlaps among the concepts. Later, they sought to discern the interrelations in commitment forms. This was an important step forward because it enhanced the conceptual understanding of multiple commitments. This conceptual work is also evident in attempts that were made to develop commitment profiles. At the same time, researchers also examined the relations between commitment forms and outcomes. This too is an important research area, with weighty implications for the predictive validity of multiple commitments. All this shows that important work has been done on multiple commitments that have expanded our understanding of this concept.

Yet, the research presented here, despite its richness and importance, is not enough. More research is essential in almost every any aspect of multiple commitments. Such future research should build the findings, conclusions, and limitations of past investigations. One contribution this volume makes is that by presenting most of what is known on multiple commitments it can help to guide future efforts on this issue. This final chapter summarizes the main findings of what is known to date about multiple commitments and offers recommendations and suggestions for future research. These are organized and presented based on the main issues covered in previous chapters.

Commitment Forms.   Much work has been done on each commitment form independently, mostly on organizational commitment and a considerable amount on job involvement, and more recently on occupational commitment. Some interesting work has also been accomplished on union commitment. Less research has been directed at work values and work group commitment. A basic question that should be addressed by future research is which of the forms constitute the notion of multiple commitments. How many forms must a given study cover to justify the researcher's claiming to have adopted a multiple commitment approach? Which should be considered forms definable as part of multiple commitment in the workplace? The first question presents us with the dilemma of how to define the use of two commitments in a single study: Is this a multiple commitment approach?

Morrow (1993) addressed this very issue, and suggested five forms that Morrow termed universal, namely, forms relevant to every employee in any setting. She suggested that all these five forms should be used in any research on multiple commitments. In specific cases other forms should be added, depending on the particular setting. For example, in a unionized organization, union commitment should be included in addition to the five forms termed universal. Still, far more work is needed on this matter. First, although Morrow included continuance organizational commitment among the five universal forms the data presented here strongly challenge the rationale for its inclusion. If this form is omitted, which form should replace it? Are four forms enough for a multiple commitment approach? A consensus seems likely that the following three forms should be included in almost any study of multiple commitments: organization, occupation, and job. Like Morrow, many will recommend the inclusion of work values such as PWE as the fourth form. What other forms should be included as the fifth one? What is the status of workgroup commitment as part of the multiple commitment approach? Should union commitment be included with every unionized setting? These are some of the questions that should be dealt with in future research. Currently a solid definition of multiple commitments should include the organization, occupation, and job foci. One or two additional foci can be added based on the specific research questions or setting.

Another interesting and important issue has resulted from the fact that very little research have addressed the relations between temporary or contingent work and multiple commitments. It is not clear to what extent the various foci of commitment at work are relevant or important to the study of contingent workers. Does the growing emergence of contingent employment suggest a need for researchers to reconsider the development of additional foci of work commitment, which may be more central or relevant to workers employed on contingent rather than more traditional employment contracts? This issue was thoroughly addressed by Gallagher and McLean Parks (2001) and should be considered in future works on commitment forms.

Measurement Issues.   Although the main argument of this volume is that the multiple commitment approach is superior to research on separate commitments, research on each commitment independently should continue even from the multiple commitments viewpoint. The main reason is that to date we still have no valid, reliable definitions and measurements for some of the forms. The recommendation of this volume is that multiple commitment definitions and measurements should be generated from definitions and measurements of separate commitments. That is, we first need solid, reliable, and valid scales for each commitment; then these can be applied in a multiple commitment approach. Multiple commitments are measured by the assembly of several measures of independent commitments, so progress in the multiple commitment approach depends on progress, particularly methodological, independently in each of the commitment forms independently. In this instance, two or three commitment forms appear capable of providing reliable, valid scales in preparation for the formulation of a multiple commitment scale. These are the affective organizational commitment scale of Meyer and Allen (1984) and the job and work involvement scales of Kanungo (1979, 1982). Other forms still must develop reliable and valid scales, which can combine with these existing ones to provide a sounder measurement of multiple commitments. Because this process may take several years, researchers should be cautious in selecting their commitment scales and avoid the problematic ones as much as possible. Another interesting factor for future consideration is measuring commitment is the crosscultural setting. Most studies dealing with the measurement of multiple commitments, for instance, have been conducted in the United States. The difficulty of applying such an instrument in, say, Japan may necessitate a different version of the scale (e.g., Hanada, 1984) and most importantly, results may be difficult to interpret in light of data gathered in other countries (e.g., Lincoln & Kalleberg, 1985). Future research should examine the scales in different cultures to ensure that measures of multiple commitments are not affected by culture, and if they are, the implications of culture on measurement should be considered in any given particular research. The development of an Islamic work ethic scale (Ali, 1988) is a good demonstration of considering culture in the measurement of multiple commitments.

Concept Redundancy.   Morrow (1983) pointed out the problem of conceptual and measurement overlap among commitment scales. The research on this issue that followed Morrow's study showed that this problem exists, but it can be tolerated. Research evidence so far has shown that organizational commitment, job involvement, and work involvement, particularly the first two scales, can be used with a minimal risk of concept redundancy. When adding other commitment forms, researchers may perhaps consider the following recommendations. First, they should use established scales, particularly those whose discriminant validity has some empirical support. Second, shorter scales are recommended over long scales. Meyer and Allen's (1984) eight-item scale or Kanungo's ten-item scale for job involvement is of reasonable length. Third, researchers should attempt to use unidimensional scales. Multidimensional scales can increase the probability of conceptual confusion among the different scales and their items, and can increase the likelihood of overlap among commitment concepts and scales. Fourth, researchers should remember that some relation among commitment foci will always exist. They should take care that the intercorrelations are not excessively high. Those above .70 definitely point to a serious redundancy problem. Correlations below .50 seem acceptable.

Typologies of Commitment.   As mentioned, unidimensional scales of commitment forms are recommended. However, in chapter 4, the main suggestion was that each commitment focus should be defined as a global commitment, which has its specific constituencies. Hunt and Morgan (1994) advanced such a typology for organizational commitment. They argued that the best way to interpret Reichers's (1985) data was to define organizational commitment as the global commitment, which has its constituencies, such as commitment to top management, to supervisor, to customer, and so on. If this is the best typology for multiple commitments—and as set forth in chapter 4 I believe it is, much more work is needed to establish it. First, conceptual work is required to define the specific constituencies for each form of commitment. Second, the relation between the constituencies and their respective global commitment must be examined. Third, the possible relation among the constituencies, their respective global commitment and outcomes, have to be explored. Questions of possible overlap among constituencies of different global commitments should be considered too. So far, the only work to follow this approach was on organizational commitment, but even here more is needed. A great deal of conceptual and empirical effort is necessary in respect of the other commitment forms.

Commitment Models.   A more recent research area is the interrelations among commitment foci. Two models of these have been advanced and examined, Randall and Cote's (1991) and Morrow's (1993). So far, the findings strongly support the superiority of Randall and Cote's model, but much more research is needed on this topic. More conceptual work is needed to produce other possible models of the interrelations among commitment forms. Whereas Randall and Cote's model seems to have received sufficient empirical support, commitment forms may be interrelated in other ways. Randall and Cote emphasized the role of job involvement as the mediating variable in the relations among commitment forms. This finding should be tested more, so as to establish the pivotal role of job involvement in commitment models.

These commitment models were tested by means of a specific combination of commitment forms, but they should also be tested with different combinations. Future research should also find out how commitment models operate when different foci are included in them. For example, how will union commitment affect the models, or in particular Randall and Cote's (1991) model which was not tested with this form? Which commitment forms should replace the continuance commitment form, that was advanced by Morrow (1993) but does not seem to be a part of any commitment model? How many forms should be included in commitment models—four, five, or more? What are the conceptual implications of including four, five, or more commitment forms in a given model? Will it affect the models conceptually and empirically? How?

Commitment Forms and Work Outcomes. The main rationale for the interest in multiple commitments is the expectation that several forms predict outcomes better than one can form. At present, evidence shows the potential of commitment forms to predict work outcomes better than one given separate commitment. Yet, much more work is needed to confirm the superiority of multiple commitments over one commitment in predicting outcomes. First, more research is needed to test behavioral outcomes as against attitudinal outcomes used by many studies. Commitment forms can almost without doubt predict attitudes or behavioral intentions better than one commitment, for example, turnover intentions. We need more data to show that the same can be said about behavioral outcomes, such as actual turnover or absenteeism. Second, there is a need to look for other outcomes that multiple commitments can predict apart from the traditional ones such as turnover, absenteeism, and performance. For example, organizational citizenship behavior (OCB) is an outcome needing to be explored more in terms of its relations with multiple commitments.

More work is required on the nature of the relations between commitments and outcomes. It seems to be more complex than a direct relation; mediators probably exist between commitment foci and outcomes. For example, turnover intentions probably mediate the relation between commitment forms and actual turnover. In addition, some commitment forms seem to mediate the relation between other forms and outcomes. Job involvement appears to play an important role in this process by mediating the relation between the exogenous and the endogenous commitment foci. Although most research tested approximately three commitment forms in one study for their relation with outcomes, future research should test more forms in one design. Particular attention should be paid to the role of occupational commitment in predicting outcomes. With some decline in the significance of organizational commitment because of workforce reduction due to changes in the economy of many countries, occupational commitment seems to be growing in importance. This should be demonstrated in its relation to outcomes.

Researchers should also look for possible moderators in the relation between commitment forms and outcomes. One's career stage or age shows promise of being such a moderator. Research evidence (Cohen, 1991; 1993d) showed the importance of this variable as a moderator in the relation between organizational commitment and outcomes. Such moderation should be tested in the relation between multiple commitments and outcomes. Other moderators should also be tested, such as occupation (Cohen & Hudecek, 1993), gender, education, and ethnicity. The moderation effect may prove stronger for some commitment forms than for others.

Commitment and Nonwork Domain.   Very little research has examined the relation between any given commitment and nonwork domain concepts, and too few have examined multiple commitments for their relation with nonwork domains. This overly neglected issue is important in light of the changes being experienced by Western society, such as the growing participation of women in the workforce, or stronger pressures on organizations to adjust to the nonwork needs of their employees. All of these magnify the importance of the relation between commitment forms and nonwork domains. Whereas nonwork concepts are being developed more in the organizational behavior literature, few of these concepts have been related to any given commitment form. Naturally, at first, more research is needed on the commitment and nonwork relation based on a conceptual framework. For example, objective nonwork concepts such as children or marital status should be tested together with attitudinal concepts such as work and nonwork conflict for their relation to commitment forms. How do these relations differ for different commitment forms?

Attention should similarly be turned to the direction of this relation; Do nonwork domain factors affect commitment forms, or is the reverse the case? For example, can a more forceful work or nonwork conflict cause enfeeblement of commitment forms, or some of them? Or can stronger commitment act to mitigate a work or nonwork conflict? Such questions call for longitudinal designs that can cope with these important but potentially fruitful, research issues. Research on the relation between multiple commitments and nonwork domains is hardly past its exploratory stage. Therefore, any research on this relation is important and can contribute to our knowledge.

Profiles of Commitment.   This was one of the earliest fields of multiple commitment research. The concepts of dual versus unilateral commitment to union and employer, or local versus cosmopolitan, were advanced in the 1950s, many years before Morrow (1983) introduced the concept of multiple commitments. This issue is perhaps one of the most interesting and inspiring areas in multiple commitments. More recent studies have introduced additional profiles, the main one being the interaction of job and organizational commitment. Characterizing employees by commitment profiles can provide valuable and also practical information for employers. For example, which profile of commitment has the best fit to the organization in terms of employees' behavior in the workplace? Which profile of commitment is better from the viewpoint of the employee's well being? It is important to relate commitment profiles to nonwork domain aspects to explore which combination of profiles can cope better with the demands of work and nonwork.

Although the issue is interesting and important, much more work is needed. First, the findings of the earlier studies have to be reexamined with more current scales, namely valid and reliable scales, to ascertain that the earlier findings were not affected by measurement problems. Conceptual work is needed to explore the possibilities of other profiles. For example, in addition to the union or organization profile, perhaps union or occupational profiles should also be explored in light of the increased importance of occupational commitment. An interaction between the job and the occupation may also prove to be an interesting profile to explore. More work is needed to relate different profiles to possible determinants, and more importantly, outcomes. More valuable findings might ensue when commitment profiles are related to outcomes by the direct approach.

Crosscultural Research on Multiple Commitments.   Most of what we know about commitment is based on American theories and findings. These theories clearly need to be tested in other cultures for us to learn whether they are generalizable. Very little research has examined commitment in settings other than the North American. Most of what we know is based on comparisons of Japanese and American organizational commitment. Frequently, this research concentrated on data from the Japanese setting, not comparing them with any other. The findings of this research revealed very few differences between the two cultures. This finding contradicted one of the most anticipated differences in commitment literature, but in no way does it mean that commitment theories and findings can be generalizable across cultures.

Far more research is required to examine other cultures. First, different cultures should be compared by means of the same scales. Such activity contrasts with research that examined only one culture and from which only limited conclusions can be drawn. Still more necessary is a comparison of multiple commitments across two or three cultures in the same research design applying the same commitment scales. Such research provides stronger data and more meaningful and generalizable comparisons.

There is a need for research on whether commitment scales are understood the same way across cultures. Do commitment items carry the same meaning in different cultures? Does a commitment item that is translated from English into Japanese carry the same meaning for Japanese employees as for American? Little research has dealt with this important issue. More is needed to study similar conceptual models across cultures, which can clarify whether similar theories hold in them. In this regard, more research is required to probe the relation between commitment forms and work outcomes. Besser (1993) pointed out the possibility that behaviors in the Japanese culture are not related to attitudes, as they are in the American culture. Cohen's (1999b) findings showed interesting differences in the multiple commitment outcome relation across two cultures, the Israeli and the Arab. All this showed the importance of testing the commitment outcome relation across cultures.

Future research across cultures should also scrutinize the difference between a cross national and a cross cultural comparison. Most research on commitment tested cross national differences. Such a comparison might be misleading because it may overlook the possibility that a given country may encompass more than one culture and that the cultural differences might be stronger than the national ones. Cohen (1999b) for example, found strong differences between Jewish and Arab nurses in Israel, a finding that supports this contention.

Finally, in all research areas, research is needed to apply longitudinal research designs. Such research is important because it can indicate which commitment forms are more stable than others and how a given commitment form at one time affects another form at a later time. Research on the commitment-outcome relations particularly will benefit from longitudinal designs. For example, which commitment form is related more strongly to a given outcome at what point of time? How short should the interval be between the measurement of a given commitment and the measurement of a given outcome for a stronger effect of that commitment form on the given outcome?

Multiple commitments is a relatively new, promising, and fascinating research area. Research on commitment will continue, despite the global changes in the technology, economy, and values of most Western countries. The findings so far have indicated many potential benefits from its study. This volume described has set out the knowledge that has accumulated on this issue so far. It has also criticized it and has signaled directions for future research. Much needs to be done to increase our understanding of this topic. This volume illustrates some of the advantages of continuing the work on multiple commitments.

Appendix A

Scales
of Commitment Forms

1. ORGANIZATIONAL COMMITMENT MEASURES

Organizational and Occupational Commitment of Alutto et al.
(1973)

A. Assume that you were offered a job in nursing (teaching). Would you leave nursing (teaching) under any of the following conditions?

1. With no increase in pay
2. With a slight increase in pay
3. With a large increase in pay
4. With no additional status
5. With a slight increase in status
6. With a large increase in status

For increased freedom, and for friendlier co-workers, etc.

From: Alluto et al., (1993). On operationalizing the concept of commitment. *Social Forces, 51,* 448–454. Copyright © the University of Northern Carolina Press. Reprinted with permission.

B. Assume that you were offered a job in nursing (teaching) but in another hospital (school district). Would you leave your current employer under any of the following conditions? (Questions are repeated as in A, above).

Note: The scale for each of the questions is: yes, definitely; uncertain; no, definitely not.

Organizational Commitment of Porter et al. (1974)

1. I am willing to put in a great deal of effort beyond that normally expected in order to help this organizational to be successful.
2. I talk up this organization to my friends as a great organization to work for.
3. I feel very little loyalty to this organization (R).
4. I would accept almost any type of job assignment in order to keep working for this organization.
5. I find that my values and the organization's values are very similar.
6. I am glad to tell others that I am part of this organization.
7. I could just as well be working for a different organization as long as the type of work was similar (R).
8. The organization really inspires the very best in me in the way of job performance.
9. It would take very little change in my present circumstances to cause me to leave this organization (R).
10. I am extremely glad that I chose this organization to work for over others I was considering at the time I joined.
11. There's not too much to be gained by sticking with this organization indefinitely (R).
12. Often, I find it difficult to agree with this organization's policies on important matters relating to its employees (R).
13. I really care about the fate of this organization.
14. For me this is the best of all possible organizations for which to work.
15. Deciding to work for this organization was a definite mistake on my part (R).

From: Mowday et al., (1979). The measures of organizational commitment. *Journal of Vocational Behavior,* 14, 224–247. Copyright © by Academic Press. Reprinted with permission of Academic Press.

Meyer and Allen (1991) Affective Organizational Commitment Scale

1. I would be very happy to spend the rest of my career with this organization.

2. I enjoy discussing my organization with people outside it.
3. I really feel as if this organization's problems are my own.
4. I think that I could easily become as attached to another organization as I am to this one (R).
5. I do not feel like 'part of the family' at my organization.
6. I do not feel 'emotionally attached' to this organization (R).
7. This organization has a great deal of personal meaning for me.
8. I do not feel a strong sense of belonging to my organization (R).

Meyer and Allen (1991) Continuance Organizational Commitment Scale

1. I am not afraid of what might happen if I quit my job without having another one lined up (R).
2. It would be very hard for me to leave my organization right now, even if I wanted to.
3. Too much in my life would be disrupted if I decided I wanted to leave my organization now.
4. It wouldn't be too costly for me to leave my organization now (R).
5. Right now, staying with my organization is a matter of necessity as much as desire.
6. I feel I have too few options to consider leaving this organization.
7. One of the few serious consequences of leaving this organization would be the scarcity of available alternatives.
8. One of the major reasons I continue to work for this organization is that leaving would require considerable sacrifice-another organization may not match the overall benefits I have here.

Meyer and Allen (1991) Normative Organizational Commitment Scale

1. I think that people these days move from company to company too often.
2. I do not believe that a person must always be loyal to his or her organization (R).
3. Jumping from organization to organization does not seem at all unethical to me (R).
4. One of the major reasons I continue to work for this organization is that I believe that loyalty is important and therefore feel a sense of moral obligation to remain.
5. If I got another offer for a better job elsewhere I would not feel it was right to leave my organization.
6. I was taught to believe in the value of remaining loyal to one organization.
7. Things were better in the days when people stayed with one organization for most of their career (R).

8. I do not think that wanting to be a 'company man' or 'company woman' is sensible anymore (R).

Meyer and Allen revised Normative Organizational Commitment Scale

1. I do not feel any obligation to remain with my current employer (R).
2. Even if it were to my advantage, I do not feel it would be right to leave my organization now.
3. I would feel guilty if I left my organization now.
4. This organization deserves my loyalty.
5. I would not leave my organization right now because I have a sense of obligation to the people in it.
6. I owe a great deal to my organization.

2. JOB INVOLVEMENT MEASURES

Job Involvement Scale of Lodhal and Kejner (1965)

1. I'll stay overtime to finish a job, even if I'm not paid for it.
2. You can measure a person pretty well by how good a job they do.
3. The major satisfaction in my life comes from my work.
4. For me, mornings at work really fly by.
5. I usually show up for work a little early, to get things ready.
6. The most important things that happen to me involve my work.
7. Sometimes I lie awake at night thinking ahead to the next day's work.
8. I'm really a perfectionist about my work.
9. I feel depressed when I fail at something connected with my work.
10. I have other activities more important than my work (R).
11. I live, eat, and breathe my work.
12. I would probably keep working even if I didn't need the money.
13. Quite often I feel like staying home from work instead of coming in (R).
14. To me, my work is only a small part of who I am (R).
15. I am very much involved personally in my work.
16. I avoid taking on extra duties and responsibilities in my work (R).
17. I used to be more ambitious about my work than I am now (R).
18. Most things in life are more important than work (R).
19. I used to care more about my work, but now other things are more important to me (R).

20. Sometimes I'd like to kick myself for the mistakes I make in my work.

From: Ludhal, T. M. & Kejner, M. M. (1965). The definition and measurement of job involvement. *Journal of Applied Psychology, 49,* 24–33. Copyright © 2002, by the American Psychological Association. Reprinted with permission.

Job involvement Measure of Kanungo (1982)

1. The most important things that happen to me involve my present job.
2. To me, my job is only a small part of who I am.
3. I am very much involved personally in my job.
4. I live, eat and breathe my job.
5. Most of my interests are centered around my job.
6. I have very strong ties with my present job, which would be very difficult to break.
7. Usually I feel detached from my job.
8. Most of my personal life goals are job oriented.
9. I consider my job to be very central to my existence.
10. I like to be absorbed in my job most of the time.

Work Involvement Measure of Kanungo (1982)

1. The most important things that happen in life involve work.
2. Work is something people should get involved in most of the time.
3. Work should be only a small part of one's life.
4. Work should be considered central to life.
5. In my view, an individual's personal life goals should be work oriented.
6. Life is worth living only when people get absorbed in work.

From: Kanungo, R. N. (1982). Measurement of TUB and work involvement. *Journal of Applied Psychology, 67,* 341–349. Copyright © 2002 by the American Psychological Association. Reprinted with permission.

The Lawler and Hall (1970) Job Involvement Scale

1. The most important things that happen to me involve my work.
2. I live, eat, and breathe my job.
3. I am very much involved personally in my work.
4. The major satisfaction in my life comes from my job.

From: Lawler, E. E., & Hall, D. T. (1970). Relationships of job characteristics to job involvement satisfaction and intrinsic motivation. *Journal of Applied*

3. WORK VALUES MEASURES

Protestant Ethic Scale (and , 1971)

1. Most people spend too much time in unprofitable amusements.
2. Our society would have fewer problems if people had less leisure time.
3. Money acquired easily (e.g., through gambling or speculation) is usually spent unwisely.
4. There are few satisfactions equal to the realization that one has done his best at a job.
5. The most difficult college courses usually turn out to be the most rewarding.
6. Most people who don't succeed in life are just plain lazy.
7. The self-made wo/man is likely to be more ethical than the wo/man born to wealth.
8. I often feel I would be more successful if I sacrificed certain pleasures.
9. People should have more leisure time to spend in relaxation (R).
10. Any wo/man who is able and willing to work hard has a good chance of succeeding.
11. People who fail at a job have usually not tried hard enough.
12. Life would have very little meaning if we never had to suffer
13. Hard work offers little guarantee of success (R).
14. The credit card is a ticket to careless spending.
15. Life would be more meaningful if we had more leisure time (R).
16. The wo/man who can approach an unpleasant task with enthusiasm is the wo/man who gets ahead.
17. If one works hard s/he is likely to make good life for her/himself.
18. I feel uneasy when there is little work for me to do.
19. A distaste for hard work usually reflects a weakness of character

From: Mirels, H. L., & Garett, J. B. (1970). The Protestant work ethic as a personality variable. *Journal of Consulting and clinical Psychology, 36*, 40–44. Copyright © 2002 by the American Psychological Association. Reprinted with permission.

Blood's (1969) Scale Of Protestant Ethic

Pro-Protestant Ethic

1. Hard work makes a man a better person.
2. Wasting time is as bad as wasting money.
3. A good indication of a man's worth is how well he does his job.

4. If all other things are equal, it is better to have a job with a lot of responsibility than one with little responsibility.

Non-Protestant Ethic

1. Whenever possible a person should relax and accept life as it is, rather than always striving for unreachable goals.
2. The principal purpose of a man's job is to provide him with the means for enjoying his free time.
3. When the hard workday is finished, a person should forget his job and enjoy himself.
4. People who 'do things the easy way' are the smart ones.

From: Blood, M. R. (1969). Work values and job satisfaction. *Journal of American Psychology, 53,* 456–459. Copyright © 2002 by the American Psychological Association. Reprinted with permission.

Work Ethic Scale by Blau and Ryan (1994)

1. If one works hard enough, he or she is likely to make a good life for him/herself.
2. If you work hard you will succeed.
3. By working hard an individual can overcome most obstacles that life presents and makes his or her own way in the world.
4. Hard work makes one a better person.
5. Hard work is a good builder of character.
6. Hard work is fulfilling in itself.
7. People should have more leisure time to spend in relaxation (R).
8. More leisure time is good for people (R).
9. Life would be more meaningful if we had leisure time (R).
10. Work takes too much of our time leaving little time to relax (R).
11. The less hours one spends working and more leisure time available the better (R).
12. Only those who depend on themselves get ahead in life.
13. One should live one's life independent of others as much as possible.
14. To be superior a person must stand-alone.
15. One must avoid dependence on other persons whenever possible.
16. You can't take it with you, so you might as well enjoy yourself (B).
17. If you've got it, why not spend it.
18. "Eat, drink and be happy, because who knows what tomorrow will bring?" may be stated strongly but nevertheless, it reflects the proper orientation toward life (R).

From: Blau, G. L., & Ryan, J. (1994). On measuring work ethic: a neglected work commitment facet. *Journal of Vocational Behavior, 51*, 435–446. Copyright © by Academic Press. Reprinted with permission.

Note: A 12-item shorter measure was suggested by using the following items: 16, 17, 18 (asceticism); 7, 8, 9 (nonleisure); 12, 13, 14 (independence); and 1, 2, 4 (hard work).

4. CAREER/OCCUPATIONAL COMMITMENT MEASURES

Career Commitment of (1985)

1. If I could get another job, different from being a nurse and paying the same amount, I would probably take it (R).
2. I definitely want a career for myself in nursing.
3. If I could do it all over again, I would not choose to work in the nursing profession (R).
4. If I had all the money I needed without working, I would probably still continue to work in the nursing profession.
5. I like this vocation too well to give it up.
6. This is the ideal vocation for a life work.
7. I am disappointed that I ever entered the nursing profession (R).
8. I spend a significant amount of personal time reading nursing-related journals or books.

From: Blau, G. L. (1985). The measurement and prediction of career commitment. *Journal of Occupational Psychology, 58*, 277–288. Reproduced with permission from the Journal of Occupational Psychology © The British Psychological Society.

Career Commitment Revised Measure of (1988)

1. If I could go into a different profession other than the current profession, which paid the same, I would probably take it (R).
2. I definitely want a career for myself in the current profession.
3. If I could do it all over again, I would not choose to work in the current profession (R).
4. If I had all the money I needed without working, I would probably still continue to work in the current vocation.
5. I like this vocation too well to give it up.
6. This is the ideal vocation for a life work.
7. I am disappointed that I ever entered the profession (R).

From: Blau, G. L. (1988). Further exploring the meaning and measurement of career commitment, *Journal of Vocational Behavior, 32,* 284–297. Copyright © by Academic Press. Reprinted with permission.

Career Commitment Revised Measure of Blau (1993)

1. If could, would go into a different occupation (R).
2. Can see self in occupation for many years.
3. Occupation choice is a good decision.
4. If could, would not choose occupation (R).
5. No money need, still continue in occupation
6. Sometimes dissatisfied with occupation (R).
7. Like occupation too well to give up.
8. Education/training not for occupation (R).
9. Have ideal occupation for life work.
10. Wish chosen different occupation (R).
11. Disappointed that entered occupation (R).

From: Blau et al. (1993). On developing a general index of work commitment. *Journal of Vocational Behavior, 42,* 298–314. Copyright © by Academic Press. Reprinted with permission.

Career Commitment Measure by Carson and Bedeian (1994).

1. My line of work/career field is an important part of who I am.
2. This line of work/career field has a great deal of personal meaning to me.
3. I do not feel "emotionally attached" to this line of work/career field (R).
4. I strongly identify with my chosen line of work/career field.
5. The costs associate with my line of work/career field sometimes seem too great (R).
6. Given the problems I encounter in this line of work/career field, I sometimes wonder if I get enough out of it (R).
7. Given the problems in this line of work/career field I sometimes wonder if the personal burden is worth it (R).
8. The discomforts associated with my line of work/career field sometimes seem too great (R).
9. I do not have a strategy for achieving my goals in this line of work/career field (R).
10. I have created a plan for my development in this line of work/career field.
11. I do not identify specific goals for my development in this line of work/career field (R).

12. I do not often think about my personal development in this line of work/career field (R).

From: Carson, K. D., & Dedian, A. G., (1994) Career commitment: construction of a measure and examination of ITS psychometric properties. *Journal of Vocational Behavior*, 44, 237–262. Copyright © by Academic Press. Reprinted with permission.

Meyer and Allen (1993) Affective Occupational Commitment Scale

1. Nursing is important to my self-image.
2. I regret having entered to the nursing profession (R).
3. I am proud to be in the nursing profession.
4. I dislike being a nurse (R).
5. I do not identify with the nursing profession (R)
6. I am enthusiastic about nursing.

Meyer and Allen (1993) Continuance Occupational Commitment Scale

1. I have put too much into the nursing profession to consider changing now.
2. Changing profession now would be difficult for me to do.
3. Too much of my life would be disrupted if I were to change my profession now.
4. It would be costly for me to change my profession now.
5. There are no pressures to keep me from changing professions (R).
6. Changing professions now would require considerable personal sacrifices.

Meyer and Allen (1993) Normative Occupational Commitment Scale

1. I believe people who have been trained in a profession have a responsibility to stay in that profession for a reasonable period of time.
2. I do not feel any obligation to remain in the nursing profession (R)
3. I feel a responsibility to the nursing profession to continue in it.
4. Even if it were to my advantage, I do not feel that it would be right to leave nursing now.
5. I would feel guilty if I left nursing.
6. I am in nursing because of a sense of loyalty to it.

From: Meyer et al. (1993). Commitment to organizations and occupations: Extension and test of three component conceptualization. *Journal of Applied*

Psychology, 78, 538–551. Copyright © by the American Psychological Association. Reprinted with permission.

5. GROUP COMMITMENT SCALES

Group Commitment (Randall and Cote's (1991) Measure)

1. How much of an opportunity do you feel you have to develop close friendship at work?
2. How much of an opportunity do you have to interact socially with your co-workers on the job?
3. How much of an opportunity in present for you to interact socially with your co-workers off the job?
4. Some of my best friends are the people I work with.
5. I feel very much part of the people I work with.
6. How frequently do you have off-the-job contacts with your work colleagues?

From: Randall, D. M., & Cote, J. A. (1991). Interrelationships of work commitment constructs. *Work and Occupations, 18,* 194–211. Copyright © 2002 by Sage Publications. Reprinted by permission of sage Publications.

Group Commitment Measure of Ellmers et al. (1998)

1. I am prepared to do additional chores, when this benefits my team.
.2. I feel at home among my colleagues at work.
3. I try to invest effort into a good atmosphere in my team.
4. In my work, I let myself be guided by the goals of my team.
5. When there is social activity with my team, I usually help to organize it.
6. This team lies close to my hart.
7. I find it important that my team is successful.

From: Ellemers et al. (1998). Career oriented versus team oriented commitment and behavior at work. *Journal of Applied Psychology, 83,* 717–730. Copyright © 2002 by the American Psychological Association. Reprinted with permission.

6. UNION COMMITMENT MEASURES

Union Commitment (Loyalty) Gordon et al. (1980)

1. I feel a sense of pride being a part of this union.
2. Based on what I know now and what I believe I can expect in the future I plan to be a member of the union as long as I am working in this branch of industry.

3. The record of this union is a good example of what dedicated people can get done.
4. The union's problems are my problems.
5. Members of this local are not expected to have a strong personal commitment to the union (R).
6. A union member has more security than most members of management.
7. I feel little loyalty toward this union(R).
8. I have little confidence and trust in most members of my union (R).
9. I talk up the union to my friends as a great organization to be member of.
10. There's a lot to be gained by joining a union.
11. Deciding to join the union was a smart move on my part.
12. My values and the union's values are not very similar (R).
13. I rarely tell others that I am a member of the union (R).
14. It's easy"to be yourself" and still be a member of the union.
15. Very little that the membership wants has any real importance to the union (R).
16. The member does not get enough benefits for the money taken by the union for initiation fees and dues (R).

Union Commitment (Responsibility to the union)
Gordon et al. (1980)

1. Even though he/she may not like parts of it, the union member must"live up to" all terms of the Articles of Agreement.
2. It's every union member's responsibility to see to it that management"lives up to" all the terms of the Articles of Agreement.
3. It is the duty of every member "to keep his/her ears open" for information that might be useful to the union.
4. It's every member's duty to support or help another worker use the grievance procedure.
5. It's every member's duty to know exactly what the Articles of Agreement entitle him/her to.
6. It's every union's member responsibility to see that other members"live up to" all the terms of the Articles of Agreement.
7. Every member must be prepared to take the time and risk of filing a grievance.

Union Commitment (Willingness to work for the union) Gordon et al. (1980)

1. I am willing to put in a great deal of effort beyond that normally expected of a member in order to make the union successful.
2. If asked, I would serve on a committee for the union.

3. If asked, I would run for an elected office in the union.
4. I doubt that I would do special work to help the union.

Union Commitment (Belief in unionism) Gordon et al. (1980)

1. My loyalty is to my work, not to the union (R).
2. As long as I am doing the kind of work I enjoy, it does not matter if I belong to a union (R).
3. I could just as well work in non-union company as long as the type of work was similar (R).

From: Gordon et al. (1980). Commitment to the union: Development of a measure and an examination of its correlates. *Journal of Applied Psychology,* 65, 479–499. Copyright © 2002 by the American Psychological Association. Reprinted with permission.

Shorter Scale of Union Commitment (Kelloway, Catano, and Southwell, 1992).

1. Loyalty—items 1, 3, 4, 9, 10, 11 from the Gordon et al.'s scale listed above (in the relevant factor).
2. Willingness to work for the union—items 1, 2, 3, from the Gordon et al.'s scale listed above (in the relevant factor).
3. Responsibility to the union—items 3, 4, 6, 7 from the Gordon et al.'s scale listed above (in the relevant factor).

(R) = Reversed item.

References

Abegglen, J. J. (1958). *The Japanese Factory*. Glencoe: Free Press.

Abrahamson, M. (1965). Cosmopolitanism, dependence-identification and geographical mobility. *Administrative Science Quarterly, 10*, 98–106.

Adler, N. J. (1983). Cross-cultural management research: The ostrich and the trend. *The Academy of Management Review, 8*, 226–232.

Agarwal, S. (1993). Influence of formalization on role stress, organizational commitment, and work alienation of salespersons: A cross-national comparative study. *Journal of International Business Studies, 24*, 715–734.

Agarwal, S., DeCarlo, T. E., & Vyas, S. B. (1999). Leadership behavior and organizational commitment: A comparative study of American and Indian salespersons. *Journal of International Business Studies, 30*, 727–743.

Agassi, J., B. (1982). *Comparing the Work Attitudes of Women and Men*. Lexington: D. C. Heath.

Ali, A. J. (1988). Scaling an Islamic work ethic. *The Journal of Social Psychology, 128*, 575–583.

Ali, A. J. (1992). The Islamic work ethic in Arabia. *The Journal of Psychology, 126*, 507–519.

Allen, N. J., & Meyer, J. P. (1990). The measurement and antecedents of affective, continuance and normative commitment to the organization. *Journal of Occupational Psychology, 63*, 1–18.

Allen, N. J., & Meyer, J. P. (1996). Affective, continuance, and normative commitment to the organization: An examination of construct validity. *Journal of Vocational Behavior, 49*, 252–276.

Allen, N. B., Miller, E. D., & Nath, R. (1998). North America. In R. Nath (Ed.), *Comparative Management*, pp. 23–54. Cambridge, MA: Ballinger.

Alutto, J. A., & Acito, F. (1974). Decisional participation and sources of job satisfaction: A study of manufacturing personnel. *Academy of Management Journal, 17*, 160–167.

Alutto, J. A., & Belasco, J. A. (1974). Determinants of attitudinal militancy among nurses and teachers. *Industrial & Labor Relations Review, 27*, 216–227.

Alutto, J. A., Hrebiniak, L. G., & Alonso, R. C. (1973). On operationalizing the concept of commitment. *Social Forces, 51*, 448–454.

Alvi, S. A., & Ahmed, S. W. (1987). Assessing organizational commitment in a developing country: Pakistan, a case study. *Human Relations, 40*, 267–280.

Amernic, J. H., & Aranya, N. (1983). Organizational commitment: Testing two theories. *Relations Industrielles, 38,* 319–341.

Anderson, C. B. (1998). The experience of growing up in a minister's home and the religious commitment of the adult child of a minister. *Pastoral-Psychology, 46*(6), 393–411.

Anderson, J. C., & Gerbing, D. W. (1988). Structural equation modeling in practice: A review and recommended two-step approach. *Psychological Bulletin, 103,* 411–423.

Angle, H. L., & Perry, J. L. (1981). Organizational commitment and organizational effectiveness: An empirical assessment. *Administrative Science Quarterly, 26,* 1–14.

Angle, H. L., & Perry, J. L. (1986). Dual commitment and labor management relationship climates. *Academy of Management Journal, 29,* 31–50.

Antonovsky, H. F., & Antonovsky, A. (1974). Commitment in an Israeli kibbutz. *Human Relations, 27,* 303–319.

Aranya, N., & Ferris, K. R. (1983). Organizational-professional conflict among U.S. and Israeli professional accountants. *The Journal of Social Psychology, 119,* 153–161.

Aranya, N., & Ferris, K. R. (1984). A reexamination of accountant's organizational-professional conflict. *The Accounting Review, 119,* 1–15.

Aranya, N., & Jacobson, D. (1975). An empirical study of theories of organizational and occupational commitment. *Journal of Social Psychology, 97,* 15–22.

Aranya, N., Lachman, R., & Amernic, J. (1982). Accountants' job satisfaction: A path analysis. *Accounting, Organizations and Society, 7,* 201–215.

Aranya, N., Pollock, J., & Amernic, J. (1981). An examination of professional commitment in public accounting. *Accounting, Organizations and Society, 6,* 271–280.

Aryee, S. (1992). Antecedents and outcomes of work-family conflict among married professional women—evidence from Singapore. *Human Relations, 45,* 813–837.

Aryee, S., & Debrah, Y. A. (1997). Members' participation in the union: An investigation of some determinants in Singapore. *Human Relations, 50,* 129–147.

Baba, V. V., & Knoop, R. (1987). Organizational commitment and independence among Canadian managers. *Relation Industrielles, 42,* 325–343.

Bailyn. L., Fletcher, J. K., & Kolb, D. (1997). Unexpected connections: Considering employees' lives can revitalize your business. *Sloan Management Review, 38*(4), 11–19.

Baird, L. L. (1969). A study of the role relations of graduate students. *Journal of Educational Psychology, 60,* 15–21.

Balfour, D. L., & Wechsler, B. (1996). Organizational commitment: Antecedents and outcomes in public organizations. *Public Productivity and Management Review, 29,* 256–277.

Bamberger, P. A., Kluger, A. N., & Suchard, R. (1999). The antecedents and consequences of union commitment: A meta-analysis. *Academy of Management Journal, 42*(3), 304–318.

Barling, J., Fullagar, C., & Kelloway, E. K. (1992). *The union and its members: A psychological approach.* New York: Oxford University Press.

Barling, J., Wade, B., & Fullagar, C. (1990). Predicting employee commitment to company and union: Divergent models. *Journal of Occupational Psychology, 63,* 49–61.

Baron R. M., Kenny, D. A. (1986). The moderator-mediator variable distinction in social psychological research: Conceptual, strategic, and statistical considerations. *Journal of Personality and Social Psychology, 51,* 1173–1182.

Bartol, M. K. (1979a). Professionalism as a predictor of organizational commitment, role stress and turnover: A multidimensional approach. *Academy of Management Journal, 22,* 815–821.

Bartol, M. K. (1979b). Individual versus organizational predictors of job satisfaction and turnover among professionals. *Journal of Vocational Behavior, 15,* 55–67.

Bashaw, R. E., & Grant, E. S. (1994). Exploring the distinctive nature of work commitments: Their relationships with personal characteristics, job performance, and propensity to leave. *Journal of Personal Selling & Sales Management, 14,* 41–56.

Bateman, T. S., & Strasser, S. (1984). A longitudinal analysis of the antecedents of organizational commitment. *Academy of Management Journal, 27,* 95–112.

Beauvais, L. L., Scholl, R. W., & Cooper, E. A. (1991). *Dual commitment among unionized faculty: A longitudinal investigation, 1,* 175–192.

Beck, K., & Wilson, C. (2000). Development of affective organizational commitment: A cross-sequential examination of change with tenure. *Journal of Vocational Behavior, 56,* 114–136.

Beck, K., & Wilson, C. (2001). Have we studied, should we study, and can we study the development of commitment? Methodological issues and the developmental study of work-related commitment. *Human Resource Management Review, 11,* 257–278.

Becker, H. S. (1960). Notes on the concept of commitment. *American Journal of Sociology, 66,* 32–40.

Becker, H. S., & Carper, J. W. (1956). The development of identification with an occupation. *American Sociological Review, 32,* 341–347.

Becker, T. E. (1992). Foci and bases of commitment: Are they distinctions worth making? *Academy of Management Journal, 35,* 232–244.

Becker, T. E., & Billings, R. S. (1993). Profiles of commitment: An empirical test. *Journal of Organizational Behavior, 14,* 177–190.

Becker, T. E., Billings, R. S., Eveleth, D. M., & Gilbert, N. L. (1996). Foci and bases of employee commitment: Implications for job performance. *Academy of Management Journal, 39,* 464–482.

Becker, T. E., Randall, D. M., & Riegel, C. D. (1995). The multidimensional view of commitment and the theory of reasoned action: A comparative evaluation. *Journal of Management, 21,* 617–638.

Bedeian, A. G., Kemery, E. R., & Pizzolatto, A. B. (1991). Career commitment and expected utility of present job as predictors of turnover intentions and turnover behavior. *Journal of Vocational Behavior, 39,* 331–343.

Bemmels, B. (1995). Dual commitment: Unique construct or epiphenomenon? *Journal of Business Research, 16,* 401–422.

Ben David, J. (1958). The professional role of the physician in bureaucratised medicine: A study in role conflict. *Human Relations, 11,* 255–274.

Bentler, P. M. (1990). Comparative fit indexes in structural models. *Psychological Bulletin, 107,* 238–246.

Bentler, P. M., & Bonett, D. G. (1980). Significance tests and goodness-of-fit in the analysis of covariance structures. *Psychological Bulletin, 88,* 588–606.

Berger, P. K., & Grimes, A. J. (1973). Cosmopolitan-local: A factor analysis of the construct. *Administrative Science Quarterly, 18,* 223–235.

Besser, T. L. (1993). The commitment of Japanese workers and U.S. workers: A reassessment of the literature. *American Sociological Review, 58,* 873–881.

Bhuian, S. N., Al-Shammari, E. S., & Jefri, O. A. (1996). Organizational commitment, job satisfaction and job characteristics: An empirical study of expatriates in Saudi Arabia. *Journal of Commerce & Management, 6,* 57–79.

Bishop, J. W., Scott, K. D., & Burroughs, S. M. (2000). Support, commitment, and employee outcomes in a team environment. *Journal of Management, 26,* 1113–1132.

Black, A. W. (1983). Some factors influencing attitudes toward militancy membership, solidarity and sanctions in a teachers' union. *Human Relations, 36,* 973–986.

Blau, G. J. (1989). Testing the generalizability of a career commitment measure and its impact on employee turnover. *Journal of Vocational Behavior, 35,* 88–103.

Blau, G., & Ryan, J. (1997). On measuring work ethic: A neglected work commitment facet. *Journal of Vocational Behavior, 51,* 435–448.

Blau, G. J. (1985a). A multiple study investigation of the dimensionality of job involvement. *Journal of Vocational Behavior, 27,* 19–36.

Blau, G. J. (1985b). The measurement and prediction of career commitment. *Journal of Occupational Psychology, 58,* 277–288.

Blau, G. J. (1986). Job involvement and organizational commitment as interactive predictors of tardiness and absenteeism. *Journal of Management, 12,* 577–584.

Blau, G. J. (1987). Using a person environment fit model to predict job involvement and organizational commitment. *Journal of Vocational Behavior, 30,* 240–257.

Blau, G. J. (1988). Further exploring the meaning and measurement of career commitment. *Journal of Vocational Behavior, 32,* 284–297.

Blau, G. J. (1999). Early-career job factors influencing the professional commitment of medical technologists. *Academy of Management Journal, 42,* 687–695.

Blau, G. J. (2001). On assessing the construct validity of two multidimensional constructs: Occupational commitment and occupational entrenchment. *Human Resource Management Review, 11,* 279–298.

Blau, G. J., & Boal, K. B. (1987). Conceptualizing how job involvement and organizational commitment affect turnover and absenteeism. *Academy of Management Review, 12,* 288–300.

Blau, G. J., & Boal, K. B. (1989). Using job involvement and organizational commitment interactively to predict turnover. *Journal of Management, 15,* 115–127.

Blau, G., Paul, A., & St. John, N. (1993). On developing a general index of work commitment. *Journal of Vocational Behavior, 42,* 298–314.

Blau, P. M., & Scott, W. R. (1962). *Formal Organizations.* San Francisco: Chandler.

Blauner, R. (1964). *Alienation and freedom: The factory worker and his industry.* Chicago: University of Chicago Press.

Blauner, R. (1969). Work satisfaction and industrial trends. In A. Etzioni (Ed.), *A sociological reader on complex organization.* New York: Holt, Rinehart and Winston.

Blegen, M. A., Mueller, C. W., & Price, J. L. (1988). Measurement of kinship responsibility for organizational research. *Journal of Applied Psychology, 73,* 402–409.

Blood, M. R. (1969). Work values and job satisfaction. *Journal of Applied Psychology, 53,* 456–459.

Bluedorn, A. C. (1982). A unified model of turnover from organizations. *Human Relations, 35,* 135–153.

Bollen, K. A. (1989). *Structural equations with latent variables.* New York: John Wiley & Sons.

Boshoff, C., & Mels, G. (2000). The impact of multiple commitments on intentions to resign: An empirical assessment. *British Journal of Management, 11,* 255–272.

Boyacigiller, N. A., & Adler, N. J. (1991). The parochial dimension: Organizational science in a global context. *Academy of Management Review, 16,* 262–290.

Bozeman, D. P., & Perrewe, P. L. (2001). The effect of item content overlap on organizational commitment questionnaire—turnover cognitions relationships. *Journal of Applied Psychology, 86,* 161–173.

Brager, G. (1969). Commitment and conflict in a normative organization. *American Sociological Review, 34,* 482–491.

Breckler, S. J. (1990). Applications of covariance structure modeling in psychology: Cause for concern. *Psychological Bulletin, 107,* 260–273.

Brewer, A., & Ko, P. (1995), Managerial strategy and nursing commitment in Australian hospitals. *Journal of Advanced Nursing 21,* 789–799.

Brief, A. P., & Aldag, R. J. (1980). Antecedents of organizational commitments among hospital nurses. *Sociology of Work and Occupations, 7,* 210–221.

Brief, A. P., & Robertson, L. (1989). Job attitude in organization: An exploratory study. *Journal of Applied Social Psychology, 19,* 717–727.

Brierley, J. A. (1996). The measurement of organizational commitment and professional commitment. *The Journal of Social Psychology, 136,* 265–267.

Brierley, J. A., & Cowton, C. J. (2000). Putting meta-analysis to work: Accountants' organizational-professional conflict. *Journal of Business Ethics, 24,* 343–353.

Brooke, P. P., Russell, D. W., & Price, J. L. (1988). Discriminant validation of measures of job satisfaction, job involvement and organizational commitment. *Journal of Applied Psychology, 73,* 139–145.

Brown, S. P. (1996). A meta-analysis and review of organizational research on job involvement. *Psychological Bulletin, 120,* 235–255.

Brown, M. (1969). Identification and some conditions of organizational involvement. *Administrative Science Quarterly, 14,* 346–355.

Brown, R. B. (1996). Organizational commitment: Clarifying the concept and simplifying the existing construct typology. *Journal of Vocational Behavior, 49,* 230–251.

Browne, M. W., & Cudeck, R. (1989). Single sample cross-validation indices for covariance structures. *Multivariate Behavioral Research, 24,* 445–455.

Buchko, A. A., Weinzimmer, L. G., & Sergeyev, A. V. (1997). A comparative analysis of organizational commitment in the United States and Russia. *Journal of Management Issues, 9,* 204–215.

Bucholz, R. (1978). An empirical study of contemporary beliefs about work in American society. *Journal of Applied Psychology, 63,* 219–227.

Busch, T. Attitudes towards management by objectives: An empirical investigation of self-efficacy and goal commitment. *Scandinavian Journal of Management, 14*(3), 289–299.

Campbell, A., Converse, P. E., & Rodgers, W. L. (1976). *The Quality of American Life.* New York: Russell Sage Foundation.

Carmeli, A., & Freund, A. (2001). *Five universal forms of work commitment, job satisfaction, and job performance: An empirical assessment.* Paper presented at the Annual Academy of Management Meetings, OB Division, Washington, DC.

Carson, K. D., & Bedeian, A. G. (1994). Career commitment: Construction of a measure and examination of its psychometric properties. *Journal of Vocational Behavior, 44,* 237–262.

Carson, K. D., & Carson, P. P. (1998). Career commitment, competencies, and citizenship. *Journal of Career Assessment, 6,* 195–208.

Cavanagh, S. J. (1996). A 'new' psychological contract for nurses: Some management implications. *Journal of Nursing Management, 4,* 79–83.

Cecil, A., & Pearson, L., & Chong, J. (1997). Contributions of job content and social information on organizational commitment and job satisfaction: An exploration in a Malaysian nursing context. *Journal of Occupational and Organizational Psychology, 70,* 357–374.

Champoux, J. E. (1981). A sociological perspective on work involvement. *International Review of Applied Psychology, 30,* 65–86.

Chang, E. (1999). Career commitment as a complex moderator of organizational commitment and turnover. *Human Relations, 52,* 1257–1278.

Chay, Y., & Aryee, S. (1999). Potential moderating influence of career growth opportunities on careerist orientation and work attitudes: Evidence of the protean career era in Singapore. *Journal of Organizational Behavior, 20,* 613–623.

Chen, X. Z., & Francesco, A. M. (2000). Employee demography, organizational commitment, and turnover intentions in China: Do cultural differences matter? *Human Relations, 53,* 869–887.

Cheung, C. K. (2000). Commitment to the organization in exchange for support from the organization. *Social Behavior and Personality, 28,* 125–140.

Cherrington, D. J. (1989). *Organizational Behavior,* Boston: Allen & Bacon.

Clugston, M. (2000). The mediating effects of multidimensional commitment on job satisfaction and intent to leave. *Journal of Organizational Behavior, 21,* 477–486.

Clugston, M., Howell, J. P., & Dorfman, P. W. (2000). Does cultural socialization predict multiple bases and foci of commitment. *Journal of Management, 26,* 5–30.

Cohen, A., Lowenberg, G., & Rosenstein, E. (1990). *Antecedents of Organizational Commitment: A Meta-Analysis*, Proceedings of the 1990 Annual Conference of the Administrative Sciences Association of Canada (Organizational Behavior Division) (pp. 40–49). British Columbia, Canada: Whistler.

Cohen, A. (1989). *Commitment to trade union: Its measurement, antecedents and its salience to other commitments in the work environment.* Unpublished doctoral dissertation, Technion-Israel Institute of Technology, Haifa, Israel.

Cohen, A. (1991). Career stage as a moderator of the relationship between organizational commitment and its outcomes: A meta-analysis. *Journal of Occupational Psychology, 64*, 253–268.

Cohen, A. (1992). Antecedents of organizational commitment across occupational groups: A meta-analysis. *Journal of Organizational Behavior, 13*, 539–558.

Cohen, A. (1993a). Work commitment in relations to withdrawal intentions and union effectiveness. *Journal of Business Research, 26*, 75–90.

Cohen. A. (1993b). Age and tenure in relation to organizational commitment: A meta-analysis. *Basic and Applied Social Psychology, 14*, 143–159.

Cohen, A. (1993c). An empirical assessment of the multi dimensionality of union participation. *Journal of Management, 19*, 749–773.

Cohen, A. (1993d). Organizational commitment and turnover: A meta-analysis. *Academy of Management Journal, 36*, 1140–1157.

Cohen, A. (1995). An examination of the relationship between work commitment and nonwork domains. *Human Relations, 48*, 239–263.

Cohen, A. (1996). On the discriminant validity of the Meyer and Allen (1984) measure of organizational commitment: How does it fit with the work commitment construct? *Educational and Psychological Measurement, 56*, 494–503.

Cohen. A. (1997a). Nonwork influences on withdrawal intentions: An empirical examination of an overlooked issue. *Human Relations, 50*, 1511–1536.

Cohen, A. (1997b). Personal and organizational responses to work/nonwork interface as related to organizational commitment. *Journal of Applied Social Psychology, 27*, 1085–1114.

Cohen, A. (1998). An examination of the relationship between work commitment and work outcomes among hospital nurses. *Scandinavian Journal of Management, 14*, 1–17.

Cohen. A. (1999a). Relationships among five forms of commitment: An empirical examination. *Journal of Organizational Behavior, 20*, 285–308.

Cohen, A. (1999b). The relation between commitment forms and work outcomes in Jewish and Arab culture. *Journal of Vocational Behavior, 54*, 371–391.

Cohen, A. (2000). The relationship between commitment forms and work outcomes: A comparison of three models. *Human Relations.*

Cohen, A., & Gattiker, E. U. (1992). An empirical assessment of organizational commitment using the side-bet theory approach. *Relations Industrielles/Industrial Relations, 47*, 439–461.

Cohen, A., & Gattiker, E. U. (1994). Rewards and organizational commitment across structural characteristics: A meta-analysis. *Journal of Business and Psychology, 9*, 137–157.

Cohen, A., & Hudecek, N. (1993). Organizational commitment–turnover relationship across occupational groups: A meta-analysis. *Group and Organization Management (formerly Group and Organization Studies), 18*, 188–213.

Cohen, A., & Kirchmeyer, C. (1994). Unions and ethnic diversity: The Israeli case of east European immigrants. *Journal of Applied Behavioral Science, 30*(2), 141–158.

Cohen, A., & Lowenberg, G. (1990). A reexamination of the side-bet theory as applied to organizational commitment: A meta-analysis. *Human Relations, 43*, 1015–1050.

Cohen, J., & Cohen, P. (1983). *Applied multiple regression/correlation analysis for the behavioral sciences* (2nd ed.). Hillsdale, NJ: Lawrence Erlbaum Associates.

Cole, E. R. (1979). *Work, mobility and participation: A comparative study of American and Japanese industry.* Los Angeles, CA: University of California Press.

Colarelli, S. M., & Bishop, R. C. (1990). Career commitment—functions, correlates, and management. *Group & Organization Studies, 15*, 158–176.

Commeiras, N., & Fournier, C. (2001). Critical evaluation of Porter et al.'s organizational commitment questionnaire: Implications for researchers. *Journal of Personal Selling & Sale Management, 21*, 239–245.

Conlon, E. J., & Gallagher, D. G. (1987). Commitment to employer and union: Effects of membership status. *Academy of Management Journal, 30*, 151–162.

Cook, J. D., Hepworth, S. J., Wall, T. D., & Warr, P. B. (1981). The experience of work: A comparison of 249 measures and their use. New York: Academic Press.

Cotton, J. L., & Tuttle, J. M. (1986). Employee turnover: A meta-analysis and review with implications for research. *Academy of Management Review, 11*, 55–70.

Cudeck, R., & Browne, M. W. (1983). Cross-validation of covariance structures. *Multivariate Behavioral Research, 18*, 147–167.

Currivan, D. B. (1999). The causal order of job satisfaction and organizational commitment in models of employee turnover. *Human Resource Management Review, 4*, 495–524.

Dalton, D. E., & Todor, W. D. (1981). Grievances filed and the role of the union steward vs. the rank and file member: An empirical test. *International Review of Applied Psychology, 30*, 199–207.

Dalton, D. R., & Todor, W. D. (1982). Antecedents of grievance filing behavior: Attitude/behavior constituency and the union steward. *Academy of Management Journal, 25*, 158–169.

Darden, W. R., Hampton, R., & Howell, R. D. (1989). Career versus organizational commitment: Antecedents and consequences of retail salespeoples' commitment. *Journal of Retailing, 65*, 80–106.

Darwish, A. Y. (2000). Organizational commitment as a mediator of the relationship between Islamic work ethic and attitudes toward organizational change. *Human Relations, 53*, 513–537.

Dean, L. R. (1954). Union activity and dual loyalty. *Industrial and Labor Relations Review, 7*, 526–536.

Decotiis, T. A., & Summers, T. P. (1987). A path analysis of a model of the antecedents and consequences of organizational commitment. *Human Relations, 40*, 445–470.

DeFillippi, R. J., & Arthur, M. B. (1996). Boundaryless contexts and careers: A competency-based perspective, In M. B. Arthur & D. M. Rousseau (Eds.), *The boundaryless career* (pp. 116–131). New York: Oxford University Press.

Derber, M., et al, (1953, 1954). *Labor-Management Relations in Illinois City: Vols. 1 & 2*. University of Illinois Press: Urbana.

Desrochers, S., & Dahir, V. (2000). Ambition as a motivational basis of organizational and professional commitment: Preliminary analysis of a proposed career advancement ambition scale. *Perceptual and Motor Skills, 91*, 563–570.

Dolen, M. R., & Shultz, K. S. (1998). Comparison of organizational, professional, university, and academic commitment scales. *Psychological Reports, 82*, 1232–1234.

Donovan, J. J., & Radosevich, D. J. (1998). The moderating role of goal commitment on the goal difficulty-performance relationship: A meta-analysis review and critical analysis. *Journal of Applied Psychology, 83*(2), 308–315.

Dooley, R. S., & Fryxell, G. E. (1999). Attaining decision quality and commitment from dissent: The moderating effects of loyalty and competence in strategic decision-making teams. *Academy of Management Journal, 42*, 389–402.

Dooley, R. S., Fryxell, G. E., & Judge, W. Q. (2000). Belaboring the not-so-obvious consensus, commitment, and strategy implementation speed and success. *Journal of Management, 26*, 1237–1257.

Dubin, R. (1956). Industrial workers' world: A study of the central life interests of industrial workers. *Social Problems, 3*, 131–142.

Dunham, R. B., Grube, J. A., & Castaneda, M. B. (1994). Organizational commitment: The utility of an integrative definition. *Journal of Applied Psychology, 79*, 370–380.

Earley, P. C. (1989). Social loafing and collectivism: A comparison of the United States and the People's Republic of China. *Administrative Science Quarterly, 34*, 565–581.

Ellemers, N., de Gilder, D., & van den Heuvel, H. (1998). Career-oriented versus team-oriented commitment and behavior at work. *Journal of Applied Psychology, 83*, 717–730.

Ellemers, N., Kortekaas, P., & Ouwerkerk, J. W. (1999). Self-categorization, commitment to the group and group self-esteem as related but distinct aspects of social identity. *European Journal of Social Psychology, 29*, 371–389.

Ellemers, N., van Rijswijk, W., Bruins, J., & de Gilder, D. (1998). Group commitment as moderator of attributional and behavioral responses to power use. *European Journal of Social Psychology, 28*, 555–573.

Erez, M., & Earley, P. C. (1993). *Culture, self-identity, and work.* New York: Oxford University Press.

Farrell, D., & Petersen, J. C. (1984). Commitment, absenteeism and turnover of new employees: A longitudinal study. *Human Relations, 37*, 681–692.

Ferris, K. R. (1981). Organizational commitment and performance in a professional accounting firm. *Accounting Organizations and Society, 6*, 317–325.

Ferris, K. R., & Aranya, N. (1983). A comparison of two organizational commitment scales. *Personnel Psychology, 36*, 87– 98.

Fineman, S. W. (1975). The work preference questionnaire: A measure of managerial need for achievement. *Journal of Occupational Psychology, 48*, 11–32.

Fishbein, M., & Ajzen, I. (1975). *Belief, attitudes, intention and behavior.* Reading, MA: Addison-Wesley.

Foa, U. G., & Foa, E. B. (1974). *Societal Structures of the Mind.* Springfield, IL: Charles C. Thomas Publishers.

Franklin, J. C. (1975). Power and commitment—an empirical assessment. *Human Relations, 28*, 737–753.

Freund, A. (2000). *Multiple commitments to work factors: A longitudinal study examining the effects of turnover in the Israeli public sector.* Unpublished doctoral dissertation, University of Haifa, Haifa, Israel.

Friedlander, F. (1970). Performance and orientation structure of research scientists. *Organization Behavior and Human Performance, 6*, 169–183.

Friedman, L., & Harvey, R. J. (1986). Factors of union commitment: The case for a lower dimensionality. *Journal of Applied Psychology, 71*, 371–376.

Frone, M. R., & Rice, R. W. (1987). Work-family conflict: The effect of job and family involvement. *Journal of Occupational Behavior, 8*, 45–53.

Frone, M. R., Russell, M., & Cooper, M. L. (1992). Antecedents and outcomes of work-family conflict: Testing a model of the work-family interface. *Journal of Applied Psychology, 77*, 65–78.

Fukami, V. C., & Larson, W. E. (1984). Commitment to company and union: Parallel models. *Journal of Applied Psychology, 69*, 367–371.

Fullagar, C. (1986). A factor-analytic study on the validity of a union commitment scale. *Journal of Applied Psychology, 71*, 129–136.

Fullagar, C., & Barling, J. (1989). A longitudinal test of the antecedents and consequences of union loyalty. *Journal of Applied Psychology, 74*, 213–227.

Fullagar, C., & Barling, J. (1991). Predictors and outcomes of different patterns of organizational and union loyalty. *Journal of Occupational Society, 64*, 129–143.

Fullagar, C., & Barling, J., Christie, P. (1991). Dual commitment in aggressive and protective unions. *Applied Psychology: An International Review, 40*, 93–104.

Fullagar, C., Gordon, M. E., Gallagher, D. G., & Clark, P. F. (1995). Impact of early socialization on union commitment and participation: A longitudinal study. *Journal of Applied Psychology, 80,* 147–157.

Fullagar, C., McCoy, D., & Shull, C. (1992). The socialization of union loyalty. *Journal of Organizational Behavior, 13,* 13–26.

Furnham, A. (1990). *The Protestant Work Ethic.* New York: Routledge.

Furnham, A., & Rose, M. (1987). Alternative ethics: The relationship between the wealth, welfare, work, and leisure ethic. *Human Relations, 40,* 561–573.

Grusky, O. (1966). Career mobility and organizational commitment. *Administrative Science Quarterly, 10,* 488–503.

Gaertner, S. (1999). Structural determinants of job satisfaction and organizational commitment in turnover models. *Human Resource Management Review, 9,* 479–493.

Gaither, C. A. (1993). Evaluating the construct validity of work commitment measures: A confirmatory factor model. *Evaluation & the Health Professions, 16,* 417–433.

Gallagher, D. G., & McLean Parks, J. (2001). I pledge thee my troth … contingently: Commitment and the contingent work relationship. *Human Resource Management Review, 11,* 181–208.

Gardner, D. L. (1992). Career commitment in nursing. *Journal of Professional Nursing, 8,* 155–160.

Goffin R. D., & Gellatly, I. R. (2001). A multi-rater assessment of organizational commitment. *Journal of Organizational Behavior, 22,* 437–451.

Goldberg, L. C., Baker, F., & Rubenstein, A. H. (1965). Local-cosmopolitan: Unidimensional or multidimensional? *American Journal of Sociology, 70,* 704–710.

Goldstein, B., & Eichorn, R. (1961). The changing Protestant ethic: Rural patterns in health, work and leisure. *American Sociological Review, 32,* 73–85.

Goldthorpe, J. H., Lockwood, D., Bechhofer, F., & Platt, J. (1968). *The affluent worker: industrial attitudes and behavior.* London: Cambridge University Press.

Goldthorpe, J. H., Lockwood, D., Bechhofer, F., & Platt, J. (1969). *The affluent worker: In the class structure.* London: Cambridge University Press.

Goldthorpe, J. H., Lockwood, D., Bechhofer, F., & Platt, J., (1971). *The affluent worker: Political attitudes and behavior.* London, Cambridge University Press.

Gomez-Mejia, L. R. (1984). Effect of occupation on task-related, contextual and job involvement orientation: A cross-cultural perspective. *Academy of Management Journal, 27,* 706–720.

Good, S. (1979). Characteristics of planners in upwardly mobile occupations. *Academy of Management Journal, 22,* 539–550.

Gordon, L. V. (1973). Work Environment Preference Schedule. The Psychological Corporation, New York.

Gordon, M. E., Beauvais, L. L., & Ladd, T. R. (1984). The job-satisfaction and union commitment of unionized engineers. *Industrial and Labor Relations Review, 37,* 359–370.

Gordon, M. E., Philpot, W. J., Burt, E. R., Thompson, C. A., & Spiller, E. W. (1980). Commitment to the union: Development of a measure and an examination of its correlates. *Journal of Applied Psychology, 65,* 479–499.

Gordon, M. E., & Ladd, R. (1990). Dual Allegiance: Renewal, recommendation, and recantation. *Personnel Psychology, 43,* 37–69.

Gottlieb, B., & Kerr, W. A. (1950). An experiment in industrial harmony. *Personnel Psychology, 3,* 445–453.

Gould, S. (1979). Characteristics of planners in upwardly mobile occupations. *Academy of Management Journal, 22,* 539–550.

Gouldner, H. P. (1960). Dimension of organizational commitment. *Administrative Science Quarterly, 4,* 468–490.

Gouldner, A. W. (1957). Cosmopolitans and locals: Toward an analysis of latent social roles. *Administrative Science Quarterly* 2, 281–306.

Gouldner, A. W. (1958). Cosmopolitans and locals: Toward an analysis of latent social identity. *Administrative Science Quarterly* 3, 444–480.

Gray, D. E. (1989). Gender and organizational commitment among hospital nurses. *Human Relations, 42*, 801–813.

Greenhaus, J. H. (1971). An investigation of the role of career salience in vocational behavior. *Journal of Vocational Behavior, 1*, 209–216.

Greenhaus, J. H. (1973). A factorial investigation of career salience. *Journal of Vocational Behavior, 3*, 95–98.

Greenhaus, J. H., & Simon, W. E. Career salience, work values and vocational indecision. *Journal of Vocational Behavior, 10*, 104–110.

Greenhaus, J. H., & Sklarew, N. D. (1981). Some sources and consequences of career exploration. *Journal of Vocational Behavior, 18*, 1–12.

Greenhaus, J. H., & Kopelman, R. E. (1981). Conflict between work and nonwork roles: Implications for the career planning process. *Human Resource Planning, 4*, 1–10.

Greer, C. R., & Stephens, G. K. (2001). Escalation of commitment: A comparison of differences between Mexican and U.S. decision-makers. *Journal of Management, 27*, 51–78.

Gregerson, H. B. (1993). Multiple commitments at work and extra-role behavior during three stages of organizational tenure. *Journal of Business Research, 26*, 31–47.

Gregersen, H. B., & Black, J. S. (1992). Antecedents to commitment to a parent company and a foreign operation. *Academy of Management Journal, 35*, 65–90.

Gregersen, H. B., & Black, J. S. (1996). Multiple commitments upon repatriation: The Japanese experience. *Journal of Management, 22*, 209–229.

Gregerson, H. B. (1993). Multiple commitments at work and extra-role behavior during three stages of organizational tenure. *Journal of Business Research, 26*, 31–47.

Griffeth, R. W., Hom, P. W., DeNisi, A. S., & Kirchner, W. K. (1985). A comparison of different methods of clustering countries on the basis of employee attitudes. *Human Relations, 38*, 813–840.

Griffeth, R. W., Hom, P. W., & Gaertner, S. (2000). A meta-analysis of antecedents and correlates of employee turnover: Update, moderator tests, and research implications for the next millennium. *Journal of Management, 26*, 463–488.

Griffin, R. W., & Bateman, T. S. (1986). Job satisfaction and organizational commitment. In C. L. Cooper & I. Roberson (Eds.), *International Review of Industrial and Organizational Psychology* (pp. 157–188). New York: John Wiley.

Grimes, A. J., & Berger, P. K. (1970). Cosmopolitan-local: Evaluation of the construct. *Administrative Science Quarterly* 15, 407–416.

Gupta, N., & Jenkins, G. D., Jr. (1991). Rethinking dysfunctional employee behaviors. *Human Resource Management Review, 1*, 39–59.

Hackett, D. R., Bycio, P., & Hausdorf, P. (1992). Further assessment of a three-component model of organizational commitment. *Academy of Management Proceedings*, pp. 212–216.

Hackett, D. R., Bycio, P., & Hausdorf, P. (1994). Further assessment of Meyer's and Allen's (1991) three-component model of organizational commitment. *Journal of Applied Psychology, 79*, 15–23.

Hackett, D. R., Lapierre, L. M., & Hausdorf, P. A. (2001). Understanding the links between work commitment constructs. *Journal of Vocational Behavior, 58*, 392–413.

Hackman, J. R., & Oldham, G. R. (1975). Development of the job diagnostic survey. *Journal of Applied Psychology, 60*, 159–170.

Hall, D. T. (1971). A theoretical model of career sub-identity development in organizational settings. *Organizational Behavior and Human Performances, 6*, 50–76.

Hall, D. T., & Schneider, B. (1972). Correlates of organizational identification as a function of career pattern and organizational type. *Administrative Science Quarterly, 17,* 340–350.

Hall, D. T., Schneider, B., & Nygren, H. T. (1970). Personal factors in organizational identification. *Administrative Science Quarterly 15,* 176–189.

Hall, R. H. (1968). Professionalism and bureaucratization. American Sociological Review, 33, 92–104.

Hall, D. T. (1972). A model of coping with role conflict: The role behavior of college educated women. *Administrative Science Quarterly 17,* 471–486.

Hall, D. T., & Hall, F. S. (1976). The relationship between goals, performance, self-image, and involvement under different organization climates. *Journal of Vocational Behavior, 9,* 267–278.

Hall, D. T., & Richter, J. (1988). Balancing work life and home life: What can organizations do to help? *Academy of Management Executive, 2,* 213–223.

Hammond, P., & Williams, R. (1976). The Protestant ethic thesis: A social psychological assessment. *Social Forces, 54,* 579–589.

Hanada, M. (1984). *12 questions regarding Japanese style management.* Tokyo, SANNO Institute of Business Administrative.

Harpaz, I. (1998a). Variables affecting non-financial employment commitment. *Applied Psychology: An International Review, 37,* 235–248.

Harpaz, I. (1998b). Cross-national comparison of religious conviction and the meaning of work. *Cross-Cultural Research, 32,* 143–170.

Harpaz, I. (1989). Non-financial employment commitment: A cross-national comparison. *Journal of Occupational Psychology, 62,* 147–150.

Harpaz, I., Claes, R., Depolo, M., & Quintanilla, A. R. (1992). Meaning of work of career starters. *International Review of Social Psychology, 5,* 81–104.

Harpaz, I., Fu, X. (1997). Work centrality in Germany, Israel, Japan, and the United States. *Cross-Cultural Research, 31,* 171–200.

Harris, C. W. (1967). On factors and factor scores. *Psychometrica, 32,* 363–379.

Harrison, J. K., & Hubbard, R. (1998). Antecedents to organizational commitment among Mexican employees of a U.S. firm in Mexico. *Journal of Social Psychology, 138,* 609–623.

Hartman, L. C., & Bambacas, M. (2000). Organizational commitment: A multi method scale analysis and test of effects. *The International Journal of Organizational Analysis, 8,* 89–108.

Hillstrom, E. L., & Stracham, M. (2000). Strong commitment to traditional Protestant religious beliefs is negatively related to beliefs in paranormal phenomena. *Psychological Reports, 86,* 183–189.

Hirschfeld, R. R., Field, H. S. (2000). Work centrality and work alienation: Distinct aspects of a general commitment to work. *Journal of Organizational Behavior, 21,* 789–800.

Ho, R., & Lloyd, J. I. (1984). Development of an Australian work ethic scale. *Australian Psychologist, 19,* 321–332.

Hoff, T. J. (2000). Professional commitment among U.S. physician executives in managed care. *Social Science & Medicine, 50,* 1433–1444.

Hofstede, G. (1980). *Cultures consequences: International differences in work related values.* Beverly Hills, CA: Sage.

Holland, J. L. (1973). *Making Vocational Choices.* Englewood Cliffs, NJ: Prentice-Hall.

House, R. J., & Rizzo, J. R. (1972). Role conflict and ambiguity as critical variables in a model of organizational behavior. *Organizational Behavior and Human Performance, 7,* 467–505.

Hovemyr, M. (1996). Forms and degrees of religious commitment: Intrinsic orientation in a Swedish context. *Journal of Psychology and Theology, 24*(4), 301–312.

Hrebiniak, L. G., & Alutto, J. A. (1972). Personal and role related factors in the development of organizational commitment. *Administrative Science Quarterly 17,* 555–573.

Hudson, R., & Sullivan, T. A. (1985). Totem or tyrant? Monopoly, regional and local sector effects on worker commitment. *Social Forces, 63,* 716–731.

Hunt, S. D., Chonko, L. B., & Wood, V. R. (1985). Organizational commitment and marketing. *Journal of Marketing, 46,* 112–126.

Hunt, S. D., & Morgan, R. M. (1994). Commitment: One of many commitments or key mediating construct? *Academy of Management Journal, 37*(6), 1568–1587.

Hunter, J. E., & Schmidt, F. L. (1990). Methods of meta-analysis: Correcting error and bias in research findings. Beverly Hills, CA: Sage.

Huselid, M. A., & Day, N. E. (1991). Organizational commitment, job involvement, and turnover: A substantive and methodological analysis. *Journal of Applied Psychology, 76,* 380–391.

Huston, T., & Levinger, G. (1978). Interpersonal attraction and relationships. In M. R. Rosenzweig & L. W. Porter (Eds.), *Annual Review of Psychology, 29,* 115–156.

Iverson, S. (1999). An event history analysis of employee turnover: The case of hospital employees in Australia. *Human Resource Management Review, 9,* 397–418.

Iverson, R. D., & Buttigieg, D. M. (1999). Affective, normative, and continuance commitment: Can the right kind of commitment be managed. *Journal of Management Studies, 36,* 307–333.

Jaros, S. J. (1997). An assessment of Meyer and Allen's (1991) three-component model of organizational commitment and turnover intentions. *Journal of Vocational Behavior, 51,* 319–337.

Jaros, S. J., Jermier, J. M., Kohler, J. W., & Sinsich, T. (1993). Effects of continuance, affective, and moral commitment on the withdrawal process: An evaluation of eight structural models. *Academy of Management Journal, 36,* 951–995.

Jauch, L. R., Glueck, F. W., & Osborn, R. N. (1978). Organizational loyalty, professional commitment and academic research productivity. *Academy of Management Journal, 21,* 84–92.

Jauch, L. R., Osborn, R. N., & Terpening, W. D. (1980). Goal congruence and employee orientations: The substitution effect. *Academy of Management Journal, 23,* 544–550.

Johnson, J. P. (1999). Multiple commitments and conflicting loyalties in international joint venture management teams. *The International Journal of Organizational Analysis, 7,* 54–71.

Johnson, M. P. (1973). Commitment: A conceptual structure and empirical application. *Sociological Quarterly,* 395–406.

Johnson, R. W., & Johnson, G. J. (1992). Differential predictors of union and company commitment: Parallel and divergent models. *Psychology, A Journal of Human Behavior, 29,* 1–12.

Johnson, R. W., & Johnson, G. J. (1995). The effects of union membership on multiple work commitments among female public sector employees *The Journal of Psychology, 129,* 181–191.

Johnson, R. W., Johnson, G. J., & Patterson, C. R. (1999). Moderators of the relationship between company and union commitment: A meta-analysis. *The Journal of Psychology, 133,* 85–103.

Joreskog, K. G., & Sorbom, D. (1989). *LISREL VII Users's Reference Guide.* Mooresville, IN: Scientific Software.

Joreskog, K. G., & Sorbom, D. (1993). *Structural equation modeling with SIMPLIS command language.* Hillsdale, NJ: Scientific Software.

Kacmar, K. M., Carlson, D. S., & Brymer, R. A. (1999). Antecedents and consequences of organizational commitment: A comparison of two measures. *Educational and Psychological Measurement, 59,* 976–994.

Kalleberg, A. L., & Mastekaasa, A. (2001). Satisfied movers, committed stayers: The impact of job mobility on work attitudes in Norway. *Work and Occupations, 28,* 183–209.

Kanter, R. M. (1968). Commitment and social organization: A study of commitment mechanisms in utopian communities. *American Sociological Review, 33,* 499–517.

Kanter, R. M. (1972). *Commitment and community: Commune and utopias in sociological perspective.* Cambridge, MA: Harvard University Press.

Kanter, R. M. (1977). *Work and family in the United States: A critical review and agenda for research and policy*. New York: Russell Sage Foundation.

Kanungo, R. N. (1979). The concept of alienation and involvement revisited. *Psychological Bulletin, 86*, 119–138.

Kanungo, R. N. (1982). Measurement of job and work involvement. *Journal of Applied Psychology, 67*, 341–349.

Keller, R. T. (1997) Job involvement and organizational commitments longitudinal predictors of job performance: A study of scientists and engineers. *Journal of Applied Psychology, 82*, 539–545.

Kelloway, E. K., & Barling, J. (1993). Members' participation in local union activities: Measurement, prediction, and replication. *Journal of Applied Psychology, 78*, 262–279.

Kelloway, E. K., Catano, V. M., & Southwell, R. R. (1992) The construct validity of union commitment: Development and dimensionality of a shorter scale. *Journal of Occupational and Organizational Psychology, 65*, 197–211.

Kim, J. (1975). Factor analysis. In Nie, N. H., Hull, C. H., Jenkins, J. G., Steinbrenner, K., & Bent, D. H. (Eds.). *SPSS: Statistical Packages for the Social Sciences*. New York: McGraw-Hill.

Kirchmeyer, C. (1995). Managing the work-nonwork boundary: An assessment of organizational responses. *Human Relations, 48*, 515–536.

Kirchmeyer, C. (1992). Nonwork participation and work attitudes: A test of scarcity vs. expansion models of personal resources. *Human Relations, 45*, 775–795.

Kirchmeyer, C. (1993a). Nonwork to work spillover: A more balanced view of the experiences and coping of professional women and men. *Sex Roles, 28*, 1–22.

Kirchmeyer, C. (1993b). *Managing the boundary between work and nonwork: An assessment of organizational practices*. Paper presented at the Annual Meeting of the Academy of Management, Atlanta, Georgia.

Kirkman, B. L., & Shapiro, D. L. (2001). The impact of cultural values on job satisfaction and organizational commitment in self-managing work teams: The mediating role of employee resistance. *Academy of Management Journal, 44*, 557–569.

Klandermans, B. (1986). Perceived costs and benefits of participation in union action. *Personnel Psychology, 39*, 379–397.

Klandermans, B. (1989). Union commitment: Replications and tests in the Dutch context. *Journal of Applied Psychology, 74*, 869–875.

Knoop, R. (1995). Relationships among job involvement, job satisfaction, and organizational commitment for nurses. *The Journal of Psychology, 129*, 643–649.

Ko, J. W., Price, J. L., & Mueller, C. W. (1997). Assessment of Meyer and Allen's three-component model of organizational commitment in South Korea. *Journal of Applied Psychology, 82*, 961–973.

Koch, J. L., & Steers, R. M. (1978). Job attachment, satisfaction and turnover among public sector employees. *Journal of Vocational Behavior, 12*, 119–128.

Kohn, M. L. (1989). *Cross-national research as an analytic strategy. Cross national research in Sociology* (pp. 77–102). Newbury Park, CA: Sage Publications.

Kornhauser, A. (1965). *Mental health of the industrial worker*. New York: Wiley.

Krausz, M., Koslowsky, M., Shalom, N., & Elyakim, N. (1995). Predictors of intentions to leave the ward, the hospital, and the nursing profession: A longitudinal study. *Journal of Organizational Behavior, 16*, 277–288.

Lachman, R., & Aranya, N. (1986a). Evaluation of alternative models of commitment and job attitudes of professionals. *Journal of Occupational Behavior, 7*, 227–243.

Lachman, R., & Aranya, N. (1986b). Job attitudes and turnover intentions in different work settings. *Organizations Studies, 7*, 279–293.

Ladd, T. R., Gordon, M. E., Beauvais, L. L., & Morgan, L. R. (1982). Union commitment: Replication and extension. *Journal of Applied Psychology, 67*, 640–644.

Landy, F. G., & Guion, R. M. (1970). Development of scales for the measurement of work motivation. *Organizational Behavior and Human Performance, 5*, 93–103.

Larwood, L., Wright, T. A., Desrochers, S., & Dahir, V. (1998). Extending latent role and psychological contract theories to predict intent to turnover and politics in business organizations. *Group & Organization Management, 23*(2), 100–123.

Lawler, E. J. (1992). Affective attachment to nested groups: A choice process theory. *American Sociological Review, 57*, 327–339.

Lawler, E. E., & Hall, D. T. (1970). Relationships of job characteristics to job involvement, satisfaction and intrinsic motivation. *Journal of Applied Psychology, 54*, 305–312.

Layder, D. (1984). Sources and levels of commitment in actor's careers. *Work & Occupations, 11*, 147–162.

Lee, S. M. (1969). Organizational identifications of scientists. *Academy of Management Journal, 12*, 327–337.

Lee, J., & Miller, D. (1999). People matter. *Strategic Management Journal, 20*, 579–593.

Lee, J. (1999). People matter: Commitment to employees, strategy and performance in Korean firms. *Strategic Management Journal, 20*, 579–593.

Lee, K., Carswell, J. J., & Allen, N. J. (2000). A meta-analytic review of occupational commitment: Relations with person-and work-related variable. *Journal of Applied Psychology, 85*, 799–811.

Lee, T. W., Ashford, S. J., Walsh, J. P., & Mowday, R. T. (1992). Commitment propensity, organizational commitment, and voluntary turnover: A longitudinal study of organizational entry processes. *Journal of Management, 18*, 15–32.

Lee, T. W., & Mowday, R. T. (1987). Voluntarily leaving an organization: An empirical investigation of Steers and Mowday's model of turnover. *Academy of Management Journal, 30*, 721–743.

Lefkowitz, J., Somers, M., & Weinberg, K. (1984). The role of need salience and/or need level as moderators of the relationship between need satisfaction and work alienation-involvement. *Journal of Vocational Behavior, 24*, 142–158.

Lensky, G. (1961). *The religious factor.* New York: Doubleday.

Leung, K. (1997). Relationships among satisfaction, commitment, and performance: A group-level analysis. *Applied Psychology: An International Review, 46*, 199–205.

Lewick, R. T. (1981). Organizational seduction: Building commitment to organizations. *Organizational Dynamics, 10*, 5–21.

Lewis-Beck, M. S. (1980). *Applied regression: An introduction.* Beverly Hills, CA: Sage.

Liebowitz, S. J. (1983). *An exploration of the relationships among union commitment, union democracy and union effectiveness.* Unpublished doctoral dissertation, University of Tennessee, Knoxville.

Lincoln, J. R., & Kalleberg, A. L. (1985). Work organization and workforce commitment: A study of plants and employees in the U.S. and Japan. *American Sociological Review, 50*, 738–760.

Lodhal, T. (1964). Patterns of job attitudes in two assembly technologies. *Administrative Science Quarterly, 8*, 482–519.

Lodhal, T. M., & Kejner, M. M. (1965). The definition and measurement of job involvement. *Journal of Applied Psychology, 49*, 2433.

London, M. (1983). Toward a theory of career motivation. *Academy of Management Review, 8*, 620–630.

London, M. (1985). Developing Managers: A guide to motivation and preparing people for successful managerial careers. San Francisco, CA: Jossey-Bass.

Louis, R. M. (1980). Career transitions: Varieties and commonalities. *Academy of Management Review, 5*, 329–340.

Luthans, F., Baack, D., & Taylor, L. (1987). Organizational commitment: Analysis of antecedents. *Human Relations, 40,* 219–236.

Loundsbery, J. W., & Hoopes, L. L. (1986). A vacation from work: Changes in work and nonwork outcomes. *Journal of Applied Psychology, 71,* 392–401.

Luthans, F., McCaul, H., & Dodd, N. G. (1985). Organizational commitment: A comparison of American, Japanese and Korean employees. *Academy of Management Journal, 28,* 213–219.

Magenau, J. M., & Martin, J. E. (1984). Patterns of commitment among rank and file union members: A canonical analysis. *Proceedings of the 37th annual meeting, industrial relations research association series* (pp. 455–464). Dallas, TX.

Magenau, J. M., Martin, J. E., & Peterson, M. M. (1988). Dual and unilateral commitment among stewards and rank-and-file union members. *Academy of Management Journal, 31,* 359–376.

March, J. G., & Simon, H. A. (1963). *Organizations.* New York: Wiley.

Marsh, R. M., & Mannari, H. (1971). Lifetime commitment in Japan: Roles, norms and values. *American Journal of Sociology, 76,* 795–812.

Marsh, R. M., & Mannari, H. (1972). A New Look at lifetime commitment in Japanese industry. *Economic Development and Cultural Change, 20,* 611–630.

Marsh, R. M., & Mannari, H. (1977). Organizational commitment and turnover: A prediction study. *Administrative Science Quarterly, 22,* 57–75.

Martin, J. E. (1981). Dual allegiance in public sector unionism: A case study. *International Review of Applied Psychology, 30,* 245–260.

Martin, J. E. (1986). Predictors of individual propensity to strike . *Industrial and Labor Relations Review, 39,* 214–227.

Martin, T. N., & Hafer, J. C. (1995). The multiplicative interaction effects of job involvement and organizational commitment on the turnover intentions of full-and part-time employees. *Journal of Vocational Behavior, 46,* 310–331.

Martin, J. E., Magenau, J. M., & Peterson, M. M. (1986). Variables related to patterns of union stewards' commitment. *Journal of Labor Research, 7,* 323–336.

Martin, T. N., & O'Laughlin, M. S. (1984). Predictors of organizational commitment: The study of part-time army reservists. *Journal of Vocational Behavior, 25,* 270–283.

Mathieu, A., Bruvold, N. T., & Ritchey, P. N. (2000). Subcultural research on organizational commitment with the OCQ invariant instrument. *Journal of Personal Selling & Sales Management, 20,* 129–138.

Mathieu, J. E., & Farr, J. L. (1991). Further evidence of the discriminant validity of measures of organizational commitment, job involvement, and job satisfaction. *Journal of Applied Psychology, 76,* 127–133.

Mathieu, J. E., & Kohler, S. S. (1990). A test of the interactive effects of organizational commitment and job involvement on various types of absence. *Journal of Vocational Behavior, 36,* 33–44.

Mathieu, J. E., & Zajac, D. M. (1990). A review and meta-analysis of the antecedents, correlates and consequences of organizational commitment. *Psychological Bulletin, 108,* 171–194.

Mayer, R. C., & Schoorman, F. D. (1992). Predicting participation and production outcomes through a two-dimensional model of organizational commitment. *Academy of Management Journal, 35,* 671–684.

McCaul, H. S., Hinsz, V. B., & McCaul, K. D. (1995). Assessing organizational commitment: An employees' global attitude toward the organization. *Journal of Applied Behavioral Science, 31,* 80–90.

McDonald, R. P., & Marsh, H. W. (1990). Choosing a multivariate model: Noncentrality and goodness of fit. *Psychological Bulletin, 107,* 247–255.

McElroy, J. C., Morrow, P. C., Crum, M. R., & Dooley, F. J. (1995). Railroad employee commitment and work-related attitudes and perceptions. *Transportation Journal, 34*(3), 13–24.

McElroy, J. C., Morrow, P. C., & Laczniak, R. N. (2001). External organizational commitment. *Human Resource Management Review, 11,* 237–256.

McElroy, J. C., Morrow, P. C., Power, M. L., & Iqubal, Z. (1993). Commitment and insurance agents job perceptions, attitudes, and performance. *Journal of Risk and Insurance, 60*(3), 363–384.

McGee, G. W., & Ford, R. C. (1987). Two (or more) dimensions of organizational commitment: Reexamination of the affective and continuance commitment scales. *Journal of Applied Psychology, 72,* 638–642.

McKelvey, B., & Sekaran, V. (1977). Toward a career-based theory of job involvement: A study of scientists and engineers. *Administrative Science Quarterly, 22,* 281–305.

Medsker, G. J., Williams, L. J., & Holahan, P. J. (1994). A review of current practices for evaluating causal models in organizational behavior and human resources management research. *Journal of Management, 20,* 239–264.

Mellor, S. (1990). The relationship between membership decline and union commitment: A field study of local unions in crisis. *Journal of Applied Psychology, 75,* 258–267.

Mellor, S. M., Mathieu, J. E., & Swim, J. K. (1994). Cross-level analysis of the influence of local union structure on women's and men's union commitment. *Journal of Applied Psychology, 79,* 203–210.

Mellor, S. M., Mathieu, J. E., Barnes-Farell, J. L., & Rogelberg, S. G. (2001). Employees' nonwork obligations and organizational commitments: A new way to look at the relationships. *Human Resource Management, 40,* 171–184.

Meyer, J. P., Stanely, D. J., Herscovitch, L., & Topolnytsky, L. (in press). Affective, continuance, and normative commitment to the organization: A meta-analysis of antecedents, correlates, and consequences. *Journal of Vocational Behavior.*

Meyer, J. P., & Allen, N. J. (1984). Testing the side bet theory of organizational commitment: Some methodological considerations. *Journal of Applied Psychology, 69,* 372–378.

Meyer, J. P., & Allen, N. J. (1991). A three-component conceptualization of organizational commitment. *Human Resource Management Review, 1,* 61–89.

Meyer, J. P., & Allen, N. J. (1997). *Commitment in the workplace: Theory, research, and application.* Thousand Oaks, Sage.

Meyer, J. P., & Herscovitch, L. (2001). Commitment in the workplace: Toward a general model. *Human Resource Management Review, 11,* 299–326.

Meyer, J. P., Allen, N. J., & Gellatly, I. R. (1990). Affective and continuance commitment to the organization: Evaluation of measures and analysis of concurrent and time-lagged relations. *Journal of Applied Psychology, 75,* 710–720.

Meyer, J. P., Paunonen, S. V., Gellatly, I. R., Goffin, R. D., & Jackson, D. N. (1989). Organizational commitment and job performance: It's the nature of the commitment that counts. *Journal of Applied Psychology, 74,* 152–156.

Meyer, J. P., Allen, N. J., & Smith, C. A. (1993). Commitment to organizations and occupations: Extension and test of a three-component conceptualization. *Journal of Applied Psychology, 78,* 538–551.

Miller, D., & Lee, J. (2001). The people make the process: commitment to employees, decision-making and performance, *Journal of Management, 27,* 163–189.

Miller, J. M., Woehr, D. J., & Hudspeth, N. (in press). The meaning and measurement of work ethic: Construction and initial validation of multidimensional inventory. *Journal of Vocational Behavior.*

Miller, D., & Lee. J. (2001). The people make the process: commitment to employees, decision-making, and performance. *Journal of Management, 27,* 163–189.

Miller, J., Kazimiers, M. S., & Schoenberg, R. J. (1981). Assessing comparability of measurement in cross-national research: Authoritarian-conservatism in different socio-cultural settings. *Social Psychology Quarterly, 44,* 178–191.

Millward, L. J., & Hopkins, L. J. (1998). Psychological contracts, organizational and job commitment. *Journal of Applied Social Psychology, 28,* 1530–1556.

Misra, S., Kanungo, R. N., Rosentiel, L. V., & Stuhler, E. A. (1985). The motivational formulation of job and work involvement: A cross-national study. *Human Relations, 38,* 501–518.

Mirels, H. L., & Garrett, J. B. (1971). The Protestant work ethic as a personality variable. *Journal of Consulting and Clinical Psychology, 36,* 40–44.

Mitra, A., Jenkins, D., & Gupta, N. (1992). A meta-analytic review of the relationship between absence and turnover. *Journal of Applied Psychology, 77,* 879–889.

Mobley, W. H. (1977). Intermediate linkages in the relationship between job satisfaction and turnover. *Journal of Applied Psychology, 62,* 237–240.

Mobley, W. H., Griffeth, R. H., Hand, H. H., & Meglino, B. M. (1979). Review and conceptual analysis of the employee turnover process. *Psychological Bulletin, 86,* 493–522.

Moon, M. J. (2000). Organizational commitment revisited in new public management. *Public Performance & Management Review, 24,* 177–194.

Morris, J. H., & Sherman, D. J. (1981). Generalizability of organizational commitment model. *Academy of Management Journal, 24,* 512–526.

Morrow, P. C. (1983). Concept redundancy in organizational research: The case of work commitment. *Academy of Management Review, 8,* 486–500.

Morrow, P. C. (1993). *The theory and measurement of work commitment.* Greenwich, CT: Jai.

Morrow, P. C., Eastman K., & McElroy, J. C. (1991). Concept redundancy and rater naivety in organizational research. *Journal of Applied Social Psychology, 21,* 219–232.

Morrow, P. C., & Goetz, J. F. (1988). Professionalism as a form of work commitment. *Journal of Vocational Behavior, 32,* 92–111.

Morrow, P. C., & McElroy, J. C. (1986). On assessing measures of work commitment. *Journal of Vocational Behavior, 28,* 214–228.

Morrow, P. C., & McElroy, J. C. (1993). Introduction: Understanding and managing loyalty in a multi-commitment world. *Journal of Business Research, 26,* 1–2.

Morrow, P. C., McElroy, J. C., & Blum, M. (1988). Work commitment among department of transportation employees. *Review of Public Personnel Administration, 8,* 96–104.

Morrow, P. C., & Wirth, R. E. (1989). Work commitment among salaried professionals. *Journal of Vocational Behavior, 34,* 40–56.

Morse, N. C., & Weiss, R. S. (1955). The function and meaning of work and the job. *American Sociological Review, 20,* 191–198.

Mottaz, C. J. (1988). An analysis of the relationship between attitudinal commitment and behavioral commitment. *Sociological Quarterly, 30,* 221–236.

Mowday, R. T., Porter, L. M., & Steers, R. M. (1982). *Employee-organizational linkage.* New York: Academic Press.

Mowday, R. T., Steers, R. M., & Porter, L. M. (1979). The measurement of organizational commitment. *Journal of Vocational Behavior, 14,* 224–247.

Mueller, C. W., Finley, A., Iverson, R. D., & Price, J. L. (1999). The effects of group racial composition on job satisfaction, organizational commitment, and career commitment. *Work and Occupation, 26,* 187–219.

Mueller, C. W., & Lawler, E. J. (1999). Commitment to nested organizational units: Some basic principles and preliminary findings. *Social Psychology Quarterly, 62,* 325–346.

Mueller, C. W., Wallace, J. E., & Price, J. L. (1992). Employee commitment: Resolving some issues. *Work and Occupation, 19,* 211–236.

Muna, F. A. (1980). The Arab Executive. New York: Macmillan.

Near, J. P. (1989). Organizational commitment among Japanese and U.S. workers. *Organization Studies, 10,* 281–300.

Near, J. P., Rice, R. W., & Hunt, R. G. (1980). The relationship between work and nonwork domains: A review of empirical research. *Academy of Management Review, 5,* 415–429.

Neubert, M. J., & Cady, S. H. (2001). Program commitment: A multi-study longitudinal field investigation of its impact and antecedents. *Personnel Psychology, 54,* 421–448.

Nogradi, G. S., & Koch, S. A. (1981). The relationship between decisional participation and commitment to the organization, community and profession among municipal recreation administrators. *Leisure Sciences, 4,* 143–159.

Norris, D. R., & Niebuhr, R. H. (1983). Professionalism, organizational commitment and job satisfaction in an accounting organization. *Accounting, Organization and Society, 9,* 49–59.

Nunnally, J. (1978). *Psychometric theory (2nd ed.).* New York: McGraw-Hill.

Nystrom, P. C. (1990). Vertical exchanges and organizational commitment of American business managers. *Group and Organization Studies, 15,* 296–312.

O'Driscoll, M. P., Ilgen, D. R., & Hildreth, K. (1992). Time devoted to job and off-job activities, interrole conflict, and affective experiences. *Journal of Applied Psychology, 77,* 272–279.

O'Reilly, C. A., & Chatman, J. (1986). Organizational commitment and psychological attachment: The effects of compliance, identification and internalization on prosocial behavior. *Journal of Applied Psychology, 71,* 492–499.

O'Reilly, C. A., & Caldwell, D. (1980). Job choice: The impact of intrinsic and extrinsic factors on subsequent satisfaction and commitment. *Journal of Applied Psychology, 65,* 559–565.

Organ, D. W., & Greene, C. N. (1981). The effect of formalization of professional involvement: A compensatory process approach. *Administrative Science Quarterly, 26,* 237–252.

Orthner, D. K., & Pittman, J. F. (1986). Family contributions to work commitment. *Journal of Marriage and the Family, 48,* 573–587.

Orzack, L. H. (1963). Work as a central life interest of professionals. In E. O. Smigal (Ed.), *Work and Leisure.* New Haven: College & University Press.

Palich, L. E., Hom, P. W., & Griffeth, R. W. (1995). Managing in the international context: Testing cultural generality of sources of commitment to multinational enterprises. *Journal of Management, 21,* 671–690.

Parasuraman, S., & Nachman, S. A. (1987). Correlates of organizational and professional commitment: The case of musicians in symphony orchestras. *Group & Organization Studies, 12,* 287–303.

Parasuraman, S. (1982). Predicting turnover intentions and turnover behavior: A multivariate analysis. *Journal of Vocational Behavior, 21,* 111–121.

Parasuraman, S. (1989). Nursing turnover: An integrated model. *Research in Nursing and Health, 12,* 267–277.

Parnell, J. A., & Hatem, T. (1999). Cultural antecedents of behavioral differences between American and Egyptian managers. *Journal of Management Studies, 36,* 399–418.

Patchen, M. (1970). *Participation, achievement and involvement on the job.* Englewood Cliffs, NJ: Prentice Hall.

Paullay, I., Alliger, C., & Stone-Romero, E. (1994). Construct validation of two instruments designed to measure job involvement and work centrality. *Journal of Applied Psychology, 79,* 224–228.

Perlow, L. A. (1998). Boundary control: The social ordering of work and family time in a high-tech corporation. *Administrative Science Quarterly, 43,* 328–357.

Perlow, L. A. (1999). The time famine: Toward a sociology of work time. *Administrative Science Quarterly, 44,* 57–81.

Pierce, J. L., & Dunham, R. B. (1987). Organizational commitment: Pre-employment propensity and initial work experiences. *Journal of Management, 13,* 163–178.

Price, J. L., & Mueller, C. W. (1981). *Professional turnover: The case of nurses.* New York: SP Medical and Scientific Books.

Porter, L. W., Crampson, W. J., & Smith, F. J. (1976). Organizational commitment and managerial turnover. *Organizational Behavior and Human Performance, 15,* 87–98.

Porter, L. W., & Smith, F. J. (1970). *The etiology of organizational commitment.* Unpublished paper, University of California, Irvine.

Porter, L. W., Steers, R. M., Mowday, R. T., & Boulian, P. V. (1974). Organizational commitment, job satisfaction and turnover among psychiatric technicians. *Journal of Applied Psychology, 59,* 603–609.

Purcell, T. V. (1954). *The worker speaks his mind on company and union.* Cambridge, MA: Harvard University Press.

Putti, J. M., Aryee, S., & Liang, T. K. (1989). Work values and organizational commitment: A study in the Asian context. *Human Relations,* 275–288.

Rabinowitz, S., & Hall, D. T. (1977). Organizational research on job involvement. *Psychological Bulletin, 84,* 265–288.

Raelin, J. A. (1989). Professional and business ethics: Bridging the gap. *Management Review, 78,* 39–42.

Ray, J. J. (1982). The Protestant ethic in Australia. *Journal of Social Psychology, 116,* 127–138.

Randall, D. M. (1987). Commitment and the organization: The organization man revisited. *Academy of Management Review, 12,* 460–471.

Randall, D. M. (1988). Multiple roles and organizational commitment. *Journal of Organizational Behavior, 9,* 309–317.

Randall, D. M. (1990). The consequences of organizational commitment: methodological investigation. *Journal of Organizational Behavior, 11,* 361–378.

Randall, D. M. (1993). Cross-cultural research on organizational commitment: A review and application of Hofstede's value survey module. *Journal of Business Research, 26,* 91–110.

Randall, D. M., & Cote, J. A. (1991). Interrelationships of work commitment constructs. *Work and Occupation, 18,* 194–211.

Randall, D. M., Fedor, D. B., & Longenecker, C. O. (1990). The behavioral expression of organizational commitment. *Journal of Vocational Behavior, 36,* 210–224.

Reed, C. S., Young, W. R., & McHugh, P. P. (1994). A comparative look at the dual commitment: An international study. *Human Relations, 47,* 1269–1293.

Reichers, A. E. (1985). A review and reconceptualization of organizational commitment. *Academy of Management Review, 10,* 465–476.

Reichers, A. E. (1986). Conflict and organizational commitment. *Journal of Applied Psychology, 71,* 508–514.

Reilly, N. P., & Orsak, C. L. (1991). A career stage analysis of career and organizational commitment in nursing. *Journal of Vocational Behavior, 39,* 311–330.

Reitz, H. J., & Jewell, L. N. (1979). Sector, locus of control and the job involvement: A six-country investigation. *Academy of Management Journal, 22,* 72–80.

Riley, M., Lockwood, A., Powell-Perry, J., & Baker, M. (1998). Job satisfaction, organizational commitment and occupational culture: A case from the UK pub industry. *Progress in Tourism and Hospitality Research, 4,* 159–168.

Ritti, R. R. (1968). Work goals of scientists and engineers. *Industrial Relations, 7,* 118–131.

Ritzer, G., & Trice, H. M. (1969). An empirical study of Howard Becker's side bet theory. *Social Forces, 47,* 475–479.

Romzek, B. S. (1989). Personal consequences of employee commitment. *Academy of Management Journal, 32,* 649–661.

Romzek, B. S. (1997). It's about time: A study of hours worked and work spillover among law firm lawyers. *Journal of Vocational Behavior, 50,* 227–248.

Ronen, S., & Shenkar, O. (1985). Clustering countries on attitudinal dimensions: A review and synthesis. *Academy of Management Review, 10,* 435–454.

Rotondi, T. (1976). Identification, personality needs and managerial position. *Human Relations, 29,* 507–515.

Rotondi, T. (1975). Organizational identification and group involvement. *Academy of Management Journal, 18,* 892–896.

Rousseau, D. M. (1995). *Psychological contracts in organizations: Understanding written and unwritten agreements.* London, UK, Sage.

Rousseau, D. M. (1998). Why workers still identify with organizations. *Journal of Organizational Behavior, 19,* 217–233.

Rosse, J. G. (1988). Relations among lateness, absence, and turnover: Is there a progression of withdrawal? *Human Relations, 41,* 517–531.

Rosse, J. G., & Hulin, C. L. (1985). Adaptation to work: An analysis of employee health, withdrawal, and change. *Organizational Behavior and Human Decision Processes, 36,* 324–347.

Rotondi, T. (1975). Organizational identification: Issues and implications. *Organizational Behavior and Human Performance, 13,* 95–109.

Rubenowitz, S., Norrigren, F., & Tannenbaum, A. S. (1983). Some social psychological effects of direct and indirect participation in ten Swedish companies. *Organizations Studies, 4,* 243–260.

Rusbult, C. E. (1980a). Commitment and satisfaction in romantic associations test of the investment model. *Journal of Experimental Social Psychology, 16,* 172–186.

Rusbult, C. E. (1980b). Satisfaction and commitment in friendships. *Representative Research in Social Psychology, 11,* 78–95.

Ruyter, K. D., & Wetzels, W. M. (1999). Commitment in auditor-client relationships: Antecedents and consequences. *Accounting, Organization and Society, 24,* 57–75.

Salancik, G. R. (1977(A)). Commitment and the control of organizational behavior and belief. In B. M. Staw & G. R. Salancik (Eds.), *New Directions in Organizational Behavior* (pp. 1–54). Chicago, IL: St. Clair Press.

Salancik, G. R. (1977(B)). Commitment is too easy. *Organizational Dynamics, 6,* 62–80.

Saleh, S. D., & Hosek, J. (1976). Job involvement: Concepts and measurements. *Academy of Management Journal, 19,* 213–224.

Saris, W., & Stronkhorst, H. (1984). *Causal modeling in non experimental research: An introduction to the LISREL approach.* Amsterdam: Sociometric Research Foundation.

Scandura, T. A., & Lankau, M. J. (1997). Relationships of gender, family responsibility and flexible work hours to organizational commitment and job satisfaction. *Journal of Organizational Behavior, 18,* 377–391.

Schnake, M. (1991). Organizational citizenship: A review, proposed model, and research agenda. *Human Relations, 44*(7), 735–759.

Schneider, B., Hall, D., & Nygren, H. (1971). Self-image and job characteristics as correlates of changing organizational identification. *Human Relations, 24,* 397–416.

Schneider, B. (1983). An interactionist perspective on organizational effectiveness. In Cameroon, K. S., & Wheaten, D. S. (Eds.), *Organizational Effectiveness: A Comparison of Multiple Models* (pp. 27–54). New York: Academic Press.

Schriesheim, C., & Tsui, A. S. (1980). *Development and validation of a short satisfaction instrument for use in survey feedback interventions.* Paper presented at the Western Academy of Management Meeting.

Scott, K. S., Moore, S. K., & Miceli, M. P. (1997). An exploration of the meaning and consequences of workaholism. *Human Relations, 50,* 287–314.

Sekaran, U. (1982). An investigation of the career salience in dual career families. *Journal of Vocational Behavior, 20,* 111–119.

Sekaran, U. (1986). Significant differences in quality of life factors and their correlates: A function of differences in career orientation or gender. *Sex Roles, 14*, 261–279.

Semyonov, M., & Lewin-Epstein, N. (1987). Hewers of wood and drawers of water: Non-citizen Arabs in the Israeli labor market. Ithaca: Cornell University, ILR Press.

Shaffer, A. M., Harrison, D. A., Matthew Gilley, K., & Luk, D. M. (2001). Struggling for balance amid turbulence on international assignments: Work-family conflict, support and commitment. *Journal of Management, 27*, 99–121.

Shamir, B. (1986). Protestant work ethic, work involvement and the psychological impact of unemployment. *Journal of Occupational Behavior, 7*, 25–38.

Sheldon, M. E. (1971). Investment and involvement as mechanisms producing commitment to the organization. *Administrative Science Quarterly, 16*, 143–150.

Sherer, P. D., & Morishima, M. (1989). Roads and roadblocks to dual commitment: Similar and dissimilar antecedents of union and company commitment. *Journal of Labor Research, 10*, 311–330.

Shore, L. M., & Wayne, S. J. (1993). Commitment and employee behavior: Comparison of affective commitment and continuance commitment with perceived organizational support. *Journal of Applied Psychology, 78*, 774–780.

Shore, L. M., & Martin, H. J. (1989). Job satisfaction and organizational commitment in relation to work performance and turnover intentions. *Human Relations, 42*, 625–638.

Shore, L. M., Newton, L. A., & Thornton, G. C. (1990). Job and organizational attitudes in relation to employee behavioral intentions. *Journal of Organizational Behavior, 11*, 57–67.

Shuval, J. T., & Bernstein, J. (1996). The dynamics of professional commitment: Immigrant physicians from the former Soviet Union in Israel. *Social Science & Medicine, 42*, 965–974.

Siders, M. A., George, G., & Dharwadkar, R. (2001). The relationship of internal and external commitment foci to objective performance measures. *Academy of Management Journal, 44*, 570–579.

Siegal, L. (1969). *Industrial Psychology (2nd ed.)*. Homewood, IL: Irwin.

Sinclair, R. R., & Tetrick, L. E. (1995). Social exchange and union commitment: A comparison of union instrumentality and union support perceptions. *Journal of Organizational Behavior, 16*, 669–680.

Singh, V., & Vinnicombe, S. (2000). What does "commitment" really mean? *Personnel Review, 29*, 228–258.

Smith, P. C., Kendall, L. M., & Hulin, C. L. (1969). *The measurement of satisfaction in work and retirement*. Chicago: Rand-McNally.

Somers, M. J. (1993). A test of the relationship between affective and continuance commitment using non-recursive models. *Journal of Occupational and Organizational Psychology, 66*, 185–192.

Somers, M. J., & Birnbaum, D. (1998). Work-related commitment and job performance: It's also the nature of the performance that counts. *Journal of Organizational Behavior, 19*, 621–634.

Sommer, S. M., Bae, S., & Luthans, F. (1996). Organizational commitment across cultures: The impact of antecedents on Korean employees. *Human Relations, 49*, 977–993.

Sorensen, J. E., & Sorensen, T. (1974). The conflict of professionals in bureaucratic organizations. *Administrative Science Quarterly, 19*, 98–106.

Spinrad, W. (1960). Correlates of trade union participation: A summary of the literature. *American Sociological Review, 25*, 237–244.

Sprecher, S., Metts, S., Burleson, B., Hatfield, E., & Thompson, A. (1995). Domains of expressive interaction in intimate relationships: Associations with satisfaction and commitment. *Family-Relations, 44*(2), 203–210.

Stagner, R., & Rosen, H. (1965). Psychology of union-management relations. California: Wadsworth Publishing Company.

Stagner, R. (1954). Dual allegiance as a problem of modern society. *Personnel Psychology, 7,* 41–46.

Stagner, R. (1956). *Psychology of industrial conflict.* New York: John Wiley & Sons.

Stagner, R. (1961). Implication of psychology in labor management relations: Comments on the symposium. *Personnel Psychology, 14,* 279–284.

Staw, B. M. (1977). *Two sides of commitment.* Paper presented at the meeting of the Academy of Management, Orlando, Florida.

Steel, R. P., & Ovalle, N. K. (1984). A review and meta-analysis of research on the relationship between behavioral intentions and employee turnover. *Journal of Applied Psychology, 69,* 673–686.

Steers, R. M. (1977). Antecedents and outcomes of organizational commitment. *Administrative Science Quarterly, 22,* 46–56.

Steers, R. M., & Rhodes, S. R. (1978). Major influences on employee attendance: A process model. *Journal of Applied Psychology, 63,* 391–407.

Steffy, B. D., & Jones, J. W. (1988). The impact of family and career planning variables on the organizational, career, and community commitment of professional women. *Journal of Vocational Behavior, 32,* 196–212.

Strauss, G. (1977). Union government in the United States: Research past and future. *Industrial Relations, 16,* 215–242.

Sullivan, S. E. (1999). The changing nature of careers: A review and research agenda, *Journal of Management, 25,* 457–484.

Super, D. E. (1970). *Work Value Inventory.* Boston: Houghton Mifflin.

Sverke, M., & Kuruvilla, S. (1995). A new conceptualization of union commitment: Development and test of an integrated theory. *Journal of Organizational Behavior, 16,* 505–532.

Sverke, M., & Sjoberg, A. (1994). Dual commitment to company and union in Sweden: An examination of predictors and taxonomic split methods. *Journal of Organizational Behavior, 16,* 505–532.

Tang, T. L. (1989). Effects of work ethic and task labels on task preference. *Journal of Psychology, 123,* 429–438

Tang, T. L. (1990). Factors affecting intrinsic motivation among university students in Taiwan. *Journal of Social Psychology, 130,* 219–230.

Tannenbaum, A. S. (1965). Unions. In J. M. March (Ed.), *Handbook of Organizations.* Chicago: Rand McNally.

Tausky, C. (1969). Meaning of work among blue-collar men. *Pacific Sociological Review, 12,* 49–55.

Templer, R. J. (1982). The emerging Black manager: A comparative study of power, commitment and supervisor perceptions. *Psychological Africana, 21,* 149–167.

Tetrick, L. E. (1995). Developing and maintaining union commitment: A theoretical framework. *Journal of Organizational Behavior, 16,* 583–595.

Tetrick, L. E., Thacker, J. W., & Fields, M. W. (1989). Evidence for the stability of the four dimensions of the commitment to the union scale. *Journal of Applied Psychology, 74,* 819–822.

Thacker, J. W., Fields, M. W., & Barclay, L. A. (1990). Union commitment: An examination of antecedents and outcomes variables. *Journal of occupational psychology, 63,* 33–48.

Thacker, J. W., & Rosen, H. (1986). Dynamics of employee reaction to company and union dual allegiance revisited and expanded. *Industrial Relations/Relations Industrielles, 41,* 128–142.

Thacker, J. W., Fields, M. W., & Tetrick, L. E. (1989). The factor structure of union commitment: An application of confirmatory factor analysis. *Journal of Applied Psychology, 74,* 228–232.

Thompson, C. A., Kopelman, R. E., & Schriesheim, C. A. (1992). Putting all one's eggs in the same basket: A comparison of commitment and satisfaction among self-and organizationally employed men. *Journal of Applied Psychology, 77,* 738–743.

Thornton, R. (1970). Organizational involvement and commitment to organization and profession. *Administrative Science Quarterly, 15,* 417–426.

Tjosvold, D., Sasaki, S., & Moy, J. W. (1998). Developing commitment in Japanese organizations in Hong Kong: Interdependence, interaction, relationship, and productivity. *Small Group Research, 29,* 560–582.

Toren, N. (1991). The nexus between family and work roles of academic women in Israel: Reality and representation. *Sex Roles, 24,* 651–667.

Trianidis, H. C., & Vassiliou, V. (1972). Interpersonal influence and employee selection in two cultures. *Journal of Applied Psychology, 56,* 140–145.

Trimpop, R. M. (1995). Union commitment: Conceptual changes in the German context. *Journal of Organizational Behavior, 16,* 597–608.

Tuma, N. B., & Grimes, A. J. (1981). A comparison of models of professionals in a research-oriented university. *Administrative Science Quarterly, 26,* 187–206.

Tziner, A. (1983). Choice and commitment to a military career. *Social Behavior and Personality, 11,* 119–128.

Van Ypreen, N. Y., Hagedoorn, M., & Geurts, S. A. E. (1996). Intent to leave and absenteeism as reactions to perceived inequity: The role of psychological and social constraints. *Journal of Occupational and Organizational Psychology, 69,* 367–372.

Vandenberghe, C., Stinglhamber, P., Bentein, K., & Delhaise, T. (2001). An examination of the cross-cultural validity of multidimensional model of commitment in Europe. *Journal of Cross-Cultural Psychology, 32,* 322–347.

Vandenberg, R. G., & Scarpello, V. (1994). A longitudinal assessment of the determinant relationship between employee commitments to the occupation and the organization. *Journal of Organizational Behavior, 15,* 535–547.

Vandenberg, R. J., & Self, R. M. (1993). Assessing newcomers' changing commitments to the organization during the first 6 months of work. *Journal of Applied Psychology, 78,* 557–568.

Vrendenburgh, D. J., & Trinkaus, J. R. (1983). An analysis of role stress among hospital nurses. *Journal of Vocational Behavior, 23,* 82–95.

Vecchio, R. P. (1980). The function and meaning of work and the job: Morse and Weiss revisited. *Academy of Management Journal, 23,* 361–367.

Vrendenburgh, D. J., & Sheridan, J. E. (1979). Individual and occupational determinants of life satisfaction and alienation. *Human Relations, 32,* 1023–1038.

Walker, J. M., & Lawler, J. J. (1979). Dual unions and political processes in organizations. *Industrial Relations, 18,* 32–43.

Wallace, J. E. (1997). Becker's side-bet theory of commitment revisited: Is it time for moratorium or a resurrection. *Human Relations, 50,* 727–749.

Wallace, J. E. (1993). Professional and organizational commitment: Compatible or incompatible? *Journal of Vocational Behavior, 42,* 333–349.

Wallace, J. E. (1995a). Corporatist control and organizational commitment among professionals: The case of lawyers working in law firms. *Social Forces, 73,* 811–839.

Wallace, J. E. (1995b). Organizational and professional commitment in professional and nonprofessional organizations. *Administrative Science Quarterly, 40,* 228–255.

Wang, J. J., & Wildman, L. (1995). An empirical-examination of the effects of family commitment in education on student achievement in 7th grade. *Journal of Research in Science Teaching, 32,* 833–837.

Warr, P. B. (1982). A national study of non-employment commitment. *Journal of Occupational Psychology, 55,* 297–312.

Warr, P. B., Cook, J., & Wall, T. D. (1979). Scales for the measurement of some work attitudes and aspects of psychological well being. *Journal of Occupational Psychology, 52*, 129–148.

Weber, M. (1958). The protestant ethic and the spirit of capitalism, Parsons, T. (translator), Scribner, New York.

Werbel, J. D., & Gould, S. (1984). A comparison of the relationship of commitment to the turnover in recently-hired and tenured employees. *Journal of Applied Psychology, 69*, 687–690.

Wetzel, K., Gallagher G. D., & Soloshy D. E. (1991). Union commitment: Is there a gender gap? *Relations Industrielles, 46*, 564–583.

White, K. (1967). Social background variables related to the career commitment of women teachers. *Personnel and Guidance Journal, 45*, 648–652.

Whitener, E. M., & Walz, P. M. (1993). Exchange theory determinants of affective and continuance commitment and turnover. *Journal of Vocational Behavior, 42*, 265–281.

Wiener, Y., & Gechman, A. S. (1977). Commitment: A behavioral approach to job involvement. *Journal of Vocational Behavior, 10*, 47–52.

Wiener, Y., & Vardi, Y. (1980). Relationships between job, organization and work outcomes: An integrative approach. *Organizational Behavior and Human Performance, 26*, 81–96.

Wiley, D. L. (1987). The relationship between work/nonwork role conflict and job-related outcomes: Some unanticipated findings. *Journal of Management, 13*, 467–472.

Williams, L. J., & Hazer, J. T. (1986). Antecedents and consequences of satisfaction and commitment in turnover models: A re-analysis using latent variables equation methods. *Journal of Applied Psychology, 71*, 219–231.

Witt, L. A. (1993) Reactions to work assignments as predictors of organizational commitment: The moderating effect of occupational identification. *Journal of Business Research, 26*, 17–30.

Wittig-Berman, U., & Lang, D. (1990). Organizational commitment and its outcomes: Differing effects of value commitment and continuance commitment on stress reactions, alienation and organization-serving behaviors. *Work & Stress, 4*, 167–177.

Wong, C., Hui, C., Wong, Y., & Law, K. S. (2001). The significant role of Chinese employees' organizational commitment: Implications for managing employees in Chinese societies. *Journal of World Business, 36*, 326–340.

Wright, T. A., & Larwood, L. (1997). Further examination of the cosmopolitan-local latent role construct. *Psychological Report, 81*, 897–898.

Yishai, Y., & Cohen, A. (1997). (Un)Representative bureaucracy: Women in the Israeli senior civil service. *Administration and Society, 28*, 441–465.

Yoon, J., Baker, M. R., & Ko, J. W. (1994). Interpersonal attachment and organizational commitment: Subgroup hypothesis revisited. *Human Relations, 47*, 329–351.

Zaccaro, S. J., & Dobbins, G. H. (1989). Contrasting group and organizational commitment: Evidence for differences among multilevel attachments. *Journal of Organizational Behavior, 10*, 267–273.

Zeffane, R. (1994). Patterns of organizational commitment and perceived management style: A comparison of public and private sector employees. *Human Relations, 47*, 977–1010.

Author Index

Note: Page numbers in *italic* indicate bibliography references.

Subject Index

Note: Page numbers in *italic* refer to figures; those in **boldface** refer to tables.

349